GEOGRAPHY AND THE ASCENSION NARRATIVE IN ACTS

The book of Acts contains a strong geographical component. Yet readings of Acts typically ignore or marginalise geography's contribution to the construction of the narrative's theology. In this book Matthew Sleeman argues that Jesus' ascension into heaven is foundational for establishing the 'spatiality' of Acts, showing that the narrative's understanding of place and space is shaped decisively by Christ's heavenly location. Drawing on recent advances in geographical theory, Sleeman offers a 'spatial' interpretation that expands our vision of how space and place inform the theological impulses of Acts. Presenting a complement to conventional 'temporal' readings of Acts, he sheds new light on the theology of the book, and suggests new ways of reading not only Acts but also other New Testament texts.

Sleeman's work combines innovative biblical scholarship with accessible and informative geographical analysis, and is suitable for those with research and teaching interests in human geography or biblical studies.

MATTHEW SLEEMAN is Lecturer in New Testament and Greek at Oak Hill Theological College, London.

SOCIETY FOR NEW TESTAMENT STUDIES
MONOGRAPH SERIES

General Editor: John M. Court

146

GEOGRAPHY AND THE ASCENSION NARRATIVE
IN ACTS

SOCIETY FOR NEW TESTAMENT STUDIES

MONOGRAPH SERIES

Recent titles in the series

Geography and the Ascension Narrative in Acts

MATTHEW SLEEMAN

CAMBRIDGE
UNIVERSITY PRESS

CAMBRIDGE UNIVERSITY PRESS
Cambridge, New York, Melbourne, Madrid, Cape Town, Singapore, São Paulo, Delhi

Cambridge University Press
The Edinburgh Building, Cambridge CB2 8RU, UK

Published in the United States of America by Cambridge University Press, New York

www.cambridge.org
Information on this title: www.cambridge.org/9780521509626

First published 2009

Printed in the United Kingdom at the University Press, Cambridge

A catalogue record for this publication is available from the British Library

Library of Congress Cataloguing in Publication data
Sleeman, Matthew, 1968–
Geography and the Ascension narrative in Acts / Matthew Sleeman.
   p. cm. – (Society for New Testament studies. Monograph series)
Includes bibliographical references.
ISBN 978-0-521-50962-6
1. Space perception in the Bible. 2. Bible. N.T. Acts – Geography.
3. Jesus Christ – Ascension. 4. Bible. N.T. Acts – Theology.
5. Bible. N.T. Acts – Criticism, Narrative. I. Title. II. Series.
BS2625.6.S59S54   2009
226.6′091–dc22

                                     2009009345

ISBN 978-0-521-50962-6 hardback

For Karen, and our children:
Phoebe, David, Thomas and Tabitha

CONTENTS

ACKNOWLEDGEMENTS

This monograph is a revised version of a PhD thesis awarded by the University of London in 2007, itself building on an earlier doctoral thesis awarded by the University of Cambridge in 1996. During my biblical studies the Revd Professor Richard Burridge has been the consummate *Doktorfater*, and Professor Judith Lieu an excellent second supervisor. I am very thankful to them, and to Dr Eddie Adam and the Revd Professor Loveday Alexander who examined the thesis and encouraged its publication.

Substantive financial support from the Latimer Trust, the Oak Hill Bursary Fund and the King's College London Theological Trust made it possible to undertake this study. This support was generously given and gratefully received. I hope that this publication is some reward for their stewardship.

I owe a great debt to the Revd Professor David Peterson, formerly principal at Oak Hill College, who was instrumental in introducing me to the academic study of Acts and in motivating me to pursue these matters. Other colleagues and students at Oak Hill provided precious friendship and stimulation throughout this project and, of the many libraries and librarians assisting with my studies, Wendy Bell stands out for especial thanks.

A study such as this reflects the influence of many different places over the years. Earlier studies as a member of St Catharine's College in the Department of Geography at the University of Cambridge helped stimulate and provoke this present work. Likewise, the many believer-spaces around the world which I have been blessed to enjoy will find their imprint here and, with it, my gratitude. Many friends have been wonderful company and comfort in many places and over the years – although too many to name here, the Clark, Cole and Lindsell families stand out as having been there along the road from geography to biblical studies and beyond.

Closer to home, my brother Jonathan and sister Rachel have helped practically with this project, as have my Mother and Father, who first taught me Acts: their example in living for Jesus still goes before me. So too does my wife Karen. She models in so many ways what it means to produce spaces 'under heaven', especially with our four children, all born under the shadow of this project. I look forward to the time and space with them granted to me, and I hope and pray we enjoy its promises together. With a gratitude to God, this book is dedicated to her and to them.

Petertide 2008
Oak Hill Theological College

PART I

Theory

1

ASCENSION SCHOLARSHIP AT THE TURN OF THE CENTURY

Half a century ago, writing about the Lukan ascension accounts, P. A. van Stempvoort declared that 'discussion never ends'. He continued: 'The flood of publications goes on from year to year. Only new points of view give one boldness to add another.'[1] This study adds a new point of view to our understanding of Jesus' ascension by examining its impact on the narrative production of space within Acts.

Part I (Chapters 1 and 2) unpacks the theory underpinning this aim, and then Part II (Chapters 3–7) applies the theory in a 'spatialised' reading of Acts 1:1–11:18. As such, this study links three poles of scholarly inquiry, namely Christ's ascension, narrative-critical readings of Acts, and the role of geography in constructing and communicating that narrative's theological message. As the opening two chapters argue, previous scholarship has failed to integrate these three considerations and each has been impoverished as a result. Instead, the ascension requires a narrative positioning within Acts, and Acts as narrative requires a heavenward orientation. Both these claims require a proper understanding of the ways in which Jesus' ascension restructures earthly places and space within the narrative.

This opening chapter positions the direction for this study within existing scholarship concerning the ascension in Acts. This task is greatly helped by Arie Zwiep's monograph on the ascension in Luke and Acts.[2] His *Forschungsbericht* deliberately addressed the previous absence of an up-to-date review of ascension literature and, by also offering a sixteen-page bibliography of ascension literature from between 1900 and 1996, Zwiep has performed an admirable service to scholarship by rectifying this deficiency.[3] This acknowledged strength within his work[4] means that the present study can focus upon particular gaps within ascension scholarship.

---

[1] Van Stempvoort 1958/9: 30.   [2] Zwiep 1997.   [3] Zwiep 1997: 1–35, 200–15.
[4] McIver 1999 specifically highlights this element of Zwiep's work for commendation.

This chapter identifies three lacunae in existing scholarship examining Christ's ascension in Acts. First, the ascension account needs better narrative positioning within Acts as a whole; second, the problematic nature of post-ascension Christological presence and absence requires further elucidation; and, third, the ascension's submerged spatiality[5] needs to be uncovered. Although interrelated and together constituting the framework for the present study, each contention will be introduced in turn, the first two being appraised in this chapter. The third lacuna, concerning setting and spatiality, is anticipated in this chapter but explored more fully in Chapter 2.

1.   A need for ascension scholarship to engage with narrative perspectives

Ascension scholarship and narrative readings

In the major examination of the Lukan ascension accounts preceding Zwiep, Mikeal Parsons's 1987 monograph distinguished traditional 'diachronic' analyses (text, source and form criticism) from more 'synchronic' (narrative literary) approaches to the text.[6] This distinction provides a taxonomy for positioning Zwiep's work and, indeed, all ascension scholarship. Assessed in its light, ascension scholarship reveals no sustained attempt, either before or after Parsons, to trace the impact of the ascension through the course of the ensuing Acts narrative.[7] John Maile came nearest to adumbrating such a project, anticipating that the ascension signals 'the same story continuing in a different mode'.[8] Yet despite his article's promise, Maile's overall thesis of the ascension as indicating Jesus' continuing ministry across Acts remained undeveloped.[9] Parsons stands as the key but lone precursor for the present study,[10] his synchronic approach to the ascension

---

[5] As Chapter 2 will elucidate, 'spatiality' is used as a summary term for 'the production of Space' (Soja 1996: 71). Throughout, *space* is 'at once result and cause, product and producer' of social life (Lefebvre 1991: 142).

[6] Parsons 1987: 18–24.

[7] Although pursuing other questions, Zwiep's *Forschungsbericht* confirms this observation.

[8] Maile 1986: 56.

[9] Maile (1986: 53 n. 68, 56 n. 77) makes reference to a thesis project which ultimately he failed to complete.

[10] Zwiep's *Forschungsbericht* passed over a branch of ascension literature, largely from the 1960s, which sought to come to terms with Bultmannian demythologising agendas (e.g. K. C. Thompson 1964, J. G. Davies 1969, Metzger 1969, Selman 1969). Importantly, these studies sought to engage with the *meaning* of the ascension, an

remaining undeveloped by subsequent scholarship. Therefore, the present study focuses on this aspect of the ascension.

Parsons intended his synchronic analysis to explore the ways in which the ascension narrative 'functions as a narrative beginning, anticipating major plot developments in the story of Acts'.[11] Adopting Marianna Torgovnick's literary theory concerning narrative closure for a reading of Acts 1, Parsons identified there a noticeably different narrative function from that evident in the Luke 24 account.[12] These differences, Parsons argued, are better explained in terms of their literary function than by recourse to interpolation or source theories.[13] His analysis of the Acts 1 account within its narrative cotext[14] identified elements of circularity, parallelism, 'empty center' narrative patterning (by which 'the characters variously respond to an absent, but curiously present Jesus'),[15] reverse linkage (whereby a sequel refers to its predecessor), and internal focalisation. Yet Parsons himself recognised the limited nature of his own inquiries at this juncture: 'Despite the number of ancillary plot strategies anticipated in Acts 1, this study is limited to the major one concerning the place of Israel in the gentile mission, reflected in the disciple's [*sic*] question and Jesus' response in Acts 1:6–8.'[16] Such an acknowledgement of the text's potential and Parsons's admission of the limited scope of his own study suggest room for further synchronic analysis of the ascension within Acts.

This present study builds on Parsons's synchronic approach, but in a new direction. It examines the ways in which Jesus' ascension structures the church[17] in Acts, and how it shapes the believers' 'spatiality', that is, the ways in which Jesus' ascension produces space and an understanding of space both within and beyond the church.[18]

Although Parsons pursued both diachronic and synchronic methods, Zwiep's subsequent analysis of the Lukan ascension maintained a

advance beyond simple hypothesising about the text's historical development. As such, at their best, they anticipated elements of later, more 'literary' readings of the ascension. K. C. Thompson 1964 provides the clearest example of these anticipations.

[11] Parsons 1987: 24.   [12] Parsons 1987: 151–86.

[13] Parsons 1987: 189–99. Maile (1986: 34–5) draws similar 'theological' conclusions.

[14] This study uses 'cotext' to mean 'the string of linguistic data within which a text is set', preserving 'context' for 'the socio-historical [geographical] realities of the Lukan text' (Green 1997b: 13, 14).

[15] Parsons 1987: 169.   [16] Parsons 1987: 159–60.

[17] 'Church' is here understood as shorthand for collective believers in Acts, eschewing any anachronistic rendering of the term (thereby heeding the warning of Lieu 2004: 91) but recognising it as one collective term among others for believers within Acts.

[18] While this study assumes Christian communities function as characters within the narrative, the understanding of space pursued here is more than simply keeping characters in their rightful (narrative) 'place' (cf. R. P. Thompson 2006).

more stridently diachronic approach to the text. Building on Gerhard Lohfink's earlier form-critical assessment of the Lukan ascension as a rapture story,[19] Zwiep compared the Lukan pericopae with other rapture stories circulating within first-century Judaism. More recent claims to reinstate Greco-Roman influences on the ascension accounts have contested Zwiep's analysis at this juncture,[20] but such debates remain firmly within the diachronic aspect of Parsons's taxonomy. For all his diachronic insights, and his acknowledgement of Parsons's synchronic advances, Zwiep did not advance the synchronic dimension to any degree.[21] Instead, his in-depth analysis of the wider Acts narrative was constrained to 'explicit' ascension texts, namely Acts 1:22; 3:19–21.[22] Reference to other parts of Acts were structured through Zwiep's concern with discrete issues arising from his thesis, such as the apologetic function of the forty days in Acts 1:3, and the ascension's relationship with parousia expectation and the outpouring of the Spirit.[23]

Since Zwiep, subsequent ascension scholarship has not returned to Parsons's synchronic approach. This is in large part because the most recent ascension research has been undertaken by systematic theologians whose approach is, by its nature, even less likely to be sensitive to narrative position.[24] More detailed examination of these systematic studies later in this chapter acknowledges their significant contributions to scholarly understanding of the ascension, but they do not position the ascension *within Acts as a narrative whole*.[25] They exhibit the same limited sensitivity to narrative cotext that Parsons correctly identified in earlier ascension scholarship.[26] Consequently Robert O'Toole's diagnosis still holds true nearly three decades after it was first made: 'The methodology used by most researchers seems too limited. They spend a good deal of time discussing Luke's treatment of the ascension and exaltation, but they do not study these two

---

[19] Lohfink 1971.   [20] E.g. Gilbert 2003: 242–7.
[21] Zwiep 2004, a monograph on Acts 1:15–26 described as a 'sequel' to his 1997 ascension monograph (p. vii), displays a sustained narrative turn (e.g. pp. 2, 136, 176–7) not evident in his ascension analysis.
[22] Zwiep 1997: 109–15.   [23] Zwiep 1997: 171–85.
[24] Farrow 1999, Burgess 2004, Dawson 2004, A. Johnson 2004.
[25] The one exception is A. Johnson 2004, but his 'narrative perichoresis' primarily addresses Trinitarian issues rather than ecclesiological matters.
[26] See Parsons 1987: 14 regarding J. Davies 1958; Parsons 1987: 191 regarding van Stempvoort 1958/9; and Parsons 1987: 204 n. 27 regarding Lohfink 1971. Indirectly, Lohfink has recognised this weakness in his earlier work (1999: 319). Yet, despite – or, perhaps more accurately, *because of* – an autobiographical confession to that effect (Lohfink 1999: 311–22), Lohfink's recent ecclesiology fails to consider the ascension's effect upon the earthly church.

events in Luke-Acts as a whole.'[27] Indeed, that this criticism can be levelled at the vast majority of previous ascension scholarship indicates the fundamental nature of the methodological divide identified by Parsons. It therefore remains evident that the ascension still requires the supplementary insights of more synchronic approaches which recognise that any search for the theology of Acts 'must struggle to reclaim the character of Acts as a narrative'.[28]

Narrative criticism and narrative setting

The paucity of synchronic readings of the ascension highlights the need to obtain methodological purchase for such a study. This need is exacerbated by the conceptual growth within Anglo-American Acts scholarship[29] of what can be termed 'narrative criticism' from its origins in the early 1980s[30] into a catch-all term for many different text-based approaches.[31]

The advent of narrative criticism promised a transformation for geography within biblical studies after decades of its neglect and abuse. The early twentieth-century original 'quest' for the historical Jesus combed the gospels for their geographical references in an atomistic fashion, only to be followed by early redaction critics dismissing these geographical references as confused and incoherent. Narrative criticism's shift from historical to literary questions suggested new horizons for understanding settings, understandings in which 'Galilee and Jerusalem are no longer simply geographical references but settings for dramatic action … rich in connotational, or associative values, and these values contribute to the meaning of the narrative for the implied reader'.[32]

---

[27] O'Toole 1979: 111; cf. also p. 112. The present study views Acts as a sequel to Luke's Gospel, acknowledging its qualified unity with Luke's Gospel. This approach resists the excesses of 'parallelomania' by granting Acts a literary life of its own, while acknowledging that challenges to Luke-Acts unity have 'probably led to a stronger, better-defended, case for the unity of Luke-Acts' (Marshall 1999: 340).

[28] Gaventa 1988: 150.

[29] The limited engagement with German-speaking scholarship within this study reflects the relative absence of such 'literary' approaches within its writings on Acts. As recently as 2006 a *German* narrative-critical theory could be judged an exegetical gap (Eisen 2006: 43), although cf. Wasserberg 1998, who adopts a hybrid methodology, bridging historical-critical and narrative-critical approaches to the text (p. 34).

[30] Rhoads 1982.

[31] The term 'narrative criticism' is retained here because of its heuristic value as a collective label for the broad raft of narrative-based approaches to biblical texts.

[32] Malbon 1992: 24, 31.

Despite this promise, however, setting has remained a relatively undeveloped ancillary to plot and action, which have been viewed as primarily driven by sequence and time.[33] The neglect of setting within narrative readings of Acts is particularly surprising, given that Acts makes more use of spatially related terms than any other NT text.[34] Also, when viewed as a narrative event, the ascension relocates a particular character (Jesus) from one *setting* to another. Given that the account is told from the spatial vantage point of the disciples who remain on earth,[35] the *settings of other characters* are also repositioned by Jesus' ascension. Such interplay of settings adumbrates a wider understanding of narrative *space*.

Given narrative criticism's sustained neglect of these matters, Matthew Skinner's recent foregrounding of narrative setting provides a helpful springboard for the reading undertaken here.[36] As Skinner muses, while lamenting the comparative lack of scholarly interest in setting compared with the literature concerning characterisation, 'Perhaps analysis of setting is about to experience a period of similar fecundity within the study of biblical narratives.'[37]

Skinner helpfully highlights that analysing setting as an aspect of narrative does not require every text to deliver 'explicit descriptions of its settings or have them figure prominently in the causes and effects of narrated events'; instead, 'no narrative can totally bracket out the notion of setting; nor can any ever exhaust all the details of any single one'.[38] Setting can dynamically shift from an apparently background position to a more active role within the narrative wherein spaces become 'thematized', 'acting places' rather than simply the place of action.[39] In short, narratives inherently assume settings, but settings are not simply a flash of 'colour', or ready-formed background scenery

---

[33]   Both Powell (1990: 69) and Marguerat and Bourquin (1999: 77) liken setting to adverbs. Although Resseguie (2005: 87–120) provides a longer introduction to setting, his discussion still lacks an integrative theory (a charge also applicable to Resseguie 2004) and is premised upon setting as 'background against which the narrative action takes place' (p. 87).

[34]   According to Parsons 1998: 158 n. 14, utilising semantic domain lexicons.

[35]   Parsons 1987: 175. Parsons's underlying understanding of point of view has stood up to scrutiny (Yamasaki 2007: 91–4). Cf. also Eisen 2006: 154–7.

[36]   Skinner 2003: 34–55.   [37]   Skinner 2003: 4 n. 5.   [38]   Skinner 2003: 34–5.

[39]   Bal 1995: 95. This is a more insightful theoretical observation than Bar-Efrat's distinction (1989: 195) between mentioning and describing sites, that is, backgrounding and foregrounding in relation to events. Bar-Efrat's categories neglect the more active and constitutive aspects of space and place.

'behind' the action.[40] Simply naming a place can evoke a host of descriptive associations which inform narrative action and, inevitably, 'Reading involves a process of spatial reconstruction or imagination.'[41]

Applying Skinner's insight to the ascension, that Acts lacks any *description* of heaven (οὐρανός) does not preclude it from functioning as a significant setting within the narrative, even though this has been an unspoken assumption of previous ascension scholarship.[42] Indeed, as the locale for the ascended Christ, the central character in Luke's first volume, its significance is worthy of further examination.

Thus the present study applies Skinner's theoretical insights in a new arena, locating them within a wider understanding of spatiality (Chapter 2) and using them to read the ascension within Acts (Chapters 3–7). Skinner has linked setting to the understanding of plot and characters within a narrative, recognising that settings 'can delimit the range of possibilities for action in a scene' and contribute to the symbolic and perceptive mood of a narrative, and that their repetition contributes towards the construction of 'archetypes and meaningful contrasts'.[43] Further, Skinner posits that settings reflexively relate with one another, and 'movement through various settings in a story can be a means of patterning events and anticipating or intensifying new horizons in the plot'.[44] Thus, Chapter 3 will argue that the fourfold repetition of οὐρανός at the outset of Acts (1:10–11) is highly important for constructing the narrative's spatiality.

Skinner's insights, taken together and applied to the ascension, anticipate οὐρανός exercising a rich functionality in the ordering of space within Acts. This study will therefore position the ascension in Acts 1 as more significant for the wider Acts narrative than previous scholarship has indicated, with commensurate benefits for reading Acts. As section two of this chapter demonstrates, this also involves revisiting characterisation within Acts: at the ascension, Jesus, as a key character within Luke-Acts, undergoes cumulative development

---

[40] Darr's reduction of setting to providing 'clues' and 'convenient markers' (Darr 1998: 70) for reading character might reflect his primary focus upon characterisation, but it falsely flattens out the dynamic and reflexive reaffirmation, negation, revision and supplementing of *settings* across Acts.

[41] Skinner 2003: 36; see also p. 36 n. 23. Regarding 'imagined' geographies within contemporary human geography, see Valentine 1999, Gregory 2000a.

[42] Parsons 1987 is an exception, but then Parsons 1998 failed to connect his insights concerning the ascension with his later examination of the narrative space of Acts. Eisen 2006 is more suggestive in this regard.

[43] Skinner 2003: 48–53, quoting from pp. 49, 51.   [44] Skinner 2003: 53.

rather than simply disappearing from the plot.[45] By sustaining Jesus as a placed character within the narrative, Acts encourages auditors[46] to appreciate his new location in heaven, by which Jesus' character becomes fused to some degree with the divine heavenly voice of Luke's Gospel.

This study anticipates that spatiality can be carried in small details within the narrative. Skinner helpfully inverts the conventional estimation that the typically limited explicit geographical description within biblical narrative makes assessment of geographical setting correspondingly harder: 'Although readers reared on modern novels may find the dearth of descriptive detail in biblical narratives unusual, it is not a unique phenomenon among the corpus of extant texts from antiquity … settings therefore could suggest rich associations among an audience without lengthy descriptions and play significant roles within the performance of the dramas.'[47] In short, limited elaboration or description of οὐρανός as Christ's new setting within Acts 1 does not preclude discernment of its significance for narrative spatiality.

While Skinner's theoretical insights helpfully inform new readings of narrative settings, Skinner notes that his work is suggestive rather than exhaustive.[48] Most importantly, full comprehension of a narrative's 'spatiality' cannot be reduced to setting, just as a narrative's understanding of *time* cannot be reduced to analysis of narrative pace. As Chapter 2 will establish, setting and space are related, even reflexive, but they are not coterminous. Skinner's failure to connect setting with space is partly exegetical, in that his analysis of Acts 21–8 does not examine the narrative's beginning, where the ascension exercises a comprehensive primacy effect over space in Acts.[49] Skinner's limited understanding of space is also theoretical, in that he interprets contemporary geographical theory too narrowly through the filter of setting. Skinner saw his own work as 'an early step toward a more comprehensive and much needed understanding

---

[45] By contrast, to cite an extreme example, the promising title of Fuller 1994 – 'The Life of Jesus, after the Ascension (Luke 24:50–53; Acts 1:9–11)' – leads to no consideration of Acts beyond 1:11!

[46] 'Auditor' is used throughout this study to refer to the intended recipient(s) of the narrative (without specifying a particular historical reconstruction), in recognition that most recipients would 'hear' rather than 'read' the text. For further discussion of orality within Acts, see Shiell 2004.

[47] Skinner 2003: 54–5 n. 92.   [48] Skinner 2003: 53.

[49] Without particular reference to spatiality, Parsons 1987: 182–4 recognises that 1:9–11 exhibits a primacy effect over narrative expectations.

of the importance of settings in Luke's narrative'.[50] This present project extends his work, utilising spatiality as a larger theoretical concept. Chapter 2, therefore, will develop an overarching understanding of space, with setting located within it, as the theoretical basis for the exegesis undertaken in Part II.

As both symptom and cause of the difficulty of theorising space, setting in itself lacks the necessary integrative analytical framework for examining space. Typically, insights concerning space remain as disparate observations regarding toponymy, topographical features, architectural design, geopolitical dimensions, and cosmological (dis) order. Rather than conducting a unified examination of space, those biblical scholars who have investigated setting have tended towards more piecemeal consideration or, at best, exploration of particular aspect(s) of space. Coming to biblical studies as a geographer, I want to bring geographical insights to bear on such a richly spatial text as Acts.

Mieke Bal has voiced the theoretical need for an integrative theory of space: 'Few concepts deriving from the theory of narrative texts are as self-evident, and yet have remained so vague, as the concept of *space*. Only a few theoretical publications have been devoted to it.'[51] For Bal, 'The relations between space and event become clear if we think of well-known, stereotypical combinations: declaration of love by moonlight on a balcony, high-flown reveries on a mountain-top, a rendezvous in an inn, ghostly appearances among ruins; brawls in cafés.'[52] Such fixed combinations form structural *topoi* and, arguably, ascension accounts could well represent such a *topos*. Indeed, historical-critical readings of the ascension, via form criticism, are already mindful of this suggestion, as Zwiep's work illustrates. Yet a *narrative* reading of the ascension requires more flexibility, since also 'the expectation that a clearly marked space will function as the frame for a suitable event may also be disappointed'.[53] Thus, mapping narrative representations of space requires sequential, cumulative, and synchronic analysis of space as it is constructed rhetorically and holistically within specific texts (in this instance, Acts) – readings which are sensitive to structural expectations but not determined by such structures.[54]

[50] Skinner 2003: 4.   [51] Bal 1995: 93.
[52] Bal 1995: 96.   [53] Bal 1995: 97.
[54] For similar theorisation concerning characterisation, see Darr 1992: 37.

Conclusion

Using Parsons's taxonomy to position existing ascension scholarship, this section has highlighted the limited synchronic analysis of the ascension within Acts as a wider narrative. It has also examined recent developments in understanding narrative setting within Acts, appropriating their strengths while looking beyond them for an adequate and integrative theory of narrative space. The overall direction of this study has been introduced through the contention that Jesus' post-ascension setting in heaven shapes other (earthly) settings, and indeed the production of space, within Acts.

2.   Christological presence *and* absence?

Existing ascension literature demonstrates an abiding scholarly tension between Christological presence and absence, and Jesus' corresponding activity or inactivity, engendered by the ascension.

Again, Parsons provides a starting point for discussion. His notion of an 'empty center'[55] to Acts, whereby Christ is a character who is 'absent but curiously present … around which both the major action and the various characters' thoughts revolve',[56] highlights the tension of post-ascension Christological presence and absence. Parsons is, however, far from being the first to raise this issue. It casts a longer shadow, within both biblical studies and systematic theology. A survey of this scholarship, even if necessarily selective, both positions this conundrum and anticipates moving beyond Parsons's formulation.

Presence and absence within biblical studies

First, the history of biblical studies reinforces the need for a *narrative* consideration of Christological presence and absence. A century ago, reflection on the ascension proclaimed an absent but active Christ, but without examining whether Acts *per se* would sustain such a conclusion.[57] Later on, mid-twentieth-century redaction criticism addressed more specifically the post-ascension Christology of Acts, but cast it in terms of a more passive absence. Under this reading, during the so-called 'epoch of the church', the Spirit substitutes for Christ, who remains in heaven until the parousia, which is now

---

[55] Parsons 1987: 160.   [56] Kreiswirth 1984: 39–40, quoted in Parsons 1987: 161.
[57] E.g. Swete 1910, MacLean 1915.

delayed until an indeterminate future time.[58] Mediation might happen through Jesus' name,[59] but Jesus is present on earth only 'as a figure from the past by means of the picture of him presented by tradition'.[60]

Charles Moule crystallised – and, to a degree, hardened – this position in the now much-quoted concept of 'absentee Christology'.[61] This hardening was not so much Moule's own work; he himself concluded that his survey of Acts 'seems to show that the Christology of Acts is not uniform, whatever may be said to the contrary',[62] and later he moderated his position further:

> The presence of the Spirit in a sense compensates for the absence (at least from sight) of the ascended Christ, and ... the presence of the Spirit continues the work of Christ. The Spirit implements in Christians the insights and the character and the activity belonging to Christ ... the Spirit communicates and extends the presence of Christ. And it is more accurate to say this than to say that the Spirit takes the place of Christ.[63]

Phrases such as 'in a sense', 'at least from sight' and 'the activity belonging to Christ' make apparent that this issue is conceptually complex. Moule's original formulation is perhaps much quoted because the phrase 'absentee Christology' deftly characterised one side of the argument and – whether Moule intended as much – lent itself as an expression of a passive Christology. There has, however, been a steady stream of those seeking to deny the applicability of an absent-and-passive Christological formulation to the post-ascension Christ in Acts.

One of the first such respondents to Moule was George MacRae, who, in 1973, commented: 'Our emphasis on the "absentee" character of the Christology of Acts is only half the story. How does the growing Christian community relate to the Christ who is exalted in heaven? Or to put the question differently, is there any sense in which the "absent" Christ is nevertheless present to his church?'[64] MacRae

---

[58] For instance, Haenchen (1971: 151) judges the Acts ascension account as understated, thereby orientating Christian disciples adjusting to life before the parousia. Similarly, van Stempvoort (1958/9) saw Luke 24 as doxological and Acts 1 as offering harder realism for the infant church.

[59] Conzelmann 1960: 178 n. 2; Haenchen 1971: 92.   [60] Conzelmann 1960: 186.

[61] Moule 1966: 179–80.   [62] Moule 1966: 181.

[63] Moule 1977: 104.   [64] MacRae 1973: 160.

then claimed 'four modes of "presence" at least', outlining four such 'senses' – the Spirit; Jesus' name; Jesus in remembered, recalled, and proclaimed history; and Jesus' model of discipleship.[65]

MacRae's work was picked up by O'Toole, who, in pressing against the bounds of Hans Conzelmann's temporal hypothesis, initially responded more to the issue of Christological passivity than to the question of absence:

> Unfortunately, Conzelmann's position has … led to the conviction on the part of some that Jesus after the ascension remains inactive in heaven. But this is not so … Jesus remains active (Acts 4:12; 5:31; 10:42; 13:38–42) through his name (2:21, 38; 3:6, 16; 4:7, 10, 12, 17, 18, 30; 5:28, 40f, 8:16 etc.), the Spirit (cf. Acts 16:7), 'witness' (Acts 18:5–10), discipleship (Acts 3:22–26; 26:23) and visions (cf. 7:54–56; 9:1–16, 27; 22:6–16, 17–22; 23:11; 26:12–18). Luke does not envisage three epochs but only two: the time before and the time after Jesus.[66]

Two years later, O'Toole advocated more firmly Christological presence as well as activity, defining Moule's 'absentee Christology' as meaning that 'the risen Jesus does little in this world; he is in heaven at the right hand of the Father'.[67] O'Toole vigorously rejected this view, concluding: 'The risen Lord acts and is present to the whole life of his church … Certainly, the Father and the Spirit are active, but a church without considerable activity on the part of the risen Christ is not Lukan.'[68] Not only was O'Toole's analysis longer than Moule's presentation of absentee Christology; it was also maximal in its search for Christological activity in Acts, appealing to evidence from twenty-two chapters of Acts.[69]

O'Toole's strident position was not without counter-presentations; J. A. Ziesler, for example, countered one important plank in the 'presence' argument, namely claims made concerning the 'name' of Jesus. Ziesler opposed the understanding that 'though Luke had removed Jesus firmly off the stage, he contrived to bring him back again through various devices, among them his "name"'.[70] Ziesler denied that Acts maintains any single 'concept of the name', claiming that a Hellenistic magical background precluded any sense of

---

[65] MacRae 1973: 160–5.   [66] O'Toole 1979: 112.
[67] O'Toole 1981: 472.   [68] O'Toole 1981: 498.
[69] The exceptional chapters being 12, 17, 24–5 and 27–8.   [70] Ziesler 1979: 28.

presence in Acts 3:16, and judged that Acts 9:34 is an anomaly, not the key to understanding healings in Acts.[71] Furthermore, Ziesler concluded, the 'name' referred to the past, not to the present. Such opposition to the post-ascension Christ being 'present' can be understood spatially as well as temporally.

The dichotomy is deep, but Parsons did not mediate between these positions. Instead he claimed O'Toole and MacRae as supportive of his own 'empty center' position (and against Moule's notion of 'absentee Christology'), and mentioned Ziesler's counter-argument only in passing.[72]

Parsons's position concerning this matter was not supported by Zwiep. In contrast Zwiep claimed that rapture Christology presents 'the almost unavoidable corollary ... that Luke advocates an "absentee christology", i.e. a christology that is dominated by the (physical) absence *and present inactivity* of the exalted Lord'.[73] Some of the aspects which O'Toole claimed as indicating an active post-ascension Christology appear less active within Zwiep's estimate that the post-ascension Christ 'does make his presence known but he does so in spiritual ways'.[74] Zwiep expounds his claim in a footnote:

> According to the Book of Acts, Jesus now acts through his name (Acts 3:16; 4:10, 30 cf. Acts 19:13), through the Spirit (Acts 10:19; 11:12; 13:2; 15:28; 16:6–7; 19:21?; 20:22–23; 21:4, 11), through visionary experiences (Acts 9:10, 12; 10:3, 11, 17, 19; 12:5; 16:8–10; 18:9–10; 22:17–18; 23:11; 26:19) and through angelic interventions (Acts 5:19; 12:7, 9, 23; 27:23), but these are all intermediary experiences.[75]

This is not unproblematic. Zwiep's crucial but rather adjectival category of 'intermediary experiences' is considerably strained by (e.g.) Acts 18:10, an issue not explored further by Zwiep. Even Moule, in his initial formulation of 'absentee Christology', had to acknowledge the 'undeniably' active Christ in 18:10.[76] Zwiep also fails to consider other important Acts references, such as 9:17, 34. He classifies Saul's Christophany in Acts 9 as a 'visionary experience' rather than 'a physical appearance of Jesus in line with the resurrection appearances', but acknowledges that 'it may be suggested that Luke would agree that Paul had had an encounter with the *exalted* lord from

---

[71] Ziesler 1979: 37–8.   [72] Cf. Parsons 1987: 162, 259 n. 69.
[73] Zwiep 1997: 182, emphasis original.   [74] Zwiep 1997: 182.
[75] Zwiep 1997: 182 n. 3.   [76] Moule 1966: 179.

heaven'.[77] Acts 9 is judged to be the terminus of such appearances, on the basis of 1 Corinthians 15:8,[78] even though his dismissive footnote (p. 182 n. 3, quoted above) makes reference to Acts 22:17–18. The same footnote provides Zwiep's only reference to 9:10, 12.

The underlying questions mount as Zwiep's main text then appeals to evidence *beyond* the Lukan corpus, first to Hebrews, before then concluding: 'Since the ascension Jesus seems to have been put on the sidetrack as it were, waiting for his glorious comeback at the parousia (cf. 1 Thess 1:10).'[79] In short, Zwiep inadequately establishes his argument from within Acts, especially if the question of presence and absence is, within Acts, a dynamic rather than a fixed hermeneutic one: '"Decisive withdrawal" obviously had meaning only to the disciples who had first known Jesus from the "earthly" side during His ministry … Paul, by contrast, began, as it were, at the opposite end.'[80]

Zwiep concluded that the ascension establishes the Jesus event 'along two separate lines', one in heaven, the other on earth.[81] The former axis is essentially passive and the latter axis functions via the Spirit, a reading reminiscent of Moule's original formulation of 'absentee Christology' but without Moule's qualifications concerning 18:10. Crucially, however, Zwiep did not explore the dialectical space *between* these 'separate' lines, the geography bound up with narrative interface of presence and absence. In short, Zwiep brought neither theology nor geography to bear in a narrative analysis of the heavenly Christ and the earthly church in Acts. This is the space the present study seeks to address.

The possibility of wider narrative referents for an active Christ within Acts, noted above, together with the pregnant import of Acts 1:1, qualify Zwiep's 'separate' lines of the ascended Christ's activity and keep open the possibility of other "activity" for the ascended Christ. Likewise, Zwiep's form-critical assessment of Saul's encounter on the Damascus road as a 'heavenly vision' misses what is arguably the key theological point of that thrice-told account within the overall narrative, namely that *Christ* continues to influence the flow of history, but in the 'wrong' epoch. Zwiep could accommodate this *temporal* aberration – 'Luke's focus is more on that which connects the two periods than that which divides them'[82] – but within Zwiep's schema the *spatial* violation of the post-ascension Christ directly intervening *on earth* is harder to bear.

---

[77] Zwiep 1997: 173, 130, emphasis original.   [78] Zwiep 1997: 172 n. 1.
[79] Zwiep 1997: 182.   [80] Moule 1957: 208.
[81] Zwiep 1997: 185.   [82] Zwiep 1997: 171.

A comparison of four scholars representing both sides of this debate, Moule and Zwiep as advocates of an absentee Christology and O'Toole and Beverly Gaventa[83] as supportive of a more active Christology, confirms this conclusion. Even allowing for the differing lengths of their analyses,[84] the comparison highlights two key issues.

First, the simple breadth of data appealed to within Acts confirms the need for a narrative reading: simple proof-texting is likely to prove insufficient in placing an argument. Critical assessment of claim and counter-claim requires a broader and more nuanced consideration than simply the piling up of citations. This is especially important given the lack of declared criteria for determining Christological activity, inactivity or intermediary activity.[85] Interpretative criteria remain subjective and frequently lacking in narrative consideration.

As a second and related issue, the diversity in verses cited from Acts by the two sides of this debate is noteworthy. Of Zwiep's 29 references, only 13 clearly match those used by O'Toole and/or Gaventa. Moule appeals to 25 references within Acts: 16 are 'shared' with O'Toole and/or Gaventa. Interestingly *all four scholars* appeal to 9:10; 16:6–7; 18:9–10 (Moule recognising it as opposing his thesis) and 23:11. Only six other references are shared by Moule and Zwiep. Both sides of the debate risk the possibility of an excluded middle, or of partial appeal to the Lukan data.

Studies of Acts, therefore, generate an oscillating debate between advocates ranged on either side of an apparent dualism:

Absence　　………………　Presence

‖　　　　　　　　　　　‖

Inactivity　　………………　Activity

Implicit alliances of absence with inactivity and of presence with activity strengthen the usually unarticulated power of the dualism.[86] The prevalence of 'in a sense' argumentation, highlighted above,

---

[83] Gaventa 2003b.

[84] Moule and Zwiep's analyses are clearly shorter than O'Toole and Gaventa's longer examinations.

[85] Gaventa 2003b makes this same observation concerning MacRae 1973 and O'Toole 1981. It is also applicable to (*inter alia*) Moule 1966 and Zwiep 1997. Gaventa 2003b defines activity of Jesus as 'when either the narrator or a character refers to an action on the part of Jesus that takes place after the ascension itself'.

[86] Cf. the geographer Sayer (1991: 284), discussing the evocative notion of 'locality': 'It is when they are aligned that dualisms are at their most seductive and dangerous. What impresses us about such thinking may have more to do with its simplicity and symmetry than its ability to interpret the world.'

betrays the limited traction of existing analyses. Even Parsons, whose narrative sensitivities contribute to his reluctance to subscribe to absentee Christology 'because of the theological baggage the term carries with it', adds an ambivalent note: 'but in a sense this idea of an absent Christ along with the idea of an ascended Lord paints in broad strokes at least part of Luke's characterization of Jesus in Luke-Acts'.[87] Taken together, these observations raise the suspicion that, upon analysis, the alignment of these categories will either break down or involve more complex relationships than is commonly realised.[88] But unless it is to run and run,[89] how is it possible to move beyond this interpretative impasse?

Presence and absence within systematic theology

If biblical studies has yet to resolve this impasse of presence and absence, then perhaps attention needs to turn elsewhere, to the systematic examinations of the ascension which represent the most recent ascension scholarship. Beginning with Douglas Farrow's monograph 'Ascension and Ecclesia',[90] these studies have offered considerable reflection on the issue of Christological presence and absence.

Beginning from the premise that 'the question about Jesus underlies the question about the church', Farrow examined the balance between Christ present and Christ absent, claiming that 'this particular ambiguity [is] at its [the church's] very heart'.[91] Farrow's organising principle makes two major advances, both of which anticipate the reading of Acts pursued here.

First, Farrow self-consciously raises Christological presence and absence as a first-order question, rather than an issue governed by a prior interpretative stance. Farrow breaks free of redaction criticism's influence (perhaps because he is a systematic theologian), judging that 'the delay of the parousia crisis was strictly a modern one'.[92] This liberates his analysis from prior historical schemas, which

---

[87] Parsons 1987: 240 n. 278. Jesus' name occurs 68 times in Acts, spread over 24 of its 28 chapters.

[88] Cf. Sayer 1991.

[89] Mark Strauss 1995: 356 raises this Christological question at the close of his monograph on the Davidic Messiah in Luke-Acts. Cf. also Tiede 1986: 280; Buckwalter 1996: 21–2, 173–92; and Turner 2000: 295–7.

[90] Farrow 1999.   [91] Farrow 1999: ix, 3.

[92] Farrow 1999: 17. As Chapter 2 demonstrates, the parousia-delay hypothesis has subdued a spatial reading of the ascension.

have dominated Acts scholarship over the last fifty years, allowing proper attention to be given to presence and absence in their own right.[93] Unlike those who view the ascension and Pentecost as neatly demarcating the period of Jesus from that of the church, Farrow judges that 'Pentecost does not *resolve* the problem of presence and absence. It *creates* it, by adding a presence which discloses the absence.'[94] Farrow has posed, therefore, a quite deliberately spatial question – 'Where is Jesus?' – at the centre of his work,[95] a question which the temporal focus of previous ascension scholarship, with its concern with forty days and parousia timings, has ignored or down-played. Further, Farrow also rejects viewing the ascension as an event with little distinct significance in the NT beyond Luke 24 and Acts 1. As such, although not engaging in narrative analysis of scripture,[96] Farrow indirectly anticipates such an approach.

Second, Farrow explicitly links the ascension with ecclesiological issues. Importantly, the ascension's impact upon believers within Acts is a more fundamental plot-line than Parsons's examination of the place of the Jews within the narrative. Farrow's re-examination of Christological presence and absence resonates with other recent eccle-siological debates,[97] further highlighting the need for a longitudinal narrative approach. Farrow's ecclesiological inquiry requires more focused narrative analysis, and Acts represents fruitful ground for such a study.

Farrow has been enthusiastically popularised by Scott Dawson, not least with regard to this problematic matter of presence and absence.[98] Dawson asks the key questions: 'If Jesus is in heaven, then can he be *with* us?' and, if so, then 'What kind of space?'[99] He also highlights Farrow's debt to T.F. Torrance's articulations of space, a legacy which has helped systematic theology move ahead of biblical studies in understanding Christ's ascension.[100] Dawson also

---

[93] Farrow here builds upon the earlier insights of Torrance 1976: 123–39.

[94] Farrow 1999: 271 n. 59, emphases original.

[95] This is the title of Farrow's fifth and central chapter (Farrow 1999: 165–254).

[96] Farrow's Acts 9 *inclusio* (Farrow 1999: 15, 273) comes closest; instead, however, Farrow's narrative follows the centuries of church history, from Origen to Barth.

[97] Both the Trinitarian notion of 'ecclesial being' developed by Volf (1998) and debate concerning whether the locus of the church is heaven or earth (Peterson 1998a, cf. Giles 1995) call out for further consideration through a narrative reading of Acts.

[98] Dawson 2004.   [99] Headings from Dawson 2004: 44–50.

[100] Torrance (1976: 130) conceptualises space as 'relational and variational'.

reiterates Farrow's concern that the ascension not be spiritualised and thereby domesticated, with Jesus 'safely diffused and dissolved into the heavens … [where] he no longer seems a threat to the rulers of the world'.[101]

Farrow's approach has also been developed by Andrew Burgess. Importantly for the present study, Burgess rejects Farrow's foundational eucharistic ecclesiology[102] as ill-defined and 'loaded with more freight than it can safely bear – especially with any New Testament mandate'.[103] Farrow has objected to this qualification of his method,[104] but it is justified, especially given the Acts narrative's sustained focus on the growing 'word' (e.g. 2:41; 4:4; 6:7; 8:4, 14, 25; 10:44; 11:1, 19; 12:24), whereas eucharistic references within Acts are at best only infrequent and ambiguous.[105] Regarding presence and absence, however, Burgess accepts Farrow's overall claim that this matter is central to understanding the ascension. Burgess pitches the issue in Barthian categories concerning the 'time between';[106] as this chapter and the next will propose, this is also a matter of the 'space between'.

The impasse in biblical studies identified earlier is encapsulated in Burgess's comment: 'The question is … "what manner of description of Jesus' presence is appropriate?"'[107] As this chapter has proposed, this question requires a narrative answer from Acts, but Burgess does not provide it. Like Farrow, Burgess comes up against a *narrative* impasse when articulating presence and absence. Regarding Acts 1:9–11, Burgess comments: 'The ascension cannot be seen as simple absence – rather it creates the possibility of *an altogether different form of presence*',[108] but then he abstracts this assertion from Acts, moving instead immediately to Barth's use of Colossians 3:1.[109] Yet whether the Acts narrative sustains this claim is of signal interest, if not utmost importance, for upholding Burgess's argument.

[101] Dawson 2004: 55.
[102] Farrow (1999: 1) illustrates this concept's early and unargued assumption within his argument.
[103] Burgess 2004: 138.   [104] Farrow 2005.
[105] The sacramental 'Christian theology of place' developed by Inge (2003) risks the same imbalance. Heil (1999) provides a sustained exposition of implicit eucharistic-spaces within Acts.
[106] Burgess 2004: 15–16 provides an introductory summary of this term.
[107] Burgess 2004: 150.   [108] Burgess 2004: 96, emphasis added.
[109] Burgess 2004: 99 n. 12.

Conclusion: presence and absence in prospect

In summary, Farrow, Dawson and Burgess provide clear evidence of systematic scholarship preceding biblical studies, highlighting the kinds of question which biblical scholars need to address if they are to move past their impasse regarding presence and absence. Yet in this matter, both biblical studies and systematic theology require more sensitivity to the narrative specificities of Acts. This suggests space for biblical studies to develop further these insights.

Bringing together this chapter's two sections, two directions for the present study can be proposed. First, the ascension needs consideration as a narrative event within Acts. This examination must include, but not be reduced to, the concept of narrative setting. Second, the ascension – especially within biblical studies – has raised tendentious understandings of Christological presence and absence, passivity and activity, within Acts. In this light, it is little wonder, perhaps, that Gaventa has eschewed 'the customary language of *geography* or *location*' when addressing these matters,[110] but systematicians have maintained at least the prospect of an alternative way forward. Yet although they ask the right questions concerning space, Farrow, Dawson and Burgess have not drawn on the theoretical insights of contemporary human geography in their readings of the ascension. Van Stempvoort's challenge, with which this chapter opened, thus provokes a new response. This study proposes that theories of space generated within the discipline of human geography will advance understanding of Christological presence and absence brought about by the ascension, a conundrum which itself indicates the need for such a spatial analysis.

Therefore the contentions made in both halves of this chapter point towards the need for a richer spatial understanding of the ascension, one informed by geographical theory. Chapter 2 will outline such theories, before subsequent chapters engage in an exegetical narrative-spatial reading of the ascension within Acts.

---

[110] Gaventa 2003b: n.p., emphasis original.

2

FINDING A PLACE FOR ASCENSION GEOGRAPHY

Both contentions made in Chapter 1, that the ascension in Acts requires a narrative reading, and that the ascension concerns problematic conceptions of Christological presence and absence, point towards the need for geographical theory to inform a richer spatial understanding of the ascension. Yet, as Chapter 1 has also shown, narrative criticism has tended to underplay the geographical or spatial aspects of the text. All too often, geography is reduced to background scenery, or considered only as a flash of 'colour', or assumed to function as an already-made 'setting' in which narrative action subsequently occurs. Geography is rarely viewed as being genuinely involved in developing the narrative and its theological message.

This chapter explores the reasons for this marginalisation of geography, arguing that it unjustifiably constrains a fully critical reading of the text, and proposes an alternative understanding of space which Part II of this study will use to read Acts. Sections 1 and 2 identify a critique of the neglect of space which has arisen within human geography. Then, after a survey of previous attempts to read scripture for its spaces (section 3), sections 4 and 5 outline and position the theory and method utilised in Part II.

1.   The forgotten place of geography

Biblical studies' neglect of geography reflects a wider marginalising of the spatial aspect of reality within modern Western social theorisation. The bounds of this disregard of geography are broad, mapping a larger intellectual stance over the past two centuries. The human geographer Ed Soja, for example, makes a wide-ranging critique of what he sees as a modernist neglect, casting it as 'historicism'. By this, Soja means 'an over-developed contextualisation of social life and theory that actively submerges and peripheralises the geographical imagination'.[1] Allan Pred, another, American, geographer whose analysis parallels that of Soja, opposes 'a privileging of history that either peripheralizes, subordinates, submerges, or devalues all that is spatial, or totally neglects any manifestation of humanly transformed nature and human geography, completely ignoring the sit(e)-uated dimension of all social life'.[2] Pred asserts that 'all histories are geographically specific … [and] All human geographies are historically specific', with the intention of '(re)discovering the unbreakable links between the historical, the geographical, and the social'.[3] Both Pred and Soja disavow splitting history from geography, seeing such divisions as part of the problem of historicism rather than a path to its resolution: 'Twentieth-century social scientists – whether of positivistic, interpretive, or Marxist persuasion – have for the most part preferred to re-represent the world in vertical, aspatial, and sequential terms, in terms of historical depth and duration, rather than in terms of horizontality, proximity, and simultaneity, rather than in terms of geographical configuration and extent.'[4]

Instead, Soja suggests addressing historicism through nothing less than 'a new critical human geography, an historical and geographical materialism'.[5] Soja's strategy involves deconstructing and recomposing 'the rigidly historical narrative' that has underpinned much of Western social theory rather than implementing 'a superficial linguistic spatialisation that makes geography appear to matter theoretically as much as history'.[6] Such an ontological realignment aims to counter the historical hermeneutic that has silenced, marginalised and excluded consideration of space.

Although Soja's diagnosis of historicism is illustrated from the wider social and political sciences, he does not extend his analysis to biblical studies.[7] As this chapter demonstrates, Soja's critique applies fruitfully to biblical studies, challenging entrenched, taken-for-granted assumptions about geography within biblical scholarship. Yet for many observers, the idea of geography as supplying a more constitutive reading strategy for scripture seems laughable. Stereotypes which equate geography with colouring in maps do not immediately suggest innovative and productive readings of scripture.

---

[1] Soja 1989: 15.   [2] Pred 1990: 6.   [3] Pred 1990: 1, 2.   [4] Pred 1990: 5.
[5] Soja 1989: 6.   [6] Soja 1989: 1, 7.
[7] Soja is a leading figure in what is termed the 'Los Angeles School' of postmodern urban geography, and this is where – in both a locational and sub-disciplinary sense – Soja's own research interests are centred.

Such stereotypes might have held true in the 1950s,[8] but since then much has changed within academic geography. A wider appreciation of its development as a scholarly discipline will render such dismissals as premature.

2.   A more dynamic place: the history of human geography

As a modern academic discipline, geography's origins lie in the colonialist days of the late nineteenth century.[9] Its initial paradigm was environmental determinism, that is, an understanding that the physical environment determines human society. Yet this paradigm not only underpinned European colonialism; it also buttressed National Socialism in 1930s and 1940s Germany. This implication with the horrors of that time led geography to a post-war retreat into regional studies, 'back into its neo-Kantian cocoon'.[10] By studying regions, geography retreated into description, away from discredited theory. Thus, shrinking to 'the explanation of geographies by geographies, geographical analysis turned into itself, the description of associated outcomes deriving from processes whose deeper theorization was left to others ... [By 1960] the discipline of modern geography was theoretically asleep'.[11] The modern stereotype of geography as maps solidified during this era as geography *became* the map and the topical organisation of its elements, both physical and human, with space and time as merely external containers or frameworks for these regional elements.

By the 1960s, however, a new generation of Anglo-American geographers had become dissatisfied with simply mapping and describing regions. Instead, they sought to bring mathematical modelling and geometry to the fore, presenting geography as 'spatial science', a newly theorised discipline which examined space as a separate structure with its own autonomous laws of construction and transformation. This period, later termed the 'quantitative revolution', was short-lived.[12] It itself experienced a crisis, as geographers realised that retreating into mathematical modelling was actually taking

[8] E.g. D. M. Smith (1984: 118, 119): 'Like so many of my contemporaries who reached the sixth form at school in the early 1950s, my first ability in geography was revealed by a capacity to draw sketch maps with extraordinary neatness ... [As an undergraduate] it was the second year before I found it necessary to enter the library.'
[9] Livingstone 1992: 216–59; cf. Driver 1992.   [10] Soja 1989: 37.
[11] Soja 1989: 38.   [12] Billinge, Gregory and Martin 1984, Barnes 2000a.

them further away from the turbulent events of the real world in the late 1960s.

In the 1970s two strands of 'postpositivist' human geography arose in reaction to the quantitative revolution. One was structuralist, predominantly Marxist, emphasising the influence of economic and political structures on the shaping and interaction of places.[13] The other strand, termed 'humanistic', consisted of various attempts to reinstate human agency at the fore of geography.[14] Both streams continued to understand 'geography' in its etymological senses, seeking to 'write the earth'.[15] In this sense, at least, they showed continuity with earlier regional manifestations of geography. But both structural and humanistic geography were attempting to theorise rather than simply describe, and thus differed from earlier regional studies. Most crucially, both strands conceived space as far more active in constituting social life than had been the case under the descriptive regional paradigm. Yet unlike 'spatial science', postpositivist geography does not view space in itself as causing or explaining anything; rather than being the specific object of study for geographers, space is essential for any social actions, actions which give meanings to places. In summary, geography now examines more than mere patterns of distribution in space: it is concerned with conceptualising the processes which produce space and create places.

In the 1980s, structuration theory attempted to unite these two poles of human geography.[16] Under this theory, human agency and social structure reflexively shape one another in the course of producing space and constructing place. Subsequently, as part of a 1990s 'postmodern wave',[17] human geography has undergone a further development, generally called 'the cultural turn'. Geographers who had been focused on social, economic and political forces have rediscovered the cultural aspects of human reality and have also interacted more with questions of 'nature'.[18]

Now more than ever, geography is dynamic and pluriform, sensitive to heterogeneity, conscious of the politics of presentation and interpretation, and eager to allow room for new and marginalised ways of writing the earth. It is a multi-headed, interdisciplinary – even 'post-disciplinary' – creature.[19] Even this brief and sketchy survey

[13] E.g. Harvey 1973; especially cf. Harvey 1969.   [14] E.g. Ley and Samuels 1978.
[15] Cf. Darby 1962.   [16] Gregory 2000b.
[17] Dear 1994.   [18] P. Crang 2000.
[19] For a revealing cross-section of this contemporary diversity, see Johnston, Gregory, Pratt and Watts 2000; cf. Soja 1996: 83–163.

demonstrates that twenty-first-century geography is far more diverse and richer theoretically than earlier, but still enduring reductionist stereotypes which reduce geography to maps. In addition, this survey has indicated the ways in which past conceptualisations of geography have fed and reinforced the historicism that Soja has criticised.

3.   Out of place: the submerged geography of biblical studies

Biblical studies has begun to cross the boundaries of historicism such that, as this chapter will indicate, there is now too vast an array of biblical studies using space for a comprehensive survey to be possible here.[20] This growth reflects, and is part of, a wider resurgence of interest in place and space.[21] A critical survey of the origins of this interest in space within biblical studies has previously been lacking;[22] providing such a survey with particular attention to Luke-Acts and the ascension will inform and position the reading method adopted in Part II of this study.

Wider biblical studies

Soja's accusation of historicism is borne out by a survey of twentieth-century theological dictionaries. Older dictionaries frequently contain articles on historiography, but they lack any geographical equivalent.[23] Becoming a repeated neglect, this absence continued into the 1980s.[24] The first dictionary article dedicated to geography did not appear until the 1990 *Dictionary of Biblical Interpretation*: even then it still presented geography as the passive handmaiden of theology without any suggestion that theology itself is inherently geographical.[25] The 1992 *Anchor Bible Dictionary* made a more concerted

---

[20] This escalation in scholarly interest has happened within the opening few years of this century: before then, an exhaustive survey was conceivable. Any review is, now, necessarily partial.

[21] For a helpful survey of scholarly examinations of place, including those in theology and religious studies, see http://pegasus.cc.ucf.edu/~janzb/place (accessed July 2008). For an introduction to these issues, see Cresswell 2004.

[22] Berquist (2002) focuses more narrowly on the immediate precursors of biblical studies' contemporary interest in 'critical spatiality'. Inge (2003: 1–32) is astute concerning academic geography, but does not connect directly with Lukan studies.

[23] E.g. Troeltsch 1913.

[24] E.g. Kent 1983, Anonymous 1987 and Hennesey 1987 each lack a geographical equivalent.

[25] Curtis 1990. Historical analysis was, as usual, well represented in this dictionary: see Downing 1990, Morgan 1990, and Stanton 1990.

attempt to cover the geographical. Its three articles addressing geographical themes highlight the submerged geography of twentieth-century biblical studies.

First, in an article entitled 'Geography and the Bible (Palestine)', Nicholas Raphael describes geography in terms of spatial science, although analysis is divided into 'physical character' and 'human geography', categories more reminiscent of regional description.[26] The latter category remains descriptive and concerned narrowly with distribution patterns. It covers the evolution of settlement patterns, landscape modification, agriculture, and towns and road networks. Not only is such 'geography' inconsistent and outdated, it is also not integrated with theology.[27]

More recent but still somewhat outdated geographical analysis was used in a second *ABD* article, 'Geography and the Bible (Early Jewish)' by Philip Alexander.[28] Alexander used the concept of 'mental maps', a concept developed in 1970s humanistic geography, with an acknowledgement that geographers 'are less tied than they used to be to the idea that the only "real" map is one that results from careful surveying and mathematical projection',[29] and a warning that maps are not always value-free. This risks maintaining a dualism between 'real' and 'imagined' space, and the implication remains – supported by Alexander's appeal to a notion of 'pure' geography for some representations – that some maps can be and indeed *are* value-free.[30] Yet maps *always* present a point of view and need to be read with a pervading hermeneutic of suspicion, a 'cartographic anxiety'.[31] The printed maps inserted in the back of modern Bibles, with their solid lines of missionary travel and discrete places giving every appearance of having been completely 'claimed' for the gospel, very easily distort readers' appreciation and understanding of the narrative-geography within Acts – especially for 'readers' raised in a culture of colonial maps with their politically implicated Euclidian distortion and obfuscation of 'on-the-ground' lived experience.[32]

---

[26] Raphael 1992. For a similar static and non-dialectical 'geography' with undertones of environmental determinism, see Wallace and Williams 1998: 8–14.

[27] Similarly, Kitchen 1955, Baly 1957, 1987.   [28] P. S. Alexander 1992.

[29] P. S. Alexander 1992: 978. Cf. P. S. Alexander 1990: 121–2.

[30] Alexander 1992: 978.   [31] Gregory 1994; cf. Harley 1989.

[32] Whitelam (2007) makes this same point regarding 'OT' cartographies, albeit with a questionable denial of *any* historical representation of historical reality (p. 75). Closer to Acts, M. B. Thompson (1998: 61) provides an initially disorienting, but more illuminating, alternative cartographic presentation of first-century Mediterranean travel routes.

Such criticisms notwithstanding, Alexander's article put geography much more on the map of biblical studies: 'The Bible played a central role in early Jewish education and scholarship, and much geographical information was conveyed in the form of commentary on the biblical geographical texts.'[33] Alexander made a particularly important recognition, paralleling secular geographical theory, that the projection of some sort of order on to space represents a fundamental and unavoidable human reality that analyses of biblical text need to consider.[34] Place and self mutually constitute each other in a reciprocal relationship which, far from rendering place as simply a marker, casts it as involved actively in the construction of meaning. By extension, places affect one another, and one type of place can tyrannise or dominate other types of place, as place both facilitates and inhibits human awareness.[35]

Alexander's instinct was right, and he tried to break out of outdated notions of geography, even if his analysis was still constrained by a notion of 'biblical geographical texts', defined in terms of their form and content. At this juncture Alexander's analysis parallels that of Shimon Bar-Efrat, who, while arguing that 'places in the narrative are not merely geographical facts, but are to be regarded as literary elements in which fundamental significance is embodied', limited his analysis to 'geographical places, such as cities and rivers, or … details within them, such as houses and rooms'.[36] Alexander did not develop a more comprehensive geographical analysis which would be sensitive to more implicit geographical information carried within, and itself shaping, the text. Thus Alexander's method gives no suggestion of a comprehensive reading strategy for a whole narrative such as Acts. That kind of methodological step will have to come from elsewhere. Consequently, although Alexander's allusion to a Genesis 10–11 'Table of Nations' tradition in Acts 2:9–11 (the only NT text he considers) might be illuminating, it is constraining if this then becomes the limit of geographical analysis. Admittedly, the restrictions of a dictionary article may have constrained analysis of this selective citation, but a text's ability to project ideas that can be

---

[33] P. S. Alexander 1992: 978.   [34] P. S. Alexander 1992: 978.
[35] Sack 1986, 1997.
[36] Bar-Efrat 1989: 194, 187. Furthermore, Bar-Efrat assumes a historicist antagonism between 'fundamentally static and unchanging' space and what he judges biblical narrative's primary concern: 'fluctuations and developments, which are a function of time' (p. 196).

presented in the form of a map remains a consistent and unnecessary limitation on Alexander's geographical analysis and method.[37]

Such reduction of geography to cartography is common within biblical studies. Sometimes it has been virtually complete;[38] in other instances it fragments geographical description into location facts for (historical) verification.[39] Yet ancient 'geographical knowledge' was not dependent upon maps, but was instead a composite of other media such as travel reports and other literary records.[40] Jacob's comments concerning the ancient Greek world also apply to biblical geographies: 'Map-making could have implied a different balance between writing and drawing ... We have to investigate the complex meaning of the Greek verb *graphein* – drawing, writing, depicting – a polsemy inherent in the term "geo-graphy".'[41] Also, as recent cultural geography declares, the 'simple overlaying of one "map" with another may be interesting but is fairly limited in scope'.[42] In other words, static comparative geography-as-cartography in itself offers little purchase on the diachronic unfolding of a narrative's spatiality.

A third *ABD* article, 'Direction and Orientation', by Joel Drinkard Jr, broke the shackles constraining geographical analysis. Its short but helpful contribution to a renewed geographical analysis of biblical texts moves beyond merely formal definitions of the geographical.[43] Rather than biblical geography being defined by form or content, Drinkard argued, all biblical texts can be assumed to have a direction and an orientation. This orientation is in part literary, in part theological: in practice, the two are combined and, within narrative, form part of the warp and weft of the text itself. Drinkard's brief article provokes three further observations. First, his observation parallels the inherent spatiality assumed by recent human geographers such as Pred, Soja and Robert Sack. Second, although Drinkard's survey did not make any reference to the NT, his

---

[37] This is especially true given the lack of an extant *Jubilees* map, and given earlier comments regarding 'cartographic anxiety'. The same observations also apply to P. S. Alexander 1997. Cf. Flanagan 1999, who only examines P. S. Alexander 1982, 1992.

[38] See, e.g., Vanderkam 1994, entitled 'Putting Them in Their Place: Geography as an Evaluative Tool'. On one level Vanderkam's subtitle is misplaced, 'geography' never being mentioned in the article. On another level, his text deconstructs its title, revealing a subdued, domesticated notion of geography.

[39] For instance, the disparate elements discussed in Grant 1992, under the title 'Early Christian Geography'.

[40] Jacob 1999: 26. Jacob describes Strabo's *Geography* as 'a literary geography that did not rely at all on map-making but on the compilation of a library'.

[41] Jacob 1999: 27.   [42] M. Crang 1998: 47.   [43] Drinkard 1992.

understanding of geography reduces any tendency to see the OT as more amenable to spatial readings of scripture.[44] Third, although Drinkard did not apply his observation to whole narratives, his recognition of a text's inherent geography opens up the possibility of reading strategies which can view complete narrative texts as integrated spatialities.

To conclude this survey of theological dictionaries, other recent publications confirm a new and growing interest in geography as constitutive of theological meaning, but also indicate that this directional shift is far from complete. In part this reflects the time-lag from conception to publication,[45] and from discipline to discipline; in part it also reflects a continued equation of geography with a background or subsidiary role in interpreting scripture.[46] Although its boundaries are being traversed, historicist marginalisation of space is far from vanquished within biblical studies.

Luke-Acts

This section outlines three different reductionist readings of geography which have informed readings of Luke-Acts. Identifying their limitations prepares for a more comprehensive spatial reading of Acts.

The reduction of Lukan geography to history

If the effects of historicism are evident in wider biblical studies, they are especially apparent in Acts scholarship. We need look no further than Conzelmann for evidence of historicism skewing readings of

---

[44] This tendency is implicit in the present 'lead' in spatial readings of the OT. See, e.g., Gunn and McNutt 2002, Berquist and Camp 2007.

[45] Hastings, Mason and Piper (2000: vii), for example, state that their volume was conceived in 1992, with publication intended to coincide with the millennium. The volume contains an article entitled 'History' (Hastings 2000), but no parallel consideration of geography.

[46] Tellingly, the editorial remit for the *Dictionary of New Testament Background* (Evans and Porter 2000) explicitly included geography. Its article on 'Geographical Perspectives in Late Antiquity' (J. M. Scott 2000) will be discussed below. Further, while a recent *Encyclopaedia of Christianity* contains an article on 'Geography of Religion' (Henkel 2001), its entry on 'History, Auxiliary Sciences to' (Giessler-Wirsig 2001) includes geography as its eighth and final 'auxiliary science'. Henkel's essay is not examined further here, given that it does not materially affect strategies for reading scripture.

Luke-Acts.[47] Hugely important in his day, Conzelmann opened up the inquiry for specifically Lukan theology, but his very success bedevilled the search for the spatial in subsequent research. Although his redactive theory concerning the composition of Luke and Acts is now dated and has been subject to critique,[48] his historicist understanding of geography has been enduring. Given the ascension's pivotal place in Conzelmann's schema, his understanding of geography requires specific critique as a ground-clearing exercise before outlining the approach adopted in this present study.

In essence, Conzelmann's thesis was historical: he proposed a crisis of history within Luke's community, provoked by a delayed parousia. Luke's solution, according to Conzelmann, was also historical, in that Luke formulated three epochs of salvation history in order to account for the ongoing life of the earthly church within secular history. Thus Conzelmann's foundational question is 'In what sense … can Luke be described as a "historian"?'[49]

In shaping his historical schema, Conzelmann's Luke manipulated geography by, for example, locating the ministries of John the Baptist and Jesus in separate regions. For Conzelmann, geography consisted of compositional 'elements' that could be manipulated by the redactor to fit historical ends.[50] Geography consisted of locational markers, whether typological (e.g. 'the lake', mountaintops) or particular (e.g. 'Jerusalem'). Once positioned, one could move on from geography to the core issues of history. Reading Conzelmann, one is left not only seeing Jesus as 'The Centre of History'[51] but also sensing that history is at the centre of understanding Jesus. This controlling role for history extends into Conzelmann's reading of Acts, where 'it is not so much developed as it is presupposed'.[52]

---

[47] E.g. Conzelmann 1960, noting its original 1954 German title, *Die Mitte der Zeit* ('The Middle of Time'). Conzelmann's later Acts commentary (Conzelmann 1987; original German publication 1963) continued in the same historicist vein. In its introduction, the only (and brief) reference to geography in Acts concerns the 'problem' of the 'we' passages (Conzelmann 1987: xl).

[48] For illustrative criticisms of Conzelmann's parousia-delay hypothesis, see Tiede 1986; Zwiep 1997: 175–80; Nolland 1998.

[49] Conzelmann 1960: 12. Cf. Conzelmann 1987: xlv–xlviii. At no point does Conzelmann explicitly frame the corresponding question regarding in what sense Luke can be described as a geographer.

[50] Part I of Conzelmann 1960 is entitled 'Geographical Elements in the Composition of Luke's Gospel' (pp. 18–94), originally 'Die Geographischen Vorstellungen als Element der Komposition des Lukas Evangeliums'.

[51] The title of Part IV of Conzelmann 1960 (170–206), originally 'Die Mitte der Geschichte'.

[52] Conzelmann 1987: xlv.

Conzelmann's historicism appropriates and uses space, dominates and controls it, even produces it in its own image. There is no comparable notion of 'salvation geography'. Yet even as Conzelmann establishes it, the issue provoking the redactor remains stubbornly geographical: Luke's community needs to understand its 'place' within what is assumed to be uneschatological history. The same is true of later developments of Conzelmann's thesis, such as the hypothesis that Luke's community faced a dual crisis of false apocalyptic hope caused by excessively imminent eschatological expectations existing alongside (potential?) loss of faith due to parousia delay.[53]

In consequence, two conclusions become clear. First, Conzelmann's analysis was a product of its time and place. His understanding of geography as merely locational markers reflected the post-war context within which he wrote.[54] More recently his bold assertions concerning Luke's geographical inconsistency and incompetence have been questioned, and Conzelmann is now seen as having underplayed Lukan geographical nuances.[55] Quite apart from whether geography can be reduced to isolated verifiable 'facts' – something that present-day geographers would oppose[56] – Conzelmann's understanding of Lukan geography still begs the question. Even allowing for Luke to have got his geographical facts 'wrong', why is Luke so interested in something he does not know about? Admittedly, the question could be reversed and marginalised, such that Luke is not concerned about geography and so has failed to 'correct' it, but this denies and undermines Luke's claim to be writing an 'orderly narrative' (Luke 1:3; cf. Acts 11:4) and the probability that Luke's 'geography', his 'writing the earth', is part of this claim. Also, the richness and sheer diversity of the geographical data within Luke's narrative overwhelm any continuing denial of the question.

---

[53] Wilson 1973: 104–7; cf. pp. 68, 80.

[54] Remarking on the forceful language of removal in Acts 3:23, and connecting such terminology with the Holocaust, Wasserberg (1998: 227 n. 35) comments on how German commentators have characteristically side-stepped the perceived harshness of this verse. Given geographers' recognition that the Holocaust was essentially spatial (Cole 2003), and that post-war geography retreated from theorising space (G. Smith 2000), it is perhaps unsurprising that post-war German biblical scholarship should also prioritise the temporal rather than the spatial.

[55] E.g. Béchard 1999. Hengel (1983: 97–128) nuances Conzelmann's geography while preserving many of his presuppositions concerning the nature of geography.

[56] Recent geographical attention has shifted from issues of falsification – issues foregrounded within historical criticism – to questions of 'dramatisation' of self and other within representations of peoples, places, landscapes and cultures (Gregory 2000a).

Second, Conzelmann illustrates the enduring hold of now out-of-date notions of geography within Lukan studies. As perhaps the most influential hand on geographical readings of Acts, Conzelmann's redactive reading of Luke's Gospel has influenced at least one generation of Lukan scholars. Yet whereas Conzelmann's tripartite conception of salvation history has been questioned for some time,[57] his understanding of geography has been curiously enduring, a resilience reflecting a wider hegemony enjoyed by historicist assumptions within the modernist West. Clearly, Conzelmann is illustrative rather than unique in this regard. Biblical studies in general has been seen as 'a necessarily historical enterprise' which has neglected a 'sociological exegesis'.[58]

The reduction of Lukan geography to cartography and tradition

If Conzelmann remains influential but is now dated, then James Scott has produced a recent and significant monograph-length examination of biblical geographies. Crucially, however, he replicates Philip Alexander's earlier limited equation of geography with what can be mapped.[59] Scott's portrayal of a *Jubilees* tradition concerning the Table of Nations, which he sees as permeating the book of Acts, therefore remains vulnerable to the criticisms raised earlier concerning Alexander's work.

Further, Scott's consistent equation of geography with tradition must, of necessity, stress continuity and uniformity. As a result it allows insufficient scope for discontinuity, for geographical change over time, for simultaneous and contested diversity, and for theological developments to initiate spatial restructuring. Such a reduced understanding of geography will unduly limit analysis of space and place. The proximity of Christ's ascension to Jerusalem, for example, does not *inevitably* underscore a tradition which casts Jerusalem as 'the omphalos connecting heaven and earth, a veritable *axis mundi* of intersecting horizontal and vertical planes'.[60] Rather, as

---

[57] Within German-speaking scholarship, see, e.g., Wasserberg 1998.
[58] Barton 1995: 67, 68.
[59] J. M. Scott 2002. This volume replicates the method and perspectives expressed in J. M. Scott 2000.
[60] J. M. Scott 2002: 57. Cf., e.g., Weaver 2004: 117–19.

cartographers now increasingly acknowledge, discontinuities are inherent within any transmission of geographical information.[61]

Therefore, as Chapter 1 has intimated, a *narrative* reading of Acts requires a much richer and more dynamic geographical imagination. Constructions of place are contested, require active maintenance, and always remain subject to possibly radical realignments. Given this geographical dialectic, change is the norm for every spatial system and for all aspects of such systems, and it is apparent *stability* which requires explanation.[62] As a consequence, Scott's centrifugal reading of Acts, whereby Jerusalem remains 'the centre and focal point ... from first to last',[63] is too rigid to contain the narrative-geographical drama of Acts. Even Scott concedes that Acts 24–8 does not fit this framework when he admits that 'only when Paul finally comes to Rome does Jerusalem recede from view'.[64]

Thus, rather than a fixed element of a 'tradition', Jerusalem needs to be read as one part of a dynamic restructuring of place and geography in Acts resulting from Christ's ascension. As such, Scott's analysis, rather than presenting a fully geographical analysis, reflects only a partial escape from the continuing dominance of historicism. Others too have advocated an unchanging place for Jerusalem within the narrative,[65] but such readings remain too earth-bound and discount the heavenly initiatives within Acts which qualify or reinterpret the role of Jerusalem and the Temple. Instead of being encapsulated in tradition, a truly spatialised ontology 'always remains open to further transformations in the context of material life. It is never primordially given or permanently fixed.'[66]

The most remarkable evidence of Scott's residual historicism is the almost total absence of any reference to geographical theory in this monograph on geography.[67] The only reference comes in the book's final sentence: 'Ultimately, a full-orbed approach to geography, such

---

[61] Monmonier 2000. This is especially important for any reconstruction of a *Jubilees* tradition, given the lack of any extant evidence of it having been mapped during the period in question (remembering, nonetheless, that maps are themselves always persuasive, subjective communications).

[62] Harvey 1996: 49–56.   [63] J. M. Scott 2002: 57.

[64] J. M. Scott 2002: 57. Yet Jews do, of course, remain in view in Rome, and Jerusalem is mentioned as late as 28:17 (Eisen 2006: 162).

[65] E.g. Chance 1988: 101–13; Moessner 1989.

[66] Soja 1989: 122. Cf. pp. 118–37, entitled 'Towards a Spatialized Ontology'.

[67] Likewise J. M. Scott (1997), despite its title mentioning 'Geographical Aspects', only once refers in its main text to geography, and then in a simple descriptive sense (p. 375).

as that currently being developed by Robert D. Sack, may be helpful in extending our geographical horizons beyond the notion of mere physical space when dealing with our ancient texts.'[68] Such an observation would be a fitting introduction, rather than a conclusion, for a volume explicitly examining geography.

Despite these criticisms, Scott clearly highlights the need for a renewed geographical analysis of biblical texts. He foregrounds the necessity of geographical readings of scripture. This is evident in his earlier, more focused examination of Luke's geographical horizon.[69] This necessity is in part historical, to limit anachronistic assumptions about ancient understandings of the world,[70] even if Scott's cartographic solution leads to a reductionistic distortion of geographical depth and risks a naïve denial of cartographic politics.[71] The necessity is also theological, given that the theology of Acts is carried within a narrative text that is inherently geographical. Scott significantly proposes 'the more difficult task of describing … from the "inside". How did the Jerusalem apostles, for example, imagine the world of their day?'[72] This question remains insufficiently answered if geography is too narrowly associated with cartography and too rigidly carried through history by a determinative tradition.

The reduction of Lukan geography to an ontological dualism

Reducing the spatial aspect of life to one discrete 'aspect' of ontological reality represents a third illegitimate definition of geography. Geography's 'quantitative revolution' attempted such a reduction and found it wanting. It is, however, an enduring tendency in Lukan studies, illustrated by the frequent but unsustainable distinction between reading Acts 1:8 as either 'mere geographical description' or 'a statement with strong ethnic connotations'.[73] Such distinctions neuter geographical analysis by creating an unjustified and indefensible dualism between the spatial and the ethnic. Like gender, ethnicity is inherently spatial (in that it produces and interprets space), and human spatiality is inadequately conceived without

---

[68] J. M. Scott 2002: 176. Scott then cites Sack 1986, 1997.
[69] J. M. Scott 1994.   [70] J. M. Scott 2002: 1–2.
[71] See especially Scott 2000. The varying estimations of geographical (that is, cartographical) knowledge in the Roman Empire (Bekker-Nielsen 1988, Woodward 2000) actually *increase* the risk of anachronistic readings from maps.
[72] J. M. Scott 2002: 2.   [73] Here, as stated by Hays 2003: 167.

reference to ethnicity.[74] The same critique can be placed against any distinction of 'theopolitical' and 'geographical' readings of Acts 1:8.[75] Rather, ontological interpenetrations mean that geography is never 'mere geography', simple common sense, 'an inevitable geographical expansion from the centre'.[76] Therefore, properly spatialised reading strategies for scripture need to be ontologically broad, and sensitive to the inherent spatiality of any and all readings of scripture.

Having observed these reductionistic outworkings of historicism in Lukan studies, attention can now turn to historicism's specific impact within ascension scholarship, and its limitations within previous attempts to read for 'ascension geography'.

The ascension

The ascension itself has been used to justify historicist interpretations of Christianity. Early twentieth-century English scholars used it to deny geography, seeing the ascension as preserving 'that which was vitally important, the universality of the religion of Christ'.[77] Universality was set dualistically against localised appropriation: 'No religion could be really universal, which proceeded from a founder whose bones remained in a known burial place.'[78]

Such aspirations to the universal, to the 'gaze from nowhere', have been criticised by advocates of 'situated knowledge' as illusory 'god tricks promising vision from everywhere and nowhere equally'.[79] The exegesis in Part II will not retreat into such ubiquity.[80] It is suspected that the conundrum of presence and absence outlined in Chapter 1 is not so easily dissolved within the Acts narrative. Also, it is anticipated that Acts will resist the historicist suggestion that 'the right hand of the Father must not be thought of as meaning a particular place or location but rather in the sense of the glory and honour which the Incarnate Word had before the creation of the world, and which returns [*sic*] to him once more'.[81]

---

[74] Cf. Hiebert 2000. Eisen (2006: 152) maintains this connection, quite rightly, with regard to Acts 1:8.

[75] E.g. Pao 2000: 93–5.   [76] Barrett 1988: 72.

[77] Latham 1926: 389.   [78] Latham 1926: 389.

[79] Haraway 1991: 191. Regarding 'situated knowledge', see also Barnes 2000b.

[80] Cf. Metzger 1969: 127: 'What is God's right hand? This is metaphorical language for divine omnipotence. Where is it? Everywhere.'

[81] Bobrinsky 1963: 109 n. 1.

Historicism, combined with modernist rationalism, has also diverted questions of ascension geography into cul-de-sac debates regarding the location and nature of heaven.[82] These are unnecessary, both in light of more recent theological reflection upon the ascension,[83] and because an ascension geography does not require heaven to be a mappable place. Even entirely mythical locations can have a powerful sense of place projected on to them, such as the so-called Mountains of the Moon, believed from classical times to hide the source of the Nile.[84] Such endowments can then exercise a powerful structuring influence on other non-mythical places and on actual social relations, as did the Mountains of the Moon from the time of Herodotus until the nineteenth century. Likewise, nationalism is widely recognised as depending upon an *imagined* sense of community that is sensed in actual places but cannot be easily reduced to a particular place.[85] Analogously, this study contends, heaven casts an influence over other places and over social relations within Acts without the need for its locative description.

The submerged theology of contemporary human geography

Given Soja's critique of historicism, and this chapter's identification of widespread evidence of historicism within biblical studies, one might ask whether geographers have engaged in corrective readings of scripture. It is noteworthy, however, that human geography has largely ignored biblical spatialities. The sporadic attempts by geographers to link their theoretical interests with theological thought have been isolated studies,[86] or have generated occasional meetings of geographers with a shared confessional concern but diverse research interests.[87] Otherwise human geography has made few steps towards interaction with academic theology.[88] Attempts at such rapprochement have received limited attention, perhaps because of unspoken

---

[82] E.g. Latham 1926: 381, who proposes that the cloud (Acts 1:9) was low-lying, so that as 'the visible body of our Lord rose to a great height into the skies' the spectacle did not cause 'panic and widespread commotion' among the citizens of Jerusalem.
[83] E.g. N. T. Wright 2003: 654–5.
[84] J. K. Wright 1925: 304–5; Thomson 1948: 275–7. Cf. D. Cosgrove 2000.
[85] B. Anderson 1983.
[86] E.g. Ley 1974, Clark and Sleeman 1991, Park 1994, and Aay and Griffioen 1998.
[87] E.g. Olliver 1989, M. Clark 1991.
[88] It remains to be seen if the 2003 revival of the American Association of Geographers' *Geography of Religions and Belief Systems* Speciality Group generates readings of scripture (see http://gorabs.org (accessed July 2008)).

limits as to what represents legitimate 'geography', even under post-modernity, or because of implicitly maintained Western rationalist divisions concerning perceived differences in epistemology.[89] Caution concerning the 'god trick', outlined above, can become an unwarranted limit on geographers' interdisciplinary interchanges. It appears that, although still fragmented and partial, the initiative for geographical readings of scripture is coming from the theological side of this interdisciplinary exchange.[90]

On balance, therefore, although geography offers new insights for reading scripture, biblical scholars rather than geographers are quicker to grasp these opportunities.

4.   Looking for its place: signposts to a properly spatialised reading method within Lukan studies

The previous section having critiqued various reductionistic renderings of geography in Lukan studies, this section looks for signposts anticipating a properly spatialised reading of Acts.

Leslie Houlden and Rowan Williams: anticipating an ascension-geography narrative

A post-historicist understanding of space justifies revisiting the specificities of Luke's ascension geography. Leslie Houlden is anticipatory in this regard. Although initially appearing to replicate a disparaging modernist understanding of the Lukan ascension as indicative of a naïve worldview when describing Luke's 'excessively wooden, map-like, literal picture of the cosmos',[91] Houlden also highlighted the importance of linking geography and the ascension for understanding Acts. First, he viewed the ascension as 'the climax or watershed of Luke-Acts and [making] sense of the conception of that novel work as a whole, with its wide historical and geographical sweep'.[92] Then, after interrogating

[89] Compare the claim that all geographies, all places, lay claim to an ultimate belief that can and should be understood as essentially 'religious' (Clark and Sleeman 1991) with the cautious response of Driver 1991. For other critiques of the erasure of religious influences in the history of geography, see Park 1994 and Livingstone 1998.

[90] The joint American Academy of Religion and the Society of Biblical Literature '*Constructions of Ancient Space*' Seminar, established between 2000 and 2005, showcased biblical scholars beginning to use spatial theory (see www.cwru.edu/affil/GAIR/Constructions/Constructions.html (accessed July 2008)). However, it did not examine Acts.

[91] Houlden 1991: 177.   [92] Houlden 1991: 178.

each of the NT writers for their understanding of where Jesus is now, Houlden judged Luke's conception as unique within the canon. Luke is unable to follow Mark to a mysterious Galilee or to maintain Matthew's 'with you always', since he is actually addressing the 'What next?' question. This forced an innovative Lukan confrontation with geography. Houlden suggested that tradition was of little use to Luke at this juncture, except in a wider, legendary sense. Although he came close to identifying an ascension geography within Acts, Houlden drew back, judging Luke's necessity as literary rather than theological: Luke needed 'simply to get Jesus suitably to heaven when the teaching retreat (or resurrection appearances as we tend to categorize them) is over. As we have seen, the destination is agreed in early Christianity, more or less; Luke alone is compelled to describe the departure.'[93]

Nevertheless, Houlden continues to read the ascension as an isolated pericope rather than as an integrated narrative event generating geographical restructuring. This veils its spatial implications for the rest of Acts. The need remains for a reading across Acts that identifies an enduring and dynamic post-ascension geography informed by the heavenly Christ.

A more differentiated – and, it is suggested, a more Lukan – earthly geography is implicit within Rowan Williams's sense of post-ascension realities diffusing across the earth:

> Jesus is 'received' in heaven, and given his authority (which is not the bestowal of any merely contingent sovereignty in or of Israel – Acts 1:6); and the universal nature of that authority is now to be realized in the world as the church's mission spread out, enacting, enacting in history [and geography!] the lordship already realized in Jesus' heavenly life.[94]

Williams's comments anticipate an implicit ascension geography wherein the believers' mission within Acts 'spreads out' – not into some unplaced history, or simply into an immediately universal and ubiquitous history, but into a spatialised history that calls out for a geographical reading.

Richard Bauckham: ontological depth

An 'ascension geography' needs to navigate between the ontological dualisms identified earlier. Bauckham is helpful in this regard. Reflecting

[93] Houlden 1991: 178.
[94] Williams 1983: 44, square-bracketed comment added.

upon mission within the Bible, Bauckham has recently highlighted the ontological depth of geography through a conception of 'representative geography' within biblical thought, whereby specific peoples and places retain their realist particularity but also stand representatively for other peoples and places.[95] This helpfully opens up the relationship between particularity and universality in biblical geography, without becoming fixated with either pole. Bauckham also takes seriously geographical development across the Testaments, an advance on the static notions of 'tradition' discussed earlier.[96] However, Bauckham's understanding of mission remains earthbound, 'from everywhere to everywhere',[97] rather than positioned under heaven. This limited understanding of the ascension ultimately constrains the advances inherent within Bauckham's reading of mission in Acts.

Joel Green: space as constitutive of theology

Joel Green has also helpfully broadened geographical readings of Luke and Acts from reductionist ontological assumptions. Sidestepping dualistic readings of Acts 1:8, Green notes: 'Geography – and especially such geographical markers as "Judea" and "Samaria" – is not a "naively given container" but rather a social production that both reflects and configures being in the world.'[98] These comments echo the assumptions of structuration theory, outlined in Section II.

In his commentary on Luke's Gospel, Green has begun to demonstrate what this means in practice. By seeing Luke's Gospel as a 'cultural product' rather than simply a narrative text existing in isolation from the world, Green suggested that Luke's narrative 'gives expression to a vision of the world'.[99] In other words, Luke produces a geography, an interpretation of history, but a worldview that cannot be simply reduced to history. Luke 'both seeks to provide an alternative view of that world [the "real" world] and chooses aspects of that world to emphasize while downplaying others'.[100] Luke's narrative orientates auditors 'toward a reconstructed vision of God and the sort of world order that might reflect this vision of God', and Lukan discipleship means aligning oneself with this vision that 'salvation embraces the totality of embodied life'.[101]

---

[95] Bauckham 2003.   [96] Bauckham 2001.   [97] Bauckham 2003: 77.
[98] Green 1997a: 15.   [99] Green 1997b: 11.   [100] Green 1997b: 12.
[101] Green 1997b: 23, 25.

Green's Luke commentary is the first major piece of Lukan scholarship that attempts to build upon the insights of recent geographical theorists. The references are limited but suggestive. In three instances (and nowhere else in his commentary) Green cites three such theorists: Pred, Soja, and Benno Werlen.[102] First, regarding Luke 10:25–37, Green emphasises that 'geographical markers are not neutral or objective, but are social products that reflect and configure ways of understanding the world'.[103] Second, while commenting on 11:31–2, Green rehearses his assessment of geography quoted at the start of this section.[104] Finally, regarding 19:45–8, Green observes that 'as a geographical location Jerusalem and the temple constitute profoundly important social products that reflect and configure ways of understanding the world Luke is portraying'.[105]

The important point is not the citing of geographical theorists *per se*, but rather the renewed readings of Luke made possible by their insights. Space is becoming, to use Bal's terminology, 'thematicised',[106] whereby rather than functioning simply as a frame or a place of action, space becomes 'an object of presentation itself, for its own sake … an "acting place" rather than the place of action'.[107] This more active function for space, moving beyond more conventional descriptive or dismissive uses of 'geography', anticipates the reading of Acts undertaken in Part II.

Admittedly, Green's explicit references to geography are few and repetitive and his geographical analysis still limited to conventional spatial markers. Yet he does adumbrate a richer geographical reading. Perhaps his forthcoming New International Commentary on the New Testament volume on Acts will undertake a more fully fledged geographical reading; certainly Acts, as a richly geographical narrative, deserves and requires such a reading.

Halvor Moxnes: a third way?

Halvor Moxnes also exhibits a geographical imagination in his reading of Luke's Gospel. Although his publications are on a smaller scale

---

[102] Soja 1989, Pred 1990 and Werlen 1993, each cited in all three instances.
[103] Green 1997b: 426 n. 99.   [104] Green 1997b: 465 n. 51; cf. 1997a: 15.
[105] Green 1997b: 692.
[106] Bal 1995: 95–6. Green uses narratological theory but, beyond making a generalised reference to Bal's narratological theory (Green 1997b: 11), does not make explicit use of her understanding of setting.
[107] Bal 1995: 95.

than Green's commentary, Moxnes opens up more fruitful trails for a sustained geographical reading of Acts. Like Soja, Moxnes reacts against an almost exclusive analytical focus on 'time'. Like Green, he suggests that recent geographical studies of place illuminate Luke's presentation of 'given' social structures and of the kingdom of God. Moxnes distinguishes three different Lukan uses of 'world'. First, there is the world that Luke assumes, that is, the world of Jesus in Palestine. Second, there is the world as Luke portrays it. Third, there is the world as Luke wants it to be. This third use challenges the assumptions of first-century Mediterranean societies in a manner reflective of a richer understanding of geography: 'It is obvious that "world" here does not just refer to a physical space, it bears the connotation of a geographic and social space that is organised and structured in a certain way.'[108]

5.   Finding its place: a spatialised reading method for Acts

Moxnes's reading of 'kingdom' in Luke, although not extended to Acts, brings this chapter to the cusp of a spatialised reading method which can examine the ascension within the narrative flow of Acts. His reading of space opens up a critical dimension to biblical geographies that includes the descriptive but moves beyond it while also reflexively returning to it.

Moxnes achieves this by drawing upon a 'grid of spatial practices' formulated by David Harvey, one-time Halford Mackinder Professor of Geography in the University of Oxford.[109] Harvey's schema assumes three categories for analysing space, each dialectically relating with the others. The first, 'material spatial practice', relates to the realm of experience. Harvey's Marxist orientation focuses on this realm as that which ensures economic production and social reproduction. Second, 'representations of space' concern perception of space. This is the realm of signs and significations, the codes and knowledge, which allow material spatial practices to be talked about and understood. Third, 'spaces of representation' in the sphere of the imagination are mental inventions which imagine new meanings or possibilities for spatial practices. Such 'spatial discourses' include utopian plans, imaginary landscapes, and even material constructs

---

[108] Moxnes 2001a: 178.
[109] See Harvey 1990: 218–23, especially Table 3.1 on pp. 220–1, employed by Moxnes 2000, 2001a, 2001c.

Table 2.1. *A three-part schema for understanding space*

Lefebvre 1974	Harvey 1990	Soja 1996	*Particular life realm*
Physical space			
Perceived space	Material spatial practice	**Firstspace**	*Experience* – the empirical
Mental space			
Conceived space	Representations of space	**Secondspace**	*Perception* – the theoretical
Social space			
Lived space	Spaces of representation	**Thirdspace**	*Imagination* – the creative

such as symbolic places, particular built environments, paintings, and museums. They imagine new meanings or possibilities for spatial practices, drawing on and challenging existing spatial practices and their ideological justifications. Crucially, Moxnes suggests, this critical third category goes beyond the strictly empirical but also challenges and can reshape the empirical. It is more suggestive than prescriptive, claiming to be both imaginative and also substantive. Assessing Jesus' effect on people as 'dislocating identities', Moxnes refuses to reduce such transformations to temporal categories of 'before' and 'now': they were also manifested spatially, for example in relation to localised identity realms such as home, family, and village.[110] This is highly suggestive for reading Acts for local expressions of what this study will term 'ascension geography'.

As such, Moxnes interacts with a major theoretical impulse within geography. Its three key theoreticians are Harvey, whose grid of spatial practices Moxnes utilises; Soja, whose concept of 'thirdspace' will underpin this present study; and the French sociologist Henri Lefebvre, whose earlier work was foundational for both Harvey and Soja.[111] These three writers' overlapping classifications are shown in parallel in Table 2.1. This broad three-part schema underpins the exegesis undertaken in Part II, which tests its utility for reading Acts.

[110] Moxnes 2000, esp. pp. 163–71. Moxnes also draws theoretical inspiration from queer theory for his concept of Jesus 'dislocating identities', citing Edelman 1994.
[111] Soja 1996; Lefebvre 1991 (original French edition, 1974). For a critique of Soja's appropriation of Lefebvre, see Elden 2001: 812–17.

Introducing thirdspace

This schema presumes that binary oppositions can be disordered, deconstructed, and tentatively reconstituted if they are 'spatialised', that is, if their position within a production of space is properly recognised. The result will be third ways which are 'both similar and strikingly different'.[112]

Soja uses three terms to articulate how this process informs our understandings of space. 'Firstspace' refers to external, material 'physical' spatiality, to the privileging of objectivity, to 'the concrete and mappable geographies of our lifeworlds'.[113] This is the realm of conventional geography and the locus for toponymy, but, in itself, this perceived space provides an incomplete and partial understanding of the world. Soja also identifies 'secondspace', that is, mental 'projections into the empirical world from conceived or imagined geographies', the privileging of 'a world of rationally interpretable signification'.[114] Secondspace is articulated in (for example) design, written text or architectural plans.

Modernist thought, according to Soja, exhibits 'a persistent tendency … to see Firstspace and Secondspace as together defining the whole of the geographical imagination, as encompassing in their varying admixtures all possible ways of conceptualizing and studying human geography and the spatiality of human life'.[115] Both opposing and feeding each other, a dialectic of firstspace and secondspace neuters geography's formative contribution to knowledge, by rendering spatiality subject to the alternate illusions of opacity and transparency.[116]

A thirdspace perspective opens up renewed ways of thinking about space, seeking 'to break out from the constraining Big Dichotomy by introducing an-Other'.[117] This is the central theme of Soja's eponymous book, a theme traced through a wide variety of spatial critics and critiques. Thirdspace generates 'an-Other form of spatial awareness', denying dualism by examining spaces as 'simultaneously real

---

[112] Soja 1996: 61.   [113] Soja 1996: 74–5.
[114] Soja 1996: 79.   [115] Soja 1999: 267.
[116] This summary is necessarily compressed: Soja 1996: 6–82 provides a longer introduction, with pp. 62–4 providing a core summary. Regarding the two meanings of the phrase 'in its place', which equate heuristically to firstspace and secondspace, see Cresswell 1996.
[117] Soja 1999: 268.

[firstspace], imagined [secondspace] and more (both and also ...)'.[118] In this manner the dialectic of history and sociality is 'spatialised', thereby becoming a trialectic. For example, spatialising Marx, people make their own geography as much as they make their own history.[119]

Any one location can and should be analysed for its manifestations of all three kinds of Sojan space. But thirdspace, as Other, continually undermines any claim of a settled firstspace–secondspace binary relationship, and opens up new ways of seeing space, being in space and ordering space, provoking 'an-Other world[s] ... space "beyond" what is presently known and taken for granted'.[120] By its nature, thirdspace is a perspective, a means of reading place, of doing 'geography'. Thirdspace is found in the 'lived space' of 'everyday life' which *is* place,[121] filled with meaning, emotion and struggle. It is politically charged space that resists the power plays and closure of materialist firstspace and ideational secondspace, being space wherein alternative territorialities and worldviews are explored. Thirdspace resides in visionary vistas that imagine new meanings or possibilities for shaping spatial practices. It is a conception of space that presents 'the radical challenge to think differently, to expand your geographical imagination beyond its current limits'.[122] Importantly for Soja, thirdspace 'must be ... guided by some form of potentially emancipatory *praxis*, the translation of knowledge into action in a conscious – and consciously spatial – effort to improve the world in some significant way'.[123] This should not endow thirdspace with a naïve, inherently positive ethic: the last century is replete with examples of how 'geographical imaginations' can be 'expanded' for good *or* ill. The geographer Susan Smith comments: 'Not all borders and margins are radical and open "thirdspaces".'[124]

It should be noted that Soja's notion of *thirdspace* is located within a wider scholarly interest in 'third space', that is, spaces 'produced by those processes that exceed the forms of knowledge that divide the world into binary oppositions'.[125] Although the present study preserves the Sojan term 'thirdspace' (and, where useful, the associated terms 'firstspace' and 'secondspace'), this schema is assumed as

---

[118] Soja 1996: 11, square-bracketed comments added; ellipsis original.
[119] Giddens 1984: 363.
[120] Soja 1996: 34. See 'Thirding-as-Othering', Soja 1996: 60–70.
[121] Soja 1996: 40 n. 18.   [122] Soja 1996: 2.   [123] Soja 1996: 22.
[124] S. J. Smith 1999: 147. Cf. Camp 2002, concerning the gendered politics implicated within the spatiality produced in Sirach.
[125] Rose 2000: 827.

positioned within a wider interest in hybrid spaces which is already permeating theological thought, but which itself requires a critical grounding within biblical studies. Christopher Baker, for example, probes what he terms 'a theology of the third space', but his biblical frame of reference is thin and fragmented and comes at the close of his analysis. That frame *is* Luke-Acts, but Baker acknowledges that this 'rich and compelling narrative' deserves a more sustained analysis for its thirdspatial potential.[126]

Thus understood and more widely positioned, thirdspace presents a perspective with suggestive potential for moving beyond ascension scholarship's straining and untheorised categories of Christological presence and absence identified in Chapter 1, by resisting binary closure and asserting a trialectic of space rather than a dialectic.[127] A thirdspatial understanding of the ascended Christ's impact on earthly spaces within Acts challenges and reshapes both (firstspace) material locations and (secondspace) ideational projections, crafting constructions of places incorporating and exceeding conventional binary oppositions. Part II of this study will exegete this assertion, through a reading searching for such spaces within Acts 1:1–11:18.

Illustrating thirdspace

Soja has been criticised for creating neologisms for their own sake and for focusing too narrowly on Los Angeles,[128] but illustrating his schema in practice helps elucidate its processes and wider analytic and interpretative applicability. As a biblical example of thirdspace, Victor Matthews presents the threshing floor of ancient Israel as functioning within the OT as more than simply a place of agricultural production. It assumes thirdspatial connotations, becoming a place of covenants and provision for the poor, where 'the old world comes to an end and a new world begins'.[129]

The example of Soja's categories in operation most frequently cited within biblical studies[130] is Rosa Parks's refusal to give up her seat on a bus to a white passenger, an event that sparked the black

---

[126] For his biblical engagement, see Baker 2007: 149–54 (151).

[127] Soja (1996: 64–5) summarises what he terms the 'trialectics of spatiality'.

[128] Elden 1997, 2001. For a sharp critique of 'postmodern urbanism', of which Soja is a leading advocate, and its neologisms, see Lake 1999.

[129] Matthews 2003: 13.

[130] Flanagan 1999, 2000, 2001. Flanagan's formulations have been influential within the Constructions of Ancient Space Seminar (Berquist and Camp 2007: ix–x).

civil-rights movement in post-war America. As a heuristic device, however, the incident does not easily and clearly identify the operations of each perspective of space, especially secondspace, and the illusory potential for a dialectical *absence* of a thirdspace perspective is not apparent.

The Christmas truces on the Western Front in 1914 provide another, clearer, illustration. There, temporarily, 'No Man's Land' became 'Every Man's Land' as physical divides between armies and mental divisions constructing 'otherness' according to conflicting national identities and military strategy and discipline gave way to another kind of space. The truces have been subjected to a comprehensive historical analysis of their causal factors and consequential meanings:[131] what is clear is that both physical and mental conceptions of space were implicit within, and were breached by, the truces. And yet the truces themselves suggest an (albeit temporary) emancipatory impulse governing space which itself is not easily contained within such binary distinctions. Therein lies the boundary-violating essence of thirdspace.

Two other examples help paint thirdspace in *literary* forms. Platform 9¾ at King's Cross Station in J. K. Rowling's *Harry Potter* novels functions as a secondspace projection inscribed in a literary 'canon' and also, now, has a firstspace position within the station's architecture,[132] but for Rowling's followers it cannot be reduced to even the sum of these two parts, since it – and King's Cross Station itself – function thirdspatially across Rowling's canon as an impetus for (re)new(ed) magical narrative worlds and, by inference, real 'muggle' worlds. Another *narrative* example is the eponymous location in Wim Wenders's 1984 film *Paris, Texas*. The viewer is never taken to this locale, seeing the place only via a battered Polaroid picture, but it orders the entire narrative, governs the movements of every major character and offers potential plot resolutions beyond the film's open-ended conclusion. As such, the comparisons with Acts are highly suggestive.

Using thirdspace to read the ascension

This narrative power of *Paris, Texas* is curiously akin to Parsons's notion of the ascended Jesus functioning in Acts as an 'empty centre',

---

[131] Brown and Seaton 1994.
[132] See www.crypto.com/photos/misc/platform9.75.html (accessed July 2008).

a concept drawn from Martin Kreiswirth's analysis of William Faulkner's novels,[133] but Sojan categories provide greater analytic purchase for reading the ascension.

First, the notion of an 'empty centre' lacks a theological dimension with its commensurate creative and critical functions, aspects which are better elucidated via the thirdspace concept. These creative and critical considerations are bound up in this study's contention that Jesus' ascension creates spaces on earth – spaces for believers – and critiques other earthly spaces. Parsons's adoption of Kreiswirth's analysis assumes that, in the course of Acts, Jesus evokes 'a broad range of responses from those who come into contact with him', since the heavenly Christ functions 'primarily as a symbol of loss'.[134] Here Parsons follows Faulkner rather than Luke. The Faulknerian characters to whom Kreiswirth here refers are a 'hopelessly wounded aviator' who is 'blind and only intermittently conscious', and 'a subjective creature of fantasy and memory … [who] thus functions less as a fully realized character than as a locus of unfulfilled desire and loss around which everything else in the novel revolves'.[135] Such categories sit awkwardly with the heavenly Christ, whose narrative space in Acts will evoke gift, growth, gain and facilitation and not simply loss.[136] Parsons's failure to develop fully from Kreiswirth's concept a *heavenwards* orientation for Jesus 'as an absent character who moves the plot line along'[137] is a telling weakness which continues through Parsons's analysis of space.[138]

Second, thirdspace provides an integrative theory of space, something lacking in Parsons's adaptation of literary analysis, allowing more analytic flexibility regarding how Christ's ascension governs the production of space on earth.

Also, thirdspace's questioning of conventional conceptions of space and place facilitates reading for the ascension's narrative-geographical impact within Acts. It would be an act of hubris to suggest that Sojan categories will *resolve* the conundrum of Christological presence and absence identified in Chapter 1, but potentially they offer insights to reposition and advance scholarly debate. Gaventa is suspicious of 'the customary vocabulary of *geography* or *location*': only sustained exegetical consideration will assess Soja's ability to illuminate Gaventa's

---

[133] Parsons 1987: 160–2.   [134] Kreiswirth 1984: 39, quoted in Parsons 1987: 161.
[135] Kreiswirth 1984: 39.
[136] Especially if 'parousia delay is an indisputable fact, but parousia-delay crisis is actually hard to find' (Nolland 1998: 65).
[137] Parsons 1987: 171.   [138] See 'Part I: Synthesis and Prospect', below.

contention that, within Acts, Jesus 'is both powerfully exalted to God's right hand and powerfully active in and among believers'.[139] Part II, therefore, will apply Soja's theory to a reading of Acts, assessing the earthly implications of an absent-but-active ascended Christ functioning thirdspatially within the narrative. Since the heavenly Christ's earthly influence in Acts is centred on those believing in him, this analysis will examine believers' space (but is not delimited by such spaces). Concerning Luke's Gospel, Moxnes has asked, 'How does Luke imagine new structures and new spatial practices when he speaks of the "Kingdom of God"?'[140] This study asks the same question concerning the post-ascension believers in Acts. It will assess how Acts develops thirdspaces, where 'new things happen and this disrupts old and dominant ways of thinking and doing ... in order to remake understandings of the world'.[141] Thirdspace renders as problematic conventional readings of the ascension as simply about departure, not least if – as Chapter 1 asserted – such readings generate an implicit and self-referencing equation of absence with inactivity. The counter-proposal made here instead probes the ascension through Sojan lenses for its influence on subsequent earthly spaces within Acts.

Narrative spaces are not coterminous with narrative *setting*: therefore, the exegesis undertaken in Part II uses the term 'spatiality' to label a bundled sense of all three Sojan categories which can be carried and communicated between settings. To cite what will become this study's foundational example, Chapter 3 identifies an 'ascension geography' within Acts 1:6–11: this spatiality is much more than mere setting, and is communicated across various settings within the narrative. Indeed, earthly setting is almost a distraction from this foundational production of space, and is revealed only *after* the ascension (1:12). As Part II's unfolding narrative commentary shows, Sojan categories allow simultaneous attention to settings *and* to wider spatiality.

Given that any location can be analysed for its manifestations of all three kinds of Sojan space, the reading undertaken in Part II refers to hyphenated spaces (e.g. 'Jerusalem-space') as a shorthand for these three spatial perspectives interacting within particular locales, groups or individuals. Such hyphenated spaces enable analytic specificity and flexibility, providing a working structure for exegesis while not imposing Sojan categories as a mechanistic

---

[139] Gaventa 2003b: n. p., emphasis original.   [140] Moxnes 2001a: 180.
[141] Rose 2000: 827.

analytical grid upon *narrative* spaces which themselves are constructed variably across the course of Acts.

Before specifying the reading method employed here, one obvious
possible criticism of applying Sojan categories to Acts needs to be
addressed. The understanding of geography proposed here, located as
it is within current theoretical scholarship, can appear open to the
charge of generating anachronistic readings when applied to ancient
texts. To adjust Tertullian's charge: 'What does Los Angeles have to
do with Jerusalem?'[142]

The charge is refuted by classicists examining ancient writers'
understandings of the relationship between history and geography.
Katherine Clarke, for example, rejects the commonly heard view that
ancient authors used geography only as a setting for history, arguing
instead that this division anachronistically reflects dominant twentieth-
century views of geography.[143] Regarding Strabo's writings, Clarke
concludes that 'ancient notions of the term γεωγραφία (geography)
and ἱστορία (history) both incorporated aspects of the modern subjects
of geography and history; in other words … separable subjects of
geography and history, as defined in the narrow, modern sense, do
not map exactly into the ancient world'.[144] Her charge, made without
reference to Soja, parallels his critique of modern historicism.

Clarke's observations also remind that a spatialised reading does not
compete with, or seek to replace, historical readings. Rather, both are
required, and complement each other, but the spatial has been unnecessarily marginalised in modern thought, and in readings of Acts.

Clarke is not alone among ancient scholars. Claude Nicolet has
claimed: 'There is … a geography of Virgil, of Horace, and of Ovid.
Indeed nearly all literature is open to a geographical reading.'[145]
Likewise James Romm has argued that Cicero's (no longer extant)
struggles with the discipline of geography suggest that geography was
much more part of the cultural mainstream in ancient times.[146]
Josephus, too, has recently received consideration for his geography,[147]
as has the Qumran community.[148]

These implications are equally applicable to reading Acts: to adapt
Nicolet's words, 'there is a geography of Luke, of Acts'. Such geographies need assessing, not least since 'the question of whether

---

[142] Cf. Tertullian, *De praescriptione haereticorum* vii (34) 9, 12.
[143] Clarke 1999: 28. Similarly Soja 1996: 167–8.   [144] Clarke 1999: 195.
[145] Nicolet 1991: 8, quoted in Romm 1992: 7.   [146] Romm 1992: 3–4.
[147] Shahar 2004.   [148] P. R. Davies 2002.

geographical features are active or passive in the literature that describes them may alter the way in which we view the literature itself".[149]

Further assumptions underpinning a reading of Acts for its spaces

The following five horizons locate the method adopted here.

First, as a working premise, the spatialised reading undertaken in Part II assumes a high degree of *geographical coherence* within Luke's account.[150] Against the common claim that Luke lacks precise knowledge of the specifics of Palestinian geography, something assumed since Conzelmann, Luke's Gospel carefully situates Jesus 'in place', in the sense of positioning him within the spatial practices of the Roman Empire and the Herodian kingdom.[151] As Chapter 3 will argue, Luke is careful at the outset of Acts to 'place' Jesus in heaven (1:10–11), his location foregrounded by redundant repetition. This, it shall be argued, provides a foundational coherence for spatiality within Acts. Crucially, then, Christ is not omnipresent in Acts: his firstspace location is *in heaven*. Immediately Sojan categories begin to assist with the problematic of presence and absence: firstspace is not the totality of spatial consideration but, nonetheless, Christ's firstspace specificity in heaven avoids the annihilation of space by ubiquity and evokes an ascension geography to be embodied among the earthly believers.[152]

Jesus' new setting in heaven does not occlude his character development within the narrative. Rather, auditors still encounter Jesus within various narrative spaces, such that they are still able to construe a cumulative and increasingly complex image of him. As will be shown, rather than instituting a passive absentee Christology, Acts

---

[149] Clarke 1999: 32. Within NT studies, for example, Bauckham's assertion that early Christians 'had a strong, lively, and informed sense of participation in a world-wide movement' (Bauckham 1998: 3) is deeply implicated in issues of geography and calls out for close geographical analyses of specific texts.

[150] 'Acts' is the product of a complex textual transmission. Assuming the NA27 edition of the Greek text as a foundational text does not preclude allowing individual manuscripts to exhibit their own spatiality. To this end, Codex Bezae [D] is increasingly well served by Rius-Camps and Read-Heimerdinger 2004, 2006.

[151] Moxnes 2001a: 182–3.

[152] Cf. Wilken 1992: 91, who claimed that 'earlier Christian sources have much to say about time, but what they say about space appears to dethrone place as the locus of the divine presence'.

continues to construe Jesus' post-ascension character as influencing the production of earthly space(s) through numerous means. Jesus, therefore, does not rest in some Platonic static state: rather, auditors' construction of his character-in-setting is aggregative across the whole narrative. Thus, 'the manner, means and timing of its accumulation is [sic] hermeneutically significant'.[153] The ascension enjoys a 'primacy effect' at the start of Acts and exerts a rhetorical function which seeks to persuade auditors to share the implied author's ideological programme, which includes a 'geography', an ordering of space. It orders key formative spatialities within the narrative, such as Saul's exemplary and intensely spatial response to the heavenly Jesus (Chapter 6), as well as more minor settings and places. In short, the ascension governs, rather than forecloses, the dialectic development of characters and settings.[154]

Second, a narrative-geographical reading also eschews reductionist notions of geography while recognising that conventional spatial elements contribute to a *broader* geographical understanding marshalled through Sojan analysis. Soja's 'dizzying' (alphabetical) list of different spatial descriptors employed by Lefebvre suggests that there is far more 'geography' within Acts than many readings have previously realised.[155] Unlike earlier reductionist readings of geography, a narrative-geographical reading assumes that it is unlikely to exhaust or control the spatiality of the text. Soja suggests that a first step in reading for space is linguistic substitution: 'Whenever you read or write a sentence that empowers history, historicality, or the historical narrative, substitute space, spatiality, or geography and think about the consequences.'[156] Yet geography's breadth is far from exhausted by such derived and preliminary considerations. Sojan categories also facilitate and expect a richer geographical ontology – the geopolitical, typological, architectural, and cosmological, not to exhaust the options.

These types of place interweave but can be analysed together using Sojan categories: thus, although mountains as places of revelation

---

[153] Darr 1998: 73, concerning characterisation.

[154] Cf. Marguerat (2002: 216), who ignores the ascension-parousia completely when claiming that Acts contains two issues not resolved within the narrative: the global reach of the witnesses (1:8) and the outcome of Paul's appeal to Caesar. This study asserts that a third such issue, 1:11, overshadows and, indeed, positions these and other spatial matters.

[155] Soja 1996: 59.

[156] Soja 1996: 183. Cf. the implementation of this approach, albeit ethnographical rather than literary, by Long 2002.

disappear in Acts after 1:12, other places reveal the spatial consequences of Christ's ascension. Part II will demonstrate that these places are diverse and many, stretching from the upper room in Jerusalem to Rome, and beyond. Simultaneously wonders, declarations, visions, and confrontations with the devil and with demons contribute to a specifically Lukan 'politics of place' begun in Luke's Gospel,[157] a rich narrative geography. The now common sensitivity to 'the land' in Luke-Acts interacts with these aspects and with other terms which presuppose a relationship to land, such as 'the promise to Abraham', 'house of Jacob', 'son of David', 'throne of David', 'gentiles' and 'all people'. Together with more obviously spatial terms such as 'Israel' and 'Jerusalem', these terms carry theological geography, as do micro-level spatialities such as table fellowship in and between Jerusalem, Samaria, Joppa and Caesarea. As elsewhere, 'A whole history remains to be written of *spaces* – which would at the same time be the history of *powers* (both these terms in the plural) – from the great strategies of geo-politics to the little tactics of the habitat.'[158]

Taken together, all these aspects broaden the data considered 'geographical' from that considered by Conzelmann, James Scott and other attempts to read Acts geographically. Rather than being easily uncovered in a concordance or immediately discovered in an atlas, the full breadth of geography requires more subtle exposition. Part II tests whether Sojan categories can provide it.

Third, as a consequence, a narrative-geographical reading of Acts assumes and highlights *a multiplicity of complex and contested spatialities* within the narrative. Soja and other human geographers have emphasised the spatial simultaneities frequently submerged by historicist focus upon temporal sequence. In the words of some classical human-geography jargon, societies are 'processually colinear, inescapably geographical, and fragmented'.[159] Exegesis therefore will not reduce space to a unilinear or aspatial totality. Interaction with existing histories and geographies, the reflexive nature of structuration, and the dynamics of power relations operating simultaneously at varying geographical and historical scales all preclude such reductionism.

---

[157] Moxnes 2001a: 183–208.
[158] Foucault 1980b: 149, emphases original. For Foucault's 'conversion' to geography, see Foucault 1980a.
[159] Pred 1990: 13–14. Cf. the different OT ideologies of 'land' identified by Habel 1995, itself a study intended in part to confront contemporary multiple claims on particular places (pp. xi–xiii).

Rather, as has been noted, spatialities unfold over the course of the narrative – developing across time and space and coexisting with other spatialities – but not in any uniform or necessarily expected manner. Their inherently uneven development produces and reflects both premeditated and unwitting actions by protagonists operating at different territorial scales. Further, the degree to which spatialities reflexively interact varies across the narrative. Peter's encounter with Cornelius (Acts 10:1–11:18), for example, presents a higher level of mutual reflexivity than is evident in Paul's encounter with the Areopagus (17:19–34). Furthermore, a narrative-geographical reading remains open to the possibility of spatial reversal within the narrative. For example, concerning the mission to the gentiles, gentile-space is introduced and opposed several times within the narrative as different geographies are suggested and interact with one another.[160] Not all spatial issues are resolved at the end of Acts to the degree auditors might expect: the question of 'the Jews' – that is, of their *place* within the narrative's economy of space – is illustrative of a limited closure which can colour readings of the whole narrative.[161]

A spatialised reading therefore expects differential responses to the proclamation of the word of God[162] in different places. By centring its reading on the ascended Christ, and claiming him as foundational for spatial ordering within Acts, such a reading expects the narrative's point of view to challenge alternative spatialities. If the dominant viewpoint of Acts is a heavenly Christocentricity, then all alternative geographies, Jewish and gentile, and their dualistic claims, come under its critique.

These complexities cast Acts as a conflict of geographies, a clash of ways to view the world. While assuming that the Christofocal worldview which dominates Acts imposes some degree of narrative coherency over alternative viewpoints, even its implications are contested and its point of view requires assertion across the narrative. Indeed, this continuing contest shapes and defines this Christocentric worldview as it takes shape *within* the locales of Acts. Any claim for 'the universality of Christ', to quote an early twentieth-century

---

[160]   This sensitivity to the contested production of space and place is comparable with Brueggemann's macro-theological categories of 'testimony' and 'counter-testimony' (Brueggemann 1997).

[161]   Cf. Tyson 1988: 124.

[162]   Concerning the word of God as being central to Acts, see O'Reilly 1987: 11; L. C. A. Alexander 1995a: 22–3; Peterson 1998c: 541 and Marguerat 2002: 37. Cf. Marshall and Peterson 1998.

presupposition concerning the ascension's consequences,[163] remains spatially contested throughout the narrative.

Fourth, the spatialities within Acts also exhibit *intratextual* and *intertextual* qualities. Commenting on the setting of Luke 4:14–30, Guy Nave underlines Nazareth's enduring intratextual effect across Luke-Acts: Luke 'is not merely concerned with a particular event on a particular day at a particular locale, rather he is concerned with the meaning of Jesus' mission as a whole and its consequences'.[164] This same principle applies to Jesus' ascension as *the* major narrative-spatial shift at the start of Acts, with its impact extending far beyond Acts 1:11. Although Acts adopts spatial assumptions from Luke's Gospel, developments in its ascension-driven narrative both build on and critique these assumptions.

A narrative-geographical reading also looks for intertextual spatiality. Adele Reinhartz has highlighted such intertextualities when judging that Susanna's garden resonates with other Hebrew gardens – most notably, Eden – and that such shared spatialities 'contribute to the ways in which these novels [Judith and Susanna] tell a larger story, that of the covenant community'.[165] Similar OT intertextual spatial influences are likely within the production of space within Acts, albeit developed and repositioned by the ascension.[166]

Fifth, assessing Jesus' ascension for its 'narrative-geography' is properly down to earth, being focused on lived experiences of space. Pred is rightly critical of theorists who do not apply their theoretical refinements to concrete, empirical studies.[167] Examining the heavenly orientation and earthly mission of the ascension-driven church within Acts responds practically to this warning, connecting geographical theory with reading practice.

This narrative-geographical reading of Acts therefore *reverses* the order of Moxnes' extrapolations from Harvey's grid of spatial practices.[168] Whereas Moxnes examined 'kingdom' in Luke's Gospel within a Palestinian context, Part II will propose that, within Acts, the kingdom's point of view arises from a heavenly perspective which

---

[163] Latham 1926: 389.   [164] Nave 2002: 24.

[165] Reinhartz 2000: 337.

[166] Comparisons with other ancient (literary) geographies are possible and necessary: L. C. A. Alexander (2005) is suggestive concerning Greco-Roman geographies, while Borgen (1997) has compared Luke's geographical horizon with that of Philo. The present study, however, limits itself to an internal analysis of narrative-theological space within Acts, judging this to be a prior necessity for wider comparative readings.

[167] Pred 1990: 25–33.   [168] Cf. Moxnes 2001a: 180.

then positions earthly spaces. Analysis therefore relates heaven with earth, examining how Luke imagines new structures and new spatial practices in light of the catalytic ascension of Christ.

Viewed thus, the interests of Acts contrast sharply with ancient 'heavenly ascent' literature, which sought to probe the secrets of otherwise hidden cosmic geographies.[169] Rather than engaging in heavenly speculation, Luke's emphasis remains resolutely earthly, consistently concerned with mortal humanity's correct response to the ascended Christ.[170] This sustained earthly point of view in Acts prevents 'the *geo*graphy of οὐρανός' becoming an oxymoron.

This focus upon lived experience acknowledges both the long tradition of geographers who have examined the internal narrative geographies of literature,[171] and the more recent recognition that power relations and social practices within narratives in turn reflect and (re)structure readers' flesh-and-blood spatial practices.[172] Successive waves of existentialist, Marxist, feminist and queer-theory geographers have acknowledged this pragmatic power of narrative, reading narrative geographies for their class, gender, ethnic, racial and sexual constructions of space and place. The same constituting power of narrative underpins the work of Green and Moxnes who, between them, bridge narrative-critical and social-scientific approaches and anticipate a *theological* reading of space and place such as is undertaken in Part II.

6.   **Conclusion**

This chapter has critiqued existing attempts to engage in a spatialised reading of scripture and presented a method for undertaking post-Conzelmann reading of Acts. It now remains, in closing Part 1, to draw together the findings of these opening two chapters in preparation for the exegesis undertaken in Part II.

---

[169] Cf. Dean-Otting 1984: 4. The genre of Acts continues to be contested (Burridge 2004: 237–9, 275–9; Phillips 2006), but the present reading does not require or presume any predetermined genre. Instead, such debates require that Acts be read for its space.
[170] O'Toole (1979: 109) makes this point regarding the Acts 1 ascension narrative itself. The rest of Acts maintains this point of view.
[171] E.g. M. Crang 1998, Duncan and Gregory 1999.   [172] E.g. Rose 1993.

SYNTHESIS AND PROSPECT

1. Synthesis

Chapter 1 has outlined the three contentions underpinning this study which, taken together, locate the horizons for this study between Jesus' ascension, a narrative appreciation of Acts, and the inherent production of space within a narrative. Chapter 2 has set the study's direction, namely to occupy the central ground among these three poles. This tri-polar analytical framework demonstrates the limitations of previous ascension scholarship, namely its insufficient connection of these three poles. First, as Chapter 1 confirmed, existing ascension scholarship lacks a narrative dimension, Parsons – the sole exception to this pattern – having made only limited steps towards a corrective reading. Also, analyses of the relationship between the ascension and space have tended to arise from systematic perspectives, thus downplaying Acts' specific narrative ordering. Chapter 1 also illustrated how biblical studies has struggled with the problematic rendering of post-ascension Christological presence and absence, judging that its analyses often polarise into untheorised dualisms.

Chapter 2 reflected at length on the production of space within a biblical narrative such as Acts. This was necessary preparation for a spatialised reading, given the prevalence of limited and reductionist understandings of geography within biblical studies. Chapter 2 also proposed reading the Acts narrative for its space using thirdspace, an approach which takes seriously the role of space in constituting narrative meaning while recognising the dynamism and diversity within narrative 'spatiality'.

One final preliminary examination remains to be made in Part I's survey, namely whether previous considerations of the production of space and geography within Acts have paid sufficient attention to the structuring effect of the ascension. The following examination of this matter completes and integrates the literature surveys and theoretical preparations made in Part I.

Earthbound readings of Acts

As Chapter 2 intimated, scholarship has not ignored the richly geographical narrative of Acts. Yet despite – or, perhaps, *because of* – this geographical texture, insufficient attention has been paid to the relationship between this geography and the ascension in Acts.

Although Chapter 1 lauded his synchronic approach to the ascension as innovative and necessary, Parsons is indicative of this neglect. Promisingly, however, in more recent work, Parsons has addressed the sense of geography communicated by Acts.[1] Not judging Luke to be a geographer *per se*, but considering him interested in geography, Parsons uses the notion of 'mental maps' (although not utilising the term) to inquire after Jerusalem's position within Luke's symbolic world. Yet what is noteworthy, given his earlier work on the ascension, is Parsons's complete lack of interest in *heaven* as part of Luke's symbolic world.

Whereas his earlier work connected the ascension with narrative concerns, Parsons fails to relate these poles to the production of space within Acts. This lack of integration appears to be predicated upon the absence of any narrative description of the heavenly realm within Acts.[2] As Chapter 2 has argued, however, narrative settings can be invoked without description: the fourfold mention of οὐρανός in Acts 1:10–11 is a more than sufficient narrative marker in this regard. Furthermore, that Christ is 'in heaven' for most of Acts should not blind readers to his narrative influence. Conversely, as has been seen, a narrative-critical reading does not mean returning to speculative or dismissive cosmological culs-de-sac.[3] Instead, it pursues the 'narrative' post-ascension Jesus, not (to mix categories dreadfully) the 'historical' post-ascension Jesus.

In Sojan terms, Parsons fails to move beyond consideration of firstspace (understood as topography) and secondspace (defined geopolitically). In contrast to Parsons's missed opportunity to connect with his own work on the ascension, the application of Sojan spatial theory to reading Acts 1:1–11:18 made in Part II will posit that – thirdspatially – the heavenly Christ persistently and decisively influences the production of earthly spaces within Acts.

This suggests that Parsons's resultant earthbound reading of Luke's symbolic world wrongly positions Jerusalem as central to the

---

[1] Parsons 1998.   [2] Parsons 1998: 160–1.
[3] Cf., for example, the insightful analysis of a three-tier vertical axis within the Lukan storyworld articulated by Eisen (2006: 166–8).

spatial vision of Luke/Acts. The present study cannot begin its contention within Luke's Gospel, but it argues that – in Acts, at least –
Parsons's reading, by ignoring the narrative place of heaven (as
Christ's post-ascension locale), distorts Luke's understanding of
space. Although Parsons identifies a Lukan ambivalence towards
Jerusalem, this is – within the narrative span of Acts – the wrong
place from which to begin analysis. Other Jerusalem-centred readings
of Acts are similarly earthbound, and reflect the same insufficient
reflection upon the ascension's function in ordering space.[4]

Part I therefore proposes that the place of Israel or Jerusalem – or
any other setting or spatial marker within Acts – cannot be understood properly without first positioning heaven within Acts' presentation of space. To do otherwise distorts the 'spatiality' of the
narrative at its outset. It is therefore insufficient to summarise Acts
as a 'Tale of Two Cities',[5] to suggest that a shift in 'maps' from
Jerusalem to Rome occurs during the middle chapters of Acts,[6] or
to delimit Luke as having 'two images of the world'.[7] In themselves,
these various reductions are all earthbound and therefore generate
insufficient and misleading renderings of Lukan space. They under-
estimate Lukan space by underplaying the key *theological* change in
geographical horizon within Acts, namely *heavenly* Christocentrism,
a change played out spatially across the narrative, towards the end of
the earth. Loveday Alexander rightly sees Acts 1:8 as already implying 'a divine bird's-eye view of the world',[8] but has not followed
through on this observation by considering the heavenly perspective
within the broader flow of Acts. This study proposes that her otherwise useful geographical observations concerning movement and
perspective within Acts will be broadened and better positioned by
considering heaven's role within the narrative.

2.   Prospect

This study aims to reshape, to respatialise, discourse concerning Acts.
Part I has proposed a narrative reading of the ascension which takes
narrative spatiality seriously, since Jesus – the ascension's central

---

[4] E.g. Bauckham 1995; J. M. Scott 2002; Marguerat and Bourquin 1999: 81; and
Marguerat's otherwise helpful analysis (2002: 239) of 'the impulse to mobility' within Acts.
[5] Parsons 1987: 156.
[6] L. C. A. Alexander suggests a transition in Acts 13 (1995b: 32), or in Acts 16 and
beyond (1995a: 31).
[7] J. M. Scott 1994, 2000.   [8] L. C. A. Alexander 1995a: 22.

character – remains a placed character within the narrative. Part II, therefore, uses the analytic lens provided by thirdspace in a reading of Acts that engages with other scholarly readings, appropriating, critiquing and extending their spatial insights. This reading applies Alexander's judgement that reading for narrative spatiality is 'a matter of paying close attention to the precise contours of the geographical information an author chooses to highlight, and to do that we need first to find a way to depict exactly the information given in the text. Only then can we proceed to evaluation of its narrative significance.'[9] The exposition of spatial theory in Chapter 2, however, has judged that previous readings of narrative geography have been insufficient for achieving this end. Additionally, Chapter 1 suggests, 'heaven' needs to be considered as a foundational *topos* within the narrative spatiality of Acts.

Part II therefore advances these claims through a reading of Acts for its spaces. Chapter 3 outlines the key exegesis of this study, mapping an 'ascension geography' of Acts from 1:6–11. It proposes that this passage's emphasis on Jesus having gone 'into heaven' reveals the essence of Lukan spatiality within Acts. Without reducing this spatiality to this one term, or reverting to imagining that narrative geography can be traced from a concordance, Chapter 3 will argue that 'heaven' presents a fruitful trail for focalising a geographical reading of the post-ascension Jesus within Acts using thirdspace analytical categories.

Chapters 4–7 extend this exegesis as far as Acts 11:18. This juncture provides a suitable narrative closure for assessing the validity of the argument pursued here, since it reflects the extent and distribution of οὐρανός references within Acts. Οὐρανός is mentioned beyond 11:10 only in relation to creation during addresses to pagan audiences (14:15; 17:24; cf. 19:35), and in retrospective references to Saul's initial encounter with Christ, itself first recounted in Acts 9 (22:6; cf. 26:13). This distribution suggests that if the narrative is structured according to ascension geography, this should be apparent by 11:18.

Given these positional findings in Part I, attention now turns to Acts 1, to the expansive horizons and open skies of the Mount of Olives.

---

[9] L. C. A. Alexander 1995b: 20.

PART II

Exegesis

3

ACTS 1:1–26

1.   Prelude

This chapter begins to apply the theoretical insights gained in Part I in a reading of Acts 1:1–11:18. This reading is 'spatial', in that it explores how space is organised and structured within Acts. Part I refuted the equation of space with emptiness, or its marginalisation as passive background. It showed how, all too often, in the face of what Soja has termed 'historicism', spatial cues can 'shrink' before temporal or materialist assumptions governing the reading process in a manner analogous to Janice Capel Anderson's observation that female characters can shrink when read within wider androcentric assumptions.[1] A spatial reading of Acts instead assumes that in Acts – like any narrative – space is produced in places, at contested sites of meaning and at varying geographical scales, each carrying theological meaning and also being shaped by theological meaning.

As Part I showed, this 'geography' is concerned with the perception, classification, division and ordering of space into places and territories, and it anticipates the articulation of a 'worldview' that is broader than the kind of information presented simply on maps. This search for the spatial in Acts therefore involves reading Acts for the geographies which actively constitute meaning within the text.

This first exegetical chapter is foundational for what follows, expounding Christ's ascension for its determinative role in ordering space within Acts. In particular, it argues that the thirdspatial effect of 1:9–11 should supplement existing readings of Acts which judge 1:8, in isolation, as setting the narrative's geographical agenda. With these matters in mind, 1:1–11, 'one of the most subtle and concentrated

---

[1] J. C. Anderson 1994: 134.

pieces of theological writing in Luke's whole enterprise',[2] launches this inquiry into the productions of space within Acts.

2.   Entering into the space of Acts (1:1–5)

The preface to Acts begins to establish the narrative's spatial ordering. Acts 1:1 makes reference to 'the first book (λόγον)',[3] which is generally assumed to be Luke's Gospel. This, together with 'all that Jesus did and taught',[4] positions the spatiality of the opening of Acts within the remit of that found in Luke's Gospel, especially if ἤρξατο assumes here – as is widely assumed – its full natural force of all that Jesus *began* to do and teach, suggesting that Acts recounts the *continuing* words and work of Jesus, perhaps, as C. K. Barrett suggests, 'through the Holy Spirit, through the church'.[5] Usually this connection between Luke and Acts is read as indicating temporal continuity; without denying such temporality, there is also a significant transmission of narrative space from Luke's Gospel, such that Acts does not begin as a spatial *tabula rasa*. Chapter 2 has already discussed Third-Gospel spatiality concerning the 'kingdom';[6] at this initial stage of the narrative, the Lukan 'journey narrative' constitutes another important prior spatial structure continuing into Acts.

Acts 1:2b–3a begins to draw upon this Lukan journey-geography. First, the apostles are characterised as having been chosen by Jesus (1:2). This, combined with their ascription as 'men of Galilee' in 1:11, evokes the journey to Jerusalem undertaken with Jesus in Luke's Gospel (a comparison revisited in 13:31). Similarly, reference to 'his suffering' recalls Jesus' death in Jerusalem, one apparent 'end' of that journey. Here, 1:3 reintroduces the risen Jesus proving himself to be alive following his suffering and now re-associating himself with his followers. Such narration itself generates spatial claims,[7] Luke having already presented Jesus as a theologically purposeful traveller (Luke

---

[2] Turner 2000: 294–5. Cf. also Wasserberg (1998: 211), who judges that 1:1–14 signals how Acts as a whole is to be read.

[3] Except where stated, all English Bible translations follow the New Revised Standard Version (NRSV).

[4] Barrett (1994: 66) sees here 'a very adequate summary of both the contents and interests of the Third Gospel'.

[5] Barrett 1994: 66.

[6] Cf. Moxnes 2000, 2001a, 2001b, 2001c.

[7] The apostles' later designation as witnesses invokes a spatiality, especially when eyewitnesses convey geographical information from or about distant places (L. C. A. Alexander 1993: 34–41, 120–3).

9:31). Here in Acts, Jesus, the 'primal missionary',[8] is once more on the move, continuing over forty days the ministry by which 'the Lord Jesus went in and out among us' (1:21; cf. Numbers 27:16–17).[9]

Despite variant readings of 1:2, ἀνελήμφθη ('he was taken up') is widely accepted as secure.[10] Its *meaning*, however, has been hotly debated and impinges upon any ascension-based reading of Acts. This is compounded by questions surrounding the meaning of the cognate noun ἀνάλημψις in Luke 9:51 (RSV: 'to be received up'; NRSV: 'to be taken up'), a NT *hapax legomenon*. Having reviewed the options at length, Parsons persuasively demonstrates that both Luke 9:51 and Acts 1:2 refer not merely to death or ascension, but to 'Jesus' entire journey back to God (burial, resurrection, exaltation)', deciding that Acts 1:2 is best translated as 'exalted'.[11] Parsons is not alone in identifying an ascension connotation within Luke 9:51.[12] This suggests that, although in a formal sense Jesus' journey begun in Luke 9:51 concluded at Jerusalem (e.g. at Luke 19:45), its horizon also extends to the ascension: for Luke, 'the journey is the first part of that ascent to heaven which he calls Jesus' ἀνάνλημψις'.[13] To argue, as did van Stempvoort,[14] that Acts 1:2 refers simply to Christ's death, requires a convincing reason for the verb ἀναλαμβάνω to have a different sense from the same word's clear meaning in 1:11, 22. His interpretation has not received wide support. Instead, as Scott Spencer suggests, 1:2, 22 present an *inclusio* which 'tie[s] the whole first chapter together around the ascension axis'.[15]

In this manner the prologue to Acts both assumes spaces from Luke's Gospel and anticipates the forthcoming ascension account.

Without replacing temporal readings, a spatially sensitive reading of 1:3b–5 indicates new insights which are more productive than the older, somewhat jaded temporal debates concerning whether the forty days mentioned in 1:3 are symbolic or literal and their

[8] Hengel 1983: 61.
[9] This 'visible demonstration of the risen Jesus as interpreter of the Scriptures concerning the kingdom of God' prepared for 'the invisible presence of the prophet-teacher working through his Spirit' (Croatto 2005: 462).
[10] Metzger 1994: 236–241 surveys the variants; see also Parsons 1987: 129, 1988: 66 and Zwiep 1996: 237–8.
[11] Parsons 1987: 125–34 (133).
[12] E.g. Tannehill 1986: 284 n. 13; cf. Tannehill 1990: 10–11; Moessner 1989: 320; Evans 1993a: 97; 1993b: 82; Mayer 1996: 69; Turner 2000: 297; and Marguerat 2002: 50–1.
[13] Talbert 1974: 115.   [14] Van Stempvoort 1958/9: 32.
[15] Spencer 1997: 23.

relationship with the shorter timescale implicit in Luke 24.[16] Attention here focuses instead on what these verses invoke regarding an ordering of space.

The differences between the Luke 24 and Acts 1 ascension accounts are best ascribed to their particular narrative positions.[17] Narrative repetition, as 'never the return of the same',[18] generates a differential which includes the passages' productions of space. Acts 1:3b illustrates this differential: Jesus is narrated as 'speaking about the kingdom of God', without this teaching's content being specified.[19] These words, combined with his convincing resurrection appearances, confirm the narrative importance of this forty-day period for instilling Jesus' ongoing spatiality and its significance within his followers (cf., e.g., 10:41). This instruction includes geographical direction: his apostles are 'ordered (παρήγγειλεν) … not to depart from Jerusalem, but (ἀλλὰ) to wait there for the promise of the Father … [which] you have heard from me' (1:4).

At this juncture in the narrative, superficially it appears that Jesus is commanding his apostles to join themselves to Jerusalem: this has led van Stempvoort (among others) to posit a centralising role for Jerusalem within Luke's spatial order.[20] But, rather, auditors of Luke know that *Jesus* and his *journeying* provided that narrative's fundamental ordering:[21] Acts 1:4 maintains the same proximity around Jesus as the hallmark of Lukan discipleship at the outset of Acts. This Christological connective, although shortly to be restructured radically by the ascension, will, as Acts unfolds, prove to be more important than physical affinity with Jerusalem.[22]

---

[16] E.g. Larkin 1997; cf. Giles 1992, Zwiep 1997.

[17] Parsons 1987: 151–86. Similarly, van Stempvoort 1958/9.

[18] Marguerat 2002: 132.

[19] Perhaps Acts 1:3 summarises Luke 24:27, 44–8, and Acts 1:8 (Croatto 2005: 462). Certainly it establishes an initial thematic emphasis on 'the kingdom of God' which contributes to a broader architectural frame within Acts (e.g. cf. 28:31). That 1:3 does not recount explicitly Jesus addressing the need to replace Judas does not preclude reading the fulfilment of Luke 22:30 as in view in Acts 1:15–26 (*contra* Estrada 2004: 177).

[20] Van Stempvoort (1958/9: 37) judges 1:4–5 as combating an early-church tendency to leave Jerusalem. It is hard to judge whether his subsequent designation of Jerusalem as 'this holy town' (p. 41) is cause or effect of his reading. Regarding Jerusalem as a focal point, see also Conzelmann 1987: 6; Fitzmyer 1998: 199–200.

[21] Marguerat 2002: 239.

[22] Rius-Camps and Read-Heimerdinger (2004: 67) also note the Hellenistic spelling Ἱεροσολύμων in 1:4 [B D, cf. ℵ] which, they judge, in D indicates 'simply … Jerusalem as a town', 'a neutral designation for the city, devoid of religious significance'. B lacks such apparently consistent secondspace differentiation (Read-Heimerdinger 2002: 343).

Acts begins, therefore, not so much with movement 'from' Jerusalem as movement 'according to' Jesus. Already the opening verses of Acts have established Jesus as the central character in the unfolding plot. In 1:4, therefore, a significant spatial differentiation is developing *within* Acts 1. Those who have accompanied Jesus from Galilee to Jerusalem and have been shaped by the experience (cf. 1:11, 22) are now receiving from Jesus a spatial manifesto with rich third-space promise but which – by inference from 1:2 – will not be accompanied by his (firstspace) presence. Jesus' instruction bears no reassurance that he will remain with them in Jerusalem. Nevertheless, although not yet explicit, Jesus' territorial imperative will continue to govern his apostles' movements during his post-ascension absence.[23] Such is the inference of 1:1.

Although the spatial import of 'the promise of the Father' is not made apparent at this narrative juncture, this does not mean the promise's outworkings are aspatial. First, 1:4 has presented an important early indication that Jesus will continue to structure believers' space within Acts. Second, the promise's spatiality will be revealed progressively and retrospectively as the narrative unfolds (e.g. 2:17; 11:16). Third, the allusion in 1:5 to John the Baptist's foretelling of the coming baptism 'with the Holy Spirit and fire' (Luke 3:16–17) is indirect but informative at the outset of the Acts narrative.[24] In Luke 3:17 (par. Matthew 3:12) John evoked the threshing floor; here its thirdspatial qualities[25] inform the spatiality latent within Acts 1. Alternatively, the silence concerning fire in 1:5 might be deliberate, either allowing it to be picked up symbolically in 2:3 or else transforming 'the fiery baptism into something less fearful'.[26] These options need not be mutually exclusive, and the latter reading, especially, creates space for the church not so apparent in Luke 3:16–17 and 12:49–50. Mention of John also evokes his wider exhortation to prepare for the coming one (Luke 3:3–18), which in turn primes the narrative for the disciples' question in Acts 1:6.

---

[23] Nothing in Acts suggests that 1:4 inhibits *any* subsequent movement away from Jerusalem: the apostles' continuance in Jerusalem under persecution (8:1) can be explained much more positively (see subsequent discussion of 6:4). Also, Acts describes apostolic departures from Jerusalem without embarrassment (e.g. 8:14; 9:32). Within the narrative, the apostles are told that the goal of their wait will come 'not many days from now'. W. Davies 1974: 265: 'It is in Jerusalem that the destiny of the disciples lies to begin with. But only to begin with!'

[24] Tannehill (1990: 12) also claims connections with Luke 11:13.

[25] Matthews 2003: 13.   [26] Dunn 1996: 9.

3.   An 'ascension geography' orienting the space of Acts (1:6–11)

The narrative slows from summary to conversation.[27] Acts 1:6, the
narrative's only words spoken by the disciples to the earthly Jesus, has
provoked much scholarly inquiry. Yet interpretations which focus
narrowly on *temporal* issues relating to 'this ... time' incur Soja's
charge of historicism. Where its spatiality has been considered, 1:6
is usually analysed within Jesus' immediate reply in 1:7–8. The reading pursued here employs Sojan categories and places 1:6 within the
larger immediate cotext of 1:6–11 in order to position the full spatial
import of 1:6 *and* Jesus' reply.

Acts 1:6 read for its space

The question of 1:6 draws auditors into the disciples' point of view.
Far from being an illegitimate question, it fits within its immediate
narrative cotext[28] and within a common concern within intertestamental Judaism whereby 'restoration' would be understood eschato-
logically in terms dependent upon Malachi 3:23 LXX (4:6).[29] Any
such restoration would be implicated within what Gerd Theissen has
termed the 'crisis over theocracy', and would be intensely geographical within all three Sojan spheres. Spatial matters would be unavoidable for anyone presenting a hope for 'Israel'.[30]

In terms of the disciples' spatiality, their question draws together
three spatial assumptions within a tightly packed inquiry concerning
the restoration of the kingdom.[31]

First, the obviously spatial presupposition which has dominated
previous geographical analysis of 1:6, such as it is, is the restoration of
the kingdom *to Israel*.[32] The appropriation of such an archaic self-
ascription[33] generates immediate questions concerning real and

---

[27] Eisen 2006: 168.
[28] Pao 2000: 95 n. 143; Turner 2000: 295, 299. Cf. Calvin 1965: 29: 'There are as
many errors in this question as words.'
[29] Barrett 1994: 76; Eisen 2006: 150.
[30] Theissen 1978: 65. Cf. also Tiede 1986: 278–80; Rius-Camps and Read-
Heimerdinger 2004: 79–82.
[31] Τὴν βασιλείαν probably means 'sovereignty', with the cotextual resonance of
recreating a former spatial reality, namely Davidic territorial domination (so Barrett
1994: 76–8; cf. Maddox 1982: 107).
[32] Rius-Camps and Read-Heimerdinger (2004: 52–3, 71–4) expound a more nationalistic D reading 'restore to (εἰς) the kingdom of Israel', but this does not materially
alter the reading pursued here.
[33] Lieu 2004: 246–9.

imagined geographies. As will be demonstrated in subsequent chapters, Acts is not assessing such geographies within simple binary categories whereby they are accepted or rejected. Thus it is insufficient simply either to accept this complex spatial presupposition at face value as representing Luke's 'approved' spatial understanding, or to dismiss it simply as a misunderstanding on the part of the disciples.[34] Although Jesus' instruction to remain in Jerusalem might fuel the former estimation (and, within the storyworld, the question itself), Jesus' subsequent reply and ascension (examined below) qualifies such readings, inscribing instead something *more*, some*where* (third-spatial) which 'extends well beyond' traditional dualisms regarding space 'in scope, substance, and meaning'.[35]

The second presupposition in 1:6 concerns *Jesus* as the agent of restoration. It assumes that Israel's restoration hope is embodied in Jesus, whom the witnesses have followed from Galilee and whose now resurrected presence suggests that restoration is possible. The extended period of Jesus' post-resurrection teaching concerning the kingdom of God (1:3) combined with his charge not to leave Jerusalem (1:4) would understandably fuel such expectations. Nevertheless, as the subsequent verses clarify, this Christological assumption requires qualification: the promise issued in 1:11 *does* anticipate Jesus' earthly proximity as 1:6 presupposes (cf. 3:21), but first *they* will be his witnesses (1:8) in his firstspace absence. Any hope for 'Israel' therefore needs to be understood within a different kind of tensive relationship, a different space, between him *and them*.

The third presupposition in 1:6 is that the restoration could possibly happen 'now'. Historicism has frequently foregrounded this presupposition, reducing its analysis to it.[36] A spatialised reading should not adopt the opposite error: 1:6 presents a spatial-temporal question, the presumption of temporal immediacy intensifying the notion of spatial restoration, around which it is tightly bound.

---

[34] *Contra* Wilson 1973: 89, 106 and Maile 1986: 51–2. At very least, the candour expressed in 1:6 enhances the account's verisimilitude (Metzger 1969: 120). Furthermore, the parallels between Acts 1 and the Emmaus road encounter (Mayer 1996) suggest unfolding understanding on the part of the apostles.

[35] Soja 1996: 11, describing thirdspace.

[36] Witherington (1998: 110), for example, structures analysis of 1:6 around timing and mortal knowledge of such scheduling. Jervell (1998: 114, emphases original): 'Die Frage ist nicht, *ob* das Reich für Israel kommen wird, sondern ausschliesslich: *Wann* kommt das Reich, ἐν τῷ χρόνῳ τούτῳ?' ('The question is not *whether* the empire will come for Israel but exclusively: *When* does the empire come, at this time?')

Taken as a whole, therefore, the question in 1:6 implies 'here', 'by you', and 'now'. The third implication, the temporal 'now', presumes the certainty of the first two spatial assumptions. In Sojan categories, 1:6 represents the immediate overlay of firstspace (location), second-space (projection), and thirdspace (aspiration), the collapsing of eschatological space and time into an immediacy of expectation.

Expanding horizons (1:7–8)

Jesus' reply in 1:7–8 begins to unravel the tightly packed spatial presumptions in 1:6.

First, 1:7 undermines any focus upon – or expectation of – mortal knowledge concerning χρόνους ἢ καιρούς, 'times or periods'. Furthermore, Jesus' pluralised answer contrasts with, and qualifies, the questioners' immediate horizon ('Is this the time?', 1:6), creating not only a timespan ('*Zeitraum*'[37]) but also room for intermediate earthly spaces (1:8 cf. 1:6). In this manner, 'the task has arisen of finding a new relationship to this world'.[38] Crucially, this 'new relationship' is not merely temporal. Beyond the numerous scholars who have undermined the previously vice-like grip of a *temporal* eschatological crisis on the interpretation of these verses,[39] the spatial reading pursued here also destabilises any easy equation of 'here' and 'now' in 1:6. In Sojan terms, Jesus distinguishes their (and his) *firstspace* location from their *secondspace* conceptualisation of restoration.

Second, rather than the question's attention remaining focused on Jesus, his reply draws attention to the soon-to-be empowered disciples as μου μάρτυρες ('my witnesses', 1:8). The genitive's syntactical ambiguity[40] unsettles the focus, both differentiating and connecting Jesus and his followers. At this stage in the narrative, the spatiality inherent within this new relationship between Jesus and his followers is not clear: further explication and clarity will come in 1:9–11.

Third, 1:8b realigns the questioners' horizons from singular 'Israel' to a string of locational markers reaching 'to the ends of the earth'. Although Jerusalem heads this string, reinforcing Jesus' spatial command in 1:4, the subsequent geographical markers dismantle any restriction of restoration-space to 'Israel', as conventionally viewed

---

[37] Jervell 1998: 114–15 (115).   [38] Haenchen 1971: 143.
[39] E.g. Franklin 1975: 27–8; Carroll 1988: 126; Brawley 1990: 43; Tannehill 1990: 19; Ellis 1991: 18 and Green 1997a: 21.
[40] An alternative meaning, if not translation, would be 'witnesses of me'.

from Jerusalem. The mention of 'Samaria' makes this clear, coming as a significant spatial jolt for any comfortable geographical assumptions in 1:6, especially if there is a second ἐν ('in') in 1:8, which would group together Judea and Samaria within a tripartite description of the mission's growth. First-century religious-ethnic politics, confirmed by previous Lukan references to Samaritans during the journey to Jerusalem (Luke 9:52–4; 10:33–7; 17:11–19), indicate that 1:8 is no 'mere geographical description'.[41] Instead, it invokes an echo-chamber of deep ethnic hostility, a contextualised location-marker 'imbued with symbolic power ... not a "naively given container" but rather a social production that both reflects and configures being in the world'.[42] In short, this anticipation of the geography of Acts, viewed from the Mount of Olives, presents a far more unsettling prospect than the disciples' immediate surrounds. Witnessing space is projected as breaching the ethnic divides that defined Israel-space, even if the nature of these breaches, significantly, is not yet defined beyond saying that it involves witnesses. This prospect anticipates uncomfortable dislocation for these witnesses. Nor is there any comforting mention of Galilean homelands as compensation.[43] Instead, there is the promise of the Spirit's power, and the prospect of a wide range of geographic locales within this worldview.

The climactic location marker ἕως ἐσχάτου τῆς γῆς, 'to the ends [lit., "end"] of the earth', signals the earth's outermost margins, not any specific or actual location.[44] The climax of 1:8 is, therefore (in Sojan terms), a secondspace marker without a specific firstspace location, the string of three firstspace locales – Jerusalem, Judea,

[41] Hays 2003: 167. Hays suggests that mention of Galilee instead of Samaria would have constituted such 'mere geography': the distinction is analytically useful, even if Hays's phrasing is antithetical to the conception of geography pursued here.
[42] Green 1997a: 15. Cf. Jervell 1998: 116: 'Die Samaritaner sind für Lukas wichtig, eben weil er sie als Juden betrachtet.' ('The Samaritans are important, even to Luke because he considers them Jews.')
[43] Perhaps Luke lacked sources concerning post-resurrection Galilee (Barrett 1994: 80; Witherington 1998: 111). It is unconvincing that Luke rejects 'die Mischbevölkerung des galiläischen Gegenden' (Jervell 1998: 116, 'the mixed population of the Galilean areas'). Schnabel (2004a: 372) harmonises from silence: '"Judea" ... evidently includes Galilee.' More suggestive from a narrative-critical perspective, Luke is preserving a special role for Galilee (see below, concerning 1:11) while also constructing a wider, geographically inclusive secondspace. Mention of Galilee at this point would distract from both these narrative functions.
[44] J. M. Scott 2002: 58–61; Schnabel 2004a: 272–376 and Sleeman 2006: 77–9 provide recent surveys of the scholarly literature supporting this contention. Both Jew and gentile are in view: 'Man sollte nicht vorschnell an Heiden denken' (Jervell 1998: 116, 'One should not think hastily of gentiles').

Samaria – concluding with a projection, a broader secondspace horizon which incorporates all earthly firstspaces within its scope.[45]

The effect on the spatial ordering of Acts is profound. Secondspace,
here characterised as witnessing space, stretches beyond the firstspace
places mentioned in 1:8 as an unconstrained prospect, anticipating
ongoing variegated encounters between witnesses and peopled places.
Thus, as the narrative reaches its firstspace climax, Rome, auditors
discover that unnamed witnesses to Christ have already preceded the
narrative's arrival there (28:14–15). Through this phrase, ἕως
ἐσχάτου τῆς γῆς, the 'eschato-logy' of Acts is clearly and undeniably
spatialised[46] and linked to witness. Simultaneously, viewed as an
expression of secondspace, Acts 1:8 does not need to carry the burden
of outlining a detailed list of contents for the forthcoming narrative.
Such secondspace unsettles firstspace allegiances to particular places,
but it cannot be abstracted from actual places such that the particularity of proximate relations dissolves away;[47] instead, the ground is
set for a thirdspace of lived experience between and beyond such
dualisms. Thus in 1:7–8 Jesus does far more than predict the witnesses' future schedule: he (re)defines their space and, with them, that
of the wider world.[48]

Decentring horizons (1:9–11)

If Jesus' reply in 1:7–8 distinguishes the disciples' secondspace from
their firstspace, can any more be said concerning their thirdspace?
Most analyses accept 1:7–8 as the totality of Jesus' response to 1:6,
such that Jesus articulates a globalised vision for the witnesses. While
valid, this takes inadequate account of Jesus' spatial realignment

---

[45] Without using Sojan categories, Pao (2000: 91–6) and Turner (2000: 300–1) draw
similar conclusions.

[46] This is a Lukan parallel to what Lincoln (1981: 5) recognises concerning the
Pauline epistles: '[Eschatological] language involves both vertical and horizontal referents, spatial and temporal categories … heaven as well as the Last Day. All too often in
treatments of eschatology the latter pole is given all the attention and the former is
virtually ignored. Both sorts of language are to be given their full weight.' Surprisingly,
given the hold of salvation history over twentieth-century Lukan studies, ἕως ἐσχάτου
τῆς γῆς has escaped being understood simply as a temporal marker. Even historicism
has its limits.

[47] O'Donovan (1989) contends that a Christian 'sense of place' resists such a dissolution: certainly Acts would confirm his contention.

[48] Tiede (1981: 49), O'Donovan (1996: 145), and N. T. Wright (2003: 655–6) probe
the *global* ramifications of 1:6–11. The increasingly global pretensions of Rome (Romm
1992: 121–39) are at least indirectly challenged by Acts 1. Cf. also Balch 2003.

which follows in 1:9–11. Jesus' ascension clarifies further the witnesses' lived experience of space by distilling their thirdspace within a distinctively heavenward Christocentric orientation.

First, it is important to note firm narrative links between 1:8 and 1:9, even if past scholarship, eager to address phenomenological issues surrounding the ascension, has emphasised the formal differences between dialogue (1:6–8) and narrated description (1:9–10). Given that 'Luke could scarcely have recounted the Ascension in the form of a dialogue',[49] these differences can be overstated. Conversely, Steve Walton, citing Josephus (*Ant.* 4.8.48) and 2 Kings 2:9–12, has suggested that it would be strange to have an ascension account without any words from the departing person.[50] Also the dialogue *is* continued in 1:11, albeit by the messengers[51] who speak for the now ascended Jesus. Marion Soards even suggests that 'since the angelic figures speak of and for the now-ascended Jesus, it is best to understand their statements in this context as a complement to, and even as a part of, Jesus' speech'.[52] At very least, the link between these speeches is confirmed by the opening words of 1:9 – καὶ ταῦτα εἰπὼν βλεπόντων αὐτῶν ('When he had said this, as they were watching...') – and by the connective in 1:10, καὶ ὡς ἀτενίζοντες ἦσαν εἰς τὸν οὐρανὸν πορευομένου αὐτοῦ (RSV: 'And while they were gazing into heaven as he went'; NRSV: 'While he was going and they were gazing up toward heaven'), this latter connective being picked up by the messengers' question in 1:11.[53] On these grounds there are clear narrative connections across 1:6–11, given existing recognition of 1:6–8 as a connected account.[54]

Thus 1:9–11 positions 1:7–8 as Jesus' final words immediately before his decisive departure from his disciples. If this opening section of Acts continues a biographical genre from Luke's Gospel, then the subject's last words are especially important for summing up his life.[55]

[49] Wilson 1973: 103.   [50] Walton 1999: 448.
[51] Rius-Camps and Read-Heimerdinger (2004: 89–91) read them as Moses and Elijah (cf. Luke 9:30; 24:4), not angels. Cf., however, Luke 24:23.
[52] Soards 1994: 23.
[53] In this characteristically Lukan narrative use of two-clause questions (Elbert 2004), the latter concept picks up previously highlighted information from the immediate cotext.
[54] Both Pao (2000: 91–6) and Turner (2000: 294–5 n. 76) claim 1:1–11 as a unified section, but then fail to integrate 1:9–11 into their analysis. In Sojan terms (although neither uses such categories), they are insightful regarding (earthly) secondspace but miss the (heavenly) thirdspace infusing 1:6–11.
[55] Burridge 2004: 74, 142, 160–1, 174–5, 202, 225.

Certainly these words are 'final and conclusive',[56] their position affording a primacy effect within the narrative. Such positioning is hermeneutically important for establishing the spatial priorities of Acts. Furthermore, given that – even if unmentioned – the speaker's body is always a spatial reference point, as the speaker of these words in Acts 1 ascends into heaven, the words just spoken cannot be detached from this profound relocation.

The emphasis of 1:10–11, running through both the narrated description and the messengers' words, is that Jesus has gone 'into heaven' (εἰς τὸν οὐρανὸν).[57] This phrase occurs four times within the space of forty-five Greek words.[58] While not unprecedented elsewhere in the narrative, such tight repetition functions as an important way in which Luke signals spatial-theological information within Acts.[59] Repetition elsewhere within the opening verses of Acts has been understood temporally, as building expectation;[60] but here in 1:10–11 repetition also functions spatially, along the lines theorised by Bal: 'information concerning space is often repeated, to stress the stability of the frame, as opposed to the transitory nature of the events which occur within it'.[61] Seen in this light, this repetition establishes more than simply 'the reality of Christ's Lordship'[62] – even allowing for the semantic ambiguity of οὐρανός to encompass visible skies and theological heaven, the repetition also declares the *space* of Christ's lordship. Simultaneously, Christ has declared earthly space for the believers: they are waiting in Jerusalem, for the promised Holy Spirit who will enable them to witness for him to the end of the earth. Now absent in firstspace terms, Christ's ascension alters his ongoing

---

[56] Haenchen 1971: 144.

[57] Cf. Zwiep (1997: 168–9), who locates the centre of gravity of the angelic message in 1:11 within the parousia, not Christ's session.

[58] Most commentators judge the omission of one of these references in 1:11 [D gig Aug^st] to be an accidental omission. Given their lack of substantiating evidence, and the counter-evidence of such repetition within Acts (see below), the claim by Rius-Camps and Read-Heimerdinger (2004: 55) that such fourfold repetition is 'suspect' remains questionable.

[59] A *BibleWorks* search of Acts, assisted by James Oakley, has highlighted other instances where fourfold repetition within the space of fifty Greek words foregrounds spatial-theological information, namely, ἱερόν ('temple'), 3:1–2; γῆ ('country'/'land'), 7:3–4; Αἴγυπτος ('Egypt'), 7:10–12. Similar repetitions orientating believer-space (especially in relation to heaven) are θεός ('God'), 5:29–32; 11:17–18; προφήτης ('prophet'), 3:21–4; κύριος ('Lord'), 9:10–11; διαφθορά ('decay'), 13:34–7; ὕδωρ ('water'), 8:36–9; and, arguably, πᾶς ('all'), 20:25–8.

[60] So L. T. Johnson (1992: 30), regarding the threefold mention of the Spirit in 1:2, 4–5, 8.

[61] Bal 1995: 97.   [62] Maile 1986: 55.

structuring influence over this believer-space. Expressed in Soja's categories, heaven – or, more accurately, *the heavenly Christ* – provokes their thirdspace within Acts. Within Acts, Jesus' ascension decentres believer-space, provoking, to adopt Soja's words, 'the radical challenge to think differently, to expand your geographical imagination beyond its current limits'.[63] This thirdspace cannot be reduced to, or separated from, firstspace and secondspace: instead it influences and critiques these other spatial perspectives.[64]

The messengers' words (1:11) further clarify the meaning of this spatial restructuring for the witnesses' world. First, the witnesses are described as 'men of Galilee'. This first (and unexplained) mention of Galilee in Acts suggests that auditors are expected to recall information concerning Galilee inscribed within Luke's Gospel. There, Galilee was the place of origin and departure for Jesus' journey to Jerusalem.[65]

Luke Timothy Johnson notes that their Galilean origins are repeatedly stressed towards the end of Luke in a series of largely Lukan emphases (Luke 22:59; 23:5, 49, 55).[66] Not only are these references towards the *end* of Luke, but, more pertinently, Galilean origins are not mentioned until the journey-makers have arrived *in Jerusalem*,[67] that is, until they have travelled with Jesus to Jerusalem, becoming 'out of place' there, dislocated, because of their allegiance to him (cf. 22:59).[68] In this narrative section even Jesus himself is characterised as a Galilean (23:6). Once the journey to Jerusalem is under way, the noun 'Galilee' is also oriented towards it (17:11).

After Acts 1:11 the adjective 'Galilean' occurs only twice more in Acts, in both instances coloured by journeying structures. The crowds who have journeyed to Jerusalem ascribe it in wonder to the Pentecost

---

[63] Soja 1996: 2.

[64] While I agree with Estrada (2004: 90) that the apostles' point of view orients the ascension account in Acts, it does not follow that '1:9–11 centres on the apostles as the primary actors ... Jesus' character declines while the apostles' character rises' (p. 93). In every sense, Jesus' character rises in these verses, as emphasised by the fourfold repetition of his destination.

[65] Jervell (1998: 117) also equates the Galilean ascription in 1:11 with the apostles' previous journey with Jesus, but does so via 13:31.

[66] L. T. Johnson 1992: 27.

[67] The only previous use of 'Galilean' in Luke (13:1, 2) is more general and does not negate the argument.

[68] *Contra* Fitzmyer (1998: 209), who generalises 'men of Galilee', judging it to indicate that the message 'is meant to be extended to all Christians'. Such extension is not established by the term, and the cotext undermines such a reading.

witnesses (2:7), an ironic wonder for auditors recalling 1:11. Its final occurrence concerns the *false* alternative journey-geography provoked by 'Judas the Galilean', who 'rose up during the census and got people (λαόν) to follow him' (5:37).

Within the cotext of Acts 1, however, these Galileans are near Jerusalem only because they have followed Jesus on his journey to the cross and now to the edge of his ascension (cf. 1:21–2). Thus the description in 1:11 defines them according to their journey with Jesus.[69] They are both 'out of place' in Jerusalem (their firstspace location) but 'in their place' by being with Jesus (their pre-ascension narrative secondspace projection) – except that Jesus has now left *them*, generating the need for these messengers. Within Luke's geography, their discipleship journey with Jesus, which has just culminated in his 'Triumphant Exit',[70] will not return them to their earthly home. Their appointed space is now defined as 'other' than Galilee (1:3–4, 8), but remains in some way connected with Jesus.

This Christological connection is sustained by the messengers' rhetorical τί ('why?') question. This question realigns those looking firstspatially for Jesus recasting their gaze towards his new heavenly location. Two formally similar Christological questions within Luke's Gospel (2:49; 24:5) help position this realignment. The first was asked by the twelve-year-old Jesus addressing his mother, regarding his location within the Temple as being 'in my Father's house'. The second was asked by 'two men in dazzling clothes' (Luke 24:4) addressing women who had come up with Jesus from Galilee (information narrated in 23:55, and declared by the messengers in 24:6). Their question undermined the women's spatial assumption locating Jesus with the dead. Now, this third such question (Acts 1:11), addressed by two similar figures to Galilean journeymen, climactically defines the *heavenly* Jesus in relation to his *earthly* followers. 'A gentle prod with a rebuking question'[71] encourages them not to hanker after a former spatial orientation, namely shared firstspace proximity with Jesus. This suggests that ἀτενίζοντες ἦσαν εἰς τὸν οὐρανὸν ('they were gazing up towards heaven', 1:10) represents more than simply narrative colouring;[72] rather, such attention risked producing a misaligned sense of place. Although 1:10–11 presents

---

[69] There is no narrative need, nor suggestion, to follow Selman (1969: 15) in suggesting that Luke is indirectly rebuking a 'Galilean' form of apocalyptic urgency.

[70] Parsons 1987: 104, 112; also Eisen 2006: 157.

[71] Tannehill 1990: 18.

[72] Cf. Barrett (1994: 84), who sees Luke as a 'descriptive writer' at this point.

heaven as a real site, the place of Jesus, it lies beyond mortal sight. Even the witnesses do not witness this heavenly locale, even though they were – in Barrett's rendering – 'straining their eyes to see'[73] into heaven, perhaps in a misplaced imitation of 2 Kings 2:9–12.

Acts allows no account of a heavenly journey through the celestial spheres for Christ, let alone for his disciples. Like other Lukan resurrection appearances, 1:6–11 avoids any suggestion of glorification.[74] Unlike accounts of heavenly journeys circulating in the first century, the knowledge gained by mortals in this instance is very much this-worldly, very much geographical. Indeed, of Mary Dean-Otting's eleven-point list of elements characterising the Jewish heavenly journey form, at least nine are subverted in some way by the Acts 1 account.[75]

The Acts narrative will articulate how Jesus, being in heaven, will inform these Galileans' spatiality, giving it a distinctive thirdspatial orientation. Their orientation has already been expounded by Jesus himself (1:8); now, his firstspace absence brings something else, qualifying and restructuring their firstspace and secondspace. That Jesus is no longer physically present on earth means that they become *necessary* witnesses. There is no means by which to access Jesus other than through *their* testimony. Even the Spirit, from Acts 2 onwards, will be 'a presence which discloses the absence'.[76] Prospectively announcing Jesus' physical return (understanding 'in the same way' in 1:11 to carry at least this meaning) delimits the remainder of the narrative within a new and enduring spatial relationship with Jesus and, short of Jesus' eventual return, precludes the possibility of a fourth such τί question concerning Jesus' whereabouts later in Acts. But, perhaps imperceptibly at this point for the first-time auditor, there is no mention of these witnesses as being present when Jesus eventually returns.

Provisional conclusions concerning ascension geography

Importantly, despite the fourfold proclamation of Christ's new location, the watching disciples are kept by the cloud from seeing the

---

[73] Barrett 1994: 82.   [74] As noted by, e.g., van Stempvoort (1958/9: 39).

[75] Dean-Otting 1984: 4–5. The two elements which in any way resemble Acts 1 are (a) that the vision overcomes the main character such that he does not request the ascent, and (b) that the journey is finite, ending with the main character returning to earth.

[76] Farrow 1999: 271 n. 59.

ascended Jesus (1:9); a clear demarcation between earth and heaven remains. This preserves ascension thirdspace as sovereignly independent of mortal control throughout Acts, an important buffer against reducing the heavenly Christ to merely firstspatial or secondspatial categories. Thus 1:9–11 engenders an enduring critical function within believer-space which will structure the unfolding narrative. Alternative (third)spatial claims confronted within Acts are judged, on its basis, as Christologically defective (e.g. 17:22–31; 19:13–16).[77]

Heavenly thirdspace also produces and defends the possibility of distinctive earthly believer-spaces in Acts. At this stage in the narrative such new spaces are still indeterminate: their geographical production still needs to be realised both by characters within the narrative and by auditors, but they have been positioned under heaven-as-Christ's-place, that is, under a Christological heaven, and have been projected through these Jerusalem-based witnesses towards the edge of the world in anticipation of a spatial-temporal eschaton. Acts 1:7–11 has qualified imminent understandings within 1:6, not only through a global understanding of the witnesses' mission, but also through a *heavenly* Christology.[78]

For the disciples, this narrative juncture launches an ongoing journey under new conditions of separation from the one who has been their guide, a separation rehearsed and anticipated in Luke's Gospel (Luke 9:1–6, 40; 10:1–20; 22:35–8). Emphatic firstspace absence infused with the promise of firstspace return (Acts 1:10–11) generates a narrative-geographical imbalance within Acts.

A continued reading through Acts will test the proposition that this heavenly thirdspace continues to govern narrative space, such that each narrative mention of heaven provokes a patterned expectation, a recollection of 1:6–11, whether as a space of anticipation ('Is this what 1:11 foretold?') or of ironic reflection ('Where is the fulfilment of 1:11?'). Such a relationship between space and event would form a fixed combination, a *topos*.[79] A spatialised reading will also assess whether such recollections of heaven also reflect and inform further developments within the geography outlined in 1:8. Simultaneously, Christ's ascension will also preserve this geography from becoming

---

[77] W. Davies (1974: 286) simultaneously reifies geography and suggests fruitful critical-geographical analysis when he states: 'Acts is open-ended: it subordinates all geography, even Rome, to theology.'

[78] Cf. the analytic notion of a 'terrestrial' Christology inhabiting Luke's Gospel (Croatto 2005: 454–8).

[79] Cf. Bal 1995: 96–7.

either 'little more than ... an inevitable geographical expansion of 1:8 from the centre'[80] or an unchanged Jerusalem-centred worldview. Rather than 1:4 orienting Acts primarily around Jerusalem,[81] 1:10–11 positions and qualifies the geography of the entire narrative as produced under a Christological heaven.

Like any thirdspace, this orientation does not reduce to materialist/ non-materialist dualisms, and indeed challenges such categories. Earthly considerations alone do not delimit Lukan organisation, categorisation and control of space, but instead Jesus' ascension generates Soja's 'real-and-imagined-and-more'[82] sense of space. This reading confirms 'kingdom' (1:3, 6) as a placed concept which is to be similarly understood, and not to be reduced to aspatial, 'spiritual' terms. Consequently, the programme for narrative space in Acts rests among 1:6; 1:8 and 1:11, and cannot be reduced to any one (or two) of these axes. Instead these three spatial axes informing Acts can be properly understood only in relation to one another.

This is central to understanding Acts 1 as providing (to rework van Stempvoort's designation) an 'ecclesiastical-geographical' rendering of the ascension. Without anachronistically presupposing any later ecclesiological structures as being assumed within Acts, this designation strips van Stempvoort's description of the Acts 1 ascension as 'ecclesial and historical' of any latent historicism and opens up its full spatial import.[83] While in agreement with his observation that 'it is remarkable how categories of space and time dominate Acts 1', a spatial analysis presents a more nuanced geography than that which, for example, sees Jerusalem as 'this holy town'.[84] The disciples' question has received much more than an expected 'yes' or 'no' answer – a new frame for narrative action and knowledge has been set in place. Acts 1:6–11 has shown that 'place' carries a surfeit of meanings, confirming it as 'one of the most multilayered and multipurpose keywords in our language'.[85] Such an enriched notion of place qualifies any narrowly earthly notion of a 'groundplan' for Acts within these formative verses.

Thus ascension geography confirms the critique of 'earthbound' readings of Acts made in Part I. Lukan spatiality must not be so falsely conflated. Marguerat, for example, although seeking *not* to reduce Acts to an axis from Jerusalem to Rome, crucially misses this

---

[80] Barrett 1988: 72.   [81] L. T. Johnson 1992: 25.   [82] Soja 1996: 11.
[83] Van Stempvoort 1958/9: 39.   [84] Van Stempvoort 1958/9: 41.
[85] Harvey 1996: 208.

heavenly thirdspace when proposing 'another paradigm, in which Jerusalem and Rome do not exclude one another, but converge to establish the identity of Christianity'.[86] Under his schema, Acts brings together the best of both places: Jerusalem's 'indefectible attachment to Torah and its hope of resurrection' and 'the universality of Roman society where the promise of salvation offered to all peoples will find its place'.[87] Quite apart from the selective optimism of these descriptions, Christological heaven is the missing thirdspace, the deconstruction of such a polarity, the alternative orientation which makes such tensions possible and which unmakes them, creating believer-spaces in Acts which are neither of these poles or simply the sum of their better parts. Such *heavenly* thirdspace is noticeably absent throughout Marguerat's otherwise thought-provoking analysis. For example, his account of 'a Lucan obsession with travel and travellers' omits the key ascension journey of 1:9–11, thereby skewing his assessment of the space of Acts.[88]

In summary, the opening verses of Acts not only introduce significant themes developed in the narrative; they also outline the spatial structure that will order the book. The ascension is *the* moment of spatial realignment in Acts (cf. 1:1–2a), and Acts as a narrative whole cannot be understood without ongoing reference to the heavenly Christ. If Soja's exposition of thirdspace responds to realignments in the (post)modern world,[89] then the ascension into heaven of the once crucified but now resurrected Galilean creates an equivalent crisis within Acts. Such crises generate arguments over space, its 'enclosures [and] exclusions' becoming 'subjects for debate and discussion … resistance and transgression' within lived experience.[90] Soja's framework suggests a fruitful way for reading space within Acts via an ascension matrix.

Whereas, with unwitting historicist irony, Philippe Menoud's translator declared that the ascension 'floats somewhere within the space of fifty days',[91] the present reading paradoxically brings the ascension down to earth and also probes the unseen heavens of

---

[86] Marguerat 2002: 66.   [87] Marguerat 2002: 76.

[88] Marguerat 2002: 237 n. 18. Cf., as noted earlier, Marguerat 2002: 216, omitting 1:11 from consideration of external prolepses within Acts.

[89] Soja 1996: 23 (cf. pp. 318–20): 'As with all other times of crisis, there are both new dangers and new opportunities unleashed by the multiplicity of confusing and often brutal events that have been shaking the world since 1989.'

[90] Soja 1996: 320.

[91] Menoud 1978a: 172; originally 'Elle flotte dans l'intervalle des cinquante jours' (Menoud 1962: 152).

1:6–11. Functioning as far more than simple setting, the geography of these verses structures the shape of the narrative and communicates the Christocentric theology of Acts 1, which in turn shapes expectation concerning the unfolding narrative.

4. Grounding ascension space (1:12–26)

The mount called Olivet

Acts 1:12 registers the witnesses obeying immediately Jesus' preascension instruction to return to Jerusalem. This occurs before the retrospective narration of the ascension's setting being 'the mount called Olivet'.

Reference to Olivet being 'near Jerusalem, a sabbath day's journey away', a distance of approximately 800 metres, has been understood as indicating *proximity* to Jerusalem,[92] leading to historical and theological conclusions which are not sustained from *within* the narrative. Wilson rightly rejects the supposition that Jewish believers in Jesus assumed Jewish Sabbath laws and applied them to their own festival,[93] and Ernst Haenchen correctly discards Chrysostom's assumption that 1:12 indicates that the ascension occurred on a Sabbath.[94] Spencer is both historicist and dismissive of multiple temporalities (and spatialities) when suggesting that 1:12 'orients the reader to the schedule governing the entire Acts journey ... "Jewish standard time"'.[95] Rather, the preceding 'ascension geography' suggests a more cautious spatial reading whereby 1:12 indicates proximity (matching Jesus' earlier command not to leave the city), but without complete identification.[96]

Understanding Olivet as close to, but separate from, Jerusalem conforms to its role within Luke's Gospel. Although Talmudic evidence considers it as part of the Temple for ritual purposes,[97] the Lukan economy of space repeatedly emphasises the Mount as functioning as the place to which Jesus came 'out' from Jerusalem while still remaining close to the city (ἐξέρχομαι, Luke 21:37; 22:39–40;

---

[92] E.g. Lohfink 1971: 207; Hengel 1983: 107.

[93] Wilson 1973: 103–4; cf. Schille 1966: 190.

[94] Haenchen 1971: 150–1.   [95] Spencer 1997: 29.

[96] Regarding this combination of separation and attachment, cf. Rius-Camps and Read-Heimerdinger 2004: 99–100, noting how D's different spellings of Jerusalem in 1:4 and 1:12 influence their reading.

[97] Lane 1974: 403.

cf. synoptic parallels; possibly, also, cf. Acts 1:21). It was a proximate but nevertheless ambiguous space in relation to the city: close enough to enable daily visits to Jerusalem but separate from the city itself. Such marginal places are likely locations for the development of thirdspace vision.[98] As a site for the ascension, the Mount functions in this manner, its spatial ambiguity reinforcing the complex spatial-theological continuity and discontinuity heralded by the ascension.

First, Luke and Acts resist any triumphalism engendered by Olivet's eschatological resonance (e.g. Zechariah 14:1–4). Despite paralleling other synoptic references to the Mount, Luke lacks an equivalent to Matthew 24:3 and Mark 13:3. The nearest Lukan equivalent, Acts 1:6, lies within a quite different cotext. Similarly, rather than stirring his followers from the Mount to take Jerusalem by eschatological force like the Egyptian prophet reported by Josephus (*Ant.* 20.169–71; *War* 2.261–3; cf. Acts 21:38), Jesus sends his disciples 'to wait for spiritual blessing, not to fight for political freedom'.[99] Admittedly, in Luke's Gospel the Mount was the site for Jesus' triumphal entry into Jerusalem (19:29, 37), but Parsons, despite coining the term 'Triumphant Exit' for the ascension from this same locale,[100] considers that Acts 1:12 primarily evokes Olivet as a site of prayer (cf. Luke 22:39–46).[101] Although both aspects remain in view, Acts 1:6–11 has adjusted the disciples' immediate eschatological expectation and reordered their orientation towards heaven (cf. Luke 19:37–8). When the disciples do pray (Acts 1:14), it will be away from the Mount and in the city where they await fulfilment.

Second, Jesus' ascension *outside* of Jerusalem (as well as his ascent 'into heaven') qualifies claims for the city to be the *omphalos* (navel) of the earth.[102] Yet 1:12 in isolation cautions against overstating this relativising argument: it is sufficient at this juncture to note the contested claims made during the church's early centuries regarding the ascension site (and the ascension narrative)[103] as evidence of the Mount's spatial ambiguity in relation to Jerusalem. The city's narrative position will become clearer in later chapters of Acts.

[98] Soja 1996: 83–105.
[99] Spencer 1997: 28. This Egyptian prophet laid claim to an exodus tradition typical of Jewish hopes of restoration (Evans 1997: 302), claims which would have been powerfully spatial.
[100] Parsons 1987: 104, 112.   [101] Parsons 1987: 196.
[102] Cf., e.g., Moessner 1989: 309; J. M. Scott 2000: 56–8 and Estrada 2004: 106.
[103] Walker 1990: 225–7, 338–45.

The upper room

Having 'entered the city' (εἰσῆλθον, 1:13) – with ὑπέστρεψαν ('returned', 1:12), a narrative marker that the ascension occurred outside Jerusalem – the witness-apostles went to the upper room (1:13).

This site is significant for Lukan space but it resists comparative positioning.[104] It is not explicitly set up either as Temple-space[105] or against Temple-space[106] unless, by not mentioning the Temple in Acts 1, Luke reinforces that only the Spirit's imposition would grant these witnesses sufficient 'power' (1:8) to confront Temple-space and its hierarchies. Equally, there is nothing obviously euchar-istic about this upper room:[107] the venue for the last supper (ἀνάγαιον μέγα, Luke 22:12) was not, as here, a ὑπερῷον, and Acts 1:13 describes a place of lodging. The narrative therefore avoids making any obvious firstspace equation of these locations, although many have so linked them,[108] but nevertheless – as subsequent sec-tions demonstrate – neither is the powerful (third)spatial resonance of that final supper with its 'dramatic and defiant production of vision-ary space'[109] completely absent in Acts 1. In terms of thirdspace, this ὑπερῷον also anticipates the later occurrences of the term in 9:37, 39 and 20:8.[110] Both these later locales are sites of resurrection and restoration to fellowship.[111] This establishes them as more than mere firstspace venues or secondspace markers for assembled

[104] Cf. Geyring 2004: 65–9.
[105] Rius-Camps and Read-Heimerdinger (2004: 100–2) make too much of perceived parallels with Luke 24.
[106] Cf. Spencer 1997: 28–9.
[107] *Contra* Menoud 1978b: 103 n. 29. Still less is this 'the alijah of the disputing rabbis' (van Stempvoort 1958/9: 39).
[108] *Contra* L. T. Johnson (1977: 176 n. 3): 'It would make excellent dramatic sense to have the restoration occur where the promise of authority was first given.' The first-spatial absence of the now ascended Christ qualifies such a parallelism. Parsons (1987: 197) claims, without any evidence – other than citing the 'suggestion' of Lake and Cadbury 1933: 10 – that 'the identification of the two seems most natural'. L. T. Johnson (1992: 34) claims more cautiously: 'Luke may have in mind the same "upper room".' Cf. Bruce (1990: 105), who sees 'some plausibility' for such a parallel, and Zwiep (2004: 129), who judges the precise location as unimportant for the narrative.
[109] Moxnes 2001a: 207.
[110] The reading of ὑπερῷον in 10:9 is poorly attested (cf. Rius-Camps and Read-Heimerdinger 2006: 225), even if that site injects thirdspatial resonance into the narra-tive (for which, see Chapter 7).
[111] *Contra* Rius-Camps and Read-Heimerdinger (2006: 249), who consider these sites as symbolising 'adherence to traditional Jewish customs and beliefs with regard to Israel'.

believers. In Acts 1, such anticipatory resonance serves an apologetic function, emphasising the reality of Jesus' resurrection and the fellowship it engenders (and contrasting it with Judas' fate), while setting down an important marker for reading spaces in Acts in relation to the now absent Christ.[112]

The assembly

The notable absence in the list of witnesses in Acts 1:13, given the list of 'apostles' in Luke 6:14–16 and given other sensitivities to presence and absence within Acts 1, is clearly Judas Iscariot, but nothing is said immediately about his absence.[113] The narrator instead first focuses on those present in the gathering (1:14–15).

These witnesses to the ascension have already been positioned in relation to journeying with Jesus (1:11). Now others also present in the upper room, introduced without explanation unless Luke's Gospel forms assumed prior knowledge, are similarly positioned. The 'women'[114] in 1:14 are probably those who followed Jesus from Galilee (Luke 23:49; cf. Luke 8:1–3) as did, according to Acts 1:23, at least two of the other men present. Luke's Gospel has also presented others as fellow travellers with Jesus (e.g. 24:13–35, noting the collective identity 'our group', ἐξ ἡμῶν, in 24:22). Jesus' mother and siblings were previously reported as making an apparently abortive attempt to travel to (with?) Jesus (8:19–21):[115] at very least, such earlier positioning emphasises their now obedient submission to Jesus' will. Luke has depicted Mary as making two earlier visits to Jerusalem, both with Jesus. The first facilitated a rich and specifically Lukan presentation of Christological space (2:22–38). The second narrated visit to Jerusalem, recounted in 2:41–51, resulted in the twelve-year-old Jesus' three-day disappearance while he took control

---

[112] Brawley (1990: 198) identifies a series of antitheses running through 1:12–25, articulating and structuring space, including 'the opposition of inside and outside, life and death'.

[113] Even if, within the narrative world, 'Judas plays the role of an absentee antagonist who tries to determine the plot even if he is not on stage' (Zwiep 2004: 176), 1:15–26 decisively shows Jesus as the more powerful 'empty center' for the believers and, by inference, for auditors.

[114] The D reading of 1:14 appears to preserve a later downplaying of the place of women (Barrett 1994: 89); the structural explanation offered by Rius-Camps and Read-Heimerdinger (2004: 46–7, 103) is unconvincing. For varying readings of how Acts 1 is gendered, compare Spencer 1997: 31 with Parsons 1990.

[115] Luke 8:19–21 remains much more (potentially) open-ended and inclusive regarding Jesus' family than Matthew 12:46–50 and Mark 3:31–5.

of his own space, before rejoining his parents and returning to Nazareth while Mary 'treasured all these things in her heart' (2:51b). Unnamed since then, Mary reappears as a named character in Acts 1:14, again in Jerusalem. These various journey motifs suggest an inversion of Charles Talbert's interpretation of the presence of these Galilean observers as guaranteeing the corporeality of the ascended Christ.[116] Without denying Talbert's reading, previous travelling proximity with the now ascended Christ also underpins this group's ongoing corporeality as *believers in him*, securing a heavenwards orientation for believer-space at the outset of Acts and precluding any reading of believer-space that ignores this heavenly dimension.

Acts 1 also draws on a variety of spatial descriptors which emphasise the assembly's Christological and heavenly orientation indicative of its constitutive connections with the now ascended Jesus. For example, most translations assume that the narrator's introductory description of the assembly as ὄχλος ὀνομάτων (1:15) represents an idiom, rendering translations such as 'company of persons' (RSV), or 'the crowd' (NRSV). Quite probably, however, the term evokes the numbered people of God and the allocation of the land in Numbers 1:18, 20; 26:53, 55.[117] Furthermore, pluralised ὀνόματα ('names') elsewhere indicates specific persons with a shared identity (cf. Revelation 3:4; 11:13); here, such identification fits with the immediately preceding naming in Acts 1:13–14 and echoes the use of 'names' in Luke 10:20.[118] Such resonances reinforce a thirdspatial understanding arising from a Christ–heaven orientation positioning the believers in Acts 1. Cotextually, this reading complements Zwiep's verdict that 'in those days' (καὶ ἐν ταῖς ἡμέραις ταύταις) and Peter's standing up (ἀναστάς) in 1:15 constitute 'biblical language' which reassures auditors that this scene is a 'continuation of the biblical drama of salvation-history'.[119] Such reassurance also concerns salvation geography. This reading is significant, given the perplexed scholarly understanding of this phrase.[120] Numbering the 'names' also recalls the numbered seventy (seventy-two) in Luke

---

[116] Talbert 1974: 112–16.   [117] Rius-Camps and Read-Heimerdinger 2004: 117.

[118] The cotext surrounding ὀνόματα in Acts 18:15 is too distant from 1:15 for useful comparisons to be made.

[119] Zwiep 2004: 130.

[120] Estrada (2004: 180) rightly concludes 'no satisfactory answer has been given to explain the mention of the "120 persons" before Peter's speech'. Cf. Barrett 1994: 96; Zwiep 2004: 132.

10:17, while introducing an emphasis on numbers that will run through the rest of Acts 1 and beyond.[121]

Additionally, the close juxtaposition of biological and associational uses of sibling language (1:14–16) emphasises and reinforces the group's unified nature based on their previous space-time with Jesus. Ἀδελφοί (1:16, lit. 'brothers'; NRSV, 'friends') is used in both Jewish and gentile contexts to indicate members of a religious community,[122] and in Acts the term has a breadth of meaning that facilitates expression of believer-space within Jewish spatial categories but without being defined by Jewish space (e.g. 22:13). Here in Acts 1 this associative quality is expressed spatially in ἐπὶ τὸ αὐτό (1:15, which the RSV rather obliquely renders 'in all', the NRSV 'together'). As well as emphasising unity, this common Acts idiom carries a sense of assembly *in a place* paralleling its Septuagintal and Qumran occurrences.[123] Here in 1:15 it also reinforces the first instance of Luke's most frequently used adverb,[124] ὁμοθυμαδόν (1:14; RSV, 'with one accord'). The narration in 1:15 of Peter standing up to speak 'among (ἐν μέσῳ) the believers' continues this sense of placed, unified embodiment.

As the first named speaker in Acts, apart from Jesus, Peter's words carry a primacy effect within the narrative. Within this unified, numbered, embodied setting, Peter makes immediate reference to the visibly shattered apostolate at its centre. Naming Judas (1:16) both concludes the list of 1:13 and overrules any sense of completion. In the verses that follow, Peter positions both Judas and the other apostle-witnesses in relation to the now heavenly Jesus, affirming that Jesus remains a point of reference for interpreting earthly events. If 1:18–19 is seen as a narrational intrusion for the sake of auditors, Peter's speech is less about the nature of Judas' death and more about the need to replace him because of his apostasy from Jesus' way.

---

[121] Nothing within the text suggests that 120 represents a maximal number for a gathering (cf. Lohfink 1999: 221), or the minimum size for a synagogue (L. T. Johnson 1992: 34, following *M.Sanh.* 1.6). Such readings cannot be clearly inferred from Acts 1, and distract from the narrative's sustained emphasis on the company as fellow travellers with Jesus. Zwiep (2004: 133), also following *M.Sanh.* 1.6, judges 120 to stand for twelve synagogues representing the Israelite tribes, a reading which anticipates fulfilment of Israel-space under the twelve (for which, see Chapter 4). Most likely the number introduces the theme of the believers' numerical growth within Jerusalem which, arguably, extends to 21:20.

[122] Bruce 1990: 108.

[123] So Bruce 1990: 108; L. T. Johnson 1992: 34; Zwiep 2004: 132–3.

[124] Ὁμοθυμαδόν occurs ten times in Acts, and otherwise appears in the NT only in Romans 15:6. Walton 2004a explicates its variegated semantic range within Acts.

Judas' spatial apostasy

Judas is described as having committed spatial apostasy. Rather than reaching the end of his journey with Jesus at Olivet and there receiving his ascension commission (cf. 1:22), Judas took a different way, reaching the Mount as ὁδηγός, 'guide', for those who arrested Jesus (1:16; cf. Luke 22:47). Although having been one of Jesus' inner circle, a confidant within his space, Judas led the Temple authorities to 'the haven Jesus retreated to at night after tense days of teaching in the temple precincts amid mounting opposition from the priestly hierarchy'.[125]

Judas is described as having been 'numbered among us' (Acts 1:17; cf. Luke 22:47), both stressing his previous position and anticipating the need to replace Judas for witness-space to be properly filled.[126] This description contributes to the numbering theme in Acts 1, already mentioned, and projects the importance of the embodied totality of the apostle-witnesses as intended by Jesus (cf. Acts 1:2), a completion confirmed later when 'one of these' must become a witness 'with us' (1:22).[127]

Although 'us' in 1:17 refers primarily to the apostolate, the cotext of Acts 1 precludes narrowly defining this group in opposition to the 120 'names' of 1:15.[128] The 120 are those addressed by Peter (1:16), among whom the apostles are 'in place'. By virtue of the wider group's connection with Jesus established in 1:15 (see above), and of the statement that Jesus himself had chosen Judas (cf. 1:2), any 'moral crisis' concerning 'honour and integrity' is primarily one facing the whole assembly, who are here dependent upon the honour of the now absent Lord.[129] If anyone's honour is defended, it is Jesus' honour, his choice of Judas being positioned within the divine plan (1:17),[130] or the consequent (and secondary) honour of the 120 as a whole. This recognition blunts Nelson Estrada's argument that 1:12–26 is about

---

[125] Spencer 1997: 28.

[126] The appointment of twelve apostles is one of six aspects of exile theology that Evans (1997: 317–18) identifies as preparatory for the geographical restructuring associated with restoration. Cf. also McKnight 2001, Meier 2001.

[127] See Chapter 4, regarding the role of the *twelve* witnesses in Jerusalem at Pentecost (Acts 2:14, 32, 37). Beutler (1981: 394) notes a 'striking' frequency of numerical adjectives connected with μάρτυς ('witness') language.

[128] Cf. Estrada 2004: 152–3.

[129] *Contra* Estrada (2004: 36), who applies these quoted terms to the apostolate, with the 120 functioning 'symbolically' as 'the ruling body of a community'.

[130] Cf. Estrada 2004: 178–84. Zwiep (2004: 3, 51–2, 146, 173, 179–81) convincingly presents the crisis as ultimately concerning *Christological* veracity.

either completion of the twelve *or* some sort of status transformation ritual undergone by the apostles. Instead, this section presents a *spatial* transformation. Judas is 'replaced' in two senses of the English verb. His *own* space is interpreted and, in 1:25, his *apostolic* space is filled by another. In sum, Peter interprets earthly space[131] in relation to the will of the now ascended Jesus, just as he will throughout his speeches within Acts. Rather than disassociating others (whether – as Estrada suggests – the eleven,[132] or the 120) from Judas' spatial apostasy, Peter correctly positions and addresses the internal workings of believer-space, just as he will in 5:1–11 and 8:20–3.[133] Within Acts, Peter brokers space according to its production arising from Christ's ascension, and he begins to do so *within* 1:12–26, not simply because of it.

In this light, the two psalms quoted in 1:20 govern directly the post-ascension apostles' space and also, indirectly, the wider believers' space, first negatively and then positively, addressing the manner in which God handles those who reject his Christ and the outworkings of such rejection within believer-space. By ascribing these psalms to David (1:16), Peter aligns allegiance to Jesus with that appropriate to David, with implications for Jesus claiming David's territorial rights and expectations.

The first quotation in 1:20 (Psalm 68:26 LXX, modified (69:25)) confirms that Judas' demise, mentioned in the narrational aside in Acts 1:18, demonstrates the divine/Davidic will. Acts 1:18–20 concludes the narration begun when Satan 'entered' (εἰσῆλθεν) Judas such that he 'went away' (ἀπελθών) from Jesus to betray him (Luke 22:3–4). It forms an oppositional contrast to that of Jesus, who has been 'taken up' (Acts 1:2, 11, 22).[134] Ben Witherington's blunt description of Judas' 'own place' in 1:25 as 'hell'[135] indicates a

---

[131] Cf. Zwiep (2004: 130, 179), who sees Peter playing 'an active role', providing 'the authentic link to the historical mission of Jesus'. This 'role' and 'link' constitute space; they do not simply interpret history.

[132] Estrada 2004: 181.

[133] Estrada mentions 5:1–11 only marginally (2004: 141, 170), and does not consider 8:20–23.

[134] This spatial opposition is much more coherent and apparent than the parallel with Luke 9:42 suggested by W. D. Davies 1974: 231.

[135] Witherington 1998: 122. Similarly Conzelmann 1987: 12 and Zwiep 2004: 166–8. Within his wider reading of possessions within Acts, L. T. Johnson (1992: 37) claims a contrast with the apostles in Luke 18:28 having left their own 'homes' (τὰ ἴδια) to follow Jesus (cf. L. T. Johnson 1977: 174–83). The distinction is not large, however: such possessions language is employed *spatially* as part of a larger presentation of the intimate connection between earthly orientation and the now heavenly Jesus.

negative space in all three Sojan senses, a contrast to Judas' former 'place' (the second[136] τόπος in 1:25) in the ministry ascribed by Jesus within the group of believers. As with Herod in Acts 12, Judas' gruesome death 'is one of the signature elements of divine retribution'.[137]

The believers' response

If apostasy is spatial, so is its solution, prefigured in the production of space presented in Peter's second psalm quotation (Psalm 108:8 LXX (109:8)). Primarily this addresses Judas' place within the apostolate, although his position as a 'name' in the sense of Luke 10:20 is also compromised. As Luke Timothy Johnson astutely comments, Judas' betrayal represented more than simply an individual's failure: rather, in a unique fashion, it 'splintered the numerical and symbolic integrity of that group which constituted the beginning and essential authority of the restored people of God' and constituted 'a threat to the fulfilment of Jesus' promise and the whole plan of God'.[138] This 'plan of God' anticipates a restored space, a renewed apostolate symbolically indicating renewed Israel.[139]

On one level, it is relatively easy to say, 'Let another take his office', but how is a replacement to be chosen, especially given the Christocentric spatial ordering established earlier in Acts 1? Acts 1:21–2 outlines the geographical criteria for inclusion, and the assembly is able to determine (at least) two suitable candidates, whose comprehensive life-geography with Jesus is apparent to all.

Although these candidates fulfil Peter's stated criteria regarding earthly experience and instruction from Jesus, they have not been chosen as apostle-witnesses by the now heavenly Christ (cf. 1:2). Jesus had chosen the original twelve and the balance of judgement suggests that Jesus also chooses this replacement apostle-witness.

The key question concerns who is 'Lord' (κύριε) in 1:24. Although later assembly prayers are specifically marked as being addressed to God (e.g. 4:24), here the recipient's identity is more ambiguous.

---

[136] The reading τόπον is 'strongly supported' in the manuscript evidence, and the alternative reading (κλῆρον, 'share') likely reflects the influence of 1:17 (Metzger 1994: 249).

[137] O. W. Allen 1995: 123.   [138] L. T. Johnson 1992: 38.

[139] Rather than being 'quite vague' on the matter (Estrada 2004: 122), the Acts narrative sufficiently highlights the need for a completed 'twelve-space', most clearly at 2:14. See, e.g., Turner 2000: 301; cf. Zwiep 2004: 49–52, 181–2.

In 1:24 this Lord is described as knowing everyone's heart (καρδιογνῶστα πάντων), which partially parallels the description of God as ὁ καρδιογνώστης θεός in 15:8,[140] but this later reference to God granting the gift of the Holy Spirit itself finds a Christological parallel in 2:33, where *Jesus* bestows the gift which he has received from the Father. Comparing 2:33 with 1:4 confirms how earthly appreciation of the post-ascension agencies of God ('the Father', cf. also in 1:7 and 2:33) and Jesus become blurred and not always easily distinguished from the earthly point of view adopted in Acts,[141] unlike their obviously clear heaven–earth differentiation within Luke's Gospel. The relatively distant parallel description of God as knowing human hearts in 15:8 does not preclude a Christological reading here,[142] and the more immediate cotext of the verbal parallel between the 'choosing' in 1:2 and 1:24 suggests a Christological identity for κύριε in 1:24. Jesus himself chose the original twelve (cf. the same verb in 1:2). Furthermore, Jesus' followers address him as κύριε in 1:6 (albeit in a very different situation) and Peter describes him as 'the Lord (κύριος) Jesus' in 1:21. If these pointers support a Christological reading of 1:24, then the cotextual requirements of continuity and completion of witness to/for *Jesus* in 1:21–2 further entrench this conclusion.[143]

This reading establishes Jesus' thirdspatial influence at this earliest post-ascension juncture. This highly significant conclusion for establishing a Christocentric spatiality within Acts is confirmed by recognising that the prayer also demonstrates the believers' agreement with Peter's *spatial* interpretation of Judas' fate. In this manner, the prayer – in this crucial post-ascension scene – continues to constitute and interpret Christocentrically the space of those who pray. Thus, in 1:25, Judas 'turned aside' from 'this ministry and apostleship', purposing 'to go [cf. Luke 22:22] to his own place'. Reading Acts for its space revises Allison Trites's conclusion that 'Luke relates prayer to his understanding of redemptive *history*'[144] as requiring a parallel

[140] So Bruce 1990: 112. L. T. Johnson (1992: 37) cites this and various scriptural references referring to God as knowing human hearts.
[141] Rowe (2006: 189, 201–2) has drawn independent but parallel conclusions from Luke's Gospel. Cf. Turner 2000: 295–7, and also Gaventa 2004: 48–9 regarding the difficulty of separating the roles of God and Jesus in Acts 20:35.
[142] Cf. Barrett 1994: 103.
[143] Zwiep (2004: 164) confuses presence and absence, apparently suggesting that the Spirit's coming *is* Jesus' return. His reasoning is unconvincing, and cuts across his earlier arguments that the crisis of Judas is a crisis for Jesus.
[144] Trites 1978: 185, emphasis added.

relation to redemptive geography whereby prayer signals a desire for, expectation of and delight in God's saving activities within the world.[145]

The implications for salvation geography arising from 1:12–26 are immense. The absent Jesus is here presented as actively directing his people during what the weight of existing scholarship would consider to be the 'wrong' epoch for such activity. Christ is active and absent, but cannot be reduced to these poles. Such irreducibility reflects the 'and more' which is constitutive of thirdspace.[146] Further, Jesus' impact is central and constitutive to the believers' economy of space, and reading Acts 1 *for its space* has led to this conclusion. Like Estrada, this present reading does not consider 1:12–26 as an 'empty interval',[147] but for reasons other than those presented by Estrada. Rather than the apostles being left alone by Jesus (pure absence), space is being reordered thirdspatially according to the ascension, acknowledging Jesus' heavenly presence with the Father, ready to pour out the Spirit (cf. Luke 24:49; Acts 2:33). In terms of narrative telling, 'replacing' Judas *after the ascension*[148] is pivotal for communicating this sustained Christological ordering of space. Similarly, Judas being replaced *prior to Pentecost* precludes reading the Spirit as the simple replacement for Christ[149] in ordering believer-space. Given the absence of any replacement process when another apostle dies (12:2), Christ's restructuring of apostle-space within 1:15–26 is presented as having an enduring narrative significance. More immediately, far from disappearing without trace from the rest of the narrative, the chosen Matthias needs to be seen, to be placed with the other eleven, come the day of Pentecost and beyond (2:14, 32, 37; 5:29). But that is to jump ahead to the next chapter.

5.   Conclusion

This chapter has been foundational for Part II of this study. Having identified elements of a Lukan spatiality extending from Luke's Gospel into Acts, it has argued that 1:6–11 provides the fundamental reordering of space which launches Luke's second volume, 1:7–11 as

---

[145] Cf. Plymale 1991: 110–11.   [146] Soja 1996: 11.

[147] Estrada 2004: 3. Cf. Dunn (1996: 15) 'empty of either [Jesus or the Spirit]'.

[148] Estrada (2004: 177) places too much interpretative weight on Jesus not having raised the matter himself in 1:3.

[149] *Contra* Zwiep 2004: 164.

a whole simultaneously embracing and breaking the binary dualisms encoded within 1:6.

Sojan analysis has enabled analysis of the apostles' rapidly unfolding spatiality within these verses and beyond, Jesus' ascension engendering a thirdspace which reinterprets both firstspace location and secondspace projection. Acts 1:9–11, through repetition, promise and narrative position, resolutely establishes narrative thirdspace as Christocentric and heavenly. This thirdspace, like the 'times or periods' in 1:7, remains independent of mortal control. Jesus' previous proximity with his followers is now replaced by firstspatial absence, but – even before Pentecost – he still relates with them from heaven.

This enduring relationship is demonstrated by the believers' obedience to Jesus' command to wait in Jerusalem. Characterised as Galileans, the disciples remain 'out of place' after Jesus' ascension, as they stay located in Jerusalem according to Jesus' word, awaiting the promised Spirit. This does not orient Acts-space around Jerusalem, important though the city is at this narrative juncture. Instead, 1:8, with its globalised secondspace projection of witness-space, casts Jerusalem as one firstspace locale alongside many others yet to be transformed by witness reaching 'to the ends of the earth'. While not obliterating Jerusalem's special status, this spatial economy does elevate it, as is evident in the ascension's setting on Olivet.

Following 1:1–11, the narrative establishes the upper room as a place earthing heavenly thirdspace in acts of resurrection and restored fellowship. A spatialised reading locates the 120 in 1:15 as an assembly of 'names', numbered, unified, prayerful, and ordered by Jesus. Their gathering forms the first post-ascension embodiment of ascension geography within Acts. Jesus' enduring influence over believer-space is evident in their acceptance of Peter's exposition of Judas-space and apostle-space in relation to the ascended Christ. Also, it is Jesus who chose Matthias as *his* 'replacement' for Judas.

This reading of Acts 1 has begun to advance the study's wider thesis, that the ascension can and should be read for its space and that its spatiality orders the wider Acts narrative. With regard to this latter claim, attention can now turn to Acts 2 and beyond.

4

ACTS 2:1–6:7

1.   Introduction

The previous chapter has argued that Acts 1:6–11 presents a comprehensive spatial vision which underpins the whole of Acts and which is developed by its wider narrative. This vision has been proposed as the key to understanding the production, presentation and evaluation of space within Acts. The present chapter now examines 2:1–6:7 for evidence of this 'ascension geography'. The chapter has two aims. First, it elucidates a spatially sensitive reading of this section of Acts. Second, it demonstrates the abiding and governing importance of the ascended Christ for understanding these spaces. As such, it begins to test the *spatial* veracity and range of the claim that 'from Acts 1 everything moves out from the ascension'.[1] Such spatiality would cast Christ's ascension as 'an expanding symbol' within Acts which 'has a persuasive effect' which acts as 'a powerful enticement [for auditors] to explore a new perspective on life'.[2] Expanding symbols are thirdspatial, in that they provide 'an area which can be glimpsed, never surveyed',[3] which hides 'residues of meaning which call for further exploration'.[4]

In Acts 1 the believers remained in a private sphere. Now, in Acts 2, the group emerges with its (dis)orienting view of space, into other more public spaces, as the descending Spirit – sent by Jesus – creates a new space within Jerusalem, one which Peter's speech helps call into being.

This chapter's six central sections examine the resultant narrative spaces in 2:1–6:7. These sections confirm that space is not coterminous with setting: different spaces are formed and defended within the

---

[1] Talbert 1974: 112.
[2] Tannehill 1984: 238, 240. Tannehill did not apply the term to the ascension. Parsons (1987: 198) applied it to Acts 1, but in relation to Luke 24.
[3] Brown 1950: 59.   [4] Tannehill 1984: 240.

same (firstspace) setting of Jerusalem. The chapter's cumulative 'reading for space' appraises Jerusalem's 'place' within the Acts narrative and its theology, avoiding reduction either to physical location or to theological projection abstracted from lived experience positioned 'under heaven'.

2.   Israel-space (Acts 2)

First mentioned explicitly in 2:5, Jerusalem constitutes the *setting* for Acts 2–7, but the *spatiality* assumed by the Pentecost narrative is that of the broader Diaspora (2:5–11, 36). Here, as a setting, Jerusalem functions as a festal centre, a firstspace actualisation of secondspace claims over 'Israel' as its covenantal centre. This territoriality is kept in view throughout Acts 2–5 by references to 'Israel' and 'Israelites'. It is here, *within* the city's spatial claims, that the ascension geography ordered by 1:6–11 makes its distinctively Christofocal thirdspace appeal.

Ascension spatiality informing Pentecost (2:2; 2:5)

The first indication in Acts 2 of this foundational ascension spatiality is 'from heaven' (ἐκ τοῦ οὐρανοῦ), an important but overlooked spatial marker in 2:2. Surprisingly, even usually exhaustive commentators ignore this reference to heaven.[5] Other commentators ascribe to it OT resonances,[6] or wider Hellenistic parallels.[7] While valid, such allusions insufficiently connect with the specific spatiality of 1:6–11. The fourfold reference to οὐρανός in 1:10–11 provides a much closer connective, but remains unmentioned by virtually all commentators.[8] Thus, 2:2 provides a largely unrecognised reference to ascension spatiality within the narrative. In short, 2:2 needs to be positioned within the ordering of space established by 1:6–11, and to be understood Christologically.

At this crucially early point in the Pentecost narrative the ambiguous nature of the heavenly phenomena draws out this Acts 1 connective. By not explaining the phenomena until 2:4, the narrative

---

[5]   E.g. Barrett 1994; Bruce 1990. 'Heaven' is more important for spatial positioning in 2:2 than 'house' (concerning which, see Green 1991: 556 n. 49; cf. Barrett 1991: 346).

[6]   E.g. L. T. Johnson 1992: 42; Fitzmyer 1998: 234, 238.

[7]   Van der Horst 1985: 49.

[8]   The exception is Turner 2000: 274. Spencer (1997: 27) comes close, but assumes wrongly that the disciples see into heaven in Acts 1.

allows room for auditors informed by Acts 1 (and, possibly, Luke 24:49) to speculate concerning their import, especially immediately after the solemn opening of Acts 2:1.[9] If prophecy is being fulfilled, then *which* prophecy from Acts 1 – 1:4, 1:11, or both? Yet even in this moment of narrative uncertainty, amid a wind/spirit ambiguity which auditors 'cannot yet distinguish',[10] explicit mention of heaven in 2:2 establishes a Christological link with the phenomena which 2:33 will later only serve to confirm. The heavenly referent recalls the Christological evocation of heaven only a chapter earlier in Acts, providing auditors cognisant of the spatial ordering of 1:6–11 with a level of knowledge greater than that ascribed to the onlookers in 2:7–13.[11] More distantly, mention of 'fire' (2:3) recalls the Baptist's (Christocentric) promise in Luke 3:16–17 (cf. Acts 1:5).

Having established a link between the ascended Christ and the descending Spirit, the next reference to heaven, following soon afterwards in 2:5, is equally significant for establishing the spatiality of Acts 2. That the bystanders are 'from every nation under heaven' (ἀπὸ παντὸς ἔθνους τῶν ὑπὸ τὸν οὐρανόν) is clearly a secondspatial ascription;[12] indeed, most commentators read this phrase as referring to the visible heavens, judging it to indicate earthly universality[13] and noting OT, intertestamental and classical parallels.[14] Yet earthbound diversity, although verifying the subsequent linguistic miracle,[15] does not determine or delimit a spatial reading of 2:5. Nor do intertextual readings preclude a thirdspatial Christological understanding of 'heaven' in 2:5, a reading which 1:9–11 and 2:2 would affirm, by which 'under heaven' is reworked with new theological meaning by which an

---

[9] Tannehill (1990: 26) likens the anticipation within 2:1a to that in Luke 9:51.

[10] Brawley 1987: 36. Barrett (1994: 113) discerns 'a vivid natural analogy'.

[11] *Contra* Tannehill 1990: 26.

[12] Any hyperbole within 'every nation' should not distract analysis of 'under heaven'. Cf., e.g., Bauckham 1996: 421. Bauckham fails to consider how thirdspace connotations within 2:5 might qualify and relativise his hierarchical and earthbound maintenance of Jerusalem's centricity.

[13] E.g. J. M. Scott 2002: 84, and Rosner 1998: 218, which cites J. M. Scott 1994: 523 as evidence that Luke's horizons extend beyond the Roman Empire. Neither Rosner nor Scott extend that horizon to heaven. Scott (1995: 163), citing Tannehill 1986: 232–7, sees a parallel with the mission of the seventy (seventy-two) in Luke 10:1–12, 17–20. Cf. Bruce 1990: 116: 'from every land where there were Jews'.

[14] E.g., variously, Haenchen 1971: 168 n. 10; Barrett 1994: 119; Fitzmyer 1998: 239 and Bauckham 2001: 472.

[15] Tannehill 1990: 27.

implicitly Christological territoriality is narrated in 2:5.[16] Without denying that Luke-Acts is aware of the visible heavens,[17] Jesus' third-space rule from heaven, laid out in 1:6–11, provokes a Christological reading of the secondspace narrated in 2:5. This narration anticipates the climax of Peter's address (2:36). Acts is already pressing its ascension-geography claims upon those gathered in Jerusalem.

Acts 2:9–11 'under heaven'

This heavenly orientation within 2:5 helps position the frequently problematic geography of 2:9–11. Various readings have been proposed to account for the list but, as Luke Timothy Johnson concludes, 'hypotheses abound, but none can be proven'.[18]

Perhaps no such hypothesis needs to be proven if 'under heaven' in 2:5 provides the key thirdspace orientation governing 2:9–11. An ascension geography building on 1:6–11 and recapitulated in 2:2, 5 relativises the need to interpret the specifics of the list by bringing it within a Christological focus. This suggests more than 2:9–11 simply *representing* 2:5.[19] Rather, as 2:30–3 will declare, 'heaven' is where Christ is enthroned, with these (and other) earthly places under his sway. This reading counters viewing 2:8–11 as an isolated or self-enclosed spatial indicator, since 2:5 effectively heads the list and relativises it through its overarching thirdspatial assumptions, assumptions soon to be expounded by Peter. It provides a spatial-theological rationale to support Marguerat's suggestion that 2:8–11 ambiguously merges the universality of prophetic eschatology with the Roman ideal of accepting foreign nations within empire.[20] Similarly, this reading realigns rather than rejects connections with existing Jewish geographical imaginations.[21]

---

[16] By seeing a possible allusion back to the Abrahamic promise and to Acts 1:8, Hays (2003: 164) approaches such a reading but does not connect 2:5 with Christ's ascension and heavenly session.

[17] DeSilva 1997: 440.

[18] L. T. Johnson 1992: 43; similarly Barrett 1994: 121–4. Sleeman (2006: 105–6) provides a more detailed excursus.

[19] So Haenchen 1971: 169.

[20] Marguerat 2002: 74. On the latter point, also Balch 2003. Narratively, Wasserberg (1998: 219–20) sees 2:9–11 as anticipating what will unfold for the nations/gentiles in Acts 10.

[21] Although Gilbert (2002; cf. 2003: 247–52) highlights helpfully the political agendas served by geography and identifies such dimensions in 2:8–11, this does not fore-close other readings (cf. Goulder 2002: 147–8).

This relativising effect of ascension geography also critiques interpretations prioritising Jerusalem's position within 2:8–11. Spencer,
for example, sees Judea-Jerusalem as orienting the places listed, and
Bauckham judges that 2:8–11 accurately represents (and advocates) a
Jerusalem-centred worldview prevalent and 'natural' within first-
century Judaism.[22] Such analyses map secondspace, even firstspace,
but lack the necessary thirdspace reflection provoked by 1:6–11.
Ascension geography theologically reflects on Christ's firstspatial
presence in heaven, *not* in Jerusalem, and restructures narrative
space according to *heavenly* thirdspace. Jerusalem-centred readings
lack theoretical realisation that space is not a static given: space is not
only produced, but also requires continual reproduction. While wel-
coming current scholarly emphasis on the narrative being 'placed'
within a geographical context, Jerusalem – unless it is to distort
readings of Acts as a whole – must itself be positioned by an ascension
geography with unfolding implications across the narrative. Otherwise Jerusalem-centred presuppositions impose a premature chauvin-
ism over the narrative.[23] Ascension geography generates room for
new conceptions of space within the narrative, wherein Jerusalem,
while still important, is not necessarily an abiding earthly thirdspatial
locus. Here, rather, in Acts 2, Jerusalem constitutes a staging-post,
albeit the foundational theatre, for the witness foretold within 1:8,
Jerusalem itself anticipating a hearing among 'every nation'. 'Judea'
is included as one of the locations recited in 2:9, and in 2:8, 11 the
crowd hear not in Hebrew or Greek, but in their own native (i.e.,
local) languages. This Pentecostal geography is not intent on abolish-
ing 'the structures of particular familiarity';[24] rather, this is 'Pentecost
in the heteropolis'[25] – or, at least, in the first of the *heteropoleis* within
Acts.[26]

The crowd is 'bewildered' (2:6); this verb συγχέω occurs in the NT
only in Acts, where it indicates a locale's incomprehension regarding
ascension geography (cf. 9:22; 19:32; 21:27, 31). Thus Jerusalem experiences the first 'space-lag' within Acts, whereby human experience

---

[22] Spencer 1997: 34; Bauckham 1996: 423.

[23] J. M. Scott (2002: 56) emphasises Jerusalem as *omphalos*, with corresponding loss
of a heavenward and Christological understanding of space. See also Curtis 1990: 688.

[24] O'Donovan (1989: 56) makes this point more generally, concerning a doctrine of
'election'.

[25] Baker 2007: 151.

[26] This is not to deny that Acts 2 is, in part, a particularistic *renewal* of Israel's
covenant. See, e.g., Panier 1991: 110 and Turner 2000: 279–89 concerning Mosaic/Sinai
parallels.

and interpretation trail behind heavenly intervention within earthly space. It *needs* the witnesses in order to understand its own place within this new spatial economy. Indeed, bewilderment (συγχέω) characterises Jerusalem's first and last narrative appearances within Acts (cf. 21:27, 31), generating a cumulative spatial irony.[27] The list in 2:8–11 therefore primarily highlights the need for witnesses, not the spatial primacy of Jerusalem. The witnesses must speak ...

Joel 3:1–5 LXX (2:28–32) ordering Pentecostal space according to 1:6–11

Peter's quotation from Joel (Acts 2:17–21), rightly seen as structuring the wider Acts narrative,[28] sustains this Christological ordering of space.[29] Although the insertion of 'in the last days' in 2:17 has often been headlined as the major adjustment of Joel within Acts 2,[30] such emphasis becomes historicist if it underplays two other variations which particularly impinge upon its production of space.[31]

First, the words 'above', 'signs' and 'below' inserted into Joel's prophecy in Acts 2:19 link heaven and earth in Acts,[32] reinforcing the narrative's ascension geography (cf. 1:10–11; 2:2), and creating 'a foothold for his [Peter's] Christological use of the Joel passage'.[33] This heaven–earth connective generates a Lukan emphasis on 'wonders and signs'.[34] 'Wonders', not mentioned in Luke's Gospel, occur in Acts only in relation to 'signs' (2:19, 22, 43; 4:30; 5:12; 6:8; 7:36; 14:3; 15:12), suggesting that the couplet functions thirdspatially by interpreting

---

[27] Jerusalem's apparent 'knowledge' of 'Galileans' (2:7; cf. 1:11) compares with the layered spatial irony within Acts 21–2, e.g. the closed doors of 21:30 (cf. the first vista of the Temple in 3:2, and another divinely opened 'door' in 14:27), the deeply ironic spatial verdict of 22:22, and 21:38 generating ironic retrospection to Gamaliel's words in 5:34–39, especially given mention of Gamaliel in 22:3.

[28] Tannehill 1990: 31, regarding Acts 2–5; Wall 1998: 443–9, regarding Acts 2–15.

[29] Particularities within the D text of 2:17–21 (outlined by Rius-Camps and Read-Heimerdinger 2004: 169, 181–4) would strengthen the reading pursued here, but the reading pursued here does not depend upon such textual tendencies.

[30] E.g. Barrett 1994: 129.

[31] Cf. six 'theologically potentially significant' changes from the LXX listed by Turner (2000: 270), and Turner's general discussion of Acts 2:17–21 (pp. 268–74).

[32] Rius-Camps and Read-Heimerdinger (2004: 183) suggest references to 2:2 and 2:3 respectively. Cf. the elliptical comments made by Bruce (1990: 121), Barrett (1994: 137–8) and Fitzmyer (1998: 253).

[33] Turner 2000: 274.

[34] The phrase occurs nine times in Acts, compared to three occurrences in the Pauline corpus.

earthly manifestations in relation to the *heavenly* Christ.[35] Within a
Jewish context, references in Acts to 'signs' without commensurate
'wonders' function critically, indicating points of view lacking
acknowledgement of this ascension ordering.[36] As Acts 8 will demonstrate, 'signs' function similarly in Samaria. Acts 8:13 reflects
Simon's inadequate grasp of ascension geography, and 'signs' in 8:6
await the ecclesial-pneumatic connection brought by the Jerusalem-
based apostles in 8:15–17.[37]

This introduces a particularising geography of 'wonders and signs'
which can be extrapolated from the couplet's distribution across Acts.
In Jewish contexts, the marker evokes a new exodus linked with
Jesus;[38] in gentile scenarios, 'signs and wonders' attest to gentile
inclusion among a renewed people of God under Christ (judging
15:12 to be reflecting upon 14:3, 8–11). 'Signs and wonders' terminology disappears after Acts 15, even where similar miraculous events
occur, suggesting that their spatial role has been fulfilled by that
narrative juncture.

Such a geography suggests that, instead of a temporal dichotomy
between 'signs' and 'wonders',[39] 'wonders and signs' are both immediate (2:43; cf. 2:22; 7:36) *and* proleptic of what is to come (2:19b–20).
Joel's 'stock-in-trade Old Testament cosmic dissolution language'
signals the beginning of the destruction of the old world order.[40]
Accepting the witnesses' message *here and now* means coming under
Jesus' *continuing* and *eschatological* territorial influence. This territoriality is confirmed by Acts omitting Joel's reference to Jerusalem as
the site for deliverance (Joel 3:5b LXX), even though it would suit the
present narrative setting and even though Acts 2:39c incorporates the
final part of Joel 3:5. The geography of Acts will be far vaster in its
scope, and would be obscured by such a particularistic and Jerusalem-
centred note at this foundational point in its exposition.

Acts 2:21 both earths and crowns this realignment of space. The
reallocation of 'Lord' from YHWH in the Joel cotext to Jesus in Acts
2:38 is established via Jesus' ascended status, expounded in 2:33–4

---

[35] Cf. Luke 24:49, where 'from on high' (cf. 1:78) and the emphatic ἐγώ ('I', i.e.,
Jesus) create a spatial conundrum awaiting resolution 'in the city'.

[36] Acts 4:16 (cf. 4:12). In 4:22 'sign' is qualified by 'of healing'.

[37] This is not to disparage the real effects of Philip's ministry; cf. Rius-Camps and
Read-Heimerdinger (2006: 142–3), who claim that Samaria's response alludes to the
rocky soil of Luke 8:4–15.

[38] O'Reilly (1987: 171–8) posits 3:22 and 7:36–7 as centring two chiasms bridging
Acts 1–5 and 6–7.

[39] Tannehill 1990: 32.   [40] Beale 2004: 212–16 (212).

(discussed below). The notion of calling upon the name of the Lord re-echoes through Acts (7:59; 9:14, 21; 22:16), always in close connection with the *heavenly* Jesus influencing earthly space. Jesus' 'name' bridges his heavenly position and his earthly influence, manifesting his *in absentia* territoriality (cf. Luke 19:11–27). Earthly 'calling' assumes 'both a sense of identity with Jesus and a confidence in Jesus' heavenly authority'.[41]

In these ways, the Joel quotation reinforces ascension geography as the interpretative guide for the ordering of space within Acts.

Peter's exposition as a Christological ordering of space (2:22–36)

Peter's subsequent argument presents a profoundly Christocentric exposition which propounds ascension geography by delineating Jesus' territoriality as stretching from Nazareth[42] (2:22) to God's right hand (2:33–6), to a spatial destiny with territorial power over the hearers.

In the pursuit of this claim, Peter is emphatic that Jesus' body did not see 'corruption' (διαφθορά), drawing on Psalm 15:9 LXX (16:9) in Acts 2:27. There, David articulates a hope that God's Holy One will not be allowed to experience corruption. In a crucial move in 2:31, Peter transposes David's hope to Jesus' flesh, having already advanced this claim negatively in 2:29 when asserting that David's nearby tomb constitutes local confirmation that the promise of Psalm 16 was *not* fulfilled in David's body. This familiar Jerusalem locale was a place of obvious decay, a thirdspace cul-de-sac signalling only 'corruption'.[43] Its alternative, anticipated in the continuing quotation from Psalm 16 in 2:28, is 'the way of life', ὁδοὺς ζωῆς, revealed 'with your presence', μετὰ τοῦπροσώπου σου. By inference, it has to allude to another, elsewhere.

David was a 'prophet'[44] (2:30), since he foresaw and spoke about the Christ's resurrection from the realms of bodily decay. Prophecy

---

[41] Wall 1998: 445.

[42] In Nazareth (Luke 4:16–30) Jesus raised programmatically the main conflict areas within Third-Gospel geography – domination of space, boundaries and cosmology (Moxnes 2001a: 194) – conflicts overflowing into Acts. Within Acts, 'Nazareth' functions as an enduring absent space, recalling these earlier conflicts. Cf. Acts 3:6; 4:10; 6:12; 10:38; 22:8; 26:9; cf. 24:5.

[43] 'Putrefaction and decay would have been graphically real for first-century Jews who practiced secondary burial' (K. L. Anderson 2006: 211 n. 57).

[44] David is never so described in the OT, although 2 Samuel 23:1–7 and 1 Chronicles 28:12 MT provide probable correlation.

here implies declaring insights concerning Christ's status, a status which results in a consequent ordering of space. This meaning casts light on the term's programmatic meaning in 2:17–18.

The logic of Peter's address could pass immediately from 2:31 on to 2:36, but first Peter must connect Jesus' present *heavenly* location with its proximate Pentecostal consequences. David 'did not ascend into the heavens' (2:34); but another has done so (cf. 1:10–11), whose outpouring of the Spirit (2:33)[45] now rewrites spatial relations between earth and heaven and upon the earth. Thus there is an enthroned Davidic king, but one enthroned in heaven. He does not reign from Jerusalem, although his territoriality clearly includes the city (cf. Luke 1:32–3, 69–71). The vindication of Jesus within Jerusalem, left open in Luke 20:17, 41–4, is now declared there.

Thus, rather than pointing to earthly Jerusalem enjoying third-space continuity within a restored Davidic kingship fulfilling patri-archal hopes, David's tomb provided a paradoxical marker to another thirdspace *elsewhere*, at God's right hand, entered into by Jesus through the apparent theological cul-de-sac of the cross (2:23, 36). The twelve witnesses' embodied proclamation (2:32, 'we all') emphasises that it is Jesus who has been so 'raised up' (ἀνέστησεν) from the dead: his destiny contrasts with David's decayed presence in earthly Jerusalem. Occurring in the NT only here and in Acts 13:35–7, where, also drawing upon Psalm 15:9 LXX (16:9), a fourfold cluster of 'corruption' references re-emphasises the contrasting destinies awaiting the corpses of Jesus and David, διαφθορά functions opposi-tionally, as a form of *anti*-thirdspace. Here lies the primary opposition in the storyworld of Acts – not between heaven and earth, but between heaven and the realm of the dead.[46]

Consequently, as well as stressing the physicality of Jesus' resurrec-tion, Jesus' *bodily* but now *non-earthly* location is being proclaimed in relation to a whole new Christofocal worldview, a reordered spatiality. Jesus' destiny – and destination – declared in Acts 2 emphasises the reordering of *earthly* space within 1:6–11 and informs a thirdspatial estimation of him.

---

[45] In what would have been 'a sharp surprise' within the storyworld of the speech, Jesus 'becomes the author of specific phenomena given to the disciples by the Spirit', thereby generating a 'high Christology' whereby Jesus acts 'in God's place' (Turner 2000: 277–8). Turner does not elaborate his phrase's spatial ambiguities, although pp. 303–6 do develop 2:33 as indicating the Spirit's role throughout the rest of Acts as Jesus' agent.

[46] Eisen 2006: 167.

In short, a comprehensive reordering of space has occurred, crucially at Jesus' ascension: Israel's abiding hope, proclaimed by apparently reliable spokespersons in Luke 1–2, has been drawn up into heaven. This surprising restructuring qualifies any immediate spatial focus upon Israel as previously conceived. Crucially, Jesus' heavenly exaltation as 'both Lord and Messiah' (2:36) informs both the speech's climax and the hearers' response.[47]

The hearers' response as modelling ascension geography (2:37–47)

By 2:36 (cf. 2:23–4) the contrasting treatments of Jesus trigger a geo/theopolitical crisis for Peter's hearers (2:37). His call for baptism in 2:38 echoes the Baptist's earlier ministry in Luke 3:3–18,[48] but here specifically realigns hearers' misplaced response to the ascended Christ. If Jesus is now exalted in heaven, then Israel must repent concerning him. Such a response to him, and to his position, entails Israel undergoing a spatial transformation through a response individualised and initiated by baptism in Jesus' name: 'the person baptized becomes the property of, is assigned to the company of, Jesus'.[49] Such repentance – as always in Acts – binds respondents to Jesus' ordering of space, to his territoriality, to ascension geography.

Acts 2:38–40 also implies that this is incorporation into a remnant forming within Israel. Given geographers' long recognition that society is not 'spaceless', happening 'on the head of a pin',[50] Peter's exhortation, pronounced in Pentecostal Jerusalem, occurs within, and provokes, a radical restructuring of Israel-space: a new Christocentric space differentiated in 2:40 'from this corrupt (σκολιᾶς) generation'. This spatial crisis is thirdspatial, occurring within Judaism, even within Jerusalem, but decentring existing firstspace and secondspace categories. In an 'effort at theological gerrymandering' within 2:40, 'the borders of eschatological judgement have been redrawn'.[51] Furthermore, this restructuring extends beyond Israel,[52] an allusion to Isaiah 57:9 in Acts

---

[47] Rowe (2007) convincingly positions 2:36 at the centre of Lukan Christology, a centre which is, of course, now heavenly. *Who* Jesus is and *where* Jesus is are mutually constituted.

[48] Tannehill (1990: 40–1) elucidates these parallels.   [49] Barrett 1994: 154.

[50] Massey 1984: 4.   [51] Wall 1998: 447–8 (447).

[52] Peter's opening words in 2:14 have already claimed an audience bigger than simply those listening in the crowd.

2:39 connecting it with the gentiles.[53] In the first instance, however, diagnosis of 'this crooked generation' borrows the language of OT judgements upon Israel's failure to keep its spatial mandate (e.g. Deuteronomy 32:5; Psalm 78:8), and heralds concurrent but bifurcating geographies within Jerusalem-space and Israel-space. The passive σώθητε (2:40, lit., 'be saved'; cf. NRSV, 'save yourselves') both echoes 2:21 and reinforces the necessary heavenly dynamic underpinning salvific incorporation. Together with 2:47, 2:38–40 demonstrates how response to the apostolic message involves more than merely privatised associative will. Rather, believers are joined to a wider social grouping, to a *space*, and constituted as believers in and by that space.

The narrator's summary of the believers' collective space generated by a now heavenly Lord (2:42–7) is strategically positioned immediately after the sermon and response. While the present passive participle σῳζομένους in 2:47 leaves the point in time of salvation open, it does at least assume that salvation has begun within this new distinctive space within Jerusalem.[54] 'Breaking of bread' (2:42), whether the eucharist or ordinary meals, suggests a distinctive spatial practice.[55] Such meals would maintain publicly the ideals of meal fellowship taught and practised by Jesus, and would anticipate the eschatological banquet projected by him.[56] Similarly, the only precursor in Acts for 'the prayers' in 2:42 is 1:24–30, a profoundly Christofocal model for prayer. Perhaps '*the* prayers' might suggest regular hours and places of prayer, possibly at the Temple[57] (2:46; 3:1; cf. 5:12, 42), routine spatial practices which would constitute the new community and which, considering Jesus' 'daily' Temple activity narrated in Luke 19:47, would connect it with the practices of Jesus. Sharing possessions (Acts 2:44–5) similarly functions as more than simply material redistribution, reflecting and generating changed – and politically charged – spatial practices reflecting this group's distinctive allegiances (see below, concerning 4:36–7).

---

[53] J. M. Scott 1995: 168 n. 156. Similarly, Pao 2000: 231–3 and Turner 2000: 270. A similar formulation in 22:21 (cf. 17:27; Ephesians 2:13, 17) confirms that 2:39, in conformity to Luke 2:30–2; 24:47 and Acts 1:8, has the gentiles within its narratival scope (Wasserberg 1998: 221–2). This grants 'all flesh' in Acts 2:17 a universal hue, something lacking in its Joel cotext.

[54] Schneider 1980–2: 289.

[55] Finger (2007: 236–42) reconstructs, based in part on social-scientific analysis, what 2:46–7a would have looked and sounded like. Regarding the contribution of sound to productions of space, cf. S. J. Smith 1994.

[56] Heil 1999: 242–3.

[57] Barrett 1994: 176–8, although cf. 1991: 347; Fitzmyer 1998: 269.

Overall, this response to Peter's call for repentance is comprehensive – conceptual, cognitive, and activist – reaching even to the heart.[58] The latter point prevents *koinonia* being reduced to the merely economic, but neither can their response be seen as merely inward. Rather, third-spatially, 2:33–47 present believers in Christ as enjoying a new union with a distinctive heavenly Lord and with one another as fellow believers. Acts 2:44 intimates that the Baptist's eschatological injunction (Luke 3:11) is here being fulfilled within Israel. Such embodiment within lived experience is truly 'a new way of being in the world',[59] a fitting response to the Baptist's Isaianic projection of space in Luke 3:5 which, other than Acts 2:40, contains the only occurrence of σκολιός ('crooked') in Luke-Acts.

3.   Temple-space

A clash of geographies

If the exalted Jesus is 'effectively the new point of contact between heaven and earth, fulfilling the role of temple in God's purpose',[60] then witness to him is unlikely to remain only on Jerusalem's streets. Instead, 2:46–5:42, as a narrative commentary on the Christological claim based on 2:21,[61] carries this claim into contact, even conflict, with the spatial claims associated with the Jerusalem Temple. The narrator's *inclusio* concerning Temple-space and home-space maintains this focus (2:46; 5:42).

The act of restoration narrated in 3:1–10 and the subsequent discourse (3:11–26) both occur within Temple-space, but cannot be reduced to it. Peter, in what is widely acknowledged to be the most eschatological passage in Acts, points *beyond* the Temple, but does so *in* the Temple. If it is true that the Jerusalem Temple represented the entire cosmos within its spatial claim,[62] then it represents no small setting, just as Pentecost was no local affair. Certainly the Temple functioned within the diverse expressions of first-century Judaism as a

---

[58] Laytham 2002: 26–7, responding to Green 2002. Cf. Gehring 2004: 79–95.

[59] Turner 2000: 422, describing 'salvation'.

[60] Peterson 1998b: 394, building on McKelvey 1969: 84–91. This chapter and the next will position and develop this assertion.

[61] Tannehill 1990: 31. Arguably, this 'narrative commentary' extends to 7:59, and beyond.

[62] So Beale 2004: 45–7, who cites a wide range of Judaic commentators constructing this view of Temple-space. None can be explicitly linked to Lukan narrative, nor denied from it: Beale is constricted to arguing on the basis of implicit compatibility and admirable 'fit' (e.g. p. 189).

locale with variegated and contested meanings. As a narrative setting, the Temple functions within Jerusalem (and thus also within some wider notions of 'Israel') as a firstspace location, a secondspace covenantal projection, and an eschatological thirdspace vision.

Recognising this comprehensive spatiality avoids reducing Temple-space to mere firstspace, and precludes simplistic suggestions that the setting *per se* indicates 'a positive comparison with … Jewish expectations',[63] that 'Peter and John are represented as devout Jews who frequent the Temple'[64] or, even, that 'The appearance of the apostles in the temple shows their attachment to this symbolic center of Jewish religion'.[65] As this chapter will demonstrate, their relationship with place – especially this place – is far more complex.[66] The apostles' attendance at the Temple could also constitute a territorial claim upon it,[67] and/or judgement upon it, missionary pragmatism,[68] or a primitive lack of alternative meeting places.[69] At this narrative juncture it remains to be shown whether the apostles order their lives according to Temple-space, or whether they attempt to order Temple-space according to their lives.[70] As it had for the earthly Jesus (e.g. Luke 19:45–7), the Temple setting generates simultaneous conflicting meanings for characters within Acts as multiple spatial strategies are ranged against one another. Therefore, it is best seen as a dynamic setting with multiple possible material and symbolic meanings, each bound within larger hierarchies of spatial presuppositions.

Ascension geography within Temple-space: the sign

After mentioning the Temple in the preceding narrational summary (Acts 2:46), the narrative enters its space for the first time in 3:1–8.[71]

---

[63] Chance 1988: 82–5 (83). [64] Barrett 1994: 176, although cf. 1991: 347–9.
[65] Tannehill 1990: 52. [66] See also Sleeman 2007. [67] Conzelmann 1987: 24.
[68] Haenchen (1971: 192 n. 7) rejects this view, proposed by Calvin 'and even Preuschen'.
[69] Fitzmyer 1998: 272.
[70] 'A continued commitment to reach out to Israel through her most sacred and central institution' (Spencer 1997: 41) is perhaps suitably ambiguous, although Acts 1–2 has cast the Twelve as eschatological witness-judges who rewrite spaces in view of Jesus' ascension.
[71] The suggestion that 2:1–13 occurred within the Temple (Bruce 1990: 116, although cf. 114; Beale 2004: 203) is unconvincing (Barrett 1994: 113–14): Acts does not *begin* at the Temple (*contra* Hengel 1983: 101). On this point, however, Spencer (1997: 32) is too oppositional.

The new setting is carefully highlighted. First, the imperfect ἀνέβαινον as Peter and John 'were going up' to this new setting (3:1) 'conveys a vivid impression: the process is unrolling before our eyes'.[72] Second, the narrator mentions 'temple' (ἱερόν) four times in 3:1–3 (thrice within an εἰς construction), the first such repetition since 'into heaven' (εἰς τὸν οὐρανόν) in 1:10–11. Third, the Temple is not entered until 3:8, once the intervening healing has occurred on its boundary.

At the Gate called Beautiful,[73] the name of Jesus, uttered on the threshold of the Temple, makes an immediate and manifest impact on the beggar's spatiality. His firstspace is transformed by new mobility,[74] and so too, possibly, is his (secondspace) status within the Temple's symbolic universe.[75] Narrative expectation, built up by the participle προσδοκῶν ('he fixed his attention', 3:5) and by the word order of Peter's reply in 3:6, gives way to this dramatically reversed spatiality described with distinctive terminology. If ἔγειρε (3:6, lit. 'rise') echoes Luke 5:23,[76] an implied continuity with Jesus' earthly ministry reinforces Peter's invocation of the now absent Jesus. Certainly Acts 3:8–9 is widely seen as alluding to Isaiah 35:6[77] with its promise of spatial transformation determined from heaven (35:4).

---

[72] Haenchen 1971: 198 n. 2, partly quoting Radermacher.

[73] Rius-Camps and Read-Heimerdinger (2004: 210–11 (211)) see this name, and the passage's verbal parallels, as echoing Genesis 3, such that this episode 'marks the beginning of a new act of divine creation, as fundamental in its nature as the first creation of the world'.

[74] Haenchen (1971: 198 n. 11) grandly misses the point that *lame* beggars *can't* be choosers when he suggests, on the ground that beggars would not arrive at the Temple so late in the day, that the time reference (3:1) is a later addition to the text. Unwittingly or not, the time reference draws attention to the beggar's constrained mobility, reinforced by the two imperfect verbs in 3:2, which Barrett (1994: 179) sees as indicating habitual actions.

[75] L. T. Johnson (1992: 65) and Spencer (1997: 45–7) suggest the man's condition had previously excluded him from the Temple. Cf. Barrett 1994: 180. Rius-Camps and Read-Heimerdinger (2004: 226) suggest that he 'clings' to Peter and John, having entered the temple (3:8b, 11), because, without undergoing any prescribed acts of purification, 'he will be dependent upon their support once he is confronted by the Temple authorities'. Note, however, their cautionary footnote (p. 211 n. 3), and that this is not the offence narrated in 4:2.

[76] So L. T. Johnson 1992: 66, although a 'strong combination' of textual witnesses [א B D cop^sa] support the shorter reading, which omits ἔγειρε (Metzger 1994: 267).

[77] So most commentators. Spencer (1997: 52) also positions the mention of 'forty years' (4:22) as evoking the exodus tradition (and, also, its geography!) under-pinning Isaiah 35:1–10. Cf. the more allegorical Rius-Camps and Read-Heimerdinger 2004: 267.

By remaining in the narrative frame, the man becomes, in Acts 3–4,[78] the embodiment of the promise made in Acts 2:21. His continued alignment with the apostles placards the spatial order they proclaim and manifest, the healing of a *lame* man who then adheres to the apostles being suitably paradigmatic and symbolic for a narrative of 'the Way'.[79] The incident's narrative length suggests more than simply 'an example of healings that happened frequently (cf. 4.30; 5.12, 15, 16)'.[80] The 'example' functions, rather, in the opposite direction: the heavenwards spatiality within the miracle, sermon and subsequent defence positions these other miracles, which are mentioned only in passing.

Given the parallels between this incident and Jesus' earlier healing of a paralytic (Luke 5:17–26), Tannehill rightly argues that the similarities between the scenes 'lie less in the healing itself than in the function of these scenes in the larger narrative'.[81] But there are spatial developments since Luke 5 which highlight the arrival of ascension geography within Temple-space. Whereas there had been observers present from Jerusalem in Luke 5:17, now this 'sign of healing' is manifest in Jerusalem itself (Acts 4:21–2). Together, the scenes demonstrate developing Christocentric space: Luke 5:24 placarded 'authority *on earth* to forgive sins'; Acts 4:12 highlights the lack of any other 'name *under heaven* … by which we must be saved', precluding any other catholocities, utopias or ultimate spatial claims.[82] Such developments reinforce the resurgent Christofocal point of view and the restructured overarching spatiality brought about by the ascension, a spatial ordering which Peter must now explain.

Ascension geography within Temple-space: Peter's discourse

As in Luke 1:10, 21, Temple-space is *peopled*, here by 'all the people' (σᾶς ὁ λαός, 3:9, 11). Consequently the miracle has a wider effect, amazing other Temple-goers (3:10), who are inclined to regard the apostles before them as having caused the miracle. This error in *spatial* discernment reminds us that ascension geography is not

---

[78] His presence in 4:14 suggests that he might have been incarcerated together with Peter and John (Gallagher 2004: 56 n. 3).

[79] Hamm 1986: 305.   [80] Barrett 1994: 175.   [81] Tannehill 1990: 51.

[82] For Tannehill (1990: 51) these markers indicate simply the 'importance and general scope' of Jesus' saving power. Read more critically, 4:12 anticipates the charges of 6:13.

self-explanatory. Once more, as in 2:14–40, interpretative witnesses (cf. 1:8) are required. Peter's immediate statement in 3:12–16 therefore clarifies space, deflecting any instrumentality from the apostles' presence to Jesus' absence, from simple firstspace (which in the circumstances could easily adhere to existing notions of Temple-space) to a more nuanced spatiality focused on the heavenly Jesus. Although the apostles are *within* Temple-space and understanding their action requires acknowledgement of that location, narrative attention highlights these witnesses proclaiming their distinctively Christocentric spatiality, not on Temple-space *per se*.

As in Acts 2, Peter's address focuses space Christologically by proclaiming the contrasting treatment of Jesus by the people and by God. A series of escalating verbs across 3:11–16 together with emphatic second-person plural pronouns and vivid repetition in 3:13–15 position the hearers as needing to repent of having 'misplaced' Jesus. More than simply restoring Jesus, God 'has glorified his servant (παῖς) Jesus' (3:13),[83] whether through Jesus' resurrection, the recent miracle[84] or, as is likely, through both these aspects.[85]

This glorification underpins what is here, by faith in Jesus' name, being manifest within Temple-space. Τὴν ὁλοκληρίαν ταύτην ('this perfect health', 3:16) 'might be deliberately evocative', this term having been used in the Septuagint to designate unblemished animals acceptable to God;[86] if so, then *Jesus* brings the wholeness required of Israel, and Luke has Peter announce this *in the Temple*, at the hour of the afternoon sacrifice.

'Ignorance' concerning Jesus, 3:17, is progressively replaced by apostolic interpretation of the prophets (3:18, 25). A fundamentally *Jesus-oriented* charge to 'repent' and 'turn to God' does not suggest that any Temple sacrifice is required for sins to be 'wiped out'. Instead, these two imperatives in 3:19 inaugurate a Christological remapping of God's people crystallised in 3:23.

The spatial ordering resulting from these imperatives is marked by 'times of refreshing' (3:20; καιροὶ ἀναψύξεως), repeated times (and places!) of relief within the present era. The plural καιροί indicates 'a number of specific points of time' (whereas the pluralised χρόνων

---

[83] '*His servant* Jesus' also recalls Isaiah 52:13 (so Haenchen 1971: 205, and others); this, with Israel (Luke 1:54) and David (Luke 1:69) referents, generates a Lukan 'servant'-line extending to Jesus.

[84] Haenchen 1971: 205.

[85] Tannehill 1990: 53 n. 12, blending resurrection and exaltation; Barrett 1994: 195.

[86] L. T. Johnson 1992: 68, citing Isaiah 1:6; Zechariah 11:16.

('time') in 3:21 is clearly future in its cotextual specification) and
wider uses and cognates of the *hapax legomenon* ἀναψύξεως suggest
'temporary relief rather than finality'.[87] The temporal language of
καιροί and χρόνοι therefore also generates a spatiality, a dynamic
geography of renewal. It reprises the same (also pluralised) terms
from Jesus' words in 1:7; what lie between these instances, of course,
are Jesus' ascension and the outpouring of the Spirit. From this
narrative standpoint, Jesus' location in heaven is not only limited
in time, but also it influences life on earth in these present days.[88]
Other narrative factors provide a broader reason for locating καιροὶ
ἀναψύξεως as prior to Christ's return, namely the believer-spaces in
2:41–7 (produced by repentance and turning), and the lame man's
healing, which has already been presented in eschatological terms
(3:8–9; cf. Isaiah 35).

Such places anticipate Jesus' return from heaven, foretold in 1:11,
which will bring 'the time of universal restoration' (3:21a, χρόνων
ἀποκαταστάσεως πάντων) as foretold by the OT prophets (3:21b),
the culmination of a worldwide blessing (3:25–6). Grammatically,
πάντων could indicate 'all people' or 'all things'; a spatialised reading,
namely 'all places', links both possibilities. This posits a creation
needing restoration, the closest reference to a Lukan 'fall'.[89]

Although there is a temporal order here, communicated by the
two sendings of Jesus in 3:26[90] and 3:20, Luke is communicating a
salvation-geographical schema through these verses, not some aspatial
chronology. Indeed, such spatial dynamics *confirm* the uncertainties of
temporal knowledge communicated in 1:7.[91] Jesus is definitively in
heaven and genuinely absent from earth during the present times and
the production of these spaces, 3:21 now cementing auditors' initial
associations of Christ with heaven, and heaven with Christ. Nevertheless, response to the absent Jesus as the foretold 'prophet like Moses'

---

[87] Barrett 1994: 205.   [88] Wasserberg 1998: 224.

[89] Stenschke 1998: 141. A narrowly nationalistic reading of Πάντων, implying '"all
things of which the prophets spoke", that is, Israel to its status of glory and blessing'
(Rius-Camps and Read-Heimerdinger 2004: 235 n. 26), is diminished by the redefinition of Israel made in 3:23.

[90] K. L. Anderson (2006: 224) argues persuasively that 3:26 refers to Jesus' resurrection rather than to his incarnation (likewise Wasserberg 1998: 226). A resurrection
reading assumes incarnation and, by creating an *inclusio* with 3:13, also assumes the
ascension within its compass.

[91] *Pace* Conzelmann (1987: 29), who sees Luke as facing problems communicating
his salvation-*historical* schema across 3:19–22. Cf. Wasserberg 1998: 222–30.

(3:22; cf. 7:37–43), here proclaimed by his witnesses, (re)defines the earthly 'people' (λαός, 3:23).

Acts therefore envisages the restored bounds of Israel as delimited by Christocentric repentance, not by firstspace territorial boundaries or secondspace ethnicity (cf. 1:6). Acts 3:22–3 builds upon 3:19, blending Deuteronomy 18:15 with Leviticus 23:29. The Deuteronomy 18 cotext rejects alternative spatialities, whether the abominable practices of the nations (18:9–14) or false prophets within Israel (18:20–3). Leviticus 23 expresses correct responses on the Day of Atonement. Acts reworks both these intertexts along Christofocal boundary lines. Peter's 'ominous conclusion' in 3:23,[92] regarding not listening to Jesus, judges the pursuit of other spatialities (even if still within the firstspace land) as breaking with covenantal thirdspace, which is now tied up with the heavenly Christ. Thereby, in the Temple of all places, Peter's hearers are informed that 'the Jew who does not turn to Christ is no longer a member of God's people!'[93]

Acts 3:23 presupposes, and the ensuing narrative almost immediately recounts, opposition to Jesus-oriented geography even – especially – within earthly Israel (cf. Luke 2:34). That Christofocal spatial reordering is presently incomplete (the implication of Acts 3:21) implies that it remains subject to resistance. Nevertheless, 3:21b–2, 24–5 claim OT spatialities as confirming this geography, thereby precluding any alternative geographical schemas assuming normative legitimacy within the storyworld.

This dynamic ascension-driven geography is also anticipated at the global scale. Strictly, reference in 3:25 to 'all the families (πατριαὶ) of the earth (γῆς)' could indicate 'all the tribes of the land', but such a narrow reading downplays the foundational scope of 1:8 and universalistic implications in the Pentecost proclamation. Instead, 3:25 recalls the Abrahamic covenant (cf. Genesis 22:18; 26:4 LXX), and also alludes back to the Table of Nations in Genesis 10–11,[94] a global reach expected of the Temple at its best (Isaiah 56:7; cf. Luke 19:46). Its spatial vision is not reserved for Israel alone, but is renewal for Israel 'first' (Acts 3:26); thus, 'as Jews they are invited to take their

---

[92] Fitzmyer 1998: 290.
[93] Haenchen 1971: 209. Cf. Lohfink 1975: 55 (emphasis original): '*Und jenes Israel, das dann noch in der Ablehnung Jesu beharrte, verlor sein Anrecht, das wahre Gottesvolk zu sein – es wurde zum Judentum!*' ('And because Israel still insisted on refusing Jesus, it lost its right to be the true people of God – it became Jewry!')
[94] J. M. Scott 1995: 168.

place [!] in the New Covenant'[95] even if the Lukan economy of space denies that this is 'new'. As Chapter 5 will show, Acts 7 asserts that, from the patriarchs onwards, blessedness was not defined simply by possession of land. Instead, it pivots on turning in faith from wickedness, as Luke's earlier exposition of 'Abrahamic' geography made clear (Luke 1:54–5, 72–5; 3:8; 13:27–9; 16:22–31; 19:9).

In this manner, an alternative salvation landscape with radical implications for the theological place of the Temple is proclaimed within the Temple. Stephen's ministry will clarify its implications, but here in Acts 3 the Temple is being shorn of its thirdspace claims, these being transferred to the heavenly Christ. As a legitimate secondspace marker, the Temple must point to him; whether it will function as such remains an open question at this narrative juncture. As a firstspace locale for such teaching, the Temple is contested space; the Temple authorities with their dominant spatial order are about to intervene.

4.   Sanhedrin-space (4:1–22)

A clash of territorialities

Although the Sanhedrin is not named until 4:15, its territoriality over Temple-space becomes explicit in 4:1, and the council itself becomes a narrative setting in 4:5. As a setting, it is 'far from a neutral stage in Luke's narrative world', since consistently within Luke-Acts 'to be found before the council is to be in a dangerous place, one that usually leads to violence against followers of the Way'.[96] This setting encapsulates a broader territoriality and generates an oppositional spatiality which can be termed Sanhedrin-space. In Acts 4–5 the apostle-witnesses twice come into direct contact with this space. These encounters provoke the apostles' articulation of their own spatial order and increase narrative tension ahead of Stephen's appearance before the council.

The Sanhedrin's initial annoyance with the apostles, as narrated in 4:2, concerns disruption of conventional Temple-space – they are

---

[95] Barrett 1994: 212. Clearly, 3:25 does not *exclude* Israel: Turner (2000: 309–12) suggests that τὰ ἔθνη ('the nations', as in Genesis 22:18 and 26:4 LXX) would have indicated gentiles, whereas πατριαὶ in 3:25 includes both Jews and gentiles. Turner (2000: 419–20) considers 'Israel' to be restored ('*in principle*', p. 419, emphasis original) by Acts 15.

[96] Skinner 2003: 121.

'teaching the people' (in the Temple) and they are 'proclaiming that in [the heavenly] Jesus there is resurrection from the dead'. This latter aspect – initially an awkward and overly specific summary of Peter's preaching in Acts 3 – concerns thirdspace which opposes the earthly spatial order of the Sadducees (23:8). Both aspects will dominate Acts 4–5, provoking the maintenance and development of the critique of Temple-space which began in Acts 3.

The territorial reach of the 'name'

Given that Acts 3 saw a new claimant for the right to define the people of God being proclaimed within the Jerusalem Temple, the question of who has authority to make such definitions and to lead this people forms an obvious narrative progression. Although the claimant is absent, proclaimed as being in heaven, 'the trial of Jesus, in effect, is reopened and fresh evidence presented by the apostles to get the Jews to change their verdict'.[97] Similarities between Jesus' trial in Luke and court appearances in Acts suggest that Luke's Gospel did not resolve the conflict; rather, with these apostle-witnesses a still contested geography of power has entered a new phase. The question linking 'power' and 'name' (4:7) indicates the personal nature of this geography – in locative and political senses, it concerns the place of Jesus. This terminology picks up Peter's earlier proclamation in 3:6, 12, 16, and the emphatic final position of 'you' (ὑμεῖς) in 4:7 links a question concerning the absent Jesus with the immediate manifestation of his influence confronting the Sanhedrin.

Peter's reply in 4:10–12 locates the name of Jesus within an ascension ordering of space already expounded in Acts 2–3, with 'under heaven' (ὑπὸ τὸν οὐρανόν, 4:12) specifically recalling the ascension geography of 1:6–11 and the expansive horizon of 2:5. As with previous references to οὐρανός, commentators simply ignore this spatiality within 4:12[98] or read it as a universalistic metaphor or a reference to the visible heavens.[99] Without denying these inferences, such readings underplay the specific Christocentric spatiality established already within the narrative. It is *from heaven* that Jesus' name functions as 'the inescapable decision point concerning salvation for Peter's hearers'.[100] In reply to 4:7, Peter's hearers, who are again

[97] Trites 1977: 129.   [98] Bruce 1990: 152; L. T. Johnson 1992: 78.
[99] Barrett 1994: 232; Fitzmyer 1998: 302; Gaventa 2003a: 93.
[100] Tannehill 1990: 61.

positioned within Israel-space (4:10), need to come to terms with both the 'power' of healing before them and the 'name' of the heavenly Christ, 4:12 precluding any 'other' (ἄλλος) or 'different kind of' (ἕτερος) earthly salvation geography.[101]

Peter and John's 'boldness' (παρρησία), recognised by the Council, sustains the connection between Jesus and Sanhedrin-space (4:13). Their boldness indicates where apostolic allegiance lies and who governs their space in this territorial confrontation. As release from gaol in 5:20 will demonstrate, Christocentric governance is not confined to the realm of ideas. Its lived experience as boldness constitutes them as witnesses, binding them to their message. As the Sanhedrin's rhetorical question in 4:16 recognises, there is an inseparability of the sign from its instigators and interpreters. The cognate verb παρρησιάζομαι is used in Acts for gospel proclamation to Jews (9:27, 28; 13:46; 14:3; 18:26; 19:8; 26:26), suggesting a cotext-specific meaning for 'boldness' here, rather than a generalised Hellenistic virtue ascribed to Luke's heroes.[102] Such boldness, fuelling conflict with the Sanhedrin, enhances the apostles' status as 'eschatological regents'[103] discharging their chief responsibility as bold and faithful witnesses to Israel. It emphasises the witnesses' persistent veracity, even before the most powerful figures in Israel, conventionally the shapers of its space. It proclaims and reflects the spatial ordering affected by the heavenly Christ, 4:13 evoking the apostles' programmatic encounter with Jesus in Acts (1:6–11).

Given the social-scientific observation that power is transmitted through space in diverse ways,[104] and that the Jesus of Acts does not abide by simple rules of proximity and distance, it is necessary to read carefully for the narrative's spatiality. Jesus is firstspatially absent, but maintaining a thirdspace presence, his heavenly status structuring the apostles' practice and proclamation of space, both here re-conceived along Christocentric lines. Peter's response to the Sanhedrin (4:8–12) articulates these dynamics, emphasising Jesus, whose remarkable presence within Acts belies his physical absence

---

[101] Cf. Rius-Camps and Read-Heimerdinger 2004: 260. Consequently, although Peter 'is still very much part of Israel', this does not mean that 'these are *his* leaders' (Rius-Camps and Read-Heimerdinger 2004: 258, emphasis original). The second claim underplays the Christologically driven developments within Acts 3–4 (not least the Bezan emphases in 4:9) and neglects any rhetorical impulse or territorial appropriation within Peter's address.

[102] Barrett 1994: 233. Cf. Haenchen 1971: 219 n. 11; Fitzmyer 1998: 302.

[103] Cf. Evans 1993c.   [104] J. Allen 2003.

from most of the narrative.[105] His and John's repeated declarations in the face of opposition (4:19, 20) add emphasis, increase narrative tension and, as 'narrative rhetoric', are 'meant to convey a message not only between characters but also from the implied author to the implied reader'.[106] That such boldness continues through Acts' open-ended conclusion (28:31) suggests that auditors might also boldly appropriate proclamation-space. Thus the issue of whom one is 'to listen to' or 'obey' (4:19, ἀκούειν; 5:29, πειθαρχεῖν), far from reflecting a Socratic prototype,[107] stakes out the particular issue at hand within narrative space. The emphatic ἡμεῖς ('we') and double negation in 4:20 indicate a clear sense of separate self-identity forming around the name of Jesus.

In contrast, Peter's Sanhedrin opponents, in a rhetorical strategy intended to distance themselves from him, appear deliberately to avoid mentioning Jesus' name (4:7, 17; 5:28). The undeniable first-space reality of the sign highlighted in 4:14, 16 and 21 silences them temporarily, but their continuing opposition to what 4:16 acknowledges is an undeniable spatial restructuring that reveals a hardness of heart[108] and characterises Israel's formal leaders as persistently disqualifying themselves by rejecting Jesus. Variations from Psalm 117:22 LXX (118:22) in Acts 4:11[109] emphasise God's reversal of the spatial order created by these 'builders' of Israel-space. This, and other Lukan 'stone' passages set within Jerusalem (Luke 19:40, 44; 20:17–18; 21:5–6), construct a crisis for them and their spatial ordering.

Acts 4:17–18 presents the Sanhedrin attempting to use its spatial power[110] to constrain the apostles by ordering them to cease their ongoing public proclamation (φθέγγεσθαι) and private teaching (διδάσκειν) in the name of Jesus. The apostles' response in 4:19–20 reiterates and reinforces their alternative understanding of the

---

[105] Jesus' personal name occurs 68 times in Acts (in all chapters except 12, 14, 23 and 27); cf. 86 times in Luke's Gospel.

[106] Tannehill 1990: 62.

[107] Such formal parallels are hard to avoid (Bruce 1990: 155, 172), but are neither required nor informative, given the specific Christocentric spatiality informing Acts.

[108] Haenchen 1971: 218–19; Fitzmyer 1998: 303.

[109] Marshall (2007: 550–1) summarises these variations.

[110] Without denying a temporal element, the charge in 4:17–18 is more spatial than Haenchen (1971: 219 n. 3) and Conzelmann (1987: 33) allow, as Barrett (1994: 235) acknowledges. Acts 5:28 presumes a spatial violation of this earlier charge, and narrated spatial expansion (5:16) immediately precedes the Sanhedrin's reintroduction into the narrative.

geography of power. 'What we have seen and heard' echoes 'all that Jesus did and taught' (1:1). Again, this weds them to the now heavenly Jesus, but now also this distinctly Christofocal heavenly orientation is articulated as satisfying God's point of view ('in God's sight', ἐνώπιον τοῦ θεοῦ).

'The people': a crisis of territorial legitimacy?

As is becoming apparent, apostolic proclamation in Acts is carefully placed within a Jerusalem shaped and inhabited by both people and power. In a dynamic and sensitive portrayal of localised power relations, ascension geography in Acts 2–7 is played out among 'the people' (ὁ λαός), being earthed in their midst and embodied within their differential response to the proclamation. If the apostles are to lead the whole house of Israel into eschatological restoration through the (re)new(ed) covenant spatiality established in 1:6–11, then 'the people' should respond to them. First mentioned in 2:47 immediately after the Pentecostal beachhead for believer-space has been established, the people form a significant spatial marker within Acts 2–6,[111] reflecting and positioning this question of leadership. Their spatial orientation reflects allegiance to one of two different leaderships with their particular projections of space.

These observations notwithstanding, from the narrative's perspective neither 'the people' nor formal earthly power is the final arbiter of leadership in Acts. The Jerusalem authorities maintain the vast majority of their firstspace territoriality in Acts 2–7, even if their theological and eschatological (thirdspace) legitimacy is – from the narrator's perspective – being eroded. Therefore, as cautionary caveats – 'in reality', 'effective leaders'[112] – illustrate, these chapters require careful spatial analysis for their narrative dynamic of power. Without presenting any ambition to snatch formal authority, Peter (especially) fulfils the functions of a true leader of the people. Popular prestige is not, however, the same as formal power, even if formal power is trimmed by popular influence. Although the people's support temporarily thwarts the Temple-space hierarchy's anti-ascension territoriality (4:21; 5:13, 26), as in the Lukan passion account,[113]

---

[111] Acts 2:47; 3:9, 11, 12, 23; 4:1, 2, 8, 10, 17, 21, 27 (plural); 5:12, 13, 20, 25, 26, 34, cf. 37; also 6:8, 12.

[112] L. T. Johnson (1992: 80), basing his argument within a literary patterning established by the prophet Moses.

[113] Concerning which, see Tannehill 1990: 60.

popular acclaim easily turns away (6:12) and is not the ultimate theological marker for legitimate leadership. Acts 5:42 sustains rather than resolves the question of leadership and, with it, the issue of wider Jerusalem spaces within this section of Acts.

Narrative attention turns instead to the ἐκκλησία-space,[114] recounting the production, maintenance and development of spaces loyal to the apostles.

5.   Ἐκκλησία-space (4:23–5:16)

The worldview of the Jerusalem believers

When released from Sanhedrin-space, Peter and John go to 'their own' (τοὺς ἰδίους, 4:23; NRSV, 'their friends'). This narrated description highlights an oppositional spatiality within existing Jerusalem-space(s) which is bifurcating into a hybrid identity at once both close to and in conflict with other Jerusalem-spaces.[115] Auditors are reminded retrospectively that Peter and John have not been isolated characters before the Sanhedrin: instead, their role within a wider collectivity is recalled (e.g. 2:41–7).

The believers[116] respond in communal prayer to the apostles' report (4:24–30), a response conforming to Jesus' call to prayer in the face of temptation made immediately before his passion (Luke 22:40, 46).[117] Here, as elsewhere in Luke-Acts, the practice and content of prayer articulates boundary markers (cf. Luke 5:33–9; 18:9–14; Acts 1:24–5). This prayer, based on Psalm 2:1–2 LXX (quoted directly in Acts 4:25–6), expounds the group's theological geography, using both the psalm and Christ's earthly passion and heavenly position to interpret their own situation. It also articulates their vision for the prayer's answer. As such, it demonstrates how Luke envisages prayer: 'It is not timeless, situationless, ahistorical [or

[114]   The word ἐκκλησία ('church') enters the narrative in 5:11.

[115]   Such a reading differs from most commentators' interest in whether such a *setting* could have the capacity to gather together the thousands of converts (e.g. Haenchen 1971: 226; Barrett 1994: 243). It correlates with the strategic desires (and varying abilities) of Diaspora Jews to form 'a virtual city within the city' (Meeks 1983: 36).

[116]   Acts 4:23–31 could present a meeting of simply the apostles, or of the wider body of believers. The spatialised reading pursued here stands either way, but, noting the change of description in 4:32, perhaps the apostles are intended here, τοὺς ἰδίους presenting an implicit alternative to Sanhedrin-space, which will itself here declare its own production of space. As Barrett (1994: 241) notes, 'if this means only the Twelve, the Twelve represent the whole Christian body'.

[117]   Tannehill 1990: 71.

aspatial] prayer so general and universally applicable that it can be related at will. No, for Luke prayer is always new because its locus is the ongoing history [and geography] of the community ... the community's placing itself [thirdspatially] alongside Jesus, again through listening to Scripture.'[118]

The spatiality of Psalm 2 is used to interpret and position the shifting geography 'in this city' (4:27). Whether Herod represents 'the kings' and Pilate 'the rulers' in 4:26,[119] or whether the political and religious authorities fulfil these respective functions so as to include the Sanhedrin in the prayer, the interpretative key to the psalm is the identity *and location* of the Lord's anointed (cf. 13:33). By reading this figure as Jesus, the believers realign the conventional Jewish hermeneutic of the gentile nations as the enemies of God's Christ. In their reordered worldview, under a Christological heaven, such secondspace is transposed. *Jerusalem* Jews opposed to the *heavenly* Jesus and his witnesses (cf. Psalm 2:6) align themselves with the enemies of Yahweh. Thus 'the peoples' of Psalm 2:1 (Acts 4:25) parallel 'the peoples of Israel' in 4:27, a unique pluralising within Acts. The original parallelism of Psalm 2:1 is shockingly preserved, this psalm of hope for Israel becoming 'a description of the opposition of many in the nation'.[120] God's exaltation of Jesus as his anointed, despite this opposition, has turned previous salvation geography upside down and inside out: firstspace is transformed. The believers see themselves as living within a reordered but enduring theological landscape, a thirdspace, aligned in a Christocentric fashion but facing opposition from relict, opposing geographies. If their wider prayer reflects Hezekiah's prayer in Isaiah 37:16–20 and 2 Kings 19:15–19,[121] then the Temple setting and the external threat of a pagan foe threatening to invade Jerusalem have been radically repositioned via Psalm 2. Rather than reflecting a persecuted community 'with its back against the wall ... [showing] little concern with making fine distinctions among who resist God's purpose in Christ',[122] they generate a dynamic worldview which is characteristic of Hebrew

---

[118] Lohfink 1999: 224–5, square-bracketed comments added.
[119] Haenchen (1971: 227) reads 'the gentiles' as Jesus' Roman executioners, and the tribes of Israel as 'the peoples'.
[120] Bock 1998: 56 n. 20.
[121] Barrett 1994: 245; Fitzmyer 1998: 306; Pao 2000: 211–12. The contrast of eschatological joy (Acts 3:8) and conflict (4:25–30) parallels the literary positioning of Isaiah 35 and 37:16–20, emphasising the need for heavenly intervention on the basis of prior promise and in response to faithful intercession within earthly trials.
[122] Spencer 1997: 53.

ethnography.[123] In this manner, 'the opponents of Jesus and the opponents of the church are viewed as one continuous group',[124] a connection which the wider narrative maintains in both explicit and more implicit ways (e.g. 9:4–5; 14:5).

Prayer facilitates the characterisation of God within the narrative by verbalising connectives between events on earth and the heavenly realm. Here, such characterisation contains another reference to οὐρανός (Acts 4:24). Once again, commentators frequently ignore or marginalise the reference, rendering it as 'a well-established liturgical form',[125] or part of a biblical *topos* communicating God as creator of all[126] and sovereign over all.[127] While partially true, these readings flatten off the specific heavenly spatiality woven through Acts and already apparent in Acts 4, now itself underpinned by God as creator. Read for its space, this is not merely 'a comforting thought for those persecuted by earthly rulers'.[128] Rather, God is portrayed as one who controls geography (4:28), with the irony of Jesus' rejection, heavenly exaltation and post-resurrection mandate functioning as the paradigmatic revelation and interpretation of this control. Like 2:19, the prayer assumes that God's 'hand' (4:30; cf. 4:28) will continue to bridge heavenly and earthly realities through 'signs and wonders'[129] within the spatial order governed by the name that the Sanhedrin has sought to forbid. This is a sustained narrative assumption: the Lord's 'hand' later leads people to faith (11:21) and also causes blindness as judgement (13:11). In 4:28 God's 'plan' (βουλή) reprises the reversal of space announced in 2:23, and later βουλή references carry territorial implications (5:38; 13:36; 20:27; also, ironically, cf. 27:12). Furthermore, the appeal to God as creator in 4:24 links Acts 4 into a much wider intertextual matrix of OT *spatiality* beyond simply that expounded in Psalm 2.[130]

The life-world of the Jerusalem believers

The subsequent filling with the Spirit and continuing bold proclamation answer the earlier prayer while also echoing Pentecost. The

[123] J. M. Scott 1995: 55.
[124] Tannehill 1990: 71 n. 26. 'Gathered together' (4:26) parallels 4:5 (cf. 4:31) and Luke 22:66.
[125] Bruce 1990: 156.   [126] L. T. Johnson 1992: 83.
[127] Fitzmyer 1998: 308.   [128] Barrett 1994: 244.
[129] Perhaps, as Barrett (1994: 249) suggests, healings are the primary expectation here. If so, then 5:15–16, as well as 4:31, 33, answers the prayer.
[130] E.g. Nehemiah 9:6, 34–5; Psalm 145:3–6 LXX (146:3–6) (cf. Acts 4:8, 12); Isaiah 42:5–6 (cf. Acts 4:27, 30; 13:47; 1:8).

shaking of 'the place' (ὁ τόπος) in 4:31 reiterates that the earth lies within God's territoriality despite concerted earthly opposition to his rule, confirming 4:24 despite 4:26. The earth as the landscape of witness projected by Jesus in 1:8 remains 'under heaven' (cf. 2:5). OT intimations of divine presence[131] and assent[132] confirm and enrich this reading. In sum this Pentecostal echo is not simply an isolated renewing of Spirit-inspired speech: rather, 4:30 casts 4:31 as reiterating the heavenly intervention within earthly geographies narrated in 2:2 and declared in 2:19a. This in turn evokes the heavenly Jesus (1:10–11), the broker of the Spirit (2:33). The Pentecostal echo sustains Christology as well as pneumatology, and, by sustaining proclamation (ἐλάλουν, 'they 'spoke', 4:31; cf. λαλεῖν, 'to speak', 4:29) 'with boldness', the Spirit upholds the spatial order of 1:6–11, in public, in Jerusalem.

That they continued speaking 'the word of God' (4:31) introduces at this crucial and informative juncture a term that will become the dominant leitmotif through Acts. This 'word' is no longer simply Jesus' teaching (Luke 5:1; 8:11, 21; 11:28); it is now the mobile divine word about Jesus and his global significance, transmitted by his followers. Their requested boldness to *continue speaking* this word (noting the present infinitive λαλεῖν, Acts 4:29) assumes a territory which conforms not only to Acts 1:8 but also to the cotext of Psalm 2:1–2, verse 8 of which proposes: 'Ask of me, and I will make the nations your heritage, and the ends of the earth [LXX τὰ πέρατα τῆς γῆς] your possession.' Thus this Lukan 'word of God' assumes a Christofocal territoriality which becomes increasingly clear and is sustained to the final verse of Acts. Such territoriality confirms earlier analysis (4:13, 19–20; also 5:29) that the witnesses function according to a spatiality outlined in embryo in 1:6–11.

Like the narrated summary confirming the space pronounced earlier at Pentecost (2:41–7), so 4:32–5 fleshes out the Spirit-filling in 4:31. It narrates Jesus' continuing thirdspace influence among 'the whole group' of 4:32, who constitute the repentant gathered from within Israel, yet still within Israel. The emphatic placement of 'one' (μία) at the end of 4:32a re-emphasises their unity. Contextually 4:32

---

[131] Rapske 1998: 251 n. 47.
[132] Bruce 1990: 159; Weaver 2004: 125–6. Rius-Camps and Read-Heimerdinger (2004: 279) suggest ὁ τόπος is the Temple and the shaking indicates divine displeasure: this reading requires greater foundation than the narrative obviously affords.

chimes with the spatiality of a Hellenistic friendship *topos*,[133] but cotextually it heralds Christocentric fulfilment of OT spatialities.[134] The description centres upon the apostles, with 'power' and 'witness' language in 4:33 evoking 1:8. This cotext suggests that the 'great grace' narrated in 4:33 indicates heavenly favour rather than simply popularity among the people. As such, believer-space mirrors Jesus' own earthly growth (Luke 2:40).

The example of Barnabas (Acts 4:36–7) illustrates this burgeoning geography on a number of levels. First, he is a Levite. This leads many commentators to discuss whether a Levite was, under OT stipulations, allowed to own land,[135] but such discussions miss the narratival emphasis on the land's sale rather than its ownership, and its sale specifically for the relief of others. The only other Levite mentioned in Luke-Acts, the one who passes by on the other side and ignores the visible need before him (Luke 10:32), provides a more apposite parabolic contrast. Here in Acts 4 a Levite takes concrete action to help others,[136] thus altering his own spatial status. This is especially pertinent if Barnabas' land was near Jerusalem, previously viewed as his token of inclusion in eschatological Israel.[137] If so, its sale and gifting represent more than a shift in Barnabas' spatial status *within* Israel. The redistribution symbolically affirms Barnabas entering into renewed Israel via another route not dependent upon physical land, that of the heavenly Jesus, mediated through his apostle-witnesses.[138]

Primarily, however, Acts presents Barnabas less as a Levite, and more as an exemplary member of this Jerusalem community. Others

[133] So L. T. Johnson 1992: 86. Cf. Haenchen 1971: 231, seeing Luke as fusing Septuagintal heritage with Greek emphases.

[134] Tannehill 1990: 47. Bruce (1990: 159) translates πλῆθος (4:32) as 'congregation', alluding to Exodus 12:6 and 2 Chronicles 31:18. In Exodus 12 LXX obedience to the conditions for the assembly defines those who are not to be 'cut off' from Israel (vv. 15, 19, ἐξολεθρευθήσεται; cf. Acts 3:23). In 2 Chronicles 31 the assembly refers to faithful priests and Levites, to whom the portion is distributed (v. 19: cf. Acts 4:36–7; 6:7).

[135] E.g. Bruce 1990: 160; Barrett 1994: 260 and Fitzmyer 1998: 322.

[136] Indeed, throughout Acts, Barnabas exercises the particularist, proximate care which O'Donovan (1989: 54) commends in the sense of 'place' demonstrated by 'the Merciful Samaritan'.

[137] As Lohfink (1999: 132) suggests. If Barnabas had acquired the land as a burial plot (as Barrett 1994: 260 suggests), its disposal would represent a richly symbolic (and, for those with vested interests in Israel-space, deeply provocative) response to the hope bound up with the heavenly Jesus.

[138] Thirdspatially, this befits a Levite whose share is in the Lord (Deuteronomy 12:12; 14:29; Joshua 14:3–4; 18:7), but Luke does not clearly indicate that the sale signifies repentant realignment towards an OT spatiality appropriate to a Levite. Also, Numbers 35:1–5 and Jeremiah 1:1; 32:7–9 allow some Levitical land ownership.

should share this same unburdened attitude towards the physical land of Israel, an attitude modelled later in the narrative in different ways by Stephen (7:2–60), Philip (8:5–40), the Ethiopian (8:39), and – eventually – by the Jerusalem believers themselves (11:18; 15:28–9). Similarly, if Barnabas' property was on Cyprus, then its sale relinquished a share in the land of his birth in order to embody his place in the community of believers, a spatial allegiance Luke would applaud more widely in his characters – and his auditors – both Jew and gentile alike. In this reading Barnabas functions as everyman, *homo geographicus*, living aright under the spatial priorities of the heavenly Christ. Even if specific mention of Barnabas' action indicates that such an act of selling and sharing was not universal, this does not detract from the narrative intention that the incident should shape auditors' attitudes to place and space. Yet the narrative also endows Barnabas with a distinctive personal spatiality[139] which informs his bridge-building appearances later in the narrative (9:27; 11:25; 13:1–15:39). The name given him by the apostles in 4:36 – he is the first named non-apostolic believer following the re-establishment of the twelve – is richly justified by his generous 'under heaven' spatial practice.

Barnabas' spatial practices contrast sharply with those demonstrated by Ananias and Sapphira in 5:1–10. They seek to obtain status within ἐκκλησία-space (by their visible show of generosity and sacrifice) while preserving wealth in another private space which remains isolated from the church and under their own control. Yet, rather than the pursuit of private space or their continued involvement in wider Israel-space,[140] their offence is *collusive deceit* against the theological integrity of ἐκκλησία-space (5:4), threatening to undermine the place and integrity of truth within the community.[141] This would discourage believer-space by undermining the legitimacy undergirding believer-space which 4:29–31 narrated as the word concerning the heavenly one.

On a number of levels their spatiality parallels that of Judas Iscariot.[142] The narrative's ideological point of view is clear that, like Judas, Ananias and Sapphira – although apparently within believer-space – operate within a different geography. In both instances, deceptive spatial collusion opposes the narrative's normative assumptions

---

[139] Haenchen 1971: 231: 'a concrete example of this spirit of sacrifice'.
[140] *Contra* Rius-Camps and Read-Heimerdinger 2004: 303, 311–14.
[141] Panier 1991: 120–1. [142] Rius-Camps and Read-Heimerdinger 2004: 311–14.

regarding discipleship through deviation motivated by Satanic influence on the heart and the hope of financial gain (Acts 5:2–4; cf. Luke 22:3–6). Consequently, their apparent gains become linked with sudden death (Acts 5:2; cf. 1:18), knowledge of which spreads within Jerusalem (5:11; cf. 1:19). Understood within a narrative-theological production of space, these connections are more convincing than seeing Ananias and Sapphira as 'opposite type cases from those of Stephen, Paul and Peter'.[143]

Acts 5:1–11 thus demonstrates how spatiality is more than simply setting: the narrative here paints minimal and inferential setting,[144] but spatiality infuses the account. Peter's response to Ananias and Sapphira fulfils (and anticipates) the judgement-space foretold by Jesus in Luke 22:30. Luke 22:31–2 – noting the distribution of plural (v. 31) and singular (v. 32) second-person pronouns – cast the whole incident within Jesus' intentions for earthly believer-space.[145] The post-ascension heavenly Christology established already within Acts precludes separating Jesus from the Holy Spirit (5:3) and God (5:4) as those against whom Ananias and Sapphira have sinned.

Certainly the offence is against heaven. In its use of the rare verb νοσφίζω in 5:2, 3, the incident reflects Joshua 7:1–26, but at a more fundamental level it also recalls Eden and the fall.[146] Both intertextual instances cast the offence as against God, as reflecting and generating sinful distortion of his ordering of lived space. Ultimately, two spatialities confront each other in Acts 5:1–10, as they do across Acts 2–5, one centred on the now heavenly Christ, the other oppositional, deceptive and earthbound.[147] That the deceptive laying at the apostles' feet in 5:2 generates Sapphira's decisive falling at Peter's feet in 5:10 leaves neither the church (5:11) nor auditors in any doubt as to which spatiality wins out, even though the need for spatial discernment remains within believer-spaces produced later in the narrative

---

[143] D. J. Davies 1995: 217. O. W. Allen (1995: 125) identifies some of these connections, and also establishes links with Herod's death in Acts 12. L. T. Johnson (1977: 192) sees here a fulfilment of 3:23.

[144] Spencer (1997: 41) makes an unsubstantiated connection with the setting of 1:13. While the *spatiality* is similar to that in 1:15–26, the text gives no reason to assume the same setting.

[145] *Contra* Haenchen 1971: 239, emphasis original: 'Peter *kills* her by announcing her husband's demise and her own imminent death.'

[146] Marguerat 2002: 172–6.

[147] Marguerat (2002: 158–78) provides a layered reading of 5:1–11 which is collective and ecclesiological rather than individualistic and soteriological. As such it fits well within a reading for spaces.

(e.g. 8:18–24). Rather than tolerating internal deceit, the narrative advocates a consistent moral-ethical ordering of space within the fellowship, thereby characterising what is meant by ἐκκλησία ('church') in Acts.

The word appears for the first time in 5:11,[148] 5:1–10 having charted the ἐκκλησία within all three Sojan categories. In their actions Ananias and Sapphira underestimated the community's third-spatial impetus, an omission underlining the vital importance the narrative places on correctly ascertaining the contours of heavenly thirdspace worked out on earth. As with Simon in Samaria (see Chapter 6), the narrative demands more than simply outward identi-fication with believer-space. It also demands a conviction of the 'heart' (5:3–4), which in Luke-Acts forms the foundational base for human identity, motivation and consequently also for human geog-raphies in all three Sojan aspects. The spatial struggles within human hearts parallel the battle for cosmic space between 'two world orders' in Luke's Gospel.[149]

The impact of believer-space upon Israel-space

Acts 5:12–16 expands and develops 5:11 by positioning the apostles at the centre of believer-space, within Temple-space (5:12–13), Jerusalem-space (5:15) and even within Judea-space (5:16; cf. 1:8). Unity within Temple-space, expressed spatially by ὁμοθυμαδόν ('all together', 5:12), recalls other such unified believer-spaces within Acts[150] but, unlike 4:32–7, the majority of this summary concerns external spatial relations. 'The rest' in 5:13 are best understood as Jerusalemites beyond believer-space, such that the statement 'none … dared to join them' indicates the absence of casual association with believer-space (especially after 5:1–11!), the apostles perceived as 'numinous figures … [who] both repel and attract'.[151] Their 'many signs and wonders' performed among the people (5:12; cf. 7:36) emphasise publicly the earth–heaven thirdspace nexus established in 1:6–11, evident in Acts 2–4 and respected after 5:1–11. Solomon's

---

[148] The inclusion of ἐκκλησία in 2:47 D is generally, and rightly, discounted as a scribal addition.

[149] Concerning which, see Moxnes 2001a: 205.

[150] Acts 1:14; 2:46; 4:24. These parallels suggest that the larger community of believers is in view here, not just the apostles (cf. Jervell 1998: 200–1, *contra* L. T. Johnson 1992: 95), albeit centred on them.

[151] L. T. Johnson 1992: 95.

Portico, within the Temple complex, houses a new, assertive and growing Temple-space,[152] entered only through being 'added to the Lord', but growing 'more than ever' (5:14; cf. 2:47, also 4:4). Allegiance to Jesus requires public spatial commitment alongside the apostles, joining their group being 'virtually equivalent to becoming a Christian'.[153] Their space is visibly distinctive firstspace, here enjoying secondspatial respect, dedicated to an absent, heavenly Lord.

Abruptly, perhaps, 5:15 introduces a notion of 'healing by sheer presence' which appears 'striking and perhaps even shocking'.[154] At the very least, judging its indefinite and implicit 'they' to indicate Jerusalem Jews beyond the believers,[155] 5:15 illustrates the popular acclaim lauded on the apostles at this narrative juncture. Such ascription to Peter alone, and the lack of explicit mention of healings by this means, might suggest a popular misconstruing of space, similar to the firstspace fixation repudiated by Peter in 3:12. More positively, however, Peter's shadow, as an extension of self connected with, but beyond, corporeal presence,[156] evokes popular responses to Jesus' ministry (Luke 6:17–19, esp. v. 19). Understood as an expansion of power beyond the individual, beyond simple presence, Acts 5:15 fits its narrative position between motifs of growth and popular acclaim, projecting Jesus-space as expanding onto the streets and, in 5:16, into Jerusalem's hinterland as both word and faith in that word strain the margins of the apostles' firstspace presence in an overflowing thirdspace impact upon the sick of the city and its surrounds. Other uses of the verb ἐπισκιάζω within Luke-Acts point to heavenly encounters,[157] suggesting that Peter's 'falling' shadow in 5:15, like the instrumental 'name' in Acts 3, reiterates ascension geography.

The narrative's first turn beyond Jerusalem into wider Judea, in 5:16, is centripetal rather than centrifugal and the development does not appear to be caused by the witnesses travelling beyond the city. In its narrative cotext, such regional influence implies the overwhelming growth of Jesus-space rather than any inherent importance of Jerusalem-space other than as the firstspace location of the

---

[152] Weaver 2004: 130–1 elucidates the power relations portrayed in 5:12–21, locating them within Jerusalem's spaces and territorialities.
[153] Barrett 1994: 274.   [154] L. T. Johnson 1992: 96.
[155] Haenchen 1971: 243; Barrett 1994: 276.
[156] The shadow 'reflects the shape of the person' (Fitzmyer 1998: 329).
[157] Within the NT, Luke 1:35; Luke 9:34 (par. Matthew 17:5; Mark 9:7) and here.

apostles.[158] Given such spectacular and extraordinary territorial success within and now beyond Jerusalem, it is unsurprising that jealousy will provoke further action against the apostles from the Temple authorities.

6.   Sanhedrin-space revisited (5:17–42)

The return to a Sanhedrin setting reinforces and develops previous estimations of their space through a repeating but escalating cycle of events (cf. 4:1–22). The apostles' insistent and repeated proclamation emphasises their grasp of ascension space. This builds narrative tension while painting narrative spatiality.

Whether from jealousy or, as is less likely, from zeal,[159] the Sanhedrin once again uses confinement to contain the expanding apostolic ministry (5:17–18).[160] This time the apostles *in toto* are imprisoned, publicly,[161] perhaps reflecting their now increased visibility as a distinct group.

Angelic release

The angelic release of the apostles from custody in 5:19–26 is an unprecedented spatial development which, nevertheless, conforms to the priorities and dynamics of ascension geography.[162] That their liberation – and the almost comedic events the next morning – constitute further answers to the prayer offered in 4:29 is confirmed by the accompanying command to continue proclaiming 'the whole message about this life' (πάντα τὰ ῥήματα τῆς ζωῆς ταύτης, 5:20), thereby proscribing verbal hesitation or deviation arising from either fear or tact. The angel's spatial power and will over mortal narrative opposition indicates that Jerusalem must not be without a witness. Jerusalem's inclusion within 1:8 and the Christocentric Psalm 2

---

[158] Cf. Cyril of Jerusalem's later chauvinistic insertion of 'to this holy Jerusalem' in 5:15 (Walker 1990: 338).

[159] Barrett (1994: 283) entertains the latter reading. Both the narrative's low estimations of the Sanhedrin's motivations and 13:45 suggest that the former reading is more likely.

[160] Skinner (2003: 91) argues that 5:18, like 12:4, demonstrates 'an attempt by authorities to separate an emissary of the Way from the public realm'.

[161] If δημοσίᾳ is understood adverbially, as it is in 16:37; 18:28; 20:20.

[162] Weaver 2004 locates this pericope within familiar cultural discourses used to legitimate new cults, acknowledging the spatial aspect of group formation and how this influences resultant texts.

landscape asserted in 4:24–30 will not be erased by local opposition.[163] Instead, the power relations assumed in 1:6–11 are strongly reasserted through a variety of settings such that 'Night or day, prison or temple make [*sic*] little difference: the work of the Sovereign Lord and his servants goes on, uninhibited by conventional maps and schedules'.[164] This assertion of heaven's intentions for human geographies, understood as bridging Sojan spatial dimensions, typifies supernatural angels throughout Luke-Acts.[165] Here, the angel emboldens by reinforcing thirdspace connectives both heavenwards (itself being characterised as 'of the Lord') and earthwards (by specifying Temple-space), in 'a reluctance to concede the temple to the mission's opponents'.[166]

The instruction to 'stand' recalls Peter's initial proclamation in 2:14, and the command to keep on speaking in the Temple to the people (λαλεῖτε ἐν τῷ ἱερῷ τῷ λαῷ) reprises 4:1, ignoring the Sanhedrin's intervention against the witnesses. Indeed, specifying this location appears guaranteed to maximise the Sanhedrin's anger and the consequent risk to the apostles. Yet at daybreak, at the first opportunity, the apostles obey the angel's command. Their collective locative stance in the Temple, regardless of the risk, also continues to answer the prayer in 4:29. Simultaneously, 5:21b–26 display – in contradistinction to the Lord and his anointed of Psalm 2 – 'the impotence of human authorities to control the course of events'[167] and their impotence to control space.

How, then, is the 'angel of the Lord' (ἄγγελος κυρίου) in 5:19 to be understood? Certainly the narrator can speak of an 'angel of God', as in 10:3, but here the description is more ambiguous. Although Conzelmann rejects any Christological connection, on the grounds that Luke 'never speaks of an angel of Christ',[168] this agency does carry Christological as well as theological import.[169] The *space* created by this angel's intervention, and the spatial practices commanded of the apostles, closely match Jesus' final instructions to these same witnesses in Acts 1:4a, 8. Further, while variously interpreted, 'this life' (5:20) is

[163] Weaver (2004: 101–2) also observes exodus connotations within Acts 5.
[164] Spencer 1997: 60.
[165] Luke 1:11, 13, 18–19, 26–38; 2:9–15, 21; 4:10 (cf. par. Matthew 4:6); 9:26 (Mark 8:38; cf. Matthew 16:27); Luke 12:8–9 (cf. Matthew 10:32–3); Luke 15:10; (16:22); 24:23 (cf. Matthew 28:2–7); Acts 6:15; 7:30, 35, 38, 53; 8:26; 10:3, 7, 22; 11:13; 12:7–11 (cf. v. 15!), 23; 23:8–9; 27:23–5.
[166] Tannehill 1990: 65.   [167] Tannehill 1990: 66.   [168] Conzelmann 1987: 41.
[169] Fletcher-Louis 1997: 51; Read-Heimerdinger 2002: 283.

understood Christologically,[170] indicating the spatiality spawned by Christ's earthly life and heavenly exaltation and now drawn by the unfolding narrative of Acts. As such, it suggests a Christological remit for the 'angel of the Lord', even allowing for a Lukan ambiguity within the title.[171]

Although focusing at length upon the subsequent proclamation and confrontation following their immediate rearrest, the narrative does pause to comment in 5:24 on the high priests being 'perplexed' concerning the apostles' 'escape'. All four occurrences of this verb within the NT demonstrate a struggle to come to terms with the Jesus event and its outworkings on earth.[172] Once the apostles are rearrested, the Sanhedrin's opening accusation (5:28) relates to their previous injunction (4:18), which has been roundly ignored in 4:23–5:16 and 5:19–25, the charge 'you have filled Jerusalem' reiterating 5:12–16 on the Sanhedrin's lips.

Apostolic response

The bold retort from 'Peter and the apostles' in 5:29 reflects the spatial framework already identified in Acts 2–5. Indeed, it elucidates the geographical nub of Acts 2–7 by confronting the question of what – and *where* – is the locus for producing and maintaining Sanhedrin-space and its Israel-space. The apostles' contrasting thirdspatial vision in 5:29–32 restates the crisis of territoriality and legitimacy which drives to the heart of the biblical imagination in a fashion which would inspire Rosa Parks and the American civil-rights movement many years later.[173] Just as 'patriarchs' in 2:29 and 7:8, 9 carries a territorial import, so in 5:30 'fathers' evokes the OT's historical geography and its resultant orderings of space. Here, however, after the spatial transposition narrated in 4:23 and articulated in 4:25–7, there is a strong ambiguity within the phrase 'the God of *our* Fathers' (5:30). Coming so soon after the contrasting allegiances laid out in

---

[170] 'The "life" and "salvation" brought by Jesus' (Haenchen 1971: 249); the new life offered by Jesus as 'the Author (ἀρχηγόν) of life' in 3:15 (Barrett 1994: 284); 'the message about an effect of the Christ event' (Fitzmyer 1998: 335). Cf. Weaver 2004: 112–14.

[171] Weaver (2004: 96–104) explores implicit theophany engendered by 'the liberating epiphanies of the ἄγγελος κυρίου' (p. 102), but does not examine the title's Christological ambiguity within Acts.

[172] Cf. Luke 9:7; Acts 2:12; 10:17. Weaver (2004: 115–16) analyses these Lukan uses, but within a theological framework lacking a Christological consideration.

[173] E.g. King 1999.

5:29, how inclusive is the possessive pronoun? It can be variously read as a claim to shared ancestry and heritage, anticipating the fulfilment of Jewish hopes, or as a claim for a contrasting and superior spiritual ancestry (anticipating the second-person rhetoric in 7:51–2) which excommunicates the Sanhedrin from Jewish hopes for having committed the most heinous misordering of space when they hanged the Messiah on a tree.

Perhaps both readings have their place,[174] suggesting that the proclamation maintains genuine connection with Jewish productions of space, even while spawning a new hybrid identity based upon the distinctive thirdspace engendered by Jesus being in heaven[175] *and* the claim to remain *within* Israel. Without this latter claim, there would be little or no conflict across Acts 4–7. If a choice must be made, then the inclusive inference within the term 'the God of our ancestors' in 22:14 favours the more inclusive reading of 5:30. Nevertheless, the surrounding cotext still casts a strong hint of judgement and separation if they refuse the repentance and forgiveness of sins offered to Israel (5:31; cf. 3:23). If it is refused, then by implication the Sanhedrin resists the Holy Spirit (5:32; cf. 7:51) and positions itself beyond the plan of God: *its* Israel-space, rather than being central to God's purposes, would have removed itself from the bounds of salvation geography. Its space, despite the apparent formal arrangements of power, is under scrutiny.

Gamaliel's spatial estimation

Gamaliel's speech (5:35–9) needs to be read within the cotext of this starkly provocative and potentially polarising presentation of space. His intervention temporarily arrests a spiralling acceleration in the Sanhedrin's aggression towards believer-space (cf. 4:17, 21; 5:33; 7:54).

Although sometimes interpreted as a positive figure within the narrative, Gamaliel does not satisfy the spatiality advocated by 1:6–11, and this is a serious shortcoming in his characterisation. Mere advocacy of non-interference is not the narrative's benchmark for response to the witnesses. Gamaliel does not become a follower of

---

[174] So Römer and Macchi 1995: 184–7.

[175] Acts 5:31 certainly projects Christ's heavenly exaltation; 'raised up' (ἤγειρεν, 5:30) could refer to his incarnation or resurrection, but both possible referents join at the ascension, its thirdspace being the overflowing sum of both these loci.

Jesus, nor does he urge repentance and faith in him. Instead, Gamaliel is 'one who can find in his way of thinking a way to cope' with the apostolic message.[176] Although he correctly recognises that popular support is a fickle thing, 'what is glaringly absent from Gamaliel's oration is any sign that he has taken seriously the apostles' witness that God raised Jesus from the dead (5:30–32)'.[177] His reply encapsulates the Sanhedrin's spatial resistance, which itself produces an anti-ascension space. Most seriously, his 'plan of action based on historical prudence ... advises a "wait and see" attitude' which masks 'an example of bad faith'.[178] Such an approach is illegitimate given the restructured geography already proclaimed in 3:23. From an auditor's point of view this is tragic irony, a verdict befitting the Sanhedrin as a collective spatiality within Luke-Acts.[179] Even Gamaliel's credentials, carefully elucidated in 5:34, serve only to highlight his incomprehension while reinforcing the impossibility of standing against the divinely sanctioned spatial restructuring that has been progressively revealed to auditors.

Yet Gamaliel does direct auditors of Acts back to the narrative and its spaces: '*Anyone who wants to discern the ways of God only has a narrative recounting the joys and more often the misfortunes of a group of believers. No other mirror is offered.* The reading of the narrative of Acts becomes ... the place to perceive the ways of God.'[180] The narrative *is* 'the place'; it provides more than temporal prediction and fulfilment; it also traces space through all three Sojan perspectives. The narrative 'assigns the reader the course of day-to-day history [and geography] as a place to discover and to celebrate the ways of God'.[181]

Thus Gamaliel's citations concerning Theudas and Judas the Galilean – as one who 'got people to follow (ἀπέστησεν) him' – misplace Jesus but ironically position him for auditors. For them, Theudas' egocentric claims form, at most, a secondary comparison with Peter's deflection of glory from himself (3:12–16). Jesus' death has *not* resulted in his followers scattering; far from it in Acts 2–7 and, as we shall observe, even less so after 8:1, 4. Such comparisons, available to auditors, highlight Gamaliel's ironic miscomprehension

---

[176] Fitzmyer 1998: 333.   [177] Darr 1992: 120.
[178] L. T. Johnson 1992: 103. Fitzmyer 1998: 333: 'There is no allusion to anything in the OT; historical examples replace that in this speech.'
[179] Darr 1998: 126.   [180] Marguerat 2002: 94, emphasis original.
[181] Marguerat 2002: 96, square-bracketed comments added.

of space.[182] His initial advice that the Sanhedrin 'keep away (ἀπόστητε) from these men' (5:38) finds an ironic counterpoint in 19:9 from one who, in 22:3, will be revealed as a student of Gamaliel.

That the Sanhedrin follows Gamaliel's advice despite the apostles' earlier declaration (5:29–30) deepens the irony: 'Gamaliel's superficially benign statement is in effect a self-condemnation. When they do not obey the prophet they are "fighting God".'[183]

In this way, irony bleeds into opposition. Even Gamaliel's words do not prevent the Jerusalem authorities increasing their persecution of the apostles: indeed, 5:39c intimates that the subsequent beating received by the apostles was part of Gamaliel's counsel. The narrated restatement in 5:40 of the earlier charge in 4:17 not to speak in the name of Jesus allows auditors no doubt as to what or, rather, who is at stake. Acts 5:41–2 reinforces this Christological landscape informing the controversy, both through the apostles accepting willingly this name and its continued proclamation, and through the alternative honour geography within which they interpret their circumstances. This oxymoronic Christocentric spatiality is now firmly established within Acts.[184] It not only reiterates the heavenward perspective for interpreting earthly events advocated by Jesus in Luke 6:22–3 as based in the prophets' experience; it also reflects the specific ascension ordering of space established in Acts 1:6–11.

7.   Ἐκκλησία-space revisited (5:42–6:7)

Although commentators divide as to whether 6:1–7 fits better with the material preceding or following it, the spatial issues raised by 6:1–7 align it better with the preceding section while acknowledging its introduction of major figures within the spatiality of Acts.[185]

---

[182]   The numbers of followers of Jesus (e.g. 4:4) far exceed those claimed for Theudas (5:36); the only other 'census' in Luke-Acts (cf. 5:37) dates Jesus' birth (Luke 2:2); Judas 'the Galilean' (Acts 5:37) contrasts with Jesus the Galilean and his Galilean followers (cf. 1:11; 2:7; 9:31).

[183]   L. T. Johnson 1992: 101; similarly Darr 1998. Cf. Weaver 2004: 132–44, regarding the mythic functions of 'the God-fighter'.

[184]   Weaver (2004: 146–7) acknowledges the reflexive links joining status and territoriality in 5:41–2 and 6:7, concluding that – within a non-triumphalist acknowledgement of continuing persecution – 'the opening of the prison is a spatial synecdoche for the opening of the city to the god's cult … so that a cult may occupy a *polis*' (p. 287).

[185]   Cf. Longenecker 2004; Yamasaki 2007: 164.

The geography of widows and of apostolic ministry

After reporting that the disciples were 'increasing in number', 6:1 introduces two groups within the nascent church without any explicit explanation.[186] 'Hellenists' and 'Hebrews' are distinguished simply by grumbling about a food distribution involving their widows. The balance of scholarly opinion distinguishes them on linguistic grounds, with liturgical and possibly doctrinal differences arising from membership of different synagogues within Jerusalem.[187]

If 6:9 provides some indirect internal narrative support for such historical reconstructions of ethnic synagogues within Jerusalem, then the problem in 6:1 arises from different firstspaces within believer-space. Different (ethnic) synagogues within Jerusalem suggest significantly different spatial patterns and relations, especially if, as Brad Blue suggests concerning Diaspora situations, 'the Jewish community ... would have spent most of the Sabbath in the precincts of the synagogue'.[188] Alternatively, Reta Finger has argued that the daily distribution concerned the whole community and that the widows were working together in the provision of these meals, suggesting that the tensions are indicative of 'when meals with deep symbolic meaning are eaten across class and ethnic boundaries – and when such women working and eating together have different ethnic customs surrounding meal preparation and organization'.[189] Under either reading, real or imagined spatial differences in Acts 6, based upon, and causing, internal distractions and divisions, present new risks to a unity premised upon 1:6–11 and expressed in 2:42, 46; some time after the descent from heaven of cosmopolitan linguistic proclamation at Pentecost, the resultant growth is bringing earthly cosmopolitan strain and dissent.

Far from being a minor or necessary hiccup in the course of church growth, 'against the backdrop of prior biblical and Lukan traditions, neglecting widows is a very serious offence'.[190] Marginalising the service of some widows, to pursue Finger's reading,[191] would be equally grievous. Either scenario risks derailing the narrative's unfolding spatiality in that the veracity of its implicit claim that the

---

[186] Other than, as Penner (2004: 277–80) notes, the (secondspatial) framework provided by 2:5–11, 36.

[187] Witherington (1998: 240–7) provides an overview on these matters.

[188] Blue 1998: 478. Pages 475–9 outline Blue's basis for such a claim, including archaeological evidence from Jerusalem (p. 479).

[189] Finger 2007: 275.   [190] Spencer 1997: 65.   [191] Finger 2007: 254–64.

community's spatial practices, oriented around the heavenly Christ, fulfil OT spatial requirements, and promises would be seriously impugned by such neglect (2:44–5; 4:34–7). Indeed, the promise of covenant-space being where there are 'no poor among you' (Deuteronomy 15:4) presumes obedience to God's command which, in the cotext of Deuteronomy 15:1–18, requires the sharing of possessions, but here in Acts 6 this project appears to be under strain.

A reading for space suggests that the apostles have a place-specific role to fulfil, a specific ministry concerning 'the word of God' (6:2) and devotion 'to prayer and to serving (τῇ διακονίᾳ) the word' (6:4). This latter verse recalls 4:31, where 'prayer' and 'the word' underlined the spatial practices of believer-space.[192] Narrating them as 'the twelve' in 6:2 collects the apostles' earlier specific function *within* the community's practices, their word ministry generating secondspatial 'signs and significations, codes and knowledge, that allow such material practices to be talked about and understood'.[193] The other nearest evidence of specifically *apostolic* prayers has been Peter and John attending prayers in the Temple (3:1).[194] Perhaps prayer is also implicit within the temple gatherings of 5:12. Certainly the Temple has been emphasised as the venue for apostolic proclamation, suggesting that the apostles have both a space-defining and a place-specific ministry within Jerusalem.

This apostolic ministry would be neglected if the apostles were to continue 'to wait at tables' (διακονεῖν τραπέζαις, 6:2). 'Tables' constitute another setting, another space within the growing church, and an 'additional'[195] responsibility for them.

Under this reading Spencer's interpretation of the apostles' response is unnecessarily negative. Rather than communicating apostolic 'reluctance to become personally involved',[196] Acts 6:1–6

---

[192] Cf. Bruce 1990: 183, and also Barrett 1994: 313 for Gerardsson's suggestive hypothesis concerning an apostolic *teaching* ministry.

[193] Harvey (1990: 218–19) describing 'representations of space', his terminology for secondspace.

[194] While it is 'unlikely' that προσευχή indicates 'a place of prayer in which the apostles were constantly to be found' (Barrett 1994: 313), 'prayer' is still a *placed* activity. The apostolic specificity within 6:4 renders it unconvincing that 'the church's regular worship is meant' (Bruce 1990: 183), or that 'prayer was regarded by Christians ... as a meritous work of piety' (Haenchen 1971: 263).

[195] Soards 1994: 56.

[196] Spencer 1997: 67. Spencer (1997: 66) judges that 6:4 marks 'a retreat from the apostles' recent blend of institutional and charitable services (including "breaking of bread") to the needy in Acts (2:42–6; 4:32–7) and reversion back to old habits of resisting Jesus' comprehensive ministerial program'.

recognises the specificity and limitations of the twelve at the point where the sustained narrative focus moves away from them. Although Finger shares something of Spencer's criticism of the twelve in 6:2, her public/private distinction concerning table setting and ministry of the word highlights the increasing spatial problematic within this pericope concerning community growth.[197] Acts 6:1–6 does not reflect necessarily 'the Twelve's somewhat imbalanced view of ministry' or that 'they still have not fully accepted Jesus' holistic model of ministry'.[198] Rather than some lesser role, the language describing the seven's appointment (καταστήσομεν) in 6:3 echoes the status and eschatological responsibility of the faithful household manager, an exemplar for believer-spaces commended by Jesus in Luke 12:42–4. The daily distribution is a διακονία, the same description applied to the apostles' specific role in Acts 1:17, 25; 6:4.[199]

In summary, the primary focus of 6:1–6 concerns the integrity of believer-space in Jerusalem as fulfilling OT spatialities, and the preservation of distinctive apostolic ministry within the city. Within it, the firstspace, secondspace and thirdspace of ascension geography articulated across Acts 2–5 are sustained and reinforced.

The geography of adhering priests and the growing word

Acts 6:7 summarises and concludes the spatial development across 2:1–6:7. First, 'the word of God continued to spread (ηὔξανεν)'. Given 5:16, and if Isaiah 2:3 is here in view,[200] then this growth is beginning to strain the bounds of the city. The narrative has presented this sustained community growth within Jerusalem (2:41, 47; 4:4; 5:14; 6:7) as dependent upon heavenly thirdspace, not upon the city *per se*. This thirdspace is tangible and visible in that the statement that 'the number of the disciples increased greatly in Jerusalem' provides parallel narration of the same growth. Just as the presence of the witnesses embodies the otherwise unseen word, so too do the growing numbers around them – believer-space (re)produced by that word[201] – with a strengthening hold on the production of space within Jerusalem.

---

[197] Finger 2007: 266.   [198] Spencer 1997: 66, 67.
[199] Tellingly, feminist scholars (e.g. O'Day 1992: 310; Martin 1995: 797) question why Tabitha's service (9:36) is *not* so described, suggesting that these male 'ministries' which share the status of διακονία (6:1, 4) also share patriarchal legitimacy.
[200] L. T. Johnson 1992: 107.
[201] 'The church is *creatura verbi*', Barrett 1994: 316; cf. Kodell 1974, Panier 1991 and Marguerat 2002: 37.

Second, such a dynamic understanding of space also helps interpret the priestly adherents to the faith narrated in 6:7. F. F. Bruce over-simplifies this dynamic when suggesting that such priestly adherents 'would strengthen the ties which bound a large proportion of the believers to the temple order'.[202] Admittedly spatial transformation according to the heavenly Christ can be resisted, even within believer-space, as is evident in 5:1–11 and 11:2, but the example of Barnabas the Levite has demonstrated that Acts advocates a more profound spatial reordering whereby, instead, believers in Acts are 'bound' to *apostolic* 'order' and, through it, to *heavenly* thirdspace. The narrative stresses thirdspace freedom from opposing human author-ities (4:19–20; 5:29, 32), allowing 6:7 to assume a significant spatial realignment of 'obedience' (ὑπήκουον) for these priests such that Luke 22:30 receives another anticipatory confirmation.[203] Acts does not intimate that priestly adherents alter the community's struc-ture;[204] rather, auditors are intended to be impressed by growth of the word of God within the narrative world, now even *within* Temple-space (assuming that these priests are based in Jerusalem).[205] They are evidence of the word triumphing within Temple-space, despite perse-cution from that sphere. Gaventa is right to see 6:7b as 'astonishing' but also as indicating that 'the gospel has now extended in a danger-ous direction'.[206] The spatial escalation across 2:1–6:7 ends with a powder-keg waiting to explode. Luke's exposition of space is far from over.

8.   Conclusion

This chapter has shown how ascension *geography* maps Tannehill's 'echo effect' within Acts 2:1–6:7 and shapes the contours of what Lohfink has termed the church's 'Jerusalem springtime' within these

---

[202] Bruce 1990: 185. Cf. Penner (2004: 281–6), who rightly highlights the internal breadth and interconnected expansion of the community, now including both priests and proselytes (cf. 2:5; 6:5), at its time (and place!) of origin.

[203] Notwithstanding that Luke 1:5–25, 57–80 provides an archetype faithful priest.

[204] Conzelmann (1987: 46) also makes this point, in contrast to the influence of priests within the Qumran community.

[205] Jeremias (1969: 203–6) estimates that there were 18,000 priests and Levites at the time. Although priests were 'obliged to follow a trade during the ten or eleven months in which their service of the Temple left them free to do so' (Haenchen 1971: 264; e.g. Luke 1:8b), those in Acts 6:7 are characterised as 'priests' and as within Jerusalem, their identity thus being bound to the Temple. At the same time, there is no reason to equate these priests with those in 4:1 (cf. Barrett 1994: 218).

[206] Gaventa 2003a: 116.

chapters through both its intimation of broader horizons and its insti-
gation of conflict within Jerusalem.[207] The crisis within Jerusalem
engendered by Jesus' new status and position which the witnesses in
Acts 2–5 'interpret and provoke'[208] cannot be properly understood
without reference to earthly space being ordered by the heavenly
Christ. Although pneumatological and ecclesial, this geography cannot
be reduced to the Spirit (or the church) 'replacing' Jesus on earth.

Acts 2:1–6:7 narrates the heavenly Jesus beginning to deploy his
apostolic and Spirit-empowered witnesses within productions of
earthly space. Ascension geography has been seen to rework various
OT spatialities. Within the Jerusalem setting, this ordering of space
addressed Israel (defined broadly, across the Diaspora), the people,
the Temple, and the Sanhedrin, as well as the believing community
itself. A latent more universal spatial projection exists (e.g. 2:39;
3:25), but 2:1–6:7 confirms Lohfink's foundation premise for a biblical theology of the church: 'God does not act anywhere and everywhere, but in a concrete place', at the time and through the people of
his choosing.[209]

This chapter has upheld the study's central premise that 1:6–11
provides an overarching ordering of space(s) within the narrative.
Yet, like recent geographical theorising, its spatial reading of 2:1–6:7
identifies 'tangled arrangements of power' which throw up 'surprising
juxtapositions' and 'no simple proximities'.[210] Importantly, this spatial reading of 2:1–6:7 has readily highlighted Jesus' active 'presence
in absence'[211] within the narrative's economy of space, confirming
Jesus' absence from earth without rendering him passive within the
present age. This ordering of space justifies seeing Jesus as a rounded
character within Acts, and demonstrates the need to spatialise and
'Christologise' discussions of 'God's superintendence of history'.[212]
Often 'wonder' (θαυμάζω) forms the appropriate initial narrative
response to ascension geography as its alignments overwhelm previous expectations of the ordering of space (2:7; 3:12; 4:13; cf. also
2:12; 3:10).

The chapter has confirmed a critical geography operating within
the narrative world, critiquing other geographies and unsettling their

---

[207] Cf. Tannehill 1984; 1990: 49–51 and Lohfink 1975: 55 regarding the 'Jerusalemer
Frühling'.

[208] Tannehill 1990: 33.   [209] Lohfink 1999: viii.   [210] J. Allen 2003: 193.

[211] The phrase is from O'Donovan 1996: 145.

[212] Cf., e.g., C. H. Cosgrove 1984, Squires 1993.

spatial arrangements. The 'restoration' of 'Israel' reworked under a Christological heaven repositions all other spaces, all other geographies. This also impacts auditors' worlds. To spatialise Lohfink:

> Apparently it makes people uncomfortable to have God [/Jesus] appear so concretely in their lives. It puts all their desires and favourite ideas in danger, and their ideas about time [and space] as well. It cannot be today [or here], because in that case we would have to change our lives [here] today. So we prefer to delay God's salvation to some future time [and/or to some distant or generalised place]. There it can rest, securely packed, hygienic, and harmless.[213]

Within the narrative, characters attempt to distance Jesus by not naming him (4:17; 5:28) and by generalising him or rendering him relative by comparison with momentary and failed geographies (5:35–9), but the narrative insists that Jesus' specific earth–heaven spatiality continues to confront and to triumph, even in the face of persecution, and that it does so publicly and in close proximity to those resisting its claims.

Just as new regimes characteristically build new landscapes,[214] so the ascension order (re)constructs new spaces within Acts. Jerusalem placing Jesus upon the tree and God then raising him to the right hand produced a crisis of space which, in narrative terms, given God's mercy in offering repentance and forgiveness of sins (signified by Jesus' earthly absence), is still being resolved. Escape from this crisis requires comprehensive reordering of spatial categories. Thus, rather than reducing to positivistic place-markers, this chapter has identified how 'social place, when it is contested within the orbit of a given social formulation, can begin to take on new definitions and meanings'.[215]

The product in 2:1–6:7 is a hybrid spatiality within Jerusalem. 'Hybrid cultures are much more than syncretism, they are not mixtures from two or more sources, but a creation of something new out of difference ... Hybridity should mean no more than that the various ways of being and thinking are continuous, recognizing that segmentation is contingent and that ruptures are willed.'[216] Thus in 2:1–6:7 a new space has been produced within Jerusalem, one which accords with Soja's definition of thirdspace as 'simultaneously

---

[213] Lohfink 1999: 136, square-bracketed comments added.
[214] Harvey 1996: 230–1.   [215] Harvey 1996: 231.
[216] Shurmer-Smith and Hannam 1994: 139.

real and imagined and more',[217] since it depends upon the heavenly Christ, an absent yet formative agent, and generates the possibility of spatial transformation according to his spatial agenda.

Two polar alternatives have previously failed to understand this space. Its identity is not subordinate to the dominant 'Other' of existing Israel-space, slavishly reproducing or opposing its past assumptions concerning space, since 1:6–11 has been shown to reposition these assumptions radically. Failure to recognise this radical change remains the major criticism of Jerusalem-centred readings of Acts: they are insufficiently sensitive to the dynamics of ascension-space. Nor is the new reality an aspatial spiritual evacuation of earthly Jerusalem, as might be suggested by Bruce's comment that 'hope of an earthly and national kingdom (cf. Mark 10:35–7; Luke 1:68–75) was recast after Pentecost as the proclamation of the spiritual kingdom of God'.[218] Place and space, although relativised by the ascension, still very much matter in this new order. Acts 2:1–6:7 presents a radical and relativising development, but specifically in Jerusalem, in the same place still occupied by a 'corrupt generation'. Earthly spaces have been 'placed' differently – reread, rewritten, realigned – in the wake of Christ's ascension, whether 'home' spaces such as Israel, 'sacred' spaces such as the Temple, or 'authoritative' spaces such as the Sanhedrin. Redefining spaces in this way has raised questions which will carry through into subsequent chapters and, ultimately, to Acts 28 and beyond.

Instead of these two polar alternatives, the believers in 2:1–6:7 find themselves, to use the categories of 'subaltern geographies', 'in ambiguous spaces, zones of transition, not just in the usual geographical sense but also in the presentation of symbolic transitions between the pure and the impure, the safe and the dangerous, the known and the unknown'.[219] Within Jerusalem, this hybrid spatiality bridges shared firstspace, ambiguous secondspace wherein more universal projections (2:39; 3:25) as yet lack the movement beyond Jerusalem projected in 1:8,[220] and divergent thirdspace.

The fulcrum of this geography is its thirdspace, which is dependent upon Christ being in heaven. This chapter has illustrated how, in the thirdspaces of post-ascension Jerusalem, 'new things happen and this

---

[217] Soja 1996: 11.   [218] Bruce 1990: 102, regarding 1:6.

[219] Shurmer-Smith and Hannam 1994: 138.

[220] This localism at this juncture limits narrative exposition of the systematic verdict that 'Jesus ascended to the Father's right hand in the sense that the whole of creation is reorganised around him' (Farrow 1999: 264).

disrupts old and dominant ways of thinking and doing', such that it is necessary 'to reconceptualize ways of thinking about space in order to remake understandings of the world'.[221] This conception of *thirdspace* helps preserve what Farrow considers to be a proper discontinuity between Jesus history and common history from the 'substitution of our own story (the story of man's [*sic*] self-elevation) as the real kernel of salvation history [and geography] in the present age [and places]'.[222] The present reading of 2:1–6:7 shows that history alone should not defend this discontinuity: it can and must also be traced in space.

Acts 2:1–6:7 suggests that the ascension's spatial challenge will eventually produce schism within Jerusalem. The reference to Christ's enemies yet to be made his footstool (2:35) is fleshed out by real characters with real spatialities within the unfolding narrative, within Jerusalem-space. Old spatialities are not immediately wiped out, but continue to exert power over the production of space. They lay claim to the same spaces (e.g. 5:12). Through 2:1–6:7 conflict has escalated; it will increase further in the next section of the narrative.

---

[221] Rose 2000: 827.   [222] Farrow 1999: 29, square-bracketed comments added.

5

ACTS 6:8-8:3

1.   Introduction

A spatialised reading of Acts 6–7

Whereas the previous chapter explored the narration of ascension geography through a variety of different settings and spatialities within Jerusalem, this chapter propounds such a geography around one character within Jerusalem, and one who is often interpreted in historicist terms.

The Jerusalem section of Acts concludes with a lengthy account of Stephen's ministry and martyrdom (6:8–7:60). The account is dominated by Stephen's speech in Acts 7, the sheer length of which indicates its importance within Acts. The speech is typically presented as historical in its orientation. Thus Soards states, without needing to justify it further, that it is 'the most prominent example of the use of the past in an address in the form of explicit citations of scripture',[1] and Gaventa is typical when summarising Acts 7 as 'Stephen's rendition of Israel's history'.[2] This historical reading also extends to authorial intent,[3] and to the speech's theology, which is itself often cast in historical terms, most usually in connection with a Deuteronomistic view of history.[4] Alternatively, the history has been viewed negatively, as purposeless for its theology[5] or as unsympathetically characterising Stephen.[6]

---

[1] Soards 1994: 60.
[2] Gaventa 2003a: 117. See also Bruce 1990: 192; L. T. Johnson 1992: 135; Barrett 1994: 337; Sennett 1994: 130; Arnold 1996; Bock 1998: 61; Neudorfer 1998: 283–4 and Marguerat 2002: 239. Although Spencer 1997: 71 describes 7:2–8 as a 'tutorial in historical geography', p. 70 describes Acts 7 globally as 'a selective and interpretive recital of key stages in Israel's biblical history'.
[3] E.g. Richard 1978: 238.   [4] E.g. Römer and Macchi 1995: 182–4.
[5] Haenchen (1971: 288) judges 7:2–8 as 'simply sacred history told for its own sake and with no other theme'.
[6] For instance, Bernard Shaw's verdict on Stephen as 'a quite intolerable young speaker', 'a tactless and conceited bore' who 'inflicted on them [the Sanhedrin] a tedious sketch of the history of Israel, with which they were presumably as well acquainted as he' (Shaw 1988: 81).

The previous chapters of this study justify asking whether these readings mask the passage's spatiality such that they could be termed historicist, according to Soja's critique of that term. This is not to deny the historical dimension which is certainly present in Stephen's address,[7] but rather to ask whether *heilsgeschichtlich* summaries[8] need to allow more room for the spatial, especially when Acts 6–7 is considered within Sojan categories and in light of Christ's ascension. This chapter looks to move beyond Tannehill's recognition that 'a leisurely summary of the story of Israel, material with which Stephen's audience would be well acquainted and quite irrelevant to the issues of the moment,' forms 'a shared history and a shared set of values … [which] contributes to the power of the speech'.[9] A spatialised reading, seeking more than mere rhetorical realignment, takes further Tannehill's suggestion that 'perhaps we need to broaden our understanding of Stephen's approach to his subject'.[10]

This chapter shows that Sojan categories, especially thirdspace, are the key to opening up a spatial reading of Acts 7. It indicates that, more than simply *containing* firstspace locational markers, the speech actively *produces* space. This will confirm the study's wider thesis by demonstrating that Christological and heavenly thirdspace is central to the production of space in Acts 7, especially if 7:56 is the true climax of the address which guides understanding of the speech as a whole. It is widely acknowledged that Stephen's address emphasises God's dealings with Israel away from the Temple;[11] 7:56 forms another – and crowning – locale for this motif, one which governs other spaces both within the speech and for its hearers/auditors. Reading Stephen's speech for this geography moves his selective inclusion and interpretation of events beyond a merely familiar history. Positioned within Sojan categories, this is more telling than simply perceiving Luke-Acts as legitimising the early Christian mission without geographical restrictions.

This chapter therefore continues an innovative reading of Acts, looking for its spaces. While acknowledging that this reading remains complementary to a historical reading rather than replacing it, the chapter argues that it casts new light on this important section of Acts.

---

[7] For instance, L. T. Johnson (1992: 124) emphasises the speech's concern for dating the events it describes.

[8] So Conzelmann 1987: 51, describing 7:2–7. Haenchen (1971: 289) sees 7:2–50 as an earlier 'history sermon' utilised by Luke.

[9] Tannehill 1990: 87, 88.   [10] Tannehill 1990: 88.

[11] Sterling (1999: 213 n. 56) rehearses the scholars recognising this point.

Delimiting Stephen's speech

The delimitation of Stephen's 'speech' to 7:2–53 is so universal as to be frequently assumed rather than argued,[12] but this logic needs revisiting as possibly reflecting a historicist reading progressing from 'then' to 'now'. Instead, this chapter proposes that the speech's concluding climax comes in 7:56. The conventional delimitation requires (or assumes) that 7:54 decisively isolates 7:56 from the main body of the speech. Confident assertions of this argument[13] ignore counterinstances within Acts (2:37; 26:24, 28), yet few, if any, commentators would treat (e.g.) 2:38–40 as anything other than an integral part, if not the climax, of the Pentecost address, as told in Acts 2.[14] Also, although Stephen did not 'look'[15] and 'see' until 7:55 (and without these actions he would not have uttered 7:56), the causal participle ὑπάρχων in 7:55 qualified by 'filled with the Holy Spirit' (which matches Stephen's previous characterisation in 6:5, 8, 10), and the combination of present participle[16] and inceptive imperfect verbs in 7:54, reduce any potential for reading 7:56 as separate from 7:2–53. Neither can 7:56 be spirited away as part of 'an epilogue to the main address in the three statements in vv. 54–60'.[17] The latter two statements, 7:59 and 7:60, are formally different from Stephen's address, being prayers addressed in the vocative, 'Lord' (κύριε), rather than proclamation beginning 'Look …' (ἰδού). Since 7:56 does indeed supply 'important information otherwise absent from the speech',[18] it should not be marooned within a separate 'section', frequently labelled in non-verbal terms describing narrative action, such as 'Stephen's Martyrdom'.[19]

Stephen's speech therefore runs until, and reaches its climax in, 7:56. There, this richly geographical speech reveals a final place, its climactic locale. The implications of this broader delimitation will become apparent below.

---

[12] See virtually any commentator. Even Tannehill (1990: 85) describes 7:53 as 'the speech's final verse'. Hamm (2003: 229) is a rare exception.
[13] E.g. Haenchen 1971: 286.
[14] Haenchen 1971: 176–89 – cf. above – delimits 'Peter's Speech at Pentecost' as 2:14–41.
[15] Cf. the same verb in 6:15; 1:10.
[16] Although an aorist participle ἀκούσαντες in D.
[17] Soards 1994: 60.   [18] Soards 1994: 69.
[19] Barrett 1994: 379–88, labelling 7:54–8:1a, having entitled 7:1–53 'Stephen's Speech' (Barrett 1994: 331–78). Bruce (1990: 209–11) at least isolates 7:54–6 as 'Stephen's Final Witness'.

2.   Positioning Stephen's speech (6:8–7:1)

Acts 6:8–7:1 resumes the motif of the increasing word of God (6:7). Stephen, one of seven recognised as being of good repute and full of the Spirit and wisdom and faith (6:3, 5), now *speaks* with irrefutable wisdom and Spirit (6:10), a characterisation which will dominate his remaining narrative contribution. Those (fellow?) synagogue members who argue with him cannot refute him (6:9–10), and instead stir up 'the people as well as the elders and the scribes' (6:12).

Such synagogue opposition inherently reflects a different ordering of space. First-century synagogues were *places*, inherently spatial, both reflecting and forming particular orderings of space within their locale.[20] Thus, while labelled 'false' by the narrator (6:13), the accusations made against Stephen arise from within a particular configuration of space. Furthermore, their accusations concern the way in which Stephen's teaching configures space, implicitly in 6:11 ('against Moses and God'), and explicitly in 6:13, 14 ('this holy place and the law'). By being 'accused of attacking the foundations of Jewish life',[21] Stephen is being charged with standing over and against the conventional or dominant Jewish ordering of space around the Temple.[22]

The charges' narrative position, so soon after mention of priestly adherents (6:7), suggests a deepening crisis for Temple-space. This reading undercuts Johnson's surprise – 'a strange sequence!'[23] – concerning 'against Moses and God' in 6:11. Although these specific charges have not previously been brought against the apostles, the resonance of spatial challenge is not new within Acts. As noted earlier regarding 2:22, mention of 'Nazareth' in 6:14 evokes the programmatic conflict of Luke 4:16–30 for auditors cognisant with Luke's Gospel. Similarly the Sanhedrin setting resumed in Acts 6:12 brings a now familiar chill of danger for believers. Here, however, for the first time in Acts, 'the people' are also hostile to the word, intensifying previous spatial struggles within Acts.

---

[20] Cf. Witherington 1998: 255–7; Hengel 1983: 54–62.   [21] Tannehill 1990: 85.

[22] The meaning of 'this place' in 21:28 confirms reading 6:13–14 as referring to Temple-space rather than synagogue-space *per se*. As Fay (2006: 268) notes, there is a patterned synonymity of Temple and Jerusalem through the opening chapters of Acts. This can be acknowledged without accepting Fay's conclusion that the Temple forms 'the narrative center of Luke-Acts' (p. 269).

[23] L. T. Johnson 1992: 109.

Stephen's characterisation builds upon earlier spatial markers in Acts and anticipates the spatiality which develops across Acts 7. First, Stephen performs 'great wonders and signs among the people [of Jerusalem]'[24] (6:8), the couplet evoking the heaven–earth axis of 2:19 already seen in Jesus' earthly ministry (2:22) and that of the apostles (2:43). In an important narrative broadening, what was sought in prayer for the twelve in 4:30 as tokens of heavenly support are here evident through Stephen. In due course Stephen will claim for Moses this 'wonders and signs' spatiality (7:36), thereby lengthening further narrative connectives which serve spatial as well as historical ends. Since Moses' 'wonders and signs', combined with 'living oracles', simultaneously expressed and shaped the abiding lived space of the Jewish people 'in Egypt, at the Red Sea, and in the wilderness' (7:36, 38),[25] Stephen's ministry claims a similar formative role in Acts.

Second, Stephen is characterised as being 'full of grace and power' (6:8). Via 4:33, this description evokes Jesus' command-promise of 1:8 with its expansive spatial projection. Such an evocation of 1:8 is reinforced by reference to 'the Spirit with which he spoke' (6:10). It is these words, rather than Stephen's miracles, which provoke opposition. The irrefutability of Stephen's teaching in 6:10 also fulfils Luke 21:15 (cf. Acts 4:14 for its fulfilment among the apostles themselves). Unlike its synoptic parallels,[26] Luke 21:15 locates this invincibility as coming directly from (the now ascended) Jesus.

Third, Stephen is characterised by 'wisdom', a further connection with Luke 21:15. Occurring only four times in Acts, and only within Acts 6–7,[27] this description, and the parallel connections established by the verb to 'appoint' or 'make' (καθίστημι) in 6:3; 7:10, 27 and 35, link Stephen with Joseph and Moses, just as Third-Gospel characterisation of Jesus' 'wisdom' connects Stephen with Jesus. In sum, these connectives foreground Stephen's words which will, in Acts 7, interpret reliably the biblical story. If, as this chapter argues, that story is inherently spatial as well as historical, then Stephen's interpretative

---

[24] Chapter 3's 'hybrid' reading prompts cautious agreement with Barrett's restricted conclusion that 'there was at this stage *and in this respect* no difference between the Jerusalem crowd and the ancient people of God' (Barrett 1994: 322, emphasis added).

[25] Acts 7:36 demonstrates 'God's dynamic guidance of his pilgrim people through hostile foreign territory and chaotic-liminal realms of sea and desert' (Spencer 1997: 76).

[26] Matthew 24:20; Mark 13:11.   [27] Acts 6:3, 10; 7:10, 22.

wisdom is also geographical; his presentation of space as well as of time is intended to guide the auditors of Acts. While Haenchen correctly surmises that in 6:10 wisdom indicates 'religious wisdom and the capacity to express it persuasively',[28] this should not become an aspatial reduction. Joseph's God-given wisdom led directly to his assumption of territorial control within Egypt; Moses' wisdom (7:22) also informed territorial change; now mention of Stephen's wisdom brings similar spatial expectation in Acts 7.

Stephen's face being 'like the face of an angel' (6:15) draws these three elements together. This facial transformation contributes to the overall rhetorical effect of the speech that follows, not least given that angels within Luke-Acts consistently (re)align Israel's space and the space of Jesus' messengers. Concurrently, Stephen mirrors Moses' shining face in Exodus 34:29–35 and Jesus' transfigured face in Luke 9:29, suggesting divine accreditation, and the consequence of 'being close to God and in God's very presence'.[29] Within the more immediate cotext of Acts 6, Stephen's face suggests that, 'false witnesses' notwithstanding, 'any observers – including the council – who dare to "look closely" at this man will detect a true "prophet like Moses"'.[30] Given that 6:15 suggests an 'exact focussing of the eyes [which] makes it impossible to dismiss the following experience … as illusion or imagination,'[31] Barrett rightly expresses surprise 'that no reaction on the part of the beholders is described'.[32] Auditors are intended to take double note: first, of Stephen's implied status, and, second, of the first hints of the incomprehension which will lead to blocked ears immediately after Stephen's speech ends (7:57).[33] In a further link with the speech's conclusion, Joseph Fitzmyer, anticipating 7:55, suggests that 6:15 implies that God's glory illuminates Stephen's face.[34]

Thus, by the time the high priest invites Stephen to utter his first recorded words in Acts (7:1), a clearly spatial expectation is established for the subsequent address.

---

[28] Haenchen 1971: 271.   [29] Witherington 1998: 259.
[30] Spencer 1997: 69–70.   [31] Haenchen 1971: 272.   [32] Barrett 1994: 330.
[33] Penner (2004: 288–91) outlines a series of contrasts between Stephen and his opponents which culminate in 6:15 and resume in 7:54.
[34] Fitzmyer 1998: 360. Fletcher-Louis (1997: 98) suggests that 6:15 and 7:53 form 'an inclusio around the lengthy sermon in Acts 7:1–53'. While recognising this parallelism, the *inclusio* is not a neat one, even if the sermon is understood to end at 7:53, since 6:15 is narrated and precedes the body of the sermon.

3. The geography of Abraham (7:2–8)

Stephen's address begins with God's dealings with Abraham. While the focus rests more on God than Abraham,[35] this potential truism must not mask the passage's inherent spatiality and production of *earthly* space.

Chronological differences from Genesis 12 have distracted some commentators away from the passage's contribution to a wider spatiality within Acts 7, typified by Haenchen's stark verdict that Luke 'wrongly' relates Abraham's journeyings.[36] Fitzmyer contests such premature closure on the issue. Instead, Luke 'is simply following a different interpretation of the Abraham story. In any case, the Lucan emphasis calls on God's initiative in calling Abraham to leave his country.'[37] In Mesopotamia, in a pagan land prior to even Abraham's interim residence in Haran, the God of glory 'appeared' (ὤφθη; Acts 7:2; Genesis 12:7) to him. In short, regardless of difficulties harmonising with other texts, Acts 7 locates the divine revelation ordering Abrahamic space as occurring *beyond* the land of Canaan.

God's promise to Abraham, activated by the relocating verb μετῴκισεν (7:4b), concerned a particular production of space. That this promised possession was not realised within Abraham's lifetime (7:5) confirms Abraham's hope as thirdspatial.[38] In Sojan terms, Abraham's firstspace experience, his material life world, although determined by the promise, lagged behind his thirdspace expectation but was formed by it. Furthermore, this divine revelation foretold the antithetical production of another future yet interim space, namely sojourning followed by slavery in Egypt (7:6), with subsequent release from that spatial oppression then leading to Abraham's promise being fulfilled in his offspring worshipping *in a particular place* (7:7).[39]

Given that Acts 7:7b does not reflect either Genesis 12 or 15, it appears to draw upon Exodus 3:12, and thus anticipate Sinai. Under this reading Acts 7:7 replaces 'mountain' with 'this place', which in cotext refers to either Jerusalem and/or the Temple (6:13–14)[40] or to

[35] Gaventa 2003a: 121.   [36] Haenchen 1971: 278.
[37] Fitzmyer 1998: 369. Cf. also Witherington 1998: 266.
[38] Davies (1974: 269–70) sketches the theological significance of Abraham lacking land at the time of the promise.
[39] Beale (2004: 216–17) notes that Genesis 12:7b concludes with the first instance of small-scale sanctuary building by the patriarchs.
[40] Conzelmann 1987: 52; Tannehill 1990: 93.

the land as a whole (7:4).[41] Todd Penner is persuasive for the latter reading, given 'the various nuances of τόπος [place] in Acts 7', including 7:33 and 7:49,[42] whereas Acts 6–7 avoids any explicit mention of the Temple. Thus, instead of emphasising the bounty of exodus (cf. Genesis 15:14), Stephen highlights its destination and goal.[43] Under this reading, Acts 7:45 fulfils 7:7,[44] which influences subsequent understanding of 7:47–52 (for which, see below). Here in 7:7, 'worship' anticipates Israel's space rightly oriented under God's intention. This anticipation, which will permeate Stephen's implications (7:39, 42–43, 51–53, 56), pervades other mentions of 'worship' throughout Luke-Acts.[45]

Thus understood, 7:6–7 introduces an important spatial concept within Stephen's speech, overlooked in much analysis. The ultimate territorial promise to Abraham is mediated through an interim space, in Egypt. Initially this interim space forms part of God's saving plan (thus 7:10–14) but then it sours and has to be evacuated, under God's chosen leader who will reorder space towards fulfilment of the earlier promise (in this instance, Moses; note the temporal links in 7:17 and 7:20). The leader's territorial advance is not only initially rejected by the people, but also the lure of the interim space pulls people back towards it (see below, concerning 7:39). This spatial paradigm within God's plan partially recurs between the wilderness and exile-space (7:41–6) but now, because of Jesus' ascension, is unfolding climactically, here, in Jerusalem-space and Temple-space.

The 'covenant of circumcision' (7:8) was an embodied representation of this divinely ordained spatial trajectory towards ultimate promised, placed fulfilment. It forms a spatial marker, assuming proper worship in the right place as necessary to its being 'the visible mark of historical continuity'.[46] Within Luke-Acts, earthly historical continuity *per se* does not equate necessarily with salvation geography. Nor does heavenly promise-fulfilment occur on a pinhead, in an aspatial realm of salvation history. Instead, the only other mention of covenant in Acts, 3:25, projects an expansive spatiality reaching to 'all the families of the earth' conforming to the approved geography of inheritance (κληρονομία) in Luke-Acts

---

[41] Witherington 1998: 266; Penner 2004: 308–9. In Jeremiah 7:3, 7, 'in this place' bridges both Temple and land.
[42] Penner 2004: 309 n. 99. Cf. Richard 1978: 326.   [43] Spencer 1997: 71.
[44] Penner 2004: 309–10.   [45] Cf. Luke 1:74; (2:37); 4:8; Acts 24:14; 26:7; 27:23.
[46] Conzelmann 1987: 52.

which is consistently earthly but with an insistent heavenly referent for its spaces.[47]

Already, this earliest section of Stephen's speech illustrates the benefits of reading for space as well as for time. Stephen affirms 'traditional estimates concerning the primacy of Israel's land, law and temple ... But a careful hearing of Stephen's complete testimony about Abraham will also pick up certain counterstrains', namely mobility, lack of ownership, and epiphanies within foreign territories.[48] Yet although this part of the speech provides 'positive description and evaluation of the non-Israelite land and (to a considerable degree) its inhabitants',[49] it does not necessarily promote a positive estimation of the Diaspora *qua* Diaspora.[50] Primarily, it liberates God's production of space from delimitation by the land or to those inhabiting the land. Rather than addressing Diaspora debates such as the resurrection status of those buried outside of the land, Acts 7 is developing towards the climactic status of Christ in heaven (7:56). Not only is this climax outside of the land; it also redefines Israel by redefining the people and the earth (3:23–6).

Thus 'the country in which *you* are now living' (7:4) provides the first hint of a polemical aspect within the address, initiating distance between Stephen and his hearers (cf. 7:51–2) and evoking the Christological contrast scheme in 2:23–4.[51] This study's earlier spatialised reading of Acts 4–5 confirms the council as 'firmly entrenched in "this land" where it seeks to delimit and protect God's interests'.[52] Like the disciples in 1:6, they restrictively conflate firstspace, secondspace and thirdspace, but – as Acts 7

---

[47] Luke 12:13–34, bookended by references to κληρονομία ('inheritance', 'treasure'), relativises Solomon's glory in 12:27 (cf. Acts 7:47) and concludes with a climactic geography of the heart (Luke 12:32–4). Luke 20:14 is positioned by 20:19, where a Lukan mention of 'the scribes' prepares for the anti-gospel spaces inhabited in Acts 4:5 and 6:12. Finally, Acts 20:32 – a key reference for auditors seeking their own co-ordinates of space – is also thirdspatial when read within the consistent Lukan use of κληρονομία.

[48] Spencer 1997: 70.

[49] Neudorfer 1998: 284, pp. 285–6 providing persuasive textual evidence for this statement.

[50] *Contra* Neudorfer 1998: 285–6.

[51] Penner 2004: 306. Barrett's suggestion (1994: 343) that the distinction in 7:4 'would be more suitable if the speaker were a Hellenist Jew normally resident in the Diaspora' ignores the rhetorical dimensions of the speech.

[52] Spencer 1997: 71.

demonstrates – they remain closed to the corrective ascension geography of 1:7–11 with its ultimate fulfilment of Abrahamic spatiality. By contrast, from Stephen's perspective 'God's interests range farther and wider',[53] in accordance with the global second-space projected in 1:8. The thirdspace aspect of ascension geography made explicit in 7:55–6 posits God's interests as also ranging higher,[54] as requiring a heavenly, Christological dimension.

Thus Abraham, the patriarch *par excellence*, is presented as an exemplar of Israel-space who anticipates a greater spatiality to come.[55]

4.   The geography of Joseph (7:9–16)

Stephen reaches over the other patriarchs (7:8), in order to recount Joseph's life for two geographical reasons.

A 'foreign' land

First, Acts 7 recounts Joseph, like Abraham, encountering God in a foreign land. No mention is made of Joseph's dreams in Canaan (Genesis 37:5–11). Rather, that 'God was with him' (Acts 7:9), even – especially (or even uniquely) – in Egypt, issues a leitmotif for the Joseph section.[56] As well as moving the children of Israel into the interim space of Egypt (cf. 7:6), 7:9–16 repeatedly demonstrates that 'alienation from household and homeland did not mean abandonment by God'.[57] The absence of a change of grammatical subject in 7:10 implies that *God* appointed Joseph as ruler over Egypt. Jacob's sending of his sons to Egypt (7:12) uses ἐξαποστέλλω, 'a verb from Luke's preferred vocabulary' which 'often connotes a commissioning by God directly or indirectly through human agents, and it assumes God's working in relation to a "plan" and recognizes

---

[53] Spencer 1997: 71.

[54] An *inclusio* concerning encountering the glory of God (7:2, 55) intimates that, like Abraham, Stephen sees and lives by the ultimate spatial principle that governs all earthly spaces – and articulates it Christologically.

[55] Penner (2004: 306–8) judges the Abraham section to structure the speech as a whole.

[56] Cf. 7:20, below. This leitmotif stands, regardless of any specific and intentional shading over onto Stephen's status within the Acts 7 cotext (for which, see Spencer 1997: 72).

[57] Spencer 1997: 72.

God's authority'.[58] Their progressive and repeated journeys to Egypt indicate an emphatic 'mobility of Israel's patriarchs beyond holy land limits'.[59]

Bruce suggests that Stephen's exposition has, thus far, proposed that God 'shows no preference for one place over another' and that God's people 'should sit loose to any earthly locality'.[60] While Bruce rightly recognises a relativising of particular firstspaces, this should not generate a denial of geography within Acts 7. Any such 'anti-geography' reading under-interprets space,[61] wrongly suggesting that the 'production' of space is optional, that the power of place can be neutralised, and ignoring the fact that while places are produced in relation to one another, this does not result in homogeneity. Stephen exhibits a more critical specificity concerning the actual dynamics of space within particular locales, since he is, instead, *remaking* and theologically critiquing the emotional bonds of place according to ascension geography. In contrast to theoretical (and mythical) iso-tropic plains, Acts 7 *emphasises* locations – for example, 7:9–12 contains a fivefold repetition of 'Egypt' within sixty-three Greek words. Rather than being cast as Other, Egypt becomes the para-doxical place where God's promises are fulfilled.[62] Also, as Witherington rightly observes, 'the first-century antipathies between Jews and Samaritans' suggest that declaring Shechem as the burial site (7:16) was unlikely to ingratiate Stephen with his audience of Judean Jews.[63] In sum, place matters; the rule of God is not rendered universal in Acts in a manner that annihilates space.[64]

Differentiation within 'Israel'

Second, 7:9–16 introduces theological-geographical differentiation within 'Israel' which responds to the accusations against Stephen,[65]

---

[58] Soards 1994: 63, μετεκαλέσατο ('called', 7:14) implying compliance with the divine will (p. 64).

[59] Spencer 1997: 72.   [60] Bruce 1990: 195, 193.

[61] At its extremes, such an 'anti-geography' reading displaces God from any involve-ment with place – e.g., Sennett's assumption (1994: 130) that 'Yahweh was a god of time rather than of place'.

[62] Richard 1978: 326.   [63] Witherington 1998: 268.

[64] Cf. the potentially simplistic (and earthbound) analysis of Kee (1989: 95), and Bruce's appeal to God's ubiquity when reading 7:47 (Bruce 1990: 206). Time might relativise place (Spencer 1997: 71–2 concerning 7:6, 8) or, arguably, time enhances it; either way, God's people are still 'placed' in their interaction with God, and the role of space and place within that interaction needs careful interpretation.

[65] Richard 1979; see also Gaventa 2003a: 123; Penner 2004: 319–20.

since Joseph's brothers are presented negatively, and Joseph positively. Reading the text with sensitivity to its geography will liberate us from simple reliance on such polemical readings[66] while still highlighting differentiation within 'Israel'. Simultaneously, the rare use of 'Canaan' (7:11; 13:19 is its only other NT occurrence) recalls 'the stubborn presence of non-Yahwistic peoples in the promised land'.[67] If Jewish retellings of the Joseph story frequently cast Joseph's brothers as envious (7:9),[68] then Stephen is rhetorically astute by introducing this important but divisive theme in a relatively innocuous manner.

Shechem

As has been seen, locating the patriarchs' burial site in Shechem (7:16) raises questions of geographical interpretation and intent, not least given the variance from the Genesis account.[69] As a first-century centre of Samaritan territory, 7:16 could anticipate the mission of Acts 8.[70] Certainly its double mention and careful wording elsewhere in Stephen's speech suggest a reason other than carelessness,[71] and a Samaritan influence appears unlikely.[72]

A sensitivity to place suggests that Acts 7:16 is not simply 'cited from memory',[73] 'a simple error'[74] or an example of 'telescoping'.[75] Given 2:29 and the covenantal hopes attached to patriarchal burial *sites* (Genesis 50:5–14, 25, 26; Exodus 13:19; Joshua 24:32), such locales bear particular thirdspace significance. Spencer hints at this richer spatiality when commenting that 'bodies are often brought back for burial to cherished family plots, rich in social and cultural significance', but then broadens his reading of 7:16 as contributing to Luke's 'polemic against those who attempt to restrict God's activity to select sacred zones'.[76] The same critique could apply equally to Shechem itself, and Spencer's first observation needs to be connected

---

[66] This reading has been subject to some legitimate criticisms. Although Soards (1994: 63 n. 148) accepts Richard (1979) with qualifications, Tannehill (1990: 87 n. 20) questions whether the patriarchs are consistently presented in a negative light: if, for example, 'great suffering' (7:11) indicates divine disfavour, then rescue from famine (7:12–15) arguably shows continuing care. Similarly, Tannehill questions whether 'Shechem' (7:16) should be read as polemical.

[67] Spencer 1997: 72.   [68] L. T. Johnson 1992: 117.

[69] For which, see Barrett 1994: 351.

[70] L. T. Johnson 1992: 118–119; Gaventa 2003a: 123–4.

[71] Spencer 1997: 73.   [72] Bruce 1987; Neudorfer 1998: 293–4.

[73] Haenchen 1971: 280.   [74] Barrett 1994: 351.

[75] Bruce 1990: 196.   [76] Spencer 1997: 73.

with the specific production of space cast across Acts by 1:6–11, whereby Stephen's patriarchal-burial geography is located within the particular presentation of space made thus far in Acts. That Stephen places the patriarchal burial site in Shechem specifically undermines ultimate thirdspace claims for 'this holy place' in Jerusalem (6:13) and, within and beyond opposing mortal realities as secondspace, anticipates the final place of the ultimate figure in Stephen's address.

Stephen's thirdspace alternative is not Shechem. Ultimately it is Jesus alive and in heaven, but this awaits a later stage in the speech, namely 7:56. When it comes, Stephen's alternative will build upon, and reinforce, the programmatic spatial claims of 1:6–11. Firstspatially, it will undermine the overweening importance of 'this holy place'. Secondspatially, it will clarify the ultimate projection of covenant geography. Thirdspatially, it will specify a Christocentric and heavenly locus. All three aspects together communicate the role of the patriarchs' geography in shaping Acts 7 (and, indeed, Acts as a whole). If 7:16 anticipates a wider Lukan narrative inclusion of the Samaritans among the Jesus-oriented people of God, it is within a comprehensive worldwide restructuring instigated by ascension geography.

5. The geography of Moses (7:17–38)

Spencer suggests that this section forms the rhetorical 'centrepiece' of Stephen's address, 'inviting careful deliberation on the part of his hearers'.[77] The critique of Israel-space, hinted at in 7:9, here 'emerges with blunt force in the recital of Moses' life'.[78] Temporally, the account divides into three forty-year divisions of Moses' life. This temporal schema need not be denied, but nor is it the totality of how Acts 7 structures information about Moses. Read for its spaces, 7:17–38 inhabits four distinct settings, which will be used here to subdivide analysis.

The situation of the Israelites in Egypt and the arrival of Moses (7:17–22)

Acts 7:17–34, building 'to a high point of expectancy', unifies what has already been said about the patriarchs with what is to come

---

[77] Spencer 1997: 74.   [78] Gaventa 2003a: 124.

concerning Moses.[79] What follows 'simultaneously resounds the crucial themes of divine necessity and control. Events now proceed in relation to God's promise(s), so that human time and life [i.e. space] are evaluated in relation to the will and work of God.'[80]

If the speech has already heralded God's oversight of his people beyond the land of Israel, a second major theme is now developed, namely Israel's rejection of God's leader. This unfolds starkly in 7:21, where the baby Moses is 'abandoned', beyond Israel-space: 'The implication is that Moses' father, acting like other Israelite fathers, simply turned his son out to die and that Moses' eventual salvation and cultivation of "wisdom" and "power" were owed exclusively to God's favor ("he was beautiful before God", 7.20) manifested through Pharaoh's daughter, of all people, and in the Egyptian court, of all places (7.21–22).'[81] Thus Stephen emphasises that the exodus, Israel's defining spatial realignment, was dependent upon one who was significantly Egyptian in upbringing and outlook.[82]

Conflict with his fellow Israelites causes Moses to flee Egypt (7:23–9)

This section establishes Egypt as the place where God's people continued to reject God's chosen rescuer. When he was aged forty, 'it came into his [Moses'] heart to visit his relatives, the Israelites' (7:23). Stephen ascribes to Moses a self-understanding that 'his brethren' should also appreciate his ministry of salvation and reconciliation (7:25–6).[83] This second mention of 'salvation' in Acts parallels the earlier proclamation of Christocentric 'under heaven' spatiality also made before the Sanhedrin (4:12). Using exodus typology to characterise salvation (7:25; cf. 3:17–26)[84] confirms that salvation involves spatial realignment as well as historical destiny.

---

[79] Tannehill (1990: 91) expounds well these connectives.
[80] Soards 1994: 64, square-bracketed comment added.   [81] Spencer 1997: 74–5.
[82] This contrasts with other Jewish retellings of Moses (Neudorfer 1998: 285; Fitzmyer 1998: 376).
[83] Penner (2004: 321) judges 'Men, you are brothers' (7:26) to evoke 7:2, highlighting a 'breakdown of *philia*' between Stephen and his opponents in 7:23–9. *Within* believer-space, that Moses 'appeared' (ὤφθη, 7:26) also recalls 7:2, and anticipates the climactic sighting in 7:55, the 'prophet like Moses' already having territorial claims upon Israel (3:22–3).
[84] Green 1997a: 21.

The Hebrews fail to understand,[85] and, as Stephen declares beyond the Exodus account, they dismiss Moses' pretensions (7:27–8; cf. 7:35a). Moses is 'thrust away', suggesting both firstspatial (i.e. physical)[86] and secondspatial (verbal-conceptual) rejection. Unlike in Exodus 2:13–14, both Hebrews are cast as wrongdoers,[87] and Moses as a neutral mediator seeking peace.[88] Because of their rebuff, not out of fear concerning Pharaoh's response (7:29; cf. Exodus 2:15), Moses flees[89] to Midian.

The theophany in Midian (7:30–4)

Clearly the drama retold in Acts 7 is not happening on a pinhead. Having settled as a resident alien with kinship ties in Midian (7:29), Moses experiences a heaven-sent phenomenon in 7:30.[90] That Moses encountered the God of his fathers (7:32) in a place (ὁ τόπος) beyond Israel which God declared to be 'holy ground' (γῆ ἁγία, 7:33) matches the dynamic and mobile patriarchal geography already expounded and decisively relativises the spatial assumptions behind the accusations in 6:13 concerning 'this holy place'. This sanctified space needs to be located within both Stephen's speech and the wider narrative. Without recourse to the narrative, Luke Timothy Johnson claims: 'The Messianists argue that this presence is among them in the Spirit.'[91] Given the limited place of the Spirit within the speech, and the climactic place given to the heavenly Christ (7:56), Christological geography, rooted in OT spatialities, and its consequent realignments

[85] L. T. Johnson (1992: 126) sees Moses' self-understanding and the two Israelites' lack of understanding as unique among Jewish retellings of the Moses story, judging it as 'a distinctive Lukan contribution ... an obvious connection to his story of Jesus ... (Acts 3:17)'. Within Acts 7, it develops the recognition scene in 7:13.
[86] L. T. Johnson 1992: 127.
[87] They 'represent the whole of strife-torn Israel' (Haenchen 1971: 281).
[88] Regarding 'peace' as Moses' intention (7:26), cf. Jesus in Luke 2:14; 19:38, 42; Acts 10:36.
[89] The verb φεύγω presents a more dramatic rendition of Moses' departure than ἀναχωρέω in Exodus 2:15 LXX – 'the LXX term gives Philo the chance to treat Moses' exile as a kind of philosophical retreat' (L. T. Johnson 1992: 127).
[90] Spencer (1997: 75) likens 7:30 to the *fire* in 2:3, but without making a connection with its heavenly origins (2:2). Barrett (1994: 360) doubts whether Luke had the same mind as Calvin (1965: 190), who saw the angel to be Christ.
[91] L. T. Johnson 1992: 128. Any relativising of Jerusalem (Spencer 1997: 75) or connections with controversies within Diaspora Judaism (Neudorfer 1998: 285) needs locating within the narrative's wider spatiality, as Acts 7 provides a commentary on the Jerusalem section of Acts (Dahl 1966: 144–7; W. D. Davies 1974: 268).

of earthly space have the better primary claim for justifying Stephen's radical re-estimations of holy space and places.

No mention is made of Moses' resistance to God's call (cf. Exodus 3:13–4:17); this would clash with his earlier characterisation (7:22, 25)[92] and would undermine the clarity of Moses' spatial consciousness which Stephen's argument requires. Moses' spatiality is also emphatically directed from above; he 'appears' to Israel because of the decisive 'appearance' to him (7:30, 35). Like other heavenly experiences recounted in Acts (1:8–11; 2:1–13),[93] Moses' epiphany results in a missionary journey that realigns the geography of salvation.[94] This realignment is initially personal, as God sends Moses back to Egypt (7:34), but Moses being sent 'to Egypt', rather than to 'Pharaoh, king of Egypt', as in Exodus 3:10 LXX, emphasises his return *to the Hebrews*. In this manner his realignment becomes corporate, as 7:35 ironically reworks 7:27–8 and underlines God's reversal of the distancing initiated in 7:27–9.

The exodus from Egypt, and the desert assembly (7:35–8)

The speech becomes rhetorically sharper in this section, through a series of statements about Moses, each beginning with a demonstrative pronoun (7:35a, 35b, 36, 37, 38),[95] a rhetorical shaping without parallel in other Jewish versions of the Moses story.[96] As well as highlighting the content of these verses, this rhetoric also recalls Peter's similar claims about Jesus (2:22–4), and 7:37 evokes Deuteronomy 18:15, which in turn recalls Acts 3:22 and the consequential Christocentric geography in 3:23. The use in 7:35 of the verb ἀρνέομαι for this rejection, rather than ἀπωθέω as in 7:27, generates further Christological paralleling, in this instance with 3:13–15.[97]

Stephen presents God sending Moses as Israel's *ruler and judge* (7:35). 'Ruler' affirms one of the two titles denied Moses by a fellow Hebrew (7:27) in a retrospective mention of earlier (now generically

---

[92] Gaventa 2003a: 126.

[93] Beyond being 'visionary experiences' (Spencer 1997: 75), these epiphanies of space exhibit clear heavenly connectives. Such heavenly dynamics will reappear in Acts (e.g. 7:56; 8:26, 39; 9:3–6, 10–16; 11:19–21; 13:2; 21:30), having been established in Luke 2:10–14; 3:22; 9:31, 51.

[94] Ἀποστέλλω performs as a powerful verb within the wider salvation geography of Luke-Acts.

[95] Gaventa 2003a: 126–7.   [96] L. T. Johnson 1992: 129.

[97] L. T. Johnson 1992: 129; see also Martín-Asensio 1999: 250–3.

pluralised) rejection of Moses. Like 'judge', the ascription confirms Moses as divinely commissioned to lead the Hebrews into redemptive spatial realignment.

Acts 7:36–8 bristles with spatial resonance. First, the exodus itself is perhaps *the* OT spatial realignment. Moses 'led them out' from Egypt (7:36, 40; cf. 13:17, where *God* leads the people out). The verb ἐξάγω also occurs in Luke-Acts when the risen Jesus leads his disciples (Luke 24:50) and during angelic releases from prison (Acts 5:19; 12:17). It indicates physical relocation under divine mandate, frequently by double agency whereby God works through a chosen agent, whether angelic or human.[98]

Second, there is a geography of Moses' 'wonders and signs' which bridges the entire exodus journey towards the land of promise (7:36).[99] This comprehensive testimony condemns the people's subsequent response to Moses' spatial trajectory. It leads to 7:37 which anticipates – for the first time in the address – the response of Stephen's hearers to the promised 'prophet like Moses'. Deuteronomy 18:15, quoted here, has already been evoked in Acts 3:22–3 to account for the restructuring of earthly Israel brought about by Jesus' heavenly rule.[100]

Third, Moses is located 'in the congregation (ἐκκλησίᾳ) in the wilderness' when receiving 'living oracles (λόγια) to give to us'[101] (7:38). This mediated pattern ('received … to give …') mirrors that of the *heavenly* Jesus brokering the Spirit (2:33). This heavenly aspect both qualifies and develops Bruce's claim that 'as Moses was with the *ekklēsia* then, so Christ, the prophet like Moses, is with his *ekklēsia* now'.[102] An absent, heavenly Christ differs significantly from a present, earthly Moses, although his firstspace *absence*, if anything, increases earthly resonance for 'a pilgrim church', to adopt Bruce's term.[103] Yet, while being 'a pure, spiritual cult' wherein 'the people of God should sit loose to any earthly locality',[104] believers are still

---

[98] Cf. 16:37, 39 and 21:38.

[99] L. T. Johnson 1992: 50, 129 links 'wonders and signs' in Egypt with Deuteronomy 34:11 and acknowledges its reflection in Acts 2:19 (cf. 2:22, 43; 6:8). Rather than reflecting simply 'stereotypical' language (p. 129), the couplet and its word order positions Moses within a distinctively Lukan spatiality.

[100] Stephen's focus on Moses as prophet is all the more significant given 'its relative absence in the parallel Jewish retellings of the exodus story' (L. T. Johnson 1992: 130).

[101] Metzger 1994: 307 provides good cotextual reasons to prefer first-person plural pronouns in 7:38, 39.

[102] Bruce 1990: 202. So also Witherington (1998: 271, citing Marshall 1980: 143), who also parallels the presence of Moses and the *presence* of Jesus. Cf. Barrett 1994: 365 regarding the likely link between this OT ἐκκλησία and that of (e.g.) 5:11.

[103] Bruce 1990: 202.   [104] Bruce 1990: 202, 193.

implicated within earthly productions of particular places.[105] This
necessitates the nurture of a proper heavenly locus for their earthly
geographies.

6.   The subsequent geography of 'our fathers' (7:39–43)

'In their hearts they turned back (ἐστράφησαν) to Egypt' (7:39)
dramatically sharpens Stephen's narration of spatial rejection, and
highlights a significant 'spatiality' of the heart underplayed by previous
Acts scholarship. Dismissive comments that 7:39 '"spiritualizes" this
return'[106] or that it is simply 'a not very clear way of expressing their
desire to return there'[107] connect insufficiently with the cumulative
production of space in Acts 7 and blunt the verse's spatial implications.
Read for its space, this 'turning' (using the verb στρέφω) powerfully
declares an interior geography of the heart, which betrayed physical
location and corrupted covenantal links with heaven, ultimately
destroying the desert generation's thirdspace projection towards
the promised land.

The 'heart' has already significantly oriented space in Acts 7. In
7:23 Moses' heart motivated him to help his brethren, thus radically
altering the Egyptian worldview established for him in 7:21–2.[108]
Now in 7:39, in firstspace terms, the Israelites remain in the wilderness, as 7:40–2 confirms – but, crucially, their secondspace desire
reverts to Egypt, expressed as a turning of the heart. Here 'Egypt'
means the land of plenty, Goshen,[109] rather than the place of slavery.
Moses' complaint that the people's spatial discontent made them
ready to stone him (Exodus 17:4), a response informing a patterned
rejection of salvation geography (Numbers 14:10), is ironically noteworthy in the cotext of Acts 7. To anticipate what lies ahead, the
'heart' will remain formative in the shaping of space later in Acts 7,
two final references confirming the characteristic spatiality diagnosed
by Stephen's address (vv. 51, 54).

---

[105] Neither Acts 7, nor Acts as a whole, dissolves the specificities of places into pure
and undifferentiated universality. O'Donovan (1989: 56) casts this preservation of the
particular and the local as true across the Christian scriptures, an observation which ties
into Christ's continuing incarnation in heaven.

[106] Haenchen 1971: 283.   [107] Barrett 1994: 366; cf. Numbers 14:3.

[108] Judging 7:23 to be a 'biblicism' (L. T. Johnson 1992: 126) underplays the heart's
spatial function, both in Acts 7 and in wider Acts (cf. 2:26, 37, 46; 4:32; 5:3, 4; 8:21, 22;
11:23; 13:22; 14:17; 16:14; 21:13; 28:27).

[109] Genesis 45:10; 46:34; 47:1, 4, 27; 50:8 (and, by implication, 50:22); Exodus
8:22; 9:26.

This heart geography is played out in the desert. In a second setting Moses is 'pushed aside' (both 7:27 and 7:39 use the verb ἀπωθέω): here, however, this is despite the ongoing wonders and signs he is performing in their midst (7:36).[110] Whereas previously the Israelites had resented Moses' 'unwelcome assistance' (7:27), now they are frustrated by his 'mysterious absence' – 'we do not know what has happened to him' (7:40).[111] This spatial absence parallels Jesus' ascended absence, although Acts 7 does not draw this out (until indirectly, but climactically, in 7:56).

The verb ἀπωθέω is used only once elsewhere in Acts, at 13:46, when Paul describes the treatment of the word of God by some Jews in Pisidian Antioch. Here, Paul and Barnabas respond by announcing a 'turning' (στρεφόμεθα) to the gentiles, their rationale from Isaiah 49:6 in Acts 13:46–7 conforming to the ascension secondspace articulated in 1:8. In 13:50 these unbelieving Jews distance themselves spatially from the missionaries, an action echoing the wilderness rebellion. In this instance, however, their rejection of 'the word of God' results in the verb στρέφω being used *against* them rather than by them.

Beyond 13:46 and 7:39 – both geographically pregnant narrative moments – στρέφω occurs only in one other place in Acts, in 7:42. There, its proximity to ἀπωθέω and to ἀπωθέω in 7:39 again implicates the heart with actual productions of space. In 7:42, however, *God* is the one turning. Tannehill's comment is apposite: 'Thus pushing aside God's message or messenger results in a fateful turning, in which people turn away from God's purpose while God's purpose turns in a new direction.'[112] But this dynamic needs to be integrated into the wider production of space within Acts and, ultimately, back to a programmatic ascension geography in Acts 1.

This heavenly connection is reinforced in 7:42: God 'turned away' and 'handed them over to worship the host of heaven'. Whether ἔστρεψεν is understood as transitive or intransitive,[113] the spatial consequence is the same: Israel's thirdspace becomes realigned towards 'the host of heaven', a fundamentally misplaced thirdspace orientation. First, OT references to the 'host of heaven' position such

[110] Acts 7:35 and 7:39 form 'a bracket around vv. 36–38, which report different facets of Moses' work with the Israelites' (Soards 1994: 65).

[111] Spencer 1997: 76.   [112] Tannehill 1990: 96.

[113] Commentators divide between an intransitive reading (e.g. Barrett 1994: 367–8) and a transitive sense (e.g. Fitzmyer 1998: 381). Both options being possible, 7:42 remains ambiguous.

devotion as clearly idolatrous.[114] Also, auditors recalling 'the heavenly host' in Luke 2:13 (the only other NT occurrence of στρατιᾶς οὐρανίου) evaluate Acts 7:42 within a framework of *Christological* spatiality and the earthly implications signalled by his birth and sealed at his ascension. To worship even those heavenly beings *who point to Christ* would result in a gross perversion of Christological ascension thirdspace, a theme ratified in 4:12 and now developing towards Stephen's examination of the Temple and the climactic 7:56.

Thus Stephen 'distils [all the Sinai wanderings] into one large act of disobedience'.[115] Acts 7 casts the wilderness as a place of Israel's disobedience, idolatry, and refusal to face up to their covenant spatiality. Acts 7:42 (cf. Amos 5:25–7) demonstrates that structured idolatry began in the wilderness by problematising and rejecting an emphatic 'to me'.[116] 'Rejoicing' and the 'work of their hands' in 7:41 carry their Septuagintal connotations of idolatrous worship.[117] Such devotion rejects God as sovereign creator, and his consequent spatiality, which in 4:24–30 underpinned ascension geography. Furthermore, in 7:35–6 'the work of their own hands' contrasts with, and rejects, Moses' divine appointment 'through the angel' (σὺν χειρὶ ἀγγέλου) as their spatial leader, and replicates their earlier incomprehension that God was bringing deliverance 'through him' (διὰ χειρὸς αὐτοῦ, 7:25). Given earlier Moses–Jesus parallels and the crisis for 'builders' announced in 4:11, auditors and, possibly, Stephen's hearers should consider implicit parallels between other works – other spaces – made by human hands in Acts (see below, concerning the Temple in 7:48) and the space-ordering ministry of Jesus, the Moses-like figure now in heaven (7:56).[118]

By quoting Amos 5:25–7, Acts 7:42–3 collapses Israel's history into its geography, implying that 'the consequences of the rejection of Moses reach all the way to the Exile'.[119] Rejecting the prophet like Moses (7:37) generates more far-reaching consequences. Tannehill's identification of a 'tragic reversal' in Acts 7, marked by three aspects of the Abrahamic promise which are first stated positively and then

---

[114] E.g. Jeremiah 19:13, Zephaniah 1:5. More widely, see Niehr 1999.

[115] Gaventa 2003a: 127.

[116] L. T. Johnson 1992: 131. See Marshall 2007: 565–6 regarding the variations among Acts 7 and Amos 5:25–7 LXX and MT.

[117] Concerning which, see L. T. Johnson 1992: 131.

[118] Cf. also, for auditors, Paul's Areopagus address (17:22–31), and Demetrius' comments to his fellow artisans (19:26).

[119] Gaventa 2003a: 127.

restated negatively,[120] needs to be read within the unfolding ascension spatiality developing across Acts 7. One aspect, the 'covenant of circumcision' (7:8) awaits discussion later in relation to 7:51. The other two factors are reversed in 7:42–3.

First, God 'resettled' (μετῴκισεν) Abraham 'to this land' (7:4) from Mesopotamia / the land of the Chaldeans (7:3, 4). The only other NT use of μετοικίζω occurs in 7:43, where God promises to 'resettle' or 'deport' the people because of their idolatry,[121] this time *beyond* Babylon, *away* from the promised land. Changing 'Damascus' in Amos 5:27 to 'Babylon' is more geographically freighted than simple retrospective reflection concerning 'the *historical* experience of the community'.[122] Barrett risks historicist myopia when concluding that 'it is by no means clear why Luke should have substituted Babylon for Damascus'.[123] The lesson is explicitly spatial: those who reject God's spatial order are themselves spatially rejected, passing even *beyond* their original place of calling by God (Acts 7:43; cf. 7:4). Thus 'the spatial cycle is complete; they begin and end "beyond Babylon"'.[124] Rhetorically, the geographical shift drives home Stephen's warning to his audience of Second-Temple officials, that 'their social-and-spatial location is no more privileged or inviolable than that of their sixth-century forebears'.[125] Alongside such vulnerability, the speech's climax in 7:56 will articulate what should now be their true point of spatial reference in light of Christ's resurrection-ascension. Just as 7:43 pivoted on the turning geography of the heart in 7:39, so, by implication, those who cling to Jerusalem and its Temple in a denial of ascension geography need to be more discerning and repentant in their spatial self-reflection.

Second, Abraham was promised that his descendants would 'worship' (λατρεύσουσίν) God 'in this place' (7:7), but in 7:42 God delivers them up 'to worship (λατρεύειν) the host of heaven'. This thirdspace perversion compounds firstspace reversal beyond Babylon, especially if Haran had been a centre of the cult of the moon god and Abraham had been plucked from such a worldview.[126] Acts 7:42 issues an ironic granting of the petition made in 7:40, 'Make gods for us who will lead the way for us': in this comprehensive spatial realignment, YHWH – rather than their self-made gods – relocates them,

[120] Tannehill 1990: 90, developing Richard 1978: 205.

[121] A similar *divine* ordering of space occurs in 17:26, albeit in a very different narrative cotext.

[122] L. T. Johnson 1992: 132, emphasis added.   [123] Barrett 1994: 371.

[124] Richard 1982: 42.   [125] Spencer 1997: 77.   [126] Bruce 1990: 192.

but 'their new gods will accompany them when they are transported beyond Babylon'.[127]

Thus narrative spatiality is one of the key means by which Stephen's speech distinguishes between true and false worship. All other references to λατρεύειν in Luke-Acts are also implicated within wider productions of space (Luke 1:74; 2:37; 4:8; Acts 24:14; 26:7; 27:23). Stephen's hearers are therefore summoned to reflect upon the spatialities producing, and produced by, their own worship, given the past and present geographies shaped by heaven. Rejecting the prophet like Moses of 7:37 is unlikely to be spatially neutral.

When read within these ongoing productions of space, the idolatry of 7:41–3 both produced and reflected idolatrous spatial structures and demonstrates an enduring spatial dynamic which informs the speech as a whole. Goshen-Egypt (7:39), Moses' absence from the people while receiving the law at Sinai on their behalf (7:40; cf. 6:13–14) and, possibly, even the Temple in Stephen's Jerusalem, might subvert divinely ordered covenant spatiality and themselves come to be subverted. Beyond the question 'Which group rightly identifies itself with the temple and its traditions?',[128] a deeper issue emerges – whether, and in what sense, the Jerusalem Temple *is* the temple of God. Stephen's address now turns to this question.

7.   The geography of divine dwelling (7:44–50)

A reading for space denies any abrupt shift as attention turns from people to sanctuaries; both are producers and products of space within 'Israel', and individuals, notably David and Solomon, remain in view. This and the preceding sections are linked by two contrasting 'types' for divine dwelling, 'the images that you made' (7:43) and the God-given 'tent of testimony' (7:44).[129] Rather than it being 'astonishing' that both should have accompanied the wilderness wanderings,[130] their coexistence emphasises the proximate and overlapping nature of spatialities, as opposed to historicist tendencies towards constructing totalising, distinct and separate 'eras'.

---

[127] Richard 1982: 43.   [128] Gaventa 2003a: 119.
[129] The mobility of the 'tent' is not emphasised to critique the Solomonic temple's fixed location. More importantly, the tent 'both registers the important general theme of "witness" (see 1:8)' and demonstrates how 'the people in former times were "not without a witness" a theme that occurs in 7:44; 14:17; 17:25b-28' (Soards 1994: 66–7).
[130] Haenchen 1971: 284; similarly Conzelmann 1987: 55.

With this in mind, understanding the place of the Jerusalem Temple within Acts 7 requires deliberation as to whether the argument's logic tends towards *rejecting*, *restraining* or *replacing* the Temple. Agreeing that 'the word "temple-criticism" is capable of several meanings'[131] provokes the employment of a spatialised reading to sift these implications.

That Acts 7 *rejects* the Temple[132] has generally been discounted, perhaps in part for its anti-Jewish tendencies, but also on the grounds that the Temple enjoys positive functions elsewhere in Luke-Acts.[133] Scholars have instead tended towards reading 7:47–50 as presenting some sort of *restraint* of claims made for the Temple, opposing 'God-in-the-box theology' whereby 'it (and perhaps it alone) is the habitation of God'.[134] Various forms for Stephen's alternative vision have been suggested under this reading: a reassertion of OT tradition affirming God's transcendence of the Temple;[135] a broadening out of sacred space from simply the Temple or from any specific place of worship in the land;[136] or a worldwide mission not tied to land.[137] Read within Sojan categories, these interpretations allow a firstspace validity for the Temple, but assume some sort of (usually correctable) secondspace error associated with it.[138]

Penner, however, has revived the rejection reading, judging that it serves the specific functions of Stephen's speech at this narrative juncture,[139] and need not overwhelm more positive portrayals of the Temple and Jewish characters elsewhere in Luke-Acts.[140]

Sojan categories suggest a synthesis, and reduce the need to choose between these differing readings.[141] Both perspectives agree that Stephen identifies a fault concerning how the Temple is functioning (whether symbolically, materially or in both these realms), but then differ as to whether Solomon's construction of the Temple was itself a fundamental misunderstanding of divinely ordered space. Given Chapter 4's earlier identification of multiple motivations informing believers' interactions with the Temple in Acts, neither argument

---

[131] Larsson 1993: 379.   [132] Barrett 1991: 352.
[133] On the latter point, Walton 2004b: 136–8.   [134] Witherington 1998: 273.
[135] Sylva 1987: 267.   [136] Richard 1978: 325–6; Witherington 1998: 266.
[137] J. J. Scott 1978; Larsson 1993: 394.
[138] Walton (2004b: 138–43) gives a recent summary and defence of this line of interpretation.
[139] Penner 2004: 310–18.   [140] Penner 2004: 315, 326.
[141] Such a spatialised and heavenward reading also casts further light on the impasse inherent within Barrett's reflections (1991: 357–67) concerning attitudes towards the Temple in Acts.

needs to be decisive. Such variegated strategies might well replicate Israel's own ambiguous relationship with the Temple from its Solomonic origins,[142] or, within Acts 7, the Temple might function as another interim space akin to Goshen – initially good, but then souring and deflecting focus away from God's ultimate peopled place glimpsed in 7:56.

The issue is defused further by Peter Doble's insistence that the Temple is *not* the primary issue in view in 7:47–50. If, instead, emphasis rests on Solomon, then the key issue is obedience or disobedience, and Solomon's subsequent disobedience (that is, *not* his building of the temple *per se*), having disqualified him from fulfilling the 'Christological conditional' incumbent upon David's son (2 Chronicles 6:16), justifies the ambiguous treatment of Solomon in Luke-Acts.[143] Peter's Pentecost sermon has already established Jesus as David's legitimate Christological heir, and him in heaven, and him as exercising thirdspatial influence over believer-space within 'Israel'. Davidic territoriality is thus exercised by David's son, but, to use Doble's phrase, 'by ascent rather than descent!'[144] At Acts 7:56 Stephen will reach the same conclusion as Peter, albeit in a different form and setting.

Where, then, does this leave the Temple? It is the final interim space of Acts 7, and, as such, should not become a lure away from ascension geography. As Stephen has demonstrated, interim spaces are liable to secondspatial misinterpretation, misaligned firstspace practices, and the misallocation of thirdspace status more properly ascribed elsewhere. Reading the Temple as an interim space imbues it with potential for its rejection, not least by God, should it resist its own restructuring within ascension geography; just as deserting Moses led to judgement in 7:39–43, so too dismissing Jesus signals the Temple's destruction on grounds other than simply its failure to conform to 7:49–50.[145] The Temple's interim status is confirmed by both Solomon's failure to fulfil the 'Christological conditional' and by Lukan narrative development concerning the Temple, most notably the Lukan tearing of the Temple veil (Luke 23:45), which signals the demise of the Temple's dominance as 'a sacred symbol of socio-religious power – a cultural center' exercising 'a world-ordering

---

[142] Doble 2000: 195, regarding 2 Chronicles 6. Cf. 3(1) Kings 8:22–53 LXX, with Solomon's sevenfold repetition of εἰσακούσῃ ἐκ τοῦ οὐρανοῦ ('hear in heaven') and his integral spatial exposition.
[143] Doble 2000: 196.   [144] Doble 2000: 186 n. 16.   [145] Kilgallen 2004: 295.

function'.[146] This collapse of the Temple's secondspace mirrors a transfer of thirdspace prerogatives to Jesus[147] (Luke 23:43), who, via his ascension, is now elevated to heaven. This restructuring of Temple-space provokes and entails a commensurate recognition of Christocentric heavenly thirdspace and its influence over all earthly spaces. First, however, Stephen addresses the spatiality of his immediate audience.

8.   The consequent geography of the Sanhedrin (7:51–4)

Historicist readings, in keeping with the majority view that Stephen's address ends at 7:53, view 7:51–3 as concluding the speech's progression from 'then' to 'now'. Thus Bruce classifies these verses as 'personal application',[148] presumably for Stephen's hearers; and Spencer, having provided geographical headings for the speech's earlier sections, trails off somewhat limply, entitling 7:51–3 'Conclusion'.[149] In contrast, a sustained spatialised reading sees here a condemnation of the Sanhedrin's spatiality following 7:2–50 and anticipating what will be proclaimed in 7:56.

The emphatic second-person pronoun 'Your fathers' (7:51; cf. 7:4) links 7:51–4 with the people and places mentioned earlier in the speech while simultaneously distancing Stephen from the Sanhedrin. It is this audience, in its post-ascension space, which now comes under Stephen's gaze, both as those 'who falsely see themselves as the temple's protectors',[150] and as the spiritual descendants of Solomon's defection from God's intention for believer-space.[151]

Acts 7:51–3 articulates how some enduring principles governing the production of space outlined in 7:2–50 apply to Stephen's hearers. First, the Septuagintal use of 'stiff-necked', a NT *hapax legomenon* in 7:51, dramatically recalls the disastrous heart-orientation of the Israelites in the wilderness recounted in 7:39,[152] as does 'uncircumcised in heart' (ἀπερίτμητοι καρδίας, 7:51), which fulfils Simeon's foundational prophecy in Luke 2:34–5 concerning a Christofocal revealing of Israelite hearts. This in turn positions διεπρίοντο ταῖς

---

[146] Green 1994: 554, 510.   [147] Cf. Walton 2004b: 144–6.
[148] Bruce 1990: 207–9.   [149] Spencer 1997: 79.   [150] Gaventa 2003a: 129.
[151] Doble (2000: 201–2) assumes a 'scriptural substructure' of Isaiah 66:1–6 as underpinning this section. Cf. Beale 2004: 133–8, appealing to 'the broader context of Isaiah' (p. 218).
[152] Cf. Exodus 33:3, 5; 34:9 LXX; Deuteronomy 9:6, 13 LXX. Its Hebrew counterpart is also in Exodus 32:9 MT; cf. Nehemiah 9:29–30.

καρδίαις (7:54), rather than simply 'denoting extreme anger',[153] as a spatial marker. An idiomatic gloss (e.g. 'they became enraged') submerges this term's spatiality by downplaying its connections with other references to the heart in Acts 7. These connectives suggest that the Sanhedrin's reaction has intensified since 5:33, the only other NT occurrence of διαπρίω. Now, from Stephen's point of view, his audience is not only 'repeating that history'[154] but also replicating that geography.

Second, the Abrahamic covenant has been perverted. Casting his audience as 'uncircumcised in heart and ear', and given his earlier positioning of the 'covenant of circumcision' (7:8) as an embodied adoption of a divinely ordained spatial trajectory, Stephen positions them as antithetical to Abraham's spatial vision. 'Circumcision, too, has gone bad.'[155] His description invokes Leviticus 26:41, which prefaces the pivot upon which God's offer of spatial renewal rests (26:41b–45) following a description of the spatial disorder arising from disobedience to God's commands (Leviticus 26:14–41a).[156] Without commensurate repentant humbling of the heart, Stephen's hearers are 'as good as (uncircumcised) heathen, not in their flesh but in readiness to hear and accept God's word'.[157] In Acts 2–7 that word concerns Jesus, who appears in 7:52 as 'the Righteous One', a title indicating his innocence and highlighting the guilt of Stephen's audience.[158] If 'uncircumcised' is 'tantamount to a charge of not belonging to the people',[159] then Stephen's Christocentric charge parallels Acts 3:23 and the assumptions within 4:25–7.

Third, if 'for ever opposing the Holy Spirit' (7:51) echoes Isaiah 63:10,[160] then Acts 7:55–6 positively parallels the prayer in Isaiah 63:15 LXX for God – having 'hardened our hearts' (63:17; cf. Acts 7:51) – to 'turn from heaven and look from your holy habitation and from your glory'.

Finally, the grinding of teeth in 7:54 is a frequent OT characterisation of 'the enemies of God or God's people',[161] and Luke 13:27–8 presents such respondents as beyond the kingdom and its abundant spatiality foretold in 13:29.

---

[153] Barrett 1994: 382.   [154] Spencer 1997: 79.   [155] Tannehill 1990: 90.

[156] Noting, too, the failure of Stephen's audience to keep 'the law [cf. 6:13] as ordained by angels' (7:53; cf. 6:15).

[157] Barrett 1994: 376.   [158] Witherington 1998: 274; cf. 3:14; 22:14 and Luke 23:47.

[159] L. T. Johnson 1992: 134.

[160] As Johnson (1992: 134) and Spencer (1997: 80) suggest.

[161] Gaventa 2003a: 130, providing supporting references.

By 7:54, therefore, the sharpest contrast has been drawn between Stephen and his hearers, with socio-rhetorical 'name calling'[162] also demarcating alternative theological spatialities. That of his audience is condemned; repeatedly the narrator has affirmed Stephen's innocence (e.g. 6:3, 5, 10). Stephen's spatial punchline, however, is yet to come.

9. The heart of Acts 7 (7:55–6)

Spencer rightly observes that 'Stephen sketches an innovative map of divine space extending above and beyond the holy land of Israel'.[163] Yet to read this map properly, it is necessary to ask not only where 'the God of glory [has] appeared' (7:2) but also where he is appearing now, which brings 7:55–6 into focus. By highlighting the geography of divine glory, the narrative probes *where* 'the Most High' (7:48) does – and does not – dwell. In responding to these questions, the map of Acts 7 leads to Christ and shapes believer-space,[164] thereby confirming the abiding structuring influence of ascension geography.

Theology and Christology are bound together in 7:55. On the one hand, the anarthrous phrase 'glory (δόξα) of God' communicates an OT background 'expressive of the resplendent aspect of Jahweh's majestic presence'.[165] Simultaneously, δόξα evokes associations with the risen – and ascended – Jesus (Luke 9:31–2; 24:26; Acts 3:13; cf. 22:11). Δόξα also reveals connotations of the coming of the heavenly Son of Man (Luke 9:26; 21:27), connotations which underpin the content of Stephen's vision.[166]

Spencer is therefore right to see Jesus and the glory of God in 7:55 as 'two magnificent sights',[167] but they function as one magnificent *site* within Acts 7. This is the culmination of what 7:49–50 projected, the heavenly 'house' not built by human hands that resolves debate concerning the cultic and cosmic dimensions of God's presence raised in these earlier verses.[168]

---

[162] Spencer 1997: 79; cf. Malina and Nehrey 1991a: 99–110.

[163] Spencer 1997: 70.

[164] Fletcher-Louis (1997: 96–106) propounds Stephen as an exemplar for believers' lives.

[165] Fitzmyer 1998: 392, citing Ezekiel 9:3; 10:19.

[166] L. T. Johnson 1992: 139. Doble (2000: 204–5) expounds 'glory' as a Lukan theme.

[167] Spencer 1997: 81.

[168] Neudorfer (1998: 283) rightly sees 7:56 as the 'almost ecstatic climax' of the verb 'to see', εἰδέναι, which weaves through the speech as a 'technical term', but this does not detract from the verse's thematic connections with 7:47–50 and 7:52.

This ascension geography encapsulated in 7:55–6 provides the narrative reason and theological motivation for Stephen's death in 7:58. Readings which terminate Stephen's speech at 7:53 tend to locate the reason for his stoning in his 'final' invective in 7:51–3. Such readings are flexible, and can be invoked to deny any anti-Temple or anti-Torah sentiments with Stephen's speech.[169] The lack of any earlier intervention from Stephen's hearers is claimed as indicating that Stephen is engaged in only conventional OT prophetic critique up until 7:51,[170] even though according to the speech's internal logic (7:52), that in itself should be enough to warrant death! If those who curtail the speech at 7:53 look elsewhere, it is naturally earlier in the speech.[171] Yet if the speech extends to 7:56, Witherington's assertion that 'it was simply good early Christian rhetorical technique to leave the possibly most objectionable part of one's speech until the end' applies most particularly to Stephen's vision of the heavenly Christ – especially if, as Witherington continues, 'there does not seem to be anything in this speech [i.e. 7:2–53] that Peter could not have said'.[172] Whether representing lynch law or due legal process,[173] the decisive immediacy of the killing therefore provokes reflection on its cause, and that directs attention to the immediately preceding vision and declaration.

Stephen was killed primarily for invoking the heavenly Christ. Within the narrative, it is a *Christological* heavenly vision which Stephen declares to his hearers,[174] whereas the narrator (7:55), not the character Stephen, recounts the vision of the glory of God.[175] That Jesus is declared to be *standing* at the right hand does not lessen the spatial impact of Stephen's final words;[176] his fatal offence is Christological.[177]

---

[169] Thus Sweeney (2002: 210) who, significantly, does not even discuss 7:55–6.

[170] Witherington 1998: 274.

[171] E.g. Fitzmyer 1998: 392.   [172] Witherington 1998: 265.

[173] Richard (1978: 281) rightly repudiates 'unwarranted textual dissection' over this question.

[174] Turner (2000: 422) is too oblique when describing 7:55–6 (and 9:13–16 and 18:9) as 'comforting visions' from the Spirit (although pp. 423–7 clarify Turner's connection between Jesus and the Spirit). Brawley (1987: 131–2) ties the vision too tightly to Jerusalem.

[175] *Contra* Barrett 1994: 383.

[176] Interpretations of ἑστῶτα ('standing', 7:55–6) are manifold: see, e.g., Barrett 1994: 384–5, and the Christological multidimensionality propounded by Chibici-Reveanu 2007.

[177] Cf. Barrett 1994: 383: 'It would be mistaken to lay too much stress on the Christological significance of the vision: its effect is to confirm what Stephen has already said.' Barrett's reading underplays the narrative position of Jesus, both as ὁ δίκαιος killed by these hearers (7:52) and as Son of Man now exalted to the right hand in glory (7:55–6).

Admittedly Stephen's hearers were set against him in 7:54, prob-ably (but not necessarily exclusively) on the basis of 7:51–3, but their response in 7:57, which leads to the stoning of 7:58, is immediately sparked by Stephen's words in 7:56. Only after 7:56 is their response counter-vocal ('a loud shout'), actively rejecting what is being heard ('they covered their ears'), and actually violent (they 'all rushed together against him').[178] This is not to underplay the shift in 7:54: that 'they became enraged and ground their teeth' at him echoes 5:33 with its desire to kill, and 7:54 is commensurate with the decisive turning of hearts in 7:39.[179] Nevertheless, the declaration of the vision in 7:56 tips the balance from desire to decision.

That Jesus is not mentioned explicitly in Stephen's address until 7:52 does not detract from the claims being made for 7:55–6, given that Luke backgrounds key characters to maintain a measure of narrative suspense.[180] Now brought to the fore, 7:55–6 proclaims Jesus as glorified in heaven, a locative interest established repeat-edly earlier in Stephen's address. Stephen's vision connects with and extends visionary geographies granted to Abraham (7:2), Moses (7:30–2) and Solomon and the prophets (cf. 7:47, 52).[181] While it positions Stephen's auditors 'on the border between heaven and earth, open and closed',[182] at a more fundamental level it presents the heavenly Jesus himself as governing these borders, with as yet unseen implications for the rest of Acts. Casting Stephen as the righteous amid the unrighteous as fraternal bonds are strained to breaking point,[183] Acts 7 shades a delicate portrait of divergent spatialities. Consequently, this is not just a vision of 'the heavenly Reality so infinitely raised above all earthly

---

[178] This unanimous rejection narrated in 7:57 echoes ironically with the unity (ὁμοθυμαδόν) of the Jerusalem believers (2:46; 4:24; 5:12). Both unities are played out within all Sojan perspectives.

[179] This stopping of ears (Acts 7:57; cf. 7:51) will continue until and beyond 28:26–7. Looking ahead, meanwhile, other 'ears' in Jerusalem will pursue the outworkings of ascension geography (11:22). Within the narrative, therefore, it is insufficient simply to say, with Haenchen (1971: 292 n. 6), that 'the custom [of stopping one's ears on hearing an unseemly word] is ancient'.

[180] Martín-Asensio 1999: 256. Thus, Martín-Asensio suggests, Stephen (6:13), Jesus (6:14), Joseph (7:9) and Moses (7:35) are each indicative of '"this very one whom men [*sic*] reject God has both chosen and blessed"' (p. 253).

[181] Spencer (1997: 81) cites 1 Kings 8:10–13; Isaiah 6:1–3 and Ezekiel 1:4–28; 8:1–4; 10:1–22. In each instance the location of the vision, and what the vision declares about that location, is of central importance.

[182] Brawley 1990: 201.   [183] Penner 2004: 295–300.

polemics', but is 'a vision of the ultimate decision which shatters the frame of earthly events'.[184]

Thus Acts 7 focuses on more than simply earthly places: Jesus' position 'at the right hand of God', far from being a 'non-question'[185] or simply 'metaphorical language for the divine omnipotence ... [i.e.] Everywhere',[186] is central to understanding Stephen's speech. It not only confirms that 'The real "place" of God's dwelling, heaven itself, is thus on Stephen's side';[187] it also functions thirdspatially, analogous to Jorge Luis Borge's literary 'Aleph', a space 'where all places are'.[188] Thus 7:55–6 addresses the accusations made against Stephen in 6:14[189] by declaring the locational status of 'this Jesus of Nazareth'[190] and forms the climactic key to the speech that sparks Stephen's subsequent death, an event which has a profound ongoing impact on the production of narrative space within Acts.

In terms of ascension geography, Stephen is stoned primarily for proclaiming his vision of Christ's new (heavenly) firstspace, a third-spatial vision which is shaping Stephen's own spatiality and that to which the preceding speech has been building. While not embedding this scene within an ascension-driven production of space, Tannehill probes some of its consequences when noting that Stephen's affirma-tion of what Jesus claimed in Luke 22:69 forms 'part of an ongoing struggle that continues to the end of Acts ... [during which] two visions of reality clash'.[191]

To the end, Stephen's geographical orientation remains a para-digm of ascension geography. He having been removed from the city (7:58),[192] his calling to the 'Lord (κύριε) Jesus' in 7:59 (κύριε in 7:60) exemplifies the injunction of 2:21 and claims its promise. Stephen's final earthly moments maintain his heavenward Christocentric thirdspace. Although he was the first believer since 1:12 to leave first-space Jerusalem, Stephen does not leave the sphere of Christocentric

---

[184] Haenchen 1971: 295.

[185] Houlden 1991: 177, addressing the literal whereabouts of Christ.

[186] Metzger 1969: 127.   [187] Fitzmyer 1998: 392.

[188] Soja (1989: 222–4; 1996: 54–60) employs Borge's 'Aleph' to articulate thirdspace.

[189] Albeit indirectly, as Penner (2004: 294–5) rightly observes. *Contra* Conzelmann (1987: 57), who, following Dibelius, judges the speech to be disconnected from the earlier accusations.

[190] Penner (2004: 292) engages in an unsubstantiated false dichotomy when judging that 'the vision is not about Jesus *per se*, but about the characterization of Stephen'.

[191] Tannehill 1990: 98.

[192] Stephen's removal in 7:58 also parallels ironically the location of Moses' 'tent of witness' (cf. 7:44; 22:20). Situated beyond the camp, this was where Moses met with God and requested to see God's glory (Exodus 33:7–11, 18).

ascension geography.[193] His fate mirrors that of previous Christocentric prophets in Jerusalem (7:51). Also, the frequent comparison with Jesus' passion is rightly made; to this must be added Stephen's continuing consciousness of the ascended Jesus, who is 'ruling with heavenly power, whom the opponents still cannot see'.[194] The same heavenly Jesus who sends the Holy Spirit in 2:33 will, Stephen trusts in 7:59, receive *his* spirit at this point of death. Meanwhile, Stephen's removal from the city, and his abiding sense of Christological providence, anticipate the greater scattering which closes the Jerusalem section of Acts (8:1).

10.   Aftermath: a restructuring of believer-space (7:57–8:3)

Looking ahead in Acts, holding to the spatial vision of 7:55–6 will enthral believers and instil hostility in opponents for long beyond Acts 7. This vision is, therefore, formative for the rest of Acts, a primary part of the layered presentation of space and place(s) which constitutes the narrative.[195]

The decisive turn within the geography of believer-space in Acts is sparked by Stephen's vision of the heavenly Christ. Acts 7:57–8:3 achieves this turn by a series of ironic effects which emphasise the role of the heavenly Christ in ordering earthly space. First, Jesus' third-space location is but the latest – and climactic – revelation of God to Israel from beyond the land of Israel.[196] Second, the introduction of Saul in 7:58, through the reference to 'feet', echoes oppositionally the earlier presentations of ἐκκλησία-space in 4:34, 37; 5:2, 10. Such parallels remain dormant for later narrative development. Third, Stephen's vision of the heavenly Christ sparks a 'severe persecution' that issues in the Jerusalem believers being 'scattered throughout the countryside of Judea and Samaria' (8:1).[197] The recurrence of three of the four spatial markers from 1:8 is not insignificant, providentially

---

[193] This narrative juncture provides another justification for Acts 2 having omitted the Jerusalem-centric Joel 3:5b (2:32) LXX.

[194] Tannehill 1990: 99–100, without the pejorative tone of Haenchen 1971: 296, viewing Stephen's death as 'piously stylized'.

[195] Acts 7 is, as Conzelmann (1987: 57) describes it, 'an edifying mediation on the history of salvation' precisely because it addresses the *geography* of salvation.

[196] Sterling (1999: 212–14) regards 7:2–53 as legitimating early Christian mission; 7:56 provides the unstated climax to his argument.

[197] Witherington (1998: 252 n. 234) does not plumb the Christocentric first principles of Luke's testimony when claiming that persecution advances the mission – it is specifically persecution following a revelation of the *heavenly* Christ.

mapping these events reminding auditors of ascension geography's expansive and as yet unfulfilled projection 'to the ends of the earth' (the fourth element, not stated in 8:1). Fourth, the narrative interweaves and contrasts the spatialities of Stephen and Saul, an interlock reprised in Paul's Christological temple vision of 22:17–21. Unwittingly, Saul advances the spread of the word by seeking its constraint (8:3; cf. 8:1, 4), thereby ironically building up the spatial order he seeks to destroy, and all this prior to his own Damascus road encounter with the heavenly Christ. Here, prior to that later revelation to both character and auditor, 8:1–3 constitutes the narrative's lowest point,[198] underlying irony notwithstanding, as destruction rather than fellowship moves from house to house (8:3; cf. 2:46). Unseen at this juncture, a greater irony awaits, with Paul's climactic description of his house-to-house ministry (20:18b–21).

Despite many scholars arguing that Luke is mistaken on the matter,[199] 8:1 claims that *all* the Jerusalem church, except the apostles, were scattered, a relocation forced by their association with Stephen's heavenly vision and its herald. Non-totalitarian conditions of state control (if, indeed, 8:1 reports an official action) would suggest a short-lived but intense burst of persecution,[200] but Acts makes extensive use of this dispersion caused by Christological space (8:4–5; 9:1–27; 11:19–21). That the apostles stay in Jerusalem confirms Chapter 4's supposition that their distinct ministry (6:2, 4) was place-specific, their immobility implying great geographic courage.[201]

In closing, Jerusalem-space is not completely abandoned and unpromising for ascension geography, even if the favour of 'the people' has turned away from the word (6:12). Jerusalem is not unremittingly bleak persecution-space: the apostles remain there and, possibly, 8:2 hints at devout Jews burying and lamenting Stephen.[202] Yet the narrative focus remains on Stephen's thirdspace

---

[198] Tannehill 1990: 100.

[199] E.g. Haenchen 1971: 297, but cf. Witherington 1998: 278.

[200] *Contra* the assumptions of Haenchen 1971: 297, Conzelmann 1987: 60–1.

[201] L. T. Johnson (1992: 141) overreaches when claiming that the narrative has presented the apostles as 'untouchable'. Suggestions that popular resentment had not yet reached the levels of 12:2–3 (Bruce 1990: 215), or that Jerusalem needed to 'remain the mother church' (Fitzmyer 1998: 397), are not easily established within the text. Fitzmyer misplaces the text's emphasis by generalising the particular, positing that the apostles' stance 'is the way Christians should react to persecution'.

[202] As Barrett (1994: 392) and Witherington (1998: 272, 277 n. 328) suggest. Tannehill (1990: 100–1) is too certain that they were 'evidently non-Christian Jews'. Cf. Fitzmyer 1998: 397: 'they more likely were sympathetic Christians who buried and mourned Stephen before their flight'.

vision of Christ and its effects rather than on Stephen's firstspace burial site – the narrative has already downplayed such mortal details for other key characters (2:29–31; 7:2, 16).

11. Conclusion

Acts 6–7 makes a profound contribution towards a spatialised understanding of Acts based upon an abiding ascension geography. The vision of a Christological heaven governing Stephen's speech in Acts 7 reiterates and develops the ascension geography identified earlier in 1:6–11. It functions as the spur for his death and the believers' consequent persecution and scattering. In this manner, the post-ascension Jesus – through his witnesses (see 22:20 concerning Stephen) – is still shaping believer-space and redefining Israel-space on earth. Acts 7 presents a more elaborate version of the worldview based on Psalm 2 outlined in Acts 4:24–30,[203] which itself explicates the underlying ordering of space established by the ascension in 1:6–11.

Acts 7 develops and confirms the fusing of the will of God with the heavenly place (and consequent earthly spaces) of Jesus, shown foundationally in 1:6–11 but now articulated in 7:56, 59, 60. The sermon enhances Luke's characterisation of God as the promise-keeper whose blessings extend to all the families of the earth, not being bound by laws governing religious praxis.[204] Thus the characterisation of both Jesus and God is bound up in the production of earthly space(s). This geography becomes apparent in a spatialised and Christological reworking of Johnson's comments that 'the focus is on God's promise and the way [place in which] it will reach fulfilment in a time [place] beyond Abraham. God [/Jesus] appears where and when he wishes, directs and moves people and issues promises that are open-ended, to be fulfilled in often surprising ways.'[205]

Building on Chapters 3 and 4, it is excessively blunt to conclude that Acts 7 represents the break with Jerusalem and Judaism.[206] Instead, the hybrid identity of Jerusalem-space drawn in Chapter 4 continues to hold, albeit with 'a significant hardening of the

---

[203] Bock 1998: 56 n. 20.   [204] Brawley 1999.

[205] L. T. Johnson 1992: 121, square-bracketed comments added.

[206] Marguerat (2002: 47–8) judges that Luke delays Jesus' denunciation of the Temple until Acts 7, so that the Temple can function positively in Acts 2–5; Phillips (2003: 159) equates Acts 7 with Abel's death in Genesis 2. Tyson (1988: 126) suggests a distinction between *individual* Jewish believers and more structured *collective* opposition after Acts 7.

opposition'.[207] This tension reflects one geographer's observation that hybridity mirrors 'the complexities and contradictions of specific contexts' and can reinscribe boundaries.[208] If typified by the Sanhedrin, then 'Jerusalem preferred to remain with the Temple and to regard that as the final mark of God's favour, rather than let it lead them to Jesus to whom it pointed'.[209] In contradistinction, 'Stephen's speech is designed to point Israel away from the temple to the resurrected and glorified Son of Man',[210] – in other words, to reorient their geography. Acts 7 continues to 'interpret and provoke'[211] the spaces of this conflictual relationship. The geography of Acts is subtle: there are still openings in the face of Jewish hostility, even in 8:1–3. Just as Jerusalem is not written off, Acts 7 leaves open whether Jerusalem will operate as a mother church in any ecclesiological sense.[212] Rejection of Stephen's spatiality does not suggest that the Jews *in toto* are in turn rejected, but does spur 'new places of God … in which his growing new "people" gather'.[213]

Building from 1:6–11 and anticipating Acts 8–11, the stage is now set for ascension geography to order further the space of the expanding church. Acts 6–7 forms an important democratising bridge to what follows in Acts 8 and beyond. The continued growth of God's word throughout Acts 6–7 has been evident in all three Sojan dimensions, especially in the summary statement of 6:7 and in Stephen's 'geography'. By inference, inhabiting ascension geography is not simply the twelve's responsibility; it is also incumbent upon those who follow them. The vistas of the heavenly Jesus which open and close the Jerusalem section of Acts provide important triangulation for this wider place-making. While not directly normative for believers,[214] Stephen's experience of the heavenly Jesus orients the earthly space of other believers within the narrative, disciples becoming aligned with the destiny of their master at all three Sojan levels. This abiding and fundamental orientation precludes any merely earthbound analysis of narrative space within Acts 1–7 or, indeed, within Acts as a whole.

The present reading of Acts 6–7 indicates that historicist descriptions of Stephen's address need to be rewritten. Stephen's speech presents the production of space, not simply a recitation of 'historical events', as expressive of God's salvific and generous activity and as

---

[207] Tannehill 1990: 86.
[208] Pratt 1999: 155.   [209] Franklin 1975: 102–3.   [210] Peterson 1998b: 379.
[211] Tannehill 1990: 33, referring to the speeches in Acts 2–5.
[212] *Contra* Franklin 1975: 103.   [213] Petersen 1978: 86.
[214] Cf. Bolt 1998: 210–14.

subject to theological critique. Thus in narrative terms, to spatialise Tannehill, 'the narrator [of spatiality] imposes story on story on story, building up mutually interpretive layers of similar [placed] events'.[215] In conclusion, a spatial reading affirms previous recognition of the importance of Stephen's speech within (Luke-)Acts by extending this significance to include the production of post-ascension space. This realisation both anticipates and structures further narrative spaces beyond 8:3, spaces to which attention now turns.

---

[215] Tannehill 1990: 97, square-bracketed comments added.

6

ACTS 8:4–9:31

1.   Introduction

After Stephen's death and its aftermath, Acts 8:4–9:31 introduces wider geographical horizons which maintain and expand the spatialised reading of Acts pursued in earlier chapters. Witness-space extends into Samaria and anticipates 'the end of the earth' through a variety of firstspace locales. Narrative firstspace is no longer restricted to Jerusalem, nor is it so closely identified with apostolic presence. Nevertheless, as this chapter demonstrates, a consistent spatial order governed by heavenly and Christocentric thirdspace based around 1:6–11 is maintained throughout this section.

The chapter explores 8:4–9:31 by dividing it into three broad arenas: Samaria (8:4–25), the Gaza road (8:26–40), and Saul's transformation (9:1–30). Together with 9:32–11:18 (Chapter 7), these arenas embed an ascension geography 'under heaven' and 'to the ends of the earth'.

2.   Samaria-space (8:4–25)

Reading Samaria-space within ascension geography

As a narrative turn, the move to Samaria needs to be positioned within the narrative-geographical flow of Acts. Most fundamentally in this regard, movement into Samaria directly evokes the expanding witness envisaged by Jesus in 1:8. It is initiated by those 'scattered' from Jerusalem (8:2, 4), a firstspace displacement resulting from Stephen's martyrdom, itself provoked by his proclamation of heavenly thirdspace (7:56). On these two counts the spatial dynamic underpinning Acts 8–11 is driven by the heavenly Christ. Although these chapters contain many supernatural agencies spurring expansion from exclusively Jewish space towards the gentiles, the initial transposition into Samaria, like 11:19–26 (which bookends the section), is presented with no explicit supernatural accompaniment beyond Stephen's prior Christophany and heaven now answering the prayer of 4:23–31 even beyond 'this city' (4:27). This presents a powerful spur for auditors, similarly lacking supernatural accompaniments, also to 'preach the word' (cf. 8:4).

Textual variants – 'a/the city of Samaria' – mean that Philip's specific destination (8:5) cannot be precisely located in firstspace, but it is nevertheless freighted with secondspace significance, his ministry being directed towards 'the people (τὸ ἔθνος) of Samaria' (8:9). Entering 'Samaria' reprises earlier narrative evocation of this space (1:8), as well as reviving Third-Gospel interest in Samaritan responses to Jesus (Luke 9:51–6; 17:11–19). Beyond historical-critical interest in Lukan topographic knowledge,[1] there lies a much richer 'geography', one encoded within the parable of the neighbourly Samaritan (10:25–37), which, 'if taken seriously, would destabilize the world of this lawyer [in Luke 10] and challenge him to embrace the new world propagated through Jesus' ministry'.[2] This 'world' is now being embraced and embodied by Philip. Such Third-Gospel antici-pations of a robust positionality beyond Jerusalem's borders inform the move across ethnic and cultural boundaries occurring here in Acts 8, emphasising the magnitude of Philip's Samaritan ministry and opposing any mythologising of the connection between Spirit and mission.[3]

Within this dynamically unfolding geography, the Samaritans' identity and status within (Luke-)Acts is ambiguous, hybrid and not easily tied down. Their territory evokes wider traditional Jewish eschatological hopes of restoration (cf. Luke 2:36; possibly Acts 1:6), although Luke 17:18 qualifies too simplistic an equation.[4] At the same time (and in the same space), Samaritans are – for Luke – at best 'heretical' Jews' rather than simply pagans or gentiles.[5] Thus a Samaritan mission indicates both universality of salvation in Christ,[6] *and* that a mission to Shem is well under way.[7] Rather than nailing down the Samaritans' identity, the Acts narrative can

---

[1] E.g. Hengel 1983: 121–6.   [2] Green 1997b: 426, 427. See also pp. 404–6.

[3] Hays 2003: 163, 166–72.

[4] Green 1997b: 626; Bauckham 2001: 469–71; cf. Jervell 1972: 124.

[5] Quoting from Gaventa 1986: 67. Cf. Jervell 1972: 113–32. Regarding Samaria's ambiguous status, see, variously, the commentators, Coggins 1982: 431–2, and Ravens 1995: 93: 'they are Israelites and not Jews'.

[6] Fitzmyer 1998: 402.   [7] J. M. Scott 1995: 168–9 n. 158.

exploit Samaria's multi-layered ambiguity as an antechamber to the nations.[8]

The narration of Philip's preaching suggests its conformity with the salvation geography envisaged in Acts 1:6–11. First, Philip's proximity to Stephen, both textually (6:5) and in his ministry's narrative position immediately after Stephen's proclamation (7:56, 59–60) has firmly confirmed Jesus in heaven, suggests that Philip, too, proclaims the *heavenly* Christ.[9] Furthermore, 8:12 links 'the name of Jesus Christ' (a frequent motif throughout Acts 2–5) with 'the kingdom of God' (last mentioned in 1:3, 6) as the content of Philip's preaching. Clearly the temporal-spatial compression in 1:6 has not obliterated the legitimacy of the 'kingdom' concept now proclaimed, here, *in Samaria*. More than simply occupying 'a general summary of Christian belief and preaching',[10] the strategically positioned references to 'kingdom of God' in Acts are 'placed' proclamations which *produce* space, triangulating with the earth–heaven coordinates of 1:6–11 to generate an interwoven theological geography of kingdom expectation across and beyond the narrative.

Samaria, with its ambiguous relationship with Judea, benefits from the 'here but not here' of this kingdom as understood within the spatial ordering developed across 1:6–11. Although Acts does not articulate any Samaritan messianic hope based around Mount Gerizim, Philip's proclamation would confront such beliefs, even if latent in this period, with the empty slopes of Olivet. Simultaneously, Acts does not present a centripetal Jerusalem; if anything, 5:16 presents centripetal *apostles* who later will become peripatetic. Acts requires no-one in Samaria (or elsewhere) to return to Jerusalem to become incorporated within its ascension geography. Nevertheless, given the Samaritans' situation, Philip's proclamation of 'the Messiah' (τὸν Χριστόν, 8:5) might well have sat lightly to 'its Judean and Davidic associations',[11] but such a scenario increases the narrative likelihood, and need, of *heavenly* thirdspace.

Second, the Lukan Philip, 'who [probably] never knew or followed Jesus in the flesh, bears the marks [the spatiality] of a true Christian

---

[8]   Eisen 2006: 165 declares Samaria to be a buffer zone: 'Demzufolge bildet Samarien gewissermaßen einen Übergangsraum zu den Völkern.' Such a hybrid space offers a suitable bridge for an expanding ascension geography, but other places will become more significant within Acts (10:1–11:30).

[9]   Also, Philip encounters Simon of Samaria, 'another claimant to be the Standing One' (Fletcher-Louis 1997: 248 n. 127).

[10]   Barrett 1994: 408.   [11]   Bruce 1990: 217.

disciple', exhibiting 'Jesus-style activity [which] flows exclusively from his relationship with the risen [and heavenly] Christ'.[12] Beyond paralleling the apostolic proclamation in Jerusalem in its content, Philip's proclamation (ἐκήρυσσεν, 8:5) picks up the same verb's climactic (and geographically expansive) use in Luke 24:47,[13] further linking Philip's ministry with Jesus himself. Further, the 'signs' accompanying his preaching (Acts 8:6) connect Philip with the Pentecostal bridging of earth and heaven (cf. 2:19).

Samaria's 'great joy' (πολλὴ χαρά, 8:8) has been variously described as reflecting messianic hope, salvific activity or miracles performed 'in that city'.[14] This breadth of readings indicates how Philip's ministry, with its proclamation, healings and exorcisms, initiates a new (heavenly messianic) thirdspatial order which transforms comprehensively existing productions of space within Samaria. Rather than resulting simply from 'God's presence and activity in the world (cf. Luke 2:10)',[15] the resultant χαρά-space reflects orientation towards an active but absent *Christ* who is determinative of earthly spaces (cf. Acts 8:12). An ascension geography is here in view.

These narrative links legitimate Philip's ministry in an unlikely setting; they also prepare to distinguish Philip's work from that of Simon. Three times the Samaritan crowds 'paid attention' (προσεῖχον) in the narrative: in 8:6 to Philip, and in 8:10, 11 (retrospectively narrated) to Simon. The durative aspect of these imperfect verbs indicates something in progress,[16] namely rival productions of Samaritan-space. Ὁμοθυμαδόν ('with one accord') intensifies their attentiveness in 8:6, and evokes earlier descriptions of unity in Jerusalem (1:14; 2:46; 4:24; 5:12; cf. 7:57). It also emphasises the transfer of allegiance from Simon to Philip,[17] a shift which is in essence territorial, a change of geography, a spatial reordering. If Philip proclaimed a great one in heaven, previously they had adhered to a great one in their midst (8:11). This Simonic geography now deserves further examination.

---

[12] Spencer 1992b: 87, square-bracketed comments added.

[13] And in Jesus' programmatic sermon (Luke 4:18, 19).

[14] Variously Barrett 1994: 404; Fitzmyer 1998: 403; Witherington 1998: 283 n. 17 and Gaventa 2003a: 135. Spencer 1997: 85–6 addresses the shock of such a response *from the Samaritans*.

[15] Haar 2003: 173.

[16] Haar 2003: 170. Similarly the present participle and imperfect passive in 8:12, cf. the enduring quality of the perfect-tense ἐξεστακέναι ('he had amazed [them]', 8:11), 'foregrounds' Simon's (territorial) influence (p. 172).

[17] Haar 2003: 171.

Simonic geography: an oppositional spatial order within Samaria

Although he is introduced in a neutral fashion (8:9),[18] Simon's identity and narrative function have been much discussed.[19] Read for his 'space', and assessed against the ascension geography of Acts, Simon is cast as the epicentre for an alternative, oppositional geography.

Magical geography?

A magical dimension infuses how Simon is characterised in Acts 8, the verb μαγεύω (8:9, 11) placing Simon in conflict with the narrative's ideological point of view and its evaluation of space. Salvation geography informs a wider Lukan disapproval of magic practices, such that magic can be distinguished from speech-acts of 'the word' in highly charged magical-theological settings such as Samaria (8:9–24), Cyprus (13:4–12) and Ephesus (19:11–20). Across Acts, an instrumental understanding of the Lukan difference between magic and Christian ministry confirms this reading.[20]

Thus Simon functions as 'a magus with magnetic power' through his syncretistic self-designation and the crowd's opinion of him (8:9–11),[21] even if Acts 8 does not ascribe the noun to him.[22] Simon's claims concerning his presence challenge and confront Philip's claims for an *absent* Jesus and *his* ascension spatiality. Jesus' warning in Luke 21:8 positions Simon's self-promotion, and Simon's implied acceptance of such ascription from others (cf. Acts 12:23) compounds this oppositional stance. Such rhetoric of personal power is not neutral in relation to geography, but rather it shapes perceptions and utilisation of space(s) and place(s) on all three Sojan

---

[18] Haar (2003: 173) denies any grammatical or cotextual reason to translate τις ironically or contemptuously.

[19] Barrett 1979 opposes reading Acts as recasting Simon as a Samaritan magician in order to discredit a popular Gnostic hero. Cf. Derrett (1982: 53) and Haar (2003: 174), who criticise Barrett's equation of Simon with fraudulent practice.

[20] Haar's suspicion (2003: 266) of 'a Lukan metanarrative about "the triumph of Christianity over magic"' excessively discounts the effects of *ascension* spatiality upon the narrative as a whole. Cf. Conzelmann 1987: 65–6; Garrett 1989: 98–9; Marguerat 2003: 117.

[21] Marguerat 2003: 118; cf. Barrett 1994: 406–7.

[22] Μάγος ('magician') implied that 'none but themselves had the ear of the gods' (Haar 2003: 2, 174).

planes. Agreeing that 'with virtually every phrase of vv. 9–11, Luke's portrait of Simon grows increasingly negative',[23] Simon is narrated as embedding an egotistical counter-geography within Samaria. Like the claims ascribed to Theudas in 5:36, Simon's claims are territorial in their implications. His geography functions in addition to, and possibly in interaction with, any messianic counter-geography indigenous to Samaria. Thus although magic represented 'a widely diffused aspect of Hellenistic religion',[24] Acts portrays specific *placed* manifestations which themselves produce particular spatialities.

A geography of money and power?

Readings of Simon as 'hungry for power (and money)'[25] also need incorporating within his territoriality. The monetary aspect of Simon's character becomes clearer in 8:18–20; initially power is more in view. If elsewhere in Luke-Acts 'power' (8:10) is frequently a (Septuagintal) metonym for the Spirit,[26] then Simon's claim directly challenges Jesus' words in 1:8 and Peter's witness concerning Jesus in 2:33. Mention of 'all of them, from the least to the greatest' as paying attention to Simon in 8:10 intensifies his territorial reach and power,[27] contrasting with the 'one accord' ascribed to Philip in 8:6. If 'great' (8:9b, 10b) denotes 'a syncretic schema where social claim blends in an irreparable way with sacred prestige',[28] Simon's status infuses material and conceptual productions of space. Similarly, Susan Garrett's instrumental reading of power, highlighting 'the power of God' as a recurring motif throughout Luke-Acts, indicates that Luke did not see power as impersonal or free-floating.[29] Instead, conceptions of power are inherently placed, as is any invocation of Jesus' name as accessing the power of God (cf. 8:12).

In short, Acts 8 presents a Simonic geography already established in, and imposing spatial order upon, Samaria. Philip preaches 'the good news about the kingdom of God and the name of Jesus Christ' (8:12) into this Simonic spatial ordering. Whereas Simon

---

[23] Gaventa 2003a: 136–7.   [24] L. T. Johnson 1992: 147.
[25] Witherington 1998: 283.
[26] Marguerat 2002: 51, citing Luke 1:17, 35; 4:14; 24:49; Acts 1:8; 8:10; 10:38.
[27] 'Power' (δύναμις) and 'to' (ἕως) in 8:10 parallel 1:8 and, in both instances, are implicated in a production of space.
[28] Marguerat 2003: 118–19.   [29] Garrett 1989: 66–8.

'speaks of himself', Philip 'proclaims the kingdom and name of the [absent but active] Other'.[30] This foundational distinction, predicated upon 1:6–11, comes to the fore as the narrative unfolds. Interweaving narrations of Simon's and Philip's spatialities, evident in both verbal repetitions[31] and distinctive differences,[32] suggest that the two are to be read against each other. This interplay is instructive and important. The apostolic visitors from Jerusalem will reveal the true standing of these spatialities *vis-à-vis* ascension geography.

The Jerusalem apostles reveal the legitimacy of Philip's geography

A reading against *the apostles?*

Tannehill harbours an implicit judgement of apostolic tardiness concerning the advance into Samaria being pioneered by non-apostles, and Spencer explicitly critiques what he judges to be apostolic resistance to 'the inclusive kingdom of God stretching beyond Jerusalem's and Israel's ethno-political borders'.[33] As previous chapters judged concerning 6:1–6 and 8:1, Sojan analysis downplays such criticisms. Tannehill's interpretation, whereby the apostles function here as 'verifiers' rather than 'initiators' of the mission,[34] simply reveals what has been the case *throughout* Acts, but what was previously masked by narrative firstspace being confined to Jerusalem and therefore synonymous with apostolic presence. Acts 8:14 is not the first instance of the apostles 'reacting to developments that take place without their planning or control';[35] rather, these 'developing places' (to invert Tannehill's comment) now occur at a distance from apostolic firstspace presence. Tannehill continues: 'The real initiative is not in earthly hands.'[36] Indeed, it has been in *heavenly* hands since 1:9. Therefore, rather than being reduced, the apostles' role is clarified in Acts 8, and the resultant 'space-lag' is not narrated as reflecting apostolic resistance to, or rejection of, such spatial expansion.[37] Rather than initially replicating earlier apostolic

[30] Marguerat 2003: 120, square-bracketed comment added.
[31] Barrett 1994: 398.   [32] Marguerat 2003: 119–20.
[33] Tannehill 1990: 104; cf. Barrett 1988: 73; Spencer 1997: 85.
[34] Tannehill 1990: 102.   [35] Tannehill 1990: 103.   [36] Tannehill 1990: 103.
[37] *Contra* Spencer 1997: 85.

antagonism towards Samaria (Luke 9:52–4),[38] the very different calling down from heaven in 8:14–17 confirms without reservation a more dynamic narration of space anticipated in Luke 9:55; 17:11–19 and Acts 1:6–11. Acts *can* reveal such hesitation (e.g. 10:1–11:18), but it is not evident here.

A hierarchical reading?

A Sojan reading also undermines Johnson's hierarchical reading of 8:14. Although 'Luke wants us to see the Twelve as a unified group', it does not follow that they are therefore 'exercising control over the mission'.[39] If anything, Acts 8 communicates a spatial liberty: the first post-ascension declaration of 'kingdom' (8:12) confirms that mission is not tied to apostolic presence. The narrative's *heavenly* 'catholicism' does not need to be 'certified by the Jerusalem leadership',[40] other than to preserve such bilateral unity on earth. Rather, the narrative presents the Samaritan converts as valid believers before 8:14; prior to the apostolic visit, 8:14 assumes Samaritan reception of the word of God, which, in Acts, is synonymous with becoming a believer (11:1; 17:11; cf. Luke 8:13). Also, these men and women previously baptised by Philip were not rebaptised by the apostles (cf. 19:1–6). Throughout Acts, baptism is the gateway, in all three Sojan senses, which leads into ascension geography, with its rewritten spaces.[41]

As 8:20 confirms, any hierarchy is heavenly, not earthly. Sending *two* apostles indicates a witnessing role is in view[42] (especially given John's virtual redundancy within the unfolding narrative), as does their explicit return to Jerusalem (8:25). Tellingly, no Samaritan is required to return with them. Rather than being bluntly hierarchical,[43] this witness role is implicitly reflexive, as 11:1–18 will make clear. In narrative terms, the lack of a Jerusalem 'church' at this time (cf. 8:1, 14) explains the lack of any debate analogous to 11:1–18. The lack of any narrated explanation even to the other apostles signals the lack of any restrictive attitude among them. Nonetheless, *visiting*

[38] Witherington 1998: 285–6.   [39] L. T. Johnson 1992: 148.
[40] L. T. Johnson 1992: 148, appealing to 11:1–18, 22. Similarly Marguerat 2002: 126. This notion of a *heavenly* Catholicism is required by any mapping of the network model of the church in Acts presented by L. C. A. Alexander 2003.
[41] Cf. Garrett 1989: 64–5; Bruce 1990: 221 and Barrett 1994: 408–9.
[42] Trites 1977: 133–5.   [43] *Contra* Conzelmann 1987: 65.

Samaria might have clarified or confirmed this perspective for the apostles.[44] A geographical reading is thereby required.

A geographical reading?

Rather than being portrayed as reluctant or hierarchical, the apostolic visit is narrated in 8:14 using explicitly geographical terms, suggesting that *where* Philip's ministry occurs motivates their visit. This does not inscribe a Jerusalem-centred worldview within Acts; rather, it recapitulates 8:1, itself evoking 1:8. Within an ascension-geography matrix, Acts 8 reflexively reorders both Jerusalem and Samaria. This reflexivity further downplays interpretations of the account as an official supervision of this expansion.[45] Rather, attention focuses on the narrative aside (8:16) concerning 'this particular and perhaps unique'[46] delay of the Spirit. It allows the apostles to *witness* (1:8! Cf. 10:44–7) the genuine nature of Samaria's reception of the word and prevents parallel politics of space[47] developing in these two places separated by long-standing antipathy.

Ultimately, the best explanation for the Spirit's delay is geographic,[48] proclamation of the kingdom in 8:12 symbolically realising the reunification of David's kingdom.[49] Earthly claims for David's city have already been circumscribed by Christ's heavenly reign (2:29, 36; 4:25–31), and David, prophetically by the Spirit, has voiced the need for apostolic unity (1:16). Now, in Sojan categories, territorial unity is established not through formal firstspace political realignment or through mere symbolism but through believer-space premised on the thirdspace word about the heavenly Christ. Its firstspaces are pluriform, multi-centred (1:8; cf. 11:17; 15:8), marked by co-operative partnership (15:3).[50] This is ironic space, solidarity found through scattering (8:4) under an absent, heavenly ruler whose bestowal of the Spirit according to his promise compels acceptance across

---

[44] Rius-Camps and Read-Heimerdinger (2006: 153–5) argue that 'the word of the Lord' and Hellenistic spelling of 'Jerusalem' within 8:25 D communicate a Bezan shift in apostolic spatial categories since 8:14.

[45] Barrett 1994: 410–11 provides a helpful broader range of possible motivations behind the apostolic visit.

[46] Witherington 1998: 289.   [47] Seccombe 1998: 359: 'Two "denominations".'

[48] Cf. Turner 2000: 360–75.   [49] Bruce 1990: 221.

[50] Tannehill (1990: 104) and Witherington (1998: 287) expound this partnership, as does Spencer (1997: 87–8), although with criticism from Turner (2000: 371).

otherwise divisive boundaries. It is based in 1:8–11, rather than 1:6, but is nevertheless intensely 'placed' rather than abstracted into a spiritualised isotropic plain.

The Jerusalem apostles reveal the illegitimacy of Simon's geography

In a sharp narrative turn, 8:18 attends again to Simon, his earlier geography (8:9–11, 13) now interacting with Peter's. Just as the apostles' visit reveals the full implications of Philip's ministry (8:15–17), so also 8:18–24 discloses the presuppositions informing Simon's spatiality, critiquing them according to ascension geography.

Simon, having been among those who believed and were baptised, had attached himself to Philip on account of 'the signs and great miracles' (8:13); now he sees something even more impressive, namely the apostles' hands conferring the Spirit (8:18). Three references to 'hands' (8:17, 18, 19) uncover the fundamental issue to be Simon's 'heart' (8:21, 22). Chapter 5 has highlighted how spatialities arise from the heart's orientation, and Chapters 3 and 4 have indicated the orienting use of possessions. Here in Acts 8, Simon reveals his own egocentric geography of power, a desire ironically fulfilled by subsequent church history bestowing his name on the offence of Simony.

Simon's function (and fault) in 8:18–23 have been much discussed.[51] On six counts the incident needs to be read for its space. First, Simon's request (8:19), given his previous egocentric territoriality and his ambiguous response to Philip's gospel, represents an attempt to buy (back) Samaria-space in all its Sojan perceptions for himself, to orient Samaria once more around himself. Second, Peter's reply (8:20) highlights Simon's risk of heading to hell[52] as an anti-ascension spatial destiny. Third, if 'you have no part or share' (8:21) echoes Deuteronomy 12:12, it inverts Deuteronomy's territorial inclusion into exclusion. Any parallel in Deuteronomy 14:27, 29 contrasts with the Levite's spatiality commended in Acts 4:36–7. Fourth, 'your heart is not right before God' (8:21) parallels the wilderness generation in Psalm 78:37 and Acts 7:36–43. Fifth, 'gall

---

[51] Cf. Witherington 1998: 285 regarding 8:13, and the varying readings of the silence regarding Simon in 8:14–17 made by Barrett (1979: 291) and Derrett (1982: 53); cf. Haenchen 1971: 304 and Barrett 1994: 413.
[52] Witherington 1998: 288.

of bitterness' in Acts 8:23, while judging Simonic counter-geography, echoes the spatial implications of idolatry and covenant-breaking in Deuteronomy 29:17 LXX (29:18): 'Simon is like the man described there as going after the gods of the nations.'[53] Sixth, 'wickedness' (ἀδικία) in Acts 8:23 echoes Judas' treacherous spatiality in 1:18. Thus Simon's money and desire for power come embedded in their own geography which can be condemned from all three Sojan perspectives: deceptive in its firstspace,[54] egotistical in its secondspace, and anti-ascension in its thirdspace grasping to control the 'gift of God' (8:20). Thus Sojan categories help position Simon's ambiguity and his complex characterisation while preserving a coherent narrative flow. If Simon is 'caught again by his past',[55] then it is a spatialised past, still very much around him.

In sum, Peter continues his earlier narrative function of discerning space by clarifying Simonic space and subjecting it to a devastating ascension-geography critique. Yet as the narration of Samaria-space closes, Peter's encounter with Simon retains an open-ended conclusion. Peter's ambiguous grammar (8:22)[56] and varying interpretations of Simon's motivation in requesting prayer (8:24), complicated by variant readings,[57] preclude final certainty concerning Simon's space. Chapter 5 noted Jerusalem-space remaining open-ended in 8:1–3, and 28:31 will similarly remain open-ended. On the macro-level at least, Acts does not foreclose spaces.

Simon's open-ended fate confirms the plasticity of place and increases the narrative's ability to influence auditors' spaces. For auditors, if Simon is judged ultimately to be outside ascension geography, he provides a salutary lesson concerning the need to maintain faithful obedience to a heavenly sovereignty rather than egotistical concepts of space; if he comes ultimately within its scope, then the same lesson assumes a more repentant hue.[58]

Under either outcome, Simon-space highlights the error of seeking to control the Spirit, whether through a desire for power (8:18b;

---

[53] Barrett 1994: 417.
[54] Fitzmyer 1998: 406: 'Even though Simon has put his faith in Christ and been baptized as a Christian, he could still find himself disoriented from God.'
[55] Marguerat 2003: 119.   [56] Barrett 1994: 415–16.
[57] Barrett (1994: 417) is dismissive of 'the Western editor's intention simply to magnify the effect on Simon of Peter's rebuke'. Rius-Camps and Read-Heimerdinger (2006: 138–9, 144–7) suggest a more nuanced (and Christological) reading of 8:20–4 D.
[58] Although not precluding it, Acts 13:11 qualifies the suggestion that 'frontier communities often demand greater flexibility and toleration' (Spencer (1997: 89).

cf. 8:9–11) or from commercial deontology (8:18–20). This reading stands whether Simon assumes a commercial[59] or a magical[60] logic, if the two can be divided. Heavenly thirdspace remains sovereignly guarded from mortal manipulation, 'gift' in 8:20 reiterating 2:33, 38 and thus connecting with the heavenly Christ. So reserved, it resists and precludes the magical triad of ego, money and manipulation,[61] or any of its constituent constructions of place. Simon appears to lack such (re-)centring: he still thinks of *his* 'place' within Samaria, failing to map himself under heaven. The resultant syncretistic tendencies[62] are resisted by the narrative. If Simon's 'conversion' (8:13) had apologetic value for the power of ascension geography, so too does his correction.

Simultaneously, Simonic space educates auditors about the need for spatial discernment. Simon provides another instructive caution concerning the deception possible within (believer-)space (cf. 5:1–11). Space exhibits an opaque quality requiring apostolic discernment. Auditors are allowed no illusion that mere firstspace association is sufficient; true conversion requires comprehensive Sojan realignment under the heavenly Christ.

Leaving Samaria-space

Coming after the ambiguous closure of Simon-space, 8:25 narrates the word still going out, its diffusion unhindered by him. Apostolic approval for Samaritan believer-space is confirmed by the intensified verbal form διαμαρτυράμενοι, which reinforces that the proclamation previously made in Jerusalem (2:40) and later reported in Cornelius' house (10:42) is made now also in Samaritan territory. Earlier, Peter and John had witnessed Christ pouring out the Spirit in Samaria (8:17; cf. 2:33); now they themselves bear witness to him, as they have done previously within Jerusalem. As noted earlier, no Samaritan converts are recorded as returning with them to Jerusalem; while Samaria is no longer the despised 'Other', neither is Jerusalem the required earthly *omphalos*.

---

[59] E.g. Derrett 1982: 61–2; Fitzmyer 1998: 401.
[60] E.g. Garrett 1989: 70; Tannehill 1990: 107.
[61] Regarding these elements as typifying the concept of 'magic' within Acts, cf. S. E. Porter 2007.
[62] Regarding which, see Marguerat 2003: 107, 122–3.

Summary: Samaria-space within Acts

Samaria-space performs several functions within Acts as a narrative geography. First, it advances the diffusion of ascension geography, Samaria representing an initial bridgehead beyond Jerusalem. Its establishment as a believer-space by Philip, a non-apostle, confirms the legitimacy for such expansion without the need for apostolic firstspace presence. Conversely, apostolic visitation to such a crucial bridgehead confirms its continuity with apostolic space according to the global projection in 1:8 and the heavenly sovereignty within ascension geography. As such, both Samaria and Jerusalem are reflexively reordered within its Christocentric economy of space. Second, the didactic qualities of Samaria-space confirm that ascension geography requires apostolic discernment of space. On the one hand, deceptive spatialities mean that expressions of ascension geography cannot be reduced to mere firstspace association, to what is seen or claimed. Equally, heavenly thirdspace resists being usurped by other spatialities, whether informed by magic, money or ego (or any combination of those). Third, the thirdspace governance of the heavenly Christ overarches these developments.[63] Jesus instigates the initial providential impetus for diffusion into Samaria (1:8; 7:56), and the Spirit's subsequent confirmation of the new enterprise involves his witnesses and assumes his Pentecostal bestowal.

3.   Desert-space (8:26–40)

'Desert-space' is a heuristic label to encapsulate this pericope; it is not intended to privilege 8:26b.

Reading desert-space within ascension geography

Although 8:26–40 is sometimes viewed as self-contained within Acts, this is misleading if it reduces this section to 'a prelude to Cornelius' conversion'.[64] Also, while the Table of Nations in Genesis 10–11 suggests that this incident launches a mission to the Hamite regions,[65] this provides at best a partial understanding of the passage's spatiality. Beyond this macro-geography, almost every aspect of the chariot-rider's description influences an auditor's understanding of

---

[63] Cf. the narrowly *theocentric* readings of Tannehill 1990: 104, 113 and Marguerat 2002: 126.
[64] Conzelmann 1987: 67.   [65] J. M. Scott 1995: 167, 169–73.

his particular spatiality, and thus of the pericope's contribution to the geographical vision of Acts. In this sense, 8:26–40 is far from isolated, even if apparently self-contained. Read for its space, it fits within, and contributes to, the wider ascension geography narrated through Acts. The initially surprising subject change to 'an angel of the Lord' in 8:26 introduces the prominence of heavenly agents throughout 8:26–40. Their prominence provides a preliminary connection with ascension geography and evokes the spatial agenda of 1:8 by moving Philip from Samaria to the socio-geographic edge of Judea. Despite most commentators linking these heavenly agencies to theological rather than Christological impulses, these agents affect the ascension-geographical will of Jesus. The liminal desert setting, unusual among Luke's typically urban locations, contributes to the incident's salvation-geographical import, especially if read in the light of ascension geography.[66] By being a gateway to the peoples of the south, by mentioning two places not visited by the narrative ('Gaza' and 'Ethiopia'), and by being oriented *away* from Jerusalem (thus inverting conventional OT expectation, cf., e.g., 7:36–45), the setting hints at – and contributes towards – ascension geography's further expansion.

Reading the chariot-rider for his spaces

The character whom Philip meets within desert-space deserves and requires careful interpretation, especially regarding his spatiality. Spencer rightly comments: 'Comprehensive examination of the Ethiopian traveller's place [NB] in ancient society in relation to standard categories of race, class, and gender uncovers a fascinating, multi-faceted character who defies easy classification.'[67] Such complexity is compounded by his places of origin, both in Jerusalem and in Ethiopia, and by this liminal locale in which Philip encounters him. Truly, ἰδού ('behold', 8:27 RSV)! Given human geography's recognition that race, class and gender are 'placed' constructs, the chariot-rider's spatiality is more comprehensive than simply his 'place of origin'; a more comprehensive reading of his space is required. Only then can the space produced by his encounter with Philip be properly positioned.

---

[66] Such a geographical reading provides a control against over-elaborating the desert's liminality. Cf. Spencer 1997: 90–1.

[67] Spencer 1997: 91.

The chariot-rider is described first as an 'Ethiopian' (ἀνὴρ Αἰθίοψ). This immediately indicates something of his spatiality.

First, for modern auditors at least, that this description indicates a black African challenges 'the Eurocentric orientation of Christian Testament studies'.[68] The suspicion of latent Eurocentricity lurks in any marginalising of this man in relation to – European – Cornelius (see below concerning his status as εὐνοῦχος), and in 'Bible atlas' maps portraying journeys in Acts which do not include him.[69] Such cartographic neglect reflects an unwarranted reduction of the narrative spatiality of Acts.

Second, his description as an Ethiopian casts him as an exotic figure. This is apparent within both classical geography[70] and OT prophetic expectation.[71] This exotic referent is often presented as prefiguring Paul's gentile mission[72] or as proleptic of universal mission.[73] Used to bookend the incident (8:27–8; cf. 8:39), his locational identity and destination maintain the global scope of 1:8 across the account and, with it, the narrative dynamics of ascension geography.

Third, Luke theologically demythologises and remythologises the Ethiopian(s) within 8:26–40. Rather than presenting a people of piety and divine favour, having power to escape the ravages of death,[74] Luke brings an Ethiopian (and an influential one at that) under the span of ascension geography as one who needs understanding of scripture and who needed – and was able – to respond when Philip 'proclaimed to him ... Jesus' (εὐηγγελίσατο αὐτῷ τὸν Ἰησοῦν, 8:35). He has a place within Luke's geography, a production of space generated by a slaughtered figure from OT prophecy. This represents another instance where 'Luke can use the slenderest of vignettes to

---

[68]   Martin 1995: 791–4 (791).
[69]   Felder 1995: 207–8; Martin 1995: 793–4. Regarding Bible atlases, van der Meer and Mohrmann (1958) do not mention Ethiopia; Jedin, Latourette and Martin (1970) and Mittmann and Schmitt (2001) do not extend south of the North African Mediterranean rim.
[70]   E.g. Romm 1992: 45–8; Borgen 1997: 19, 26. Marguerat (2002: 252) sees Luke 'evoking the magic of the borders'.
[71]   A. Smith (1995: 226) describes Ethiopians in both Hellenistic and Septuagintal worldviews as 'wealthy, wise, and militarily mighty', citing 2 Samuel 18:21–33; 1 Kings 10; 2 Chronicles 12:2–3 (par. 1 Kings 14:25); 2 Chronicles 14:9–15; Psalm 68:29–36; Isaiah 18:1, 2; Isaiah 45:14 and Daniel 11:43.
[72]   E.g. Witherup 1992: 72.   [73]   E.g. Tannehill 1990: 108–9; Gaventa 2003a: 140.
[74]   Romm 1992: 58. This remythologising point remains valid even if some ancient conceptions of Ethiopians were also eurocentrically negative, as Parsons (2006: 123–41) suggests.

serve his larger literary purposes',[75] purposes which include communicating a spatial vision.

The chariot-rider's characterisation (and spatiality) become more complex with his description as a 'eunuch' (εὐνοῦχος). He is so described five times in 8:26–39, although it is noteworthy that, within Luke's delicate portrayal of the man, his geographical origins ('an Ethiopian ... of the Ethiopians', 8:27) co-ordinate his identity within 8:27–33 and are reasserted by his onward journey continued in 8:39. In between, the subsequent fourfold emphasis on him as 'the eunuch' clusters within 8:34–9.[76]

Εὐνοῦχος is best understood anatomically. Interpreting it as meaning 'official' renders the subsequent word δυνάστης ('court official') tautological.[77] Alternatively, δυνάστης could be appositional,[78] but 'the combination of physical defect and high office is not unusual',[79] and, in the context described here, it is likely. It would, however, have generated 'status inconsistency' within Jerusalem,[80] Deuteronomy 23:2 casting him as one with 'no place in the covenant community'.[81] Thus Luke's nuanced description of the man communicates much regarding his likely recent experience of Jerusalem-space, especially given the narrative's recent presentation of that space as unsympathetic to those who do not conform to its spatial expectations. Divided into its various restrictive zones and subject to policing (cf. 4:1), Temple-space would have made these spatial expectations very real to an Ethiopian eunuch.[82] That Luke's other uses of the verb προσκυνέω are ambiguous, if not verging on negative, colours interpretation of Acts 8:27.[83] Combined with the earlier narration of Jerusalem-space souring for believers, it is quite possible that the pluperfect verb ἐληλύθει ('had come') followed by a future participle,

---

[75] L. T. Johnson 1992: 158, referring to Luke's apologetic use of the chariot-rider's exotic status and social rank.
[76] *Contra* Pao (2000: 141), who judges that 'the designation "eunuch" floods the text', although this skewed distribution reinforces Pao's conclusions regarding an Isaiah 56:3–4 influence over Acts 8:26–40.
[77] Tannehill 1990: 109 n. 16. *Contra* Haenchen 1971: 310; A. Smith 1995: 227.
[78] Wasserberg 1998: 259.   [79] Barrett 1994: 425.   [80] Witherington 1998: 295.
[81] Spencer 1997: 93; cf., more extensively, 1992a: 168–72. *Contra* W. D. Davies 1974: 274.
[82] Barrett (1991: 353; cf. 1994: 425) connects him with the Temple. Witherington (1998: 297) makes an intriguing suggestion, locating him in 'the synagogue of the Freedman, perhaps?'
[83] Luke 4:7, 8; Acts 7:43; 10:25; 24:11. Luke 24:52, an exception to this reading, is textually problematic and has Jesus as its object.

προσκυνήσων ('to worship'), signals a frustrated desire,[84] rendering possible the speculation that 'his arduous journey had proved useless'.[85] Rather than primarily positioning the eunuch, 8:27 first contributes to the narrative's unfolding positioning of Jerusalem.

The main reason behind resistance to an anatomical reading of εὐνοῦχος is that it confirms his gentile status, presenting a conflict with Cornelius as the 'first' gentile convert in Acts.[86] Existing literature proposes three 'solutions'. First, a Table-of-Nations distinction between the Hamite chariot-rider and the Japhethite Cornelius appears to blunt Jew–gentile categories.[87] Yet these are the very categories highlighted in Acts 10–11, suggesting that this is at best a partial answer. Second, the chariot-rider can be cast as a Jew, but this is unconvincing.[88] Alternatively, Luke is judged to have left the man's identity ambiguous, whether out of respect for an original (Hellenistic) source which cast him as a gentile convert or because Luke did not realise he was a gentile.[89] Again, neither suggestion is convincing.

A fourth proposal, fitting better within the overarching spatiality of Acts, questions the very need for a 'first' gentile convert to function as some sort of status symbol within Acts. Such primacy presumes a historicist reading, whereas an ascension geography with expansive secondspace downplays a singular trophy 'first' and suggests that multiple 'firsts' are more communicative of the spatial projection assumed in 1:6–11.[90] Heavenly thirdspace de-centres and erodes the need for temporal primacy.[91] As a spatial narrative, Acts exhibits a pluriform interest in how different gentiles are converted in different places in different ways through different ministers of the word. In sum, effectively 'this is how things happen with the word!'

---

[84] Rius-Camps and Read-Heimerdinger 2006: 157.

[85] Gage and Beck 1994: 36.

[86] Wilson 1973: 171. Cf. Haenchen 1971: 314–16, Tannehill 1990: 110–11 and Barrett 1994: 421.

[87] Gage and Beck 1994: 35; J. M. Scott 1995: 170–1.

[88] For instance, Rius-Camps and Read-Heimerdinger (2006: 156–7) make him, effectively, an uncircumcised Jew in order to protect Cornelius' perceived place in the narrative.

[89] Wilson 1973: 172.

[90] Thus, for example, the gospel reaches Damascus (9:3) and even Rome (28:15), 'ahead' of the narrative, without need for narrative comment(ary). If Acts has any intentional primacy it is in 11:26.

[91] Bruce's unwitting struggle to escape historicist assumptions (1989: 377–80) is informative here.

Sojan narrative analysis can be taken a step further. Acts 15:7, rather than making an explicit or necessary claim to primacy for Cornelius, emphasises *firstspace interaction* ('among you').[92] In contrast, 8:26–40 remained an essentially private encounter (albeit proleptic of the gospel's global reach), an individual returning to a distant home and not affecting other believers. Thus, from the point of view of the narrative's wider believer-spaces (that is, the point of view of the 'us' of Luke 1:1), the eunuch is the first *secondspace* gentile believer in that with his conversion the *concept* of gentile conversion is broached; Cornelius and his household are the first *firstspace* gentile believers in that with them the *materiality* of gentile-space is breached by the word, water and Spirit. The eunuch is described, whereas Cornelius is named (in Acts 10, but not in Acts 11, where secondspace is again to the fore). Crucially, both are governed by heavenly third-space, with mortal believer-heralds needing heavenly assistance in order to realise Christ's spatial will expressed in 1:6–11. The two episodes are separated by Saul's heavenly call (cf. 9:15–16). Spatially it becomes a moot point as to whether 8:26–40 marks 'an even more radical stage in the rise of the gentile mission' than 10:1–11:18.[93] Instead, there is room to consider how Luke establishes a deliberate and dramatic correspondence between the two episodes.[94] Interpretation is delivered from 'needing' the Ethiopian to be a proselyte or even a Jew.[95]

Importantly, read simultaneously for his space, 'a court official of the Candace, queen of the Ethiopians', presents a powerful figure brought into the orbit and under the authority of the good news about Jesus, with clear apologetic import.[96] The chariot-rider's identity as εὐνοῦχος eludes reduction to either anatomy or power.

A proleptic realisation of a spatial ingathering which incorporates foreigners and eunuchs as envisaged by Isaiah 56:3–8 is possible, despite Isaiah 56 being neither cited nor alluded to in Acts 8:26–40.[97]

---

[92] No primacy is required by 'in the early days' (15:7), and 'first' in 15:14 compares Peter's ministry to Cornelius (15:7–10) with Barnabas and Paul's *later* gentile ministry (15:12).

[93] Barrett 1994: 420.   [94] Tannehill 1990: 110–11; Spencer 1992b: 186.

[95] See, variously, the awkward argumentation of Wilson 1973: 171–2; Gaventa 1986: 67, cf. p. 104; L. T. Johnson 1992: 159; Felder 1995: 206–7; Fitzmyer 1998: 410, 412 and Witherington 1998: 280, 293 n. 53. Unnecessarily, Wasserberg (1998: 258–9) considers that 11:19 indicates the chariot-rider is a Jew or a proselyte. Barrett (1994: 426) provides the best one-line conclusion: 'He was certainly a rare bird.'

[96] A. Smith 1995: 228; Witherington 1998: 295.

[97] R. J. Porter (1988: 55) posits the narratively probable suggestion that Philip would have made use of the Isaiah scroll, suggesting Isaiah 54:9–10; 55:1 as other possible intertexts implicit within Acts 8:35.

Isaiah 56:7 informed Jesus' critique of Temple-space in Luke 19:46 (par. Matthew 21:13), and the use of κωλύω ('prevent', Acts 8:36) concerning the chariot-rider's entry into Christian-space through baptism suggests that such incorporation would have been problematic within his previous Jerusalem-space[98] (and, quite possibly, within the Israel-space assumed in 1:6). The catalyst for a contrasting and expansive hospitality is Philip's Christological reading of the OT (8:35). As has been seen, similar Christological readings earlier in Acts have culminated in the realisation of ascension ordering of spaces, and Isaiah 56:3–8 provides an intertextual commentary on the geography unfolding in Acts.[99]

Philip's encounter with the chariot-rider as an act within ascension space

Sojan categories also enable analysis of the pericope's central encounter.

Firstspace initiative and invitation: the opening interchange (8:29–31)

The narrative emphasises Philip's instruction to approach the chariot ('Go over … and join', 8:29). His resultant proximity ('Philip ran up to itand heard', 8:30) is embedded within the narrator's fourfold emphasis in 8:28–32 concerning the rider 'reading',[100] twice specified as 'the prophet Isaiah' (8:28, 30, cf. also 8:32–3). This firstspace proximity, progressively instigated by heavenly agents in 8:26 and 8:29, is a vital prerequisite for Philip's subsequent proclamation of Jesus, especially if the chariot-rider was of higher social standing than Philip.[101] Given commentators' unwillingness to distinguish these heavenly agencies from each other,[102] the general recognition of *theological* import without commensurate *Christological* interpretation is surprising. Philip is guided according to the will of Jesus, revealed in 1:8, to proclaim Jesus

---

[98] Cf. Deuteronomy 23:2.

[99] Denova (1997: 34) suggests that this Isaianic dynamic is to the eunuch first, and then to the foreigner.

[100] This act of reading seems more important than mere ownership or possession of the scroll in positioning the man (*pace* Spencer 1997: 92). Its repeated mentions occur within the span of sixty Greek words, cf. the tighter parameters for such repetition utilised in Chapter 3.

[101] Barrett 1994: 427.   [102] E.g. L. T. Johnson 1992: 155.

to this character who is so exquisitely 'placed' within ascension geography. Jesus, although absent, is still ordering space.

The opening interchange between Philip and the chariot-rider (8:30–1) confirms a firstspace connection between them, and anticipates the Ethiopian's need for an interpreter of the secondspace encoded within the Isaiah scroll before him. His attitude contrasts sharply with that of the Samaritan Simon.[103] Whereas Simon remained ambiguous in relation to Philip, this man is sharply delineated from the outset. Secondspace interpretation begins with the particular scripture finally revealed to auditors in 8:32–3, and will lead to the heavenly Jesus in 8:35.

Secondspace interpretation: the Isaiah quotation (8:32–3; Isaiah 53:7–8)

Reading the version of Isaiah 53:7–8 recorded in Acts 8:32–3 for its space illuminates its function within the narrative,[104] developing its Christological and exegetical functions previously observed by others. For example, Spencer's observation that a Christological reading of Isaiah 53 'challenges this traditional [first-century] world and ultimately *makes room* for the devout eunuch within the scriptural-messianic community'[105] suggests a need to analyse the spaces and places of both that 'world' and that envisaged by such a reading of Isaiah. The quotation's ambiguity, encapsulated in the eunuch's question in 8:34, concerns particular (re)productions of space: the 'who' of the prophecy relates to the 'where' of its fulfilment.

The Isaiah passage's ambiguities concern the prophecy's ordering of space. First, ἡ κρίσις αὐτοῦ ἤρθη (8:33a) can be understood as 'justice was denied him' (so RSV, NRSV) or that 'his condemnation was taken away'. Second, τὴν γενεὰν αὐτοῦ ('his generation', 8:33b) can refer to his family history, or to his own generation. Third, αἴρεται ἀπὸ τῆς γῆς ἡ ζωὴ αὐτοῦ (8:33c) can be read as meaning either that his life is 'taken away' (NRSV), or that it is 'taken up' (RSV) in the sense of resurrection. Further, the conclusion of Isaiah 53:8 ('stricken for the transgression of my people') is *not* narrated

---

[103] Spencer 1997: 84–5, 92.
[104] Pao 2000: 142: 'The only scriptural quotation in Acts that comes from the voice of the narrator.'
[105] Spencer 1992a: 155, emphasis added.

in Acts.[106] Earlier observations regarding Acts 2 omitting Joel 3:5b LXX for spatial reasons find parallels here. Quoting all of Isaiah 53:8 would be 'anticlimactic' if the verb αἴρεται in Acts 8:33c is understood as referring to Jesus' exaltation to heaven.[107]

This reading of 8:33, acknowledging the Isaianic restoration project's inherent spatiality,[108] brings it under an ascension rubric for space. If the Isaiah quotation is pivotal within 8:26–40, then the section reveals the eunuch, with his carefully narrated spatial identity, as one concerned with his own participation within the geography intimated in Isaiah, but not knowing the subject of the prophecy. This connection of the Isaiah text with ascension geography becomes clearer if 'his generation' in 8:33b is understood as an exultant secondspatial marker – '"race" in the sense of spiritual descendants' – rather than a lamentation, such that 'the number of his disciples will grow incalculably, because he has become the Exalted'.[109] Indeed, 8:33b makes little sense if taken in any other way.[110]

This vast progeny is thirdspatial, in that its envisaging generates the prospect of alternative covenantal spatial relations within which there is a place for the eunuch. Thus read, Isaiah 53 contrasts with his restricted experience within Israel-space and, depending on the identity of the central figure, raises hope for him within *Isaiah*-space, wherever that is (or was, or might be) realised.

Whether Isaiah's ordering of space interweaves with the Ethiopian's own spatial status crucially requires Philip's interpretation. In the course of communicating an ascension ordering of space, Acts has already interpreted OT texts in what are, beyond the believers' circles, unexpected ways (e.g. 2:25–8; 4:25–6). The content of Philip's explanation of Isaiah-space is not recorded (cf. 8:35), but is explicitly Christological and is implicitly dependent upon a broader scriptural base than simply Isaiah 53:7–8.[111] The wider narrative answers Isaiah's question concerning who can describe the servant's generation: Philip

[106] Its exclusion on dogmatic grounds, to avoid connecting sin and death with a sacrifice (e.g. Haenchen 1971: 311 n. 3; Spencer 1992b: 175–6), fails to convince, not least given 20:28 and Luke 22:19–20 (cf. Seccombe 1981: 259; Witherington 1998: 298 and Peterson 2004). In terms of spaces, it is precisely Christ's spatial substitution for him, Christ's exclusion from the ἐκκλησία of Deuteronomy 23:2, that renders possible the more expansive territoriality of Isaiah 56:3–8.
[107] Conzelmann 1987: 68. Spencer (1992b: 176–7) also sees an ascension referent here.
[108] There is a need to 'spatialise' Pao 2000, especially pp. 140–2 concerning 8:26–40.
[109] Haenchen 1971: 312. Similarly Spencer 1992b: 178–83.   [110] Barrett 1994: 431.
[111] Cf. Luke 24:25b–27, 44–8; Acts 18:28; 28:23; and R. J. Porter 1988.

is able to do so. Within the narrative's span, that holy generation 'now finds its true place in Jesus' messianic community: the open household of God'.[112] 'Its true place', however, includes thirdspatial orientation towards the heavenly Christ and cannot be reduced to earthly believer-space alone.

Thirdspace implications: the eunuch's third question (8:36)

The eunuch's final question concerns entry into this Isaianic-Christologic ascension geography through baptism, the characteristic portal for ascension geography within Acts. Luke foregrounds this baptism-space through a fourfold reference to water within 8:36–9.[113] Such baptism-space operates on all three Sojan planes. As *thirdspace*, its liminality proffers a new world to the eunuch.[114] Now found in a desert place, moving away from Jerusalem on the road heading to the end of the earth, these waters – imagined within 1:8 categories – exhibit enriched *secondspatial* qualities. The baptism's precise *firstspace* setting, which has unnecessarily dominated discussion of its spatial significance,[115] is actually its least important spatial aspect.[116] The thirdspatial reading pursued here replaces this misplaced emphasis with a more appropriate exposition of the spatiality within 8:26–40.

On the lips of an Ethiopian eunuch, 'prevent' in 8:36 is theologically freighted, just as it will be on Peter's lips in Cornelius' house (10:47) and within the Jerusalem congregation (11:17). The verb is also spatially freighted: its uses in Acts in non-baptismal contexts – 16:6; 24:23; 27:43 – relate to the control of place and spaces. Here in 8:36–8, the eunuch's spatial and theological status are inseparable,[117] extending further the realisations of ascension geography made in Acts 1–7.

---

[112] Spencer 1992a: 161.

[113] The scholarly consensus discounting '8:37' as a later scribal addition means that the fourfold repetition is as tight as that of εἰς τὸν οὐρανόν in 1:10–11.

[114] Spencer, a strong advocate of the liminal qualities of setting in 8:26–40, misses this observation.

[115] E.g. Rapuano 1990; Horton and Blackley 2000 and various commentators.

[116] Haenchen (1971: 312), albeit for historical-critical reasons, assesses attempts to locate the site 'as touching as they are vain'.

[117] Cf. Jesus' use of the verb κωλύω in Luke 11:52; 18:16.

Onward journeys

After the pause necessitated by the baptism, the movement character-ising Acts 8–11 resumes,[118] and further reinforces ascension geogra-phy. In 8:39 the eunuch continues 'on his way rejoicing (χαίρων)', such joy within Luke-Acts often communicating salvation-geographical restructuring (e.g. 5:41; 11:23; 13:48; 15:31). Later church tradition that he carried the gospel to Ethiopia has no explicit basis in Acts, but it concurs with the spatial tenor of the narrative. If Psalm 67:32 LXX (68:31) is in view,[119] then its fulfilment is oriented towards the heavenly Jesus (cf. Acts 8:35) rather than Jerusalem-space.

Also, Philip is 'snatched away' by 'the Spirit of the Lord'[120] from the baptismal waters and propelled 'in real, spatial terms'[121] to Azotus for further proclamation northwards up the Mediterranean coast (8:39–40). At this narrative juncture, ἕως ('until', 8:40) forms a spatial boundary-marker, recalling the far horizon projected by 1:8. Expansive missionary secondspace continues to unfurl, rendering firstspace dynamically mobile.

Given that Azotus is Ashdod, one of the five ancient Philistine towns, Martin Hengel suggests that Philip's northwards evangelisa-tion represents eschatological reversal of the curse in Zephaniah 2:4.[122] Witherington judges that this suggestion is speculative,[123] and certainly Acts is not explicit in making this connection. For a spatially conscious auditor, however, such spatial inference would echo earlier Philip-led reversals in Acts 8 regarding Samaritans and a eunuch.[124] Philip's final movement here is still very much in char-acter, as he continues proclaiming Christ within liminal settings. Thus,

---

[118] Marguerat 2002: 236–9 explores the narrative function of travel within Acts.

[119] Witherington 1998: 301.

[120] The Spirit confirms retrospectively Philip's pioneering ministry, mirroring 8:17. Again, commentators typically project this heavenly agency on to God, without considering either the Spirit in Acts as facilitating Jesus' spatial order, or Philip's continuing exile from Jerusalem as resulting from the Christophany in 7:56. So, e.g., L. T. Johnson 1992: 157; Barrett 1994: 434 and Marguerat 2002: 97–8. Philip's dis-appearance echoes Luke 24:31 and even, with qualifications, Jesus' ascension (Mayer 1996: 87).

[121] Haenchen 1971: 313, reflecting *within* the storyworld in light of OT prece-dents. In 2 Corinthians 12:2, 4; 1 Thessalonians 4:17 and Revelation 12:5 the verb indicates heavenly rapture; here, however, the result is resolutely earthly, albeit for the further implementation of ascension geography.

[122] Hengel 1979: 79.   [123] Witherington 1998: 300 n. 91.

[124] Conzelmann (1987: 68 n. 3) and Spencer (1992b: 152) consider Zephaniah 2–3 in relation to the Ethiopian.

at the end of this particularly dynamic chapter Philip's procla-mation of the good news (εὐηγγελίζετο) 'to all the towns' along the 55-mile distance to Caesarea (8:40), rather than being Lukan hyperbole,[125] maintains a characteristically expansive scope for proclamation.

Summary: desert-space within Acts

Desert-space performs several functions within Acts as a narrative geography. First, it presents another location, and an unlikely loca-tion, for gospel proclamation beyond Jerusalem. Unlike Samaria, it is oriented away from Jerusalem, and the new convert has no direct contact whatsoever with the apostles in Jerusalem. Philip's liberty to evangelise in their firstspace absence is amply confirmed. Also, if Samaria-space constituted the initial expansion of believer-space beyond Jerusalem, desert-space, again in keeping with the second-space projection in 1:8, powerfully anticipates 'the end of the earth'. Not even Samaria and Jerusalem combined (cf. 1:6, a restored Israel?) can fully delimit the thirdspatial aspirations of ascension geography. Instead, an unlikely character from an unlikely place anticipates secondspatially what Cornelius' conversion will realise in the believing community's firstspace: namely that, within the bounds of the known earth, salvation geography cannot and should not be delimited to particular kinds of person. The thirdspace governance of Christ, proclaimed by Philip, overarches these obser-vations. Finally, as a didactic narrative of space, desert-space lacks the ambiguity of Samaria-space: unlike Simon, the Ethiopian is an exemplar for ascension geography, a high point in its exposition across Acts.

4.   Saul-space (9:1–30)

Acts 9:1–30 bridges several narrative settings, but this complex of scenes constitutes an integral and dynamic 'spatiality' justifying the term *Saul-space*. Concerned with more than mere setting, a reading for space probes these verses for the spatial reorientations brought about by the Damascus road encounter and its repercussions, locat-ing its impact within an abiding and developing ascension geography. Saul's initial stratagem is presented as 'an exact case of what Gamaliel

---

[125] So Fitzmyer 1998: 415; cf. L. T. Johnson 1992: 157.

has warned against' in 5:38–9,[126] and the heavenly response is devastatingly Christological. Within the narrator's point of view this is no mere theological lesson; as will be shown, it is profoundly Christological, a Christocentric ordering of space, not merely a divine spatial economy. Substantiating this claim will also bolster the earlier Christological reading of Acts 8 and will support the reading of Acts 10 in the next chapter, extending the argument that the narrative geography of Acts is structured within an ascension framework.

Reading Saul's oppositional space within ascension geography (9:1–2)

Acts 9:1 surprisingly and masterfully recalls 7:58 and 8:1, 3. That Saul is 'still breathing threats and murder' sustains Stephen's verdict in 7:52. Instead of abating with time, Saul's fierce opposition is narrated as having grown in space. Just as 8:1 presented the believers no longer confined to Jerusalem, now 9:1–2 presents their persecutor similarly expanding.[127] Saul, as he too travels out from Jerusalem, initiates an accelerating antithetical territoriality seeking to counter that proposed in 1:8.[128] His 'indiscriminate readiness to arrest Christians of both sexes'[129] maintains his intention in 8:3, while contrasting with the reception of the gospel in Samaria (8:12).

Saul's space is narrated as persecuting-space in all three Sojan dimensions. Bringing believers back 'bound to Jerusalem' (9:2) aims to confine their firstspace, reverse their secondspace and confound their thirdspace claims. This strategy is recounted three times in Acts 9 (9:1–2, 13–14, 21). This repeated telling is more than ironic:[130] it highlights Saul's spatial intent and his subsequent transformation, itself recounted three times (Acts 9, 22, and 26).

---

[126] Rapske 1998: 238, within a section (pp. 238–9) entitled 'Saul Opposes the Plan *of God*' (emphasis added). In Acts 9, Jerusalem-space again fails to assert its territoriality over ascension geography, an inability prevalent in Acts 2–7 (cf., also, Simon's failure to impose his territoriality, 8:4–25). Instead, Saul/Paul's power, initially from the Jerusalem Temple, 'is subverted by Jesus, who appears to Paul from heaven' (Robbins 1991: 216).

[127] Acts does not narrate the word reaching Damascus (135 miles NNE of Jerusalem) but assumes it. In distance, Saul's journey there far exceeds anything narrated thus far in Acts.

[128] This spatial contrast remains valid even if believer-space is 'a heterodox movement within Judaism' (Fitzmyer 1998: 424). The 'movement' (*sic!*) shares material space and even elements of ideational space, but is clearly divergent in thirdspace, as Chapter 4 indicated and 9:5 will confirm.

[129] Barrett 1994: 448.   [130] Spencer 1997: 95.

Yet Luke Timothy Johnson rightly notes: 'However important Paul turns out to be, he is *not* Luke's main character.'[131] Luke's concern is Christological, focusing upon 'the direct intervention of the risen Jesus in history [and geography]'.[132] Jesus' spatiality is to the fore.

Christological intervention in space

Saul (9:3–9)

And so Saul journeyed towards Damascus (9:3). Although it is a common Greek verb, πορεύομαι has previously been used in Acts only for movement by Jesus or his followers in service of him. The sole exception, Judas' counter-movement in 1:25, confirms Saul's present journey as antithetical to the Christocentric ordering of space within Acts, especially given the absolute use of ὁδός ('the Way') in 9:2. Indeed, 'by this time a careful reader of Luke-Acts would expect retribution, but it does not come'.[133] Instead, Saul's ὁδός (9:17) becomes 'a place of radical change',[134] a classic visionary thirdspace locale informing Acts' wider programme (cf. 2:17).

The reference to 'heaven' in 9:3 is normally addressed by commentators in a form-critical fashion, which underplays its connections with the ascension in Acts 1.[135] Such analyses fail to address this passage's radical formal difference from OT theophanies, namely its clear *Christophanic* emphasis, an observation missed by those commentators who instead position Saul's encounter within divine providence.[136] This lacuna is indicative of a sustained failure to recognise and consider the abiding impact of ascension geography on the ongoing narrative structure (and theology) of Acts. It leads to many commentators insisting upon describing Acts 9 as a theophany, despite the narrative's unambiguous marking of it as a Christophany.[137]

---

[131] L. T. Johnson 1992: 167, emphasis original.

[132] L. T. Johnson 1992: 167, square-bracketed comment added.

[133] O. W. Allen 1995: 126, but judging Saul's offence as against God, rather than against Jesus.

[134] Marguerat 2002: 255.

[135] E.g. Conzelmann 1987: 71; L. T. Johnson 1992: 162–3; Townsend 1998: 96 n. 42 and Gaventa 2003a: 148.

[136] E.g. Lohfink 1976: 89–90, regarding Acts 9–10; Rapske 1998: 238–9; Squires 1998: 31 and Turner 2000: 421–2; cf. 423–7. Tannehill (1990: 115–19) creates unnecessary Christological distance by persistently referring to 'the Lord', having headlined 'divine initiatives in the lives of Philip and Saul' (p. 113).

[137] Barrett (1994: 448–9; cf. 453) is explicit in submerging this Christophany under theophanic categories.

Other commentators have been more willing to label 9:3–6 as a Christophany, but have not integrated this insight within their wider narrative theology. Witherington, for example, acknowledges 9:3–6 as a Christophany, but later reverts to referring to *God* controlling its course.[138] Fitzmyer labels 9:3–6 as 'a revelatory Christophany', but then isolates it as unique within Acts in a manner which the narrative does not support, given the narrative significance of this and other Christophanic spaces within Acts (cf., e.g., 7:55–6; 9:10–17; 18:9–10; 22:17–21; 23:11).[139] More astutely, Jacob Jervell has labelled Saul's Acts 9 encounter as 'the last and biggest Christophany, long after the other Christophanies took place'.[140]

Recognising 9:3–6 as a Christophany clarifies that Saul is being drawn into ascension geography. Saul does not need convincing about *the God* of his fathers; rather, his encounter is primarily *Christological*, with consequential effects on Saul's theology. Whereas the ascension functioned as 'decisive withdrawal' for those who had known Jesus during his earthly ministry, Saul begins 'at the opposite end'.[141] Previously he had assumed an absentee Christology inasmuch as Jesus of Nazareth was *not* the messiah. Saul requires what the overwhelming vision in Acts 9 recounts: a Christology communicating presence, agency and specificity. It establishes him as a witness, but of the heavenly Jesus, not of the earthly Jesus as was stipulated in 1:21–2.

As a Christophany, rather than making *Saul* 'the locus of conjunction between earth/heaven, darkness/light, hidden/seen, blindness/sight, empty/full',[142] the Damascus road re-emphasises *Jesus* as focalising such liminalities, as the one still actively constituting space at these boundaries within the ongoing Acts narrative. This continuing active and constitutive agency simultaneously strengthens and denies the conventional dualism linking Luke's Gospel and Acts, that Jesus is both the proclaimer and the proclaimed.[143] Such deconstruction of conventional dualisms is typical of Soja's notion of thirdspace.[144]

---

[138] Witherington 1998: 316, 318. Similarly Rius-Camps and Read-Heimerdinger 2006: 186.

[139] Fitzmyer 1998: 420. Cf. also Selman 1969: 18; Jervell 1998: 278 and Tuckett 2001: 144 n. 31. Occasionally parallels are drawn with 7:55–6, e.g. Gaventa 1986: 55–6; Spencer 1997: 96–7.

[140] Jervell 1998: 278: 'Die letzte und grösste Christophanie, lange nachdem die anderen Christophanien stattfanden. Denn dass es sich hier um eine Christophanie handelt, lässt sich nicht bezweifeln.'

[141] Moule 1957: 208.   [142] Brawley 1990: 201.   [143] E.g. Marshall 1999: 347–9.

[144] Soja (1996: 5–6) outlines 'thirding-as-othering'.

The cumulative narrative effect, becoming clear across the chapters of Acts but especially apparent at 7:55–6 and now in 9:3–6, is that Jesus is absent but not inactive, a 'rounded' character within the narrative. Acts 9:3–6 is best read as combining theophanic elements within a Christological presentation for theological effect. The various possible interpretations of 9:3b, the suggestive double vocative ('Saul, Saul', 9:4)[145] and echoes of Septuagintal language for divine commission within 'get up and enter' (9:6)[146] are indicative of this narrative blurring of categories.

Commentators frequently compare Jesus' self-identification with believers (9:4–5) with other NT texts,[147] but 9:4–5 first needs to be understood within a distinctively Lukan frame of spatial reference. That all three Lukan accounts of Saul's conversion share the verbatim acknowledgement that the heavenly Jesus identifies himself with his followers confirms 9:4 as an important marker of Luke's narrative intent, confirming an active heavenly Christ executing the ascension geography outlined in 1:6–11.

Saul's responding question (9:5) enhances the scene's dramatic potential, and allows the accusation to be repeated.[148] It also provokes an explanation of this searching and incursive spatiality. Saul's use of 'Lord' is best viewed as ironic, again blurring theological and Christological categories, reflecting either Saul's ignorance concerning who is addressing him,[149] or Saul's failure to realise that the Lord before him is Jesus.[150] The emphatic 'I' (ἐγώ) and 'you' (σύ) accentuate the distance between Jesus and Saul, and underscore the Jesus' revelation that all Saul's previous narrative energies label him as a persecutor of Jesus.[151] Simultaneously, the stark and arresting use of Jesus' personal name emphasises him as 'alive in a new and more powerful way, and identified with his followers'.[152]

The ἀλλά ('but') in 9:6 functions as the pivot for the resultant 'new and powerful' production of space in the remaining narrative, altering

---

[145] Gaventa (1986: 57–8; 2003a: 148) and Bruce (1990: 235) see OT theophanic parallels here. Cf. also, however, Luke 8:24; 10:41; 22:31.

[146] Compare Gaventa 2003a: 149; Bruce 1990: 234–5 and Barrett 1994: 448–9.

[147] Matthew 25:35–40, 42–5 is a common parallel drawn: e.g. Bruce 1990: 235. Fitzmyer (1998: 425) also cites Luke 10:16, and Witherington (1998: 317) includes Romans 8:17 and Philippians 3:10.

[148] Gaventa 1986: 58–9.   [149] Gaventa 1986: 58; 2003a: 149.

[150] L. T. Johnson 1992: 163. Cf. Jervell 1998: 280.

[151] Gaventa 1986: 58; 2003a: 149.   [152] L. T. Johnson 1992: 163.

this encounter 'from an accusation to a commission'.[153] Saul's first-space destination initially remains unaltered, but 9:6b suggests some transformation being engineered by a thirdspace paradigm crisis heralding some profound reorientation. The contrasting reaction of his travel companions (9:7) emphasises the importance of Saul's experience above theirs,[154] focusing the ensuing narrative on him and his spatiality. The short-term provisional instruction 'stresses how completely Saul is thrown on the (direct or indirect) guidance of the Lord. He who a moment ago was so powerful has now become utterly powerless.'[155] Saul is instantly drawn into the spatial orbit of Jesus, the master of geography. All this happens far from the Jerusalem Temple, or any other place with prior claims to mediate between earth and heaven. This confirms what was proclaimed in Acts 7 and enacted in Acts 8: ascension geography is not tied to particular firstspaces. Clearly, the geography expressed here is theologically deeper than attempts to locate precise grid references for Saul's encounter.[156]

Rather than being empowered by the high priest, Saul enters Damascus under Christ's command and, blinded by him, led by the hand (9:8). Conzelmann is probably right that this blindness is less punishment and more another stress on the helplessness of Saul,[157] although some temporary intimation of judgement is not necessarily excluded.[158] In this state, he is dependent on others, a pattern which will continue until his escape in 9:29–30.[159] In thirdspatial terms, blindness removes Saul's ability to navigate and influence space, heightening narrative expectation for further Christological intervention in Saul's life. Saul's three-day disorientation intensifies the importance of what has happened and contrasts with the auditor's attention, already oriented heavenwards, which remains thus directed as the narrative moves to another site within Damascus.

Ananias (9:10–14)

Ananias' and Saul's 'double vision' (9:10–12) communicates Saul's commission,[160] and, together with the *third* such communication

---

[153] Gaventa 1986: 59. Importantly, however, Saul's call to a changed way of life makes this more than simply another prophetic call (Fitzmyer 1998: 421).
[154] Gaventa 1986: 59; 2003a: 150.   [155] Haenchen 1971: 322.
[156] Cf. Haenchen 1971: 321 n. 2.   [157] Conzelmann 1987: 72.
[158] Hamm 1986: 71. Seeing a parallel with 13:11, Rius-Camps and Read-Heimerdinger (2006: 178) identify a 'punishment'. This is not clear: Saul's fast in 9:9 may or may not represent an act of penitence.
[159] Spencer 1997: 95–6.   [160] Lundgren 1971: 121; Lohfink 1976: 74.

mentioned in 9:16, further highlights the active ordering of earthly space *by Christ*.[161] Luke's presentation of two individuals' space interwoven under the direction of the heavenly Christ generates a profound and sustained thirdspace effect[162] which the narrative will carry forward in Saul's experience: 'I myself will show him' (9:16). These 'multiple visions' in Acts 9 mirror the 'multiple experiences' of the risen Jesus in Luke 24 which generate 'a community experience and narrative'.[163] This stylistic similarity also confirms a continuing Christology in Acts (cf. 1:1). The succession of visions recorded here, combined with Ananias' recognition of the 'Lord' calling him, and his immediate response, suggests that Acts presents the earliest believers as 'familiar with this kind of direct communication from the divine'.[164]

The 'direct communication' is, however, from Jesus, not God. That Ananias' vision from 'the Lord' (9:10) is *from Jesus* is confirmed by 9:17. Thus the heavenly Christ remains explicitly active within Acts 9, marking 9:3–6 as part of the ongoing narrative rather than as a unique and isolated Christological phenomenon. The heavenly Christ is able to call both foe and follower by name (9:4, 10), and orders people and events *within firstspace*.[165] Ananias' initial verbal response (9:10), an OT stereotypical formula,[166] again positions a Christophany within theophanic categories.

Christ's announcement of the double vision provokes Ananias' resistance to visit Saul (9:13–14). As a 'disciple' (9:10), Ananias has reason to fear Saul's murderous intentions narrated in 9:1, and 9:13–14 characterises him as knowing Saul's plans. Presenting Saul's intentions as apparently public knowledge increases their magnitude (this was no mere private vendetta) and, correspondingly, reinforces the power of Jesus' sovereign interventions.

Saul's location 'at the house of Judas' (ἐν οἰκίᾳ Ἰούδα, 9:11) probably contributes to Ananias' hesitation. Commentators frequently rush to make Judas a believer, despite the absence of any narrative confirmation.[167] If anything, the narrative suggests that Judas was

---

[161] *Contra* Gaventa 2003a: 146 (emphasis added): '*God* directs Ananias to Saul.'

[162] This spatialises Johnson's description (1992: 164) of 9:12 as 'a masterful way of merging individual experiences into a shared narrative'.

[163] L. T. Johnson 1992: 168.   [164] Rius-Camps and Read-Heimerdinger 2006: 182–3.

[165] Haenchen 1971: 323: 'Ananias is given Saul's exact address.'

[166] Gaventa 2003a: 151.

[167] E.g. Barrett 1994: 453; Spencer 1997: 97–9 and Fitzmyer 1998: 427. Cf. the more circumspect Bruce 1990: 237. Rius-Camps and Read-Heimerdinger (2006: 183) propose an unconvincing allegorical reading of the directions in 9:11 as indicating a faithful household of John the Baptist's disciples.

not a believer. Ananias' fear appears misplaced if he is simply to visit the home of another believer in Damascus who is hosting Saul. Instead, Ananias' entire attitude appears premised upon Saul still occupying his anti-believer space with its associated practices, with no hint of Saul's transformation being expressed to him in the details outlined in 9:11–12. On a common-sense level, it is hard to see why, within the storyworld, those who led Saul into Damascus would seek out a believer to house their blind companion – more likely Saul, who had prepared for this visit (9:1–2), would follow through on his expected arrangements for arrival there. The Saul presented as blinded and helpless when arriving in Damascus in 9:8 is unlikely to have been proactive in seeking out a local Christian lodging. Thus Judas-space would be at best neutral for Ananias, most likely an unknown space or, at worst, colluding with the anti-Christian operation headed by Saul. To judge otherwise is to make too much of the vision in 9:4–6, which has not instructed Saul to go to a specific house in Damascus, at this (still pre-Ananias) stage in the narrative.

Ananias' resistance to Jesus' instructions represents an ascension-geography space-lag within the narrative.[168] Auditors are confident that Jesus has changed Saul's spatiality, at least in principle, but Ananias responds from knowledge of Saul's previous spatial strategies. This is the inverse of 1:6: there, the disciples over-realised their immediate space; here, Ananias under-realises his immediate space. In both instances Jesus clarifies ascension geography. Initially Jesus' more specific instructions increase Ananias' resistance, a sharp contrast with earlier instances of supernatural instruction in Acts being met by prompt obedience (5:20–1; 8:26–7; 9:6–8). Ananias initiates a strand of 'unbelieving believers' resisting or rejecting spatial changes determined from heaven (cf. 9:26; 11:2; 12:15–16).[169] Admittedly the change in Saul figures far larger within Acts, but Jesus' transformation of Ananias' life-world is also noteworthy within an analysis of the narrative's ascension geography.

Ananias' resistance helps auditors cope with the narrative's rehabilitation of Saul,[170] and communicates spatial principles for interpreting their worlds. Given the narrative's encouragement for auditors

---

[168] Tannehill (1990: 117) provides a temporal understanding of this point: Jesus as 'Overruler' causes recalculations regarding 'the future'. Simultaneously, however, Jesus overrules by reshaping *space*.

[169] Nonetheless, Ananias' hesitation is exceptional, rather than legitimated, within the narrative.

[170] L. T. Johnson 1992: 164; Gaventa 1986: 62.

to identify with ordinary believers,[171] Ananias' processing of space indicates how auditors might engage with their worlds: spatial arrangements will not always be immediately appreciated or even comprehended within ascension-geography categories. Sometimes space is perplexing, even for apostles (10:17), and auditors should expect ongoing spatial correction across all three Sojan dimensions. Indeed, it is probable that auditors will react 'against' the narrative's sense of space (perhaps, like Ananias, out of perceived defence of believer-space) but, nevertheless, they are encouraged to allow the narrative to correct their spatiality, and to learn to 'read' places and spaces in the light of revealed heavenly priorities, even heavenly direction. Ananias' resistance also reinforces the narrative's spatial expectations by reiterating earlier information emphasising the genuine intent and structured power behind Saul's original spatial plans within rhetoric recalling 2:21 (9:14). Barrett captures well the incongruity of the scene: 'Ananias fears that Saul is still out to persecute, and, presumably, that the prayer and vision are a hoax (a hoax, we must add, that had apparently taken in the Lord).'[172]

Saul's future spatiality, revealed to Ananias (9:15–16)

Jesus' explicit response to Ananias' counter-testimony[173] reinforces the narrative's earlier spatial assumptions while recasting Saul within them. Jesus' declaration of Saul's new spatial horizons picks up on – and reverses – Ananias' objections, objections expressed within the ascension-geographic discourse apparent across Acts 2–8, reframing 'how much' (ὅσα, 9:13, 16; cf. 8:3) and his 'name' (ὄνομα, 9:14, 15; cf. 2:21). Although references to Jesus' name diminish after Acts 9,[174] from here on 'the name' is inscribed in Saul's every movement, and therefore infuses the narrative. Like earlier references to 'the name' in Acts 2–5, 9:15–16 also generates its own complex 'echo effect'[175] across Acts. This is crucial for understanding the abiding nature of ascension geography across the whole span of Acts[176] and is indicative

---

[171] Bolt 1998: 210–14.   [172] Barrett 1994: 454.
[173] Adopting terminology from Brueggemann 1997: 317–32.
[174] Tannehill 1990: 49.
[175] To parallel Tannehill (1984), who identified this phenomenon concerning Jesus' 'name' within Acts 3–5.
[176] *Contra* Hedrick 1981: 419: 'The commissioning statement contained in 9:13–16 plays no part in the narrative, except to secure the services of Ananias as the "handy man" of the Lord.' Hedrick fundamentally misunderstands the pericope by

of how the later narrative progressively assumes Christological heavenly thirdspace.

Acts 9:15–16 is pivotal for the spatial progression of the remaining narrative. As a programmatic manifesto, only 1:8 exceeds its narrative impact. Indeed, it clarifies the course of 1:8 within the rest of Acts, linking ascension geography to the spatiality of Saul.

Spoken by the heavenly Christ, 9:15–16 anticipates what a self-consciously 'under heaven' spatiality will mean for Saul/Paul. Jesus' comprehensive reordering of Saul's reality, when understood third-spatially, initiates a Christological forcing of geography matching Marguerat's reading of 'a divine forcing of history'.[177] Thus, even the heuristic category 'missionary journey' needs to be located under the overarching spatiality of 9:15–16 and, consequently, within 1:6–11. Acts 9:15–16 confirms an inceptive reading of 1:1, recalling (and extending) Jesus' words in Luke 21:12. The rest of Saul's narrative life not only will reveal information about Saul/Paul, but will also contribute to Christology, both in speech and deed (cf. Acts 26:23). For the rest of the Acts narrative, Saul/Paul is where he is, doing what he is doing, and saying what he is saying, solely because of his encounter with the heavenly Christ. Such Christological control of space to the very end of Acts (and beyond) will be confirmed and further specified by 23:11 projecting Saul/Paul towards Rome.[178] Such Christological specifications provide vital clarifying shape and interpretative positioning to the common (although in itself insufficient) claim that 1:8 represents the geography of Acts.

Jesus' tripartite ordering of Saul-space extending 'before Gentiles and kings and before the people (υἱῶν) of Israel' (9:15) has been subject to contradictory interpretations.[179] Witherington observes that 'the order of this list is odd but no doubt intentional', judging it as Luke's indication of 'the comprehensive scope of Saul's commission'.[180] But

concluding it at 9:18a and ignoring 9:20, the climactic gateway into the remaining Acts narrative. Hedrick similarly ignores the geographically climactic 26:20, 23 by foreshortening analysis there to 26:12–18.

[177] Marguerat 2002: 196.

[178] Acts 22:19 projects a Christological reading of 23:11. Other tertiary markers (tertiary in the sense that 9:15–16 is a secondary marker of 1:8) include 18:9–10 and 20:35.

[179] For instance, Johnson (1992: 165) considers that the word order emphasises the Jews, whereas Barrett (1994: 456) judges them 'almost an afterthought'. Köstenberger and O'Brien (2001: 141 n. 115) prioritise the 'gentiles' as 'a new development'. Gaventa (1986: 63) proposes a progression from those who receive Paul's preaching to those who reject it, whereas Witherup (1992: 81) posits an ironically reversed ordering.

[180] Witherington 1998: 319.

this 'comprehensive scope' does not translate easily into a framework for dividing the Pauline section of Acts, despite attempts in this direction.[181] While broadly illustrative of what is to come, the narrative recounting Paul's overall spatial reach for the gospel proves to be more complex than any simple tripartite or taxonomic summary,[182] and the lack of programmatic order within 9:15 allows it to play a more delicate narrative role. As an invocation of Christological space, 9:15 develops the comprehensive span of the gospel anticipated in 8:26–39 but does not overwhelm the later telling of Peter's experiential realisation of this scope within Cornelius-space (10:1–11:18). Saul's commission is revealed, but its narrative fulfilment lies several chapters ahead and specific 'fulfilment' of 9:15 stretches until and beyond Acts 25. Prolepsis here in Acts 9 positions providence across Acts as both Christological in revelation and spatial in scope.[183]

Clearly, the Christophany in 9:3–6 and Jesus' emphatic identification of Saul as his chosen instrument with a particular and unusually expansive mission in 9:15 project Saul as more than simply another convert.[184] With its insistence that Saul 'must suffer' (δεῖ ... παθεῖν), 9:16 mirrors Jesus' predictions of his own passion (Luke 9:22; 17:25; 22:15; 24:26, 46). Although hardships within discipleship are not Saul's exclusive realm (cf. Acts 14:22), something particular is here in view. Παθεῖν, suggesting physical suffering even to death, will become the hallmark of *Saul's* future spaces, having been (with its cognate adjective) consistently applied in Luke-Acts to Jesus' passion.[185] This avoids triumphalism and sets the tenor of the text: 'The narrator never stops his text on the success of the preaching of Paul, but rather re-starts it, always anew, with the continuation of a voyage that becomes a path of suffering.'[186] Luke has already mirrored Jesus' passion in Stephen's death;[187] now he does the same in Saul's *life*. Any attempt to explicate space faces the limitations of

---

[181] Cf., e.g., Trites 1977: 140; Fitzmyer 1998: 428–9 and Gaventa 2003a: 152.

[182] Without reducing Paul's spatial reach to mere physical distance, the estimation that Paul travelled *c*. 15,500 miles during his ministry (Schnabel 2004b: 1551) is indicative of its complexity.

[183] Neither of these points is drawn out by Marguerat (2002: 93), who sees the 'programmatic function' of divine interventions as marking that 'God precedes history', such that 'in the book of Acts, the *narrative function* of *divine* predictions is no longer in need of demonstration' (p. 248, emphasis added), citing, *inter alia*, 1:8 and 9:15–16, and Squires 1993, esp. pp. 103–54.

[184] The verb which is cognate to 'chosen' in 9:15 (ἐκλέγομαι) elsewhere in Acts indicates individuals chosen for a particular role (1:2, 24–5; 6:5; 15:7, 22, 25).

[185] Skinner 2003: 96–7.   [186] Marguerat 2002: 40.

[187] Tannehill 1990: 99–100, 114 n. 4.

the English language, but Barrett's observation that Jesus 'himself will show him [Saul] what the future holds for him'[188] cannot be narrowly temporal. Rather than anticipating some unplaced future, Saul's vocation, his life as an unfolding and space-producing narrative whole, is here in view. This initiates a much more extended and *spatialised* narrative modelled upon Jesus, Saul's 9:15–16 spatiality extending over *all* the various spaces he occupies in the later narrative (cf. 26:23b). It connects Paul the missionary (Acts 13–20) with Paul the prisoner (Acts 21–8).[189] As a result, Paul's persevering ministry at the close of Acts redounds not to Paul's, but to *Jesus*', credit.[190]

Although 9:15–16 fuses suffering and mission, this is more than a simple dialectic.[191] The narrative spaces generated by this fusion are re-imagined in light of the heavenly Christ, the speaker of these words, producing his spatiality projected in 1:7–11. In a classic third-space reworking, Saul's subsequent narrative spaces are positioned within an ascension geography wherein his personal and intensely earthly sufferings link with, and are reworked by, the heavenly Christ.

Nevertheless, this is not a novel and separate narrative development. Saul/Paul is unique, but not totalising: firstspace diffusion according to 1:8 remains pluriform in the narrative. His mission relates with that of other believers within the storyworld (his is no solo endeavour) and contributes to the spatiality commended (commanded) to auditors in 1:8. Therefore, despite the specificities of Saul/Paul's calling, any auditors who themselves adopt his thirdspatial 'hope' (23:6; 24:15; 26:6–7; 28:20) are implicated within Jesus' spaces, within his spatiality. Acts as a narrative whole is an ascension geography text.

Ananias and Saul meet (9:17–19a)

Belatedly, Ananias obeys the vision, his actions in 9:17 mirroring the verbs in 9:13. Addressing Saul as 'brother' (ἀδελφέ) reflects a changed

---

[188] Barrett 1994: 450.

[189] Skinner 2003: 170, 182–3. Unfortunately, Skinner undermines the Christological implications of his own reading when commenting (p. 189, emphasis original): 'The reader knows that Paul enters them [= custody places] as *God's* representative and vessel.'

[190] Skinner (2003: 163) sees the final scene as redounding to *God's* credit. This conclusion places too much emphasis on 28:15 and ignores or downplays the Christocentric nature of 9:15–16. At this juncture, Skinner's spatial analysis of Acts 21–8 requires greater connection with an underlying *ascension* spatiality.

[191] Peterson (1998b: 543) comments: 'As he [Paul] endures suffering he learns to use it to serve the gospel.' Properly positioned in relation to a heavenly locus (cf. Peterson 1998a), this generates a robust Lukan theology of suffering (cf. also Brawley 1987: 40) and of mission (see, e.g., Tannehill 1990: 119–120; Skinner 2003).

attitude from the designation 'this man' in 9:13. Throughout Luke-Acts ἀδελφός indicates a 'fellow insider': here, the cotextual balance suggests (proleptic) description of Saul as a fellow believer in Christ. Similarly 'on your way here' (ἐν τῇ ὁδῷ ᾗ ἤρχου) bridges the transition in Saul's identity, bringing together the believer-space descriptor in 9:2 with that of Saul's interrupted journey. Both exist under the appearing Jesus. Ananias' climactic declaration 'and be filled with the Holy Spirit', especially given 9:15–16, evokes 1:8 and its surrounding ascension geography. Bestowing the Spirit is clearly not an apostolic prerogative, and here it happens beyond Israel.[192] All this is because 'the Lord ... has sent me', that is, because Jesus has reordered Ananias' boundaries. The restricted scope of Ananias' words in 9:17, together with Jesus having announced in 9:16 that he himself would inform Saul of his mission, communicates that Saul's spatial vision, which will inform so much of the shape of Acts, derives directly from Jesus.[193]

In rapid succession, Saul is healed of his blindness, undergoes baptism, and takes food for physical refreshment (9:18–19a), underlining the immediate and complete transformation of Saul which will dominate the remaining narrative. Such healing, narrated from Saul's point of view,[194] signals Jesus-space akin to Luke 4:18 (Isaiah 61:1 LXX) and Luke 7:22 (par. Matthew 11:5). Heavenly grace finds fruition in Saul.[195]

Saul's new spatiality

Within Damascus (9:19b–25)

With 9:19b–20, Saul arises from the private sphere he has occupied since 9:8. As he re-emerges as an active character, Saul inhabits, articulates and creates a radically new Saul-space. Two changes of setting reinforce this spatial realignment. First, in 9:19b Saul consorts 'with the disciples (μαθητῶν) in Damascus', the very people he so vigorously opposed in 9:1–2. Such immediate and inseparable association with other believers continues throughout Acts.

Second, Saul 'immediately' begins proclaiming Christ in the synagogues of Damascus (9:20). As well as initiating Luke's Pauline

---

[192] W. D. Davies 1974: 274 (cf. 167), without further justifying his designation of Damascus: 'Paul himself was given the Spirit, not in the land, but in Damascus, a famous "haven for heretics".'

[193] *Contra* Spencer 1997: 98; Marguerat 2002: 100.   [194] Yamasaki 2007: 171.

[195] O. W. Allen (1995: 128–9) identifies here a literary 'Salvation of a Tyrant' type-scene.

priority for mission in any new place, these settings prove Saul's new apologetic-missionary impulse. His locale, his firstspace, remains that intended when he left Jerusalem (9:2), but his practices there reflect a radically altered thirdspace hope. That 'the Son of God' (9:20) is unusual Lukan terminology should not divert attention from the obvious Christological nature of Saul's proclamation. As a self-expressed answer to his own question in 9:5, these first words spoken by Saul in Acts confirm that 9:1–30 needs to be understood Christologically. Saul now works to advance Jesus' 1:8 agenda, not oppose it. Also, it is highly likely that the narrative assumes that Saul's proclamation, like Stephen's, would include Jesus' ascension and heavenly session.

Furthermore, the proclamation–suffering dynamic within 9:20–5 already begins to fulfil Jesus' commission in 9:15–16. Similarities with Jesus' synagogue proclamation in Luke 4:16–30[196] suggest Saul's character and setting have been transformed along Christofocal lines, even if, tellingly, Jesus is physically absent. Such similarities, together with Saul's declaration being congruent with apostolic witness in Jerusalem[197] and Philip's proclamation in Samaria (Acts 8:12), yet 'without any hint of instruction',[198] contribute to a projection of narrative space ordered by the heavenly Jesus in conformity to his final pre-ascension words in 1:8.

Like Ananias a few verses earlier, the Damascus synagogues experience a 'space-lag' in relation to Saul. Four verbs in 9:21–2 – 'heard', 'amazed', 'said' and 'confounded' (ἐξίστημι, ἀκούω, λέγω and συγχύννω) – reprise 2:6–8, where another Christological realignment of earthly space from heaven caused a similar 'space-lag' among observers/hearers of the resultant space. Once again those who hear are confounded by the message and the messenger, and a divided response is again implied (9:23, 25). This will be so all the way to 28:24. The synagogues' surprise in 9:21 revives memory of 2:21 and 2:38, further embedding Saul within ascension geography. Their response also echoes Ananias' knowledge of Saul's plans in 9:13–14, reinforcing the public and premeditated nature of Saul's previous spatial plans for the 'disciples' within these synagogues (9:2). Their surprise therefore emphasises Saul's failed intent, and the consequent

---

[196] Witherington 1998: 320, following Esler 1987: 235; also Neirynck 1999.
[197] An allusion to Psalm 2:7 in Acts 9:20 mirrors 4:24–30; cf. 13:33 (Fitzmyer 1998: 434).
[198] Barrett 1994: 450. Saul is unusual, not paradigmatic in this regard; cf. 2:42–7 (Turner 1998: 340).

extremity of the change wrought in him. Saul remaining within the setting 'expected' for the execution of his original plans compounds this emphasis. The lack of any explanation for his changed perform-ance within this setting reinforces what auditors already know con-cerning this transformation. Ironically, Saul exercises a different kind of Jerusalem-space accreditation, 5:33–9 rather than 9:1–2!

That the hearers' surprise spurs Saul's proclamation of Jesus to new strength (9:22)[199] engenders a primacy effect concerning Saul's ability to shape space Christologically.

A plot to kill Saul (9:23) introduces the mortal threat which stalks Saul for most of Acts.[200] This threat, reflecting 9:16, forecloses Saul's presence within the Damascus synagogues. The one who came to persecute in Damascus synagogues is now himself persecuted there as opponents are perpetually 'watching'[201] the city gates (cf. 12:10) in order to constrain Saul's movements and complete their hostile inten-tions. Auditors are not told how Saul comes to know of the plot against him (9:24), a gap allowing scope for providential interpreta-tion (as, similarly, at 9:30). Yet Saul's survival in this and subsequent hostile narrative-spaces indicates Christological protection, not sim-ply *God's* providential care.[202]

With the Jerusalem believers (9:26–8)

That Saul leaves Damascus only when in mortal danger (9:25) keeps his distinctive spatiality in view.[203] Returning to Jerusalem (cf. 9:1–2), Saul tries to make contact with the believers there, in the first instance

---

[199] Barrett 1994: 464: 'If ἐνεδυναμοῦτο is middle it will simply mean that Saul grew stronger; if it is passive it will mean that he was strengthened by God – which is in any case implied.' The Acts 9 cotext suggests an actively Christological dimension to such strengthening.

[200] Not all Jews are uniformly enemies of the way: from 9:22 onwards, Acts distin-guishes believing and non-believing 'Jews' (Salmon 1988: 81). Cf., similarly, Weatherly (1994), concerning responsibility for Jesus' death. Given the degree of spatial sensitivity being identified in Luke's work, it is hard to see him viewing the situation in less subtle terms.

[201] Johnson (1992: 171) notes that παρατηρέω is 'used in the Gospel for hostile attention paid to Jesus by his opponents (Luke 6:7; 14:1; 20:20)'. Saul occupies the same kind of space as Jesus, albeit, at least within the narrative of Acts, with a different outcome.

[202] Brawley (1987: 40–1) cites 18:9–10; 19:21; 23:11 and 26:16–17 as emphasising *God's* providential care. These citations also merit a robustly Christological reading.

[203] Tannehill (1990: 122) rightly opposes Haenchen's supposition (1971: 336) that Luke's 'conviction [is] that Paul must have lost no time in seeking out the Twelve, the fount of all legitimacy'. Commentators assemble around questions of dating and

'the disciples' who, within the narrative, have returned since 8:1 or are post-Stephen converts.

Ananias' initial 'space-lag' (9:13–14) is repeated by these Jerusalem disciples who, similarly, are disoriented by Saul's transformation. Saul seeks to join their space,[204] but, unlike the Damascus disciples of 9:19b, they lack an Ananias who has had a clarifying vision from Christ. Saul's reputation as destroyer of believer-space blocks him, 9:26 suggesting the fear of 'a surreptitious infiltrator, perhaps an agent provocateur',[205] until Barnabas vouches for him to the apostles.[206]

As in 4:36–7, Barnabas is presented as a spatially astute character, able to detect the contours and consequences of a dynamically changing salvation geography (cf. also 11:22–6). Here, he discerns the true impact of Saul's visit to Damascus. Stressing 'the name of Jesus' in 9:27 connects Saul's Damascus-based activity with the apostles' Jerusalem-based ministry described in Acts 2–5 and decimated by Saul's earlier persecution in 8:1–3. The heavenly Jesus is the shared (thirdspace) connection between the persecuted and their former persecutor, expressed visibly in 9:28. If Luke, through Barnabas, is 'building a shared story',[207] then it becomes a shared *geography* both for characters and auditors.

Barnabas' spatial discernment is especially astute if 9:27 reads ὅ τι ἐλάλησεν αὐτῷ ('what he had said to him'), rather than ὅτι … ('and that he had spoken to him').[208] Bruce also suggests that this reading, as well as coming more naturally between two πῶς clauses, aligns better with 9:6. This reading also presents Saul's commission from Jesus (9:15–16), with its distinctive Christocentric spatiality, as pivotal within Barnabas' communication with the Jerusalem believers. It engenders an awareness of Saul's heavenly commission and subsequently realigned spatiality which itself spatialises any

sequence (e.g. Witherington 1998: 324), paying little attention to parallel questions regarding spatial dynamics. Both are needed, lest the imbalance reflect and create historicist tendencies.

[204] Κολλᾶσθαι, the verb translated 'join' (cf. 8:26), suggests both 'spatial proximity' and 'the alliance of hearts and minds' (Haenchen 1971: 242 n. 5).

[205] Barrett 1994: 467. Similarly Bruce 1990: 243, regarding 9:26.

[206] Barnabas, rather than Saul, is the more likely subject of διηγήσατο ('described') in 9:27 (Barrett 1994: 469). The counter-argument presented by Rius-Camps and Read-Heimerdinger (2006: 197 n. 109) fails if 9:27 reads ὅ τι (for which, see below).

[207] Johnson 1992: 172.

[208] So Bruce 1990: 243. Barrett (1994: 469) suggests, beyond the admittedly weak external attestation (945 1704 *al*), that this reading 'could be intended in many other MSS in which no spaces are left between words and letters'.

characterisation of Barnabas as exhibiting an 'openness to new developments in the mission',[209] or as a 'go-between or mediator ... [who is] living up to his nickname'.[210]

No immediate reason is given for Barnabas' intervention, but the etymology narrated in 4:36 and the editorial summary in 9:31 position his creating of shared space in 9:27. Throughout Luke-Acts, 'encouragement' (παράκλησις) indicates a strengthening of third-spatial perspective (cf. also Luke 2:25; 6:23–4; Acts 13:15 and the ensuing address; 15:31). Functionally Barnabas' reassurance parallels the heavenly Jesus' assurance to Ananias; Saul's personal transformation *is* legitimate, and can and should be incorporated into their production of space reflecting their adherence to ascension geography. Yet Spencer rightly highlights the lack of any visionary confirmation;[211] in this regard, Barnabas' discernment moves closer to the kind of spatial discernment auditors of Acts are likely to have to perform, if they are discerning themselves as living 'under heaven', where such visions are not normative for their experience. The lack of any expressed motivation for Barnabas' actions in Acts 9 typifies all his movements in Acts, rendering him as astute concerning spatial discernment while casting him as an 'everyman' figure who exemplifies salvation geography for auditors. His actions are to be interpreted providentially, within the heavenly and Christofocal frame of reference which the narrative has established for its production of space.

That the apostles accept Barnabas' testimony concerning the Christophany and publicly associate with Saul[212] (9:28) and that the brethren rally around Saul (9:30) provide further evidence that the narrative characters assume a more active Christology than that advocated by modern proponents of absentee Christology.

Within Jerusalem (9:29–30)

Being in Jerusalem but within this new spatial ordering brings Saul into contact and conflict with 'the Hellenists' (9:29). Witherington locates this group as 'presumably in the synagogue of the Freedmen

---

[209] Tannehill 1990: 123, likening this attestation to that of other 'approved' men (6:3; 10:22; 16:2 and 22:12). Saul, however, is qualitatively different, having been previously 'attested' *by Jesus*. Matthias (1:26) provides the nearest comparison.

[210] Witherington 1998: 326.   [211] Spencer 1997: 101.

[212] Haenchen 1971: 332: 'seen walking arm-in-arm, as it were, in the streets and lanes of that city'. Rius-Camps and Read-Heimerdinger (2006: 197–8) suggest shared ministry at this time and place.

mentioned in Acts 6:9, which involved Greek-speaking Jews from Paul's native region of Cilicia'.[213] Even if this identification is over-specific (although not precluded by the narrative), the verbs 'spoke' and 'argued' (συζητέω and λαλέω) parallel 6:9–10, intimating that Saul assumes Stephen's ministry. Both forms in 9:29 are imperfect, implying repetition, a sustained realignment of space. The response of Saul's hearers also mirrors that granted to Stephen: Saul's life comes under threat, leading to his departure from the city. Once more he is dependent upon other believers, his space being bound with theirs.

Acts 9:25 and 9:30 present Saul as a journeyman cast in the same destiny as Jesus, continuing to travel through a providential land-scape which needs to be read Christocentrically. Thus travelling to Tarsus begins Saul's journey 'far away to the Gentiles' (22:21).[214] Since flight from Jerusalem has previously proved providential for the word's growth (8:1–4), auditors might expect similar rapid resolution following Saul's departure in 9:30, especially given Jesus' words in 9:15–16. Yet Saul's relocation to Tarsus,[215] although perhaps predi-cated as evangelistic by his previous proclamation in Damascus and Jerusalem, burns on a slower narrative fuse. Auditors' expectations are delayed. Acts 9:31 will, however, sustain a heavenward focus on the growth of believer-space.

Summary: Saul-space within Acts

Acts 9:1–30 only introduces Saul-space; later, it will come to domi-nate chapters 13–28. As a justification for an ascension-geography reading of Acts, it is highly significant that 9:1–30 is so resolutely Christocentric and anticipatory of the second half of Acts. The Christophanies of Acts 9, especially Jesus' identification with believers in 9:4–5, retrospectively confirm that the spatiality of Acts 1–8 has been Christological and 'under heaven'. As is emphasised in different spaces and by different characters, the transforming power of ascension geo-graphy dominates this early Saul-space. This power is enhanced by Saul's initial opposition, the dramatic change evident in Damascus and Jerusalem, and unbelief regarding this change which confounds

---

[213] Witherington 1998: 325.

[214] This is not to deny a continuing place for the Jews within Saul's geography (see 26:17, 23). Bauckham (2000: 177) reads Saul here as making 'a new start', understanding the prophetic programme revealed by Christ as directing him first to Tarsus (cf. Isaiah 60:9; 66:19; Galatians 1:21) in a westward arc from Jerusalem, to the Japhethites.

[215] Revealed retrospectively as Saul's birth place (22:3).

outsiders and requires thirdspatial clarification for believers – either directly from the heavenly Christ (9:15–16), or through the spatially astute Barnabas (9:27). Such clarification ensures that the growth of ascension geography is not thwarted or distorted by fearful thinking disconnected from the work of the heavenly Christ. Even the apostles, who legitimated and interpreted Samaria-space within that geography, appear dependent upon Barnabas for their initial (albeit then immediate) affirmation of Saul's legitimate place within believer-space. Also, continuing a dynamic apparent in Acts 7–8, Saul's departure from Jerusalem (9:30) contributes towards the city's progressive marginalising within the Lukan economy of space. Clearly, this is not absolute rejection, but when he is rejected there, the Spirit-filled Saul embodying Christological space freely moves on elsewhere.

5.   Acts 9:31: a conclusion for Acts 6:8–9:30

Read for its space, 9:31 summarises the spatial maturation revealed in Acts, especially developments since the last such verse, 6:7. Since then, Luke has conveyed 'the sense of growth in numbers, the exemplary devotion of the disciples, the geographical spreading out of the church, and also the increase in danger as time went on'.[216] The present examination would also add that Luke is communicating that these fruits arise from the heavenly Christ overseeing this pivotal section of Acts. Within 9:31, this is communicated by the church being described as being 'built up' (οἰκοδομουμένη). The passive voice suggests divine-Christological agency, and the verb, previously used in 7:47, 49, evokes for the church the geography of the divine 'house' (οἶκος) which Stephen contested and redefined.[217]

That the singular ἐκκλησία ('church') in 9:31 describes believers across a region has provoked much debate.[218] It is often understood as the Jerusalem church now in dispersion,[219] but an ascension-geography reading suggests a thirdspace unity rather than simply a retrospective reference to an earlier ecclesial form. The singular ἐκκλησία at this narrative juncture confirms a heavenly locus, a

---

[216] Witherington 1998: 326.
[217] The verb's only other occurrence, in Acts is, tellingly, in 20:32. Examining the rich and ironic geography of οἰκοδομέω in Luke's Gospel unfortunately lies beyond the scope of the present study.
[218] Beyond the commentators, see Kodell 1974: 515; Giles 1985; 1995 and the response from Peterson (1998a); and Béchard 1999: 689 n. 44.
[219] Bruce 1990: 245–6; Giles 1995: 85–6. Cf. Metzger 1994: 322–3.

unity overseen by Christ, that believer-space in Acts remains more than the combination of material and ideational unity. Growth is more than external numbers or internal piety: it is also connected with the Spirit-bestowing Christ in a manner not reducible to 'external' or 'internal' dimensions.[220] The heavenly 'me' in 9:4 embraced believers at least in Jerusalem and Damascus, and also probably those scattered elsewhere (cf. 8:1).

Acts 9:31 employs 'Judea' in the same narrow sense as 1:8, apparently including Jerusalem within it. This shifts focus from the city to the region, anticipating 9:32–43. 'Samaria' recalls 8:4–25, linking it together with Judea and Galilee as the ἐκκλησία and thereby confirming and expanding that earlier section's narrative conclusions. Mention of 'Galilee' without prior narrative exposition has variously been explained as due to limitations in Luke's knowledge,[221] limited converts in that region,[222] or Luke's desire to emphasise that the earthly locus lies elsewhere.[223] None of these theories is convincing within the narrative's own terms. More persuasive is that Luke wanted to show that believers had settled in all Jewish regions.[224] Mention of Galilee in 9:31 also demonstrates the more general principle within Luke's presentation of space: not all developments of ascension geography need to be, indeed perhaps *should be*, revealed. Gaps communicate heavenly providence, and unexpected earthly growth of the word confirms such providence: 'Disciples of the Lord and witnesses to the gospel are liable to pop up anywhere.'[225] In short, rather than demarcating a clear boundary for the mission, 9:31 narrates a widening horizon which Acts will not contain, a shifting focus which contributes to the narrative's intent.

The 'comfort' engendered by the Holy Spirit is linked to growing numbers, but also, in immediate narrative cotext, with the third-spatial ministry of Barnabas in 9:27. The 'peace' enjoyed in 9:31 is similarly multifaceted, its spatiality bridging all three Sojan aspects. First, it is the antithesis of the fear engendered by Saul which constrained the church's spatial practices in 9:13–14, 26. Even if they were not carried back bound to Jerusalem (9:2), Saul had constrained the mentality and practices of believer-space. Thus also the abatement

---

[220] Cf. Calvin 1965: 274–5.   [221] Conzelmann 1987: 75; Witherington 1998: 126.
[222] Barrett 1994: 473; Witherington 1998: 326.   [223] Hengel 1983: 110.
[224] Barrett 1994: 472. See also the earlier discussion of Galilee's absence in 1:8, in Chapter 3.
[225] Spencer 1997: 97, regarding 9:2.

of his persecution widened the church's lived space, allowing the progress of the word to continue.

Further, if the Christ-event brings peace (e.g. 10:36), then that 'Christ-event' extends to include Christ's intervention within Acts 9 and the missions of Acts 8. Across these chapters, the heavenly Christ is presented clearly providing for, and defending, the spatial needs of his people. In these ways, this summary embeds Luke's unfolding understanding of geography.

7

ACTS 9:32–11:18

1.   Introduction

This final exegetical chapter completes an exposition of the narrative impact of ascension geography as far as Acts 11:18, beginning with an examination of how space is ordered within Peter's ministry in Lydda and Joppa (9:32–43). In its narrative position this section builds upon the territoriality expressed in 9:31 and the heavenly Christological focus sustained across 9:1–30. Then the chapter's largest sections examine the production and use of space within Cornelius' interaction with Peter, and in Peter's subsequent interactions with the Jerusalem church (10:1–11:18), identifying a deliberate spatiality within what is widely recognised to be a finely crafted and climactic narrative section. All these sections sustain the reading begun in previous chapters: the ascended Christ continues to exercise a structuring influence over the production of space within the theological narrative which is Acts.

2.   Peter-space: continuing ascension geography (9:32–43)

Narrative attention returns to Peter, the key mortal character in 1:12–6:7, but not mentioned since 8:25. Acts 9:32 presents Peter's territorial reach as congruent with that of the summary statement made in 9:31. Whether πάντων (9:32) is understood as 'all' believers or 'all' places, it securely locates Peter's present activities within the remit of 9:31.[1] While formally Gaventa is correct that the motivation for Peter's journey remains unclear,[2] the lack of definition continues the broad overview perspective of the preceding verse while the cumulative theological motivation for movement within Acts[3] suggests a

---

[1] Cf. seeing πάντων as simply another example of Lukan hyperbole (so Fitzmyer 1998: 444).
[2] Gaventa 2003a: 158.
[3] Marguerat 2002: 234–7 (234): 'in Acts, the Word travels and makes people travel'.

missionary dimension with Peter's movements.[4] The claim that Peter is on a tour of inspection too readily assumes similarities with (and such a tour in) 8:14–25.[5] Instead, more generally, 9:32 continues to expound movement from Jerusalem to Judea and Samaria (1:8) without becoming a detailed gazetteer of different locales, connecting 9:31 with Peter's subsequent activities in Lydda and Joppa.

Aeneas-space (9:33–5)

The briefly sketched account of Peter's healing of Aeneas in Lydda[6] highlights Peter's words in 9:34, 'Aeneas, Jesus Christ heals you.' Jesus himself is declared as bringing healing to Aeneas. A spatialised reading renders this as more significant than commentators' perennial concern with Aeneas' spiritual status.[7] Likening 9:34 with earlier instances where the 'name' of Jesus is operative within the narrative (e.g. 3:6, 12, 16)[8] ignores the lack of such mediation in 9:34 and the more explicitly active Christology consequently presented. This *difference* from earlier healings indicates that 9:34 is an important narrative marker, explaining 'what the name of Jesus means when the phrase is used'.[9]

First, within the narrative flow of Acts 9, Aeneas becomes the third person to have his spatiality fundamentally reordered by *Jesus himself*. It is insufficient to describe 9:34 as reflecting the work of 'the deity'.[10] Instead, an active but absent Christ structures space across at least the full span of Acts 9.[11] Spencer begins to connect this Christological observation with the construction of space within the narrative world: 'It is not so much that Peter heals in imitation of Jesus as that *Jesus himself* continues to heal through Peter. Though

---

[4] E.g. Bruce 1990: 246. Hengel (1983: 112–17) suggests a division between Philip's (Hellenistic) ministry in 8:40 and what is now Peter's (Jewish) itinerary in the same area.

[5] Cf., e.g., Haenchen 1971: 338; Conzelmann 1987: 76 and Witherington 1998: 328.

[6] Twenty-five miles NW of Jerusalem, 10–11 miles SE of Joppa (cf. 9:38).

[7] Exemplified by Haenchen 1971: 338; Bruce 1990: 247; Tannehill 1990: 125; Barrett 1994: 480; Fitzmyer 1998: 444 and Gaventa 2003a: 158.

[8] E.g. Conzelmann 1987: 76; Tannehill 1990: 126.   [9] Barrett 1994: 481.

[10] As does A. Smith 1995: 225–6.

[11] Cf. Lohfink (1976: 89–90), who neglects this narrative extension of active Christological interventions beyond 9:1–30, failing to include 9:34 in 'a whole series of direct divine [*sic*] interventions … described in such a way that the course of events really unfolds only due to these continuous interventions'. These observations concerning Acts 9 also need connecting to 'the serial nature of epiphanies' in Acts, as perceived by Weaver (2004: 283), recognising a dimension missing in Weaver's analysis, namely, that Christology is infused within and across such encounters.

absent in body, the exalted Jesus remains a force to be reckoned with on the mission field.'[12] Jesus' power is emphasised by Aeneas 'immediately' getting up, the adverb paralleling the instantaneous Christological impact in Saul's life recounted in 9:18, 20.

Such active Christology reinforces Jesus as absent in material terms (firstspace) but realigning material space. His presence is thirdspatial in that its locus lies within and beyond either material space or ideational space, that is, beyond either Peter's presence (cf. 3:12) or Peter's words in themselves. Instrumental power depends upon the absent Jesus, who, although backgrounded, remains a key character[13] in producing space. As such, more than being an exception to neat formulations of 'absentee' Christology, 9:34 constitutes an important element within ascension geography which, framed within Sojan categories, provides a sustained and stable interpretative framework for understanding Christology and the production of space across Acts.[14]

Also, the healing of Aeneas occurs *after* the Christophanic crux in 7:55–6, which heightened auditors' expectations for such interventions from heaven. Brawley observes that 'through Peter's announcement Jesus crosses the boundary between malady and healing'.[15] Such rhetoric of 'boundary-crossing' fits with Jesus' enduring thirdspace capacity within the narrative, a capacity which Soja's frame of reference casts as 'simultaneously real and imagined and more'.[16] It is now necessary to examine Tabitha-space for similar activity.

Tabitha-space (9:36–42)

Acts 9:36–42, although lacking the explicit declaration in 9:34,[17] maintains a strong connection between the heavenly Christ and the production of Tabitha-space. First, the consequential focus of both incidents is 'the Lord' (9:35; 9:42). Second, Peter's prayer (9:40) still distinguishes him from the source of resurrection power, and that power, in cotext, is best understood Christologically.[18] Third, 9:36 describes Tabitha as a 'disciple', the feminine form μαθήτρια being a

---

[12] Spencer 1997: 106, emphasis original.   [13] Cf. Martín-Asensio 1999: 267.
[14] Gaventa (2003b: n.p.) claims that 'this direct comment … serves to interpret the earlier healings', retrospectively positioning *all* previous Petrine miracles as Christological.
[15] Brawley 1990: 201–2.   [16] Soja 1996: 11.
[17] Although various 'Western' texts have Christological inclusions within 9:40 (see Rius-Camps and Read-Heimerdinger 2006: 207, 215).
[18] Tannehill 1990: 126; Witherington 1998: 333.

hapax legomenon paralleling the masculine μαθητής,[19] which is ascribed to Ananias (9:10) and initially contested concerning Saul (9:26), both of whom encountered the heavenly Jesus within Acts 9. Also, the heavenly Christ has identified himself already in 9:4–5 with the unnamed male and female 'disciples' of 9:1–2. Fourth, the widely acknowledged narrative pairing of Aeneas' healing with Tabitha's resurrection suggests that the former incident's active Christology can be assumed, although unstated, within 9:36–42. Narrative cotext and cumulative effect therefore undermine the view that 'the Christological focus, so evident in Peter's words to Aeneas, falls out'.[20] Rather, as 7:55–60 showed, 9:34 anticipated and 10:42 will confirm (also on Peter's lips), the heavenly Jesus marshals the boundary between life and death. This Christological connection *within* Acts is more persuasive than links drawn with Mark 5:40–1 (cf. Luke 8:54) or 2 Kings 4:33.[21]

This Christofocal function extends beyond distinguishing Christian charismata from occult forces,[22] and is more than a vehicle by which Peter stirs up faith in Jesus.[23] It also extends the active Christology within 9:1–30 into new settings and sustains it across Peter's ministry within Acts. This latter observation is more significant than any (derivative) 'heightening of Peter's potency',[24] still less any supposed 'widening of his compassion', compared with 5:1–10 and 6:1–6.[25]

Within this Christological ordering, Tabitha's spatiality – like that of other believers in Acts – exists 'under heaven'. Acts 9:37 might suggest that Tabitha hosts the Joppan believers;[26] certainly her 'good works and acts of charity' (9:36; cf. 9:39) exemplify the spatial practices generating fellowship-space earlier in Acts (2:42–7; 4:32–7). Both her death and her restored life attest to this production of space (9:39, 41). The open outcome in Acts 9:41b, like other suggestive closures in Acts, invites auditors to shape their own space along similar lines, through both material practices and hope placed in the heavenly Christ (9:42; cf. 9:35). Once again, this earthly salvation

[19] Reimer (1995: 34–5) emphasises this gender equality, but not on the grounds of equal connection with the heavenly Christ.
[20] Brawley 1990: 202.
[21] Barrett 1994: 485: 'If Luke had intended to evoke memories of words which in his gospel he does not use he would have done so more effectively.'
[22] Marguerat 2003: 114–15.   [23] Fitzmyer 1998: 443; cf. 444–6.
[24] Spencer 1997: 102. Cf. O'Day 1992: 309.   [25] Spencer 1997: 102–3.
[26] So Spencer 1997: 107–8.

geography both depends upon, and generates, heavenly shaping of earthly spaces.

The narration of this increasing response to (and from) the heavenly Lord ends with Peter located at the edge of the territory he has reached thus far within Acts; he is in Simon the tanner's house, by the sea, in Joppa.[27] He is at a distant boundary of Judea,[28] having come thus far in response to the disciples' request in 9:38 to 'come to us'. Here, the preposition ἕως occurs with a spatial pronounal marker: like 8:40, it gauges progress towards the preposition's foundational appearance in Acts, where it measured the global expanse of 1:8. Acts 10 will reveal what will cause Peter to move on from this locale, thereby expanding his firstspace practices and his secondspace vision. The narrative of Christological spatial intervention from heaven is far from complete.

3.   Peter-space and Cornelius-space: both 'under heaven' (Acts 10)

The sheer length devoted to the Cornelius account, and Luke's widely recognised repetitions employing 'functional redundancy',[29] indicate the importance of this narrative within Acts. These qualities also point towards its spatiality. As Marie Rosenblatt observes regarding 22:1–22, repetition from shifting points of view 'creates the illusion that the story is present, not distant. The reader is brought close to some events, the ones which absorb and preoccupy the text's telling space.'[30] Rosenblatt's comments apply more widely within Acts and more directly to spatiality. Acts 22 utilises narrative space and generates a narration *about* space. Here in Acts 10–11, shifting points of view provoke a pondering of the narrative, whereby retold events are, in Rosenblatt's terms, 'stilled' and various narrative frames and cotexts generate a 'narrative hologram'.[31] Rosenblatt casts this in terms of the narrative's temporal moments, but this 'hologram' effect is spatial as well as temporal: different narrative spaces – together with the heavenly referent in Acts – enable triangulation between tellings, generating a composite view of space. Regarding Cornelius within Acts, such triangulation reaches from 10–11 as far as 15:7–11, generating (to quote Rosenblatt concerning Saul's conversion)

---

[27] Cf. Philip's territorial reach by 8:40.
[28] Cf. Hengel 1983: 117.   [29] Witherup 1993.
[30] Rosenblatt 1990: 104.   [31] Rosenblatt 1990: 104.

'a longer "run" on the stage of Acts than other events'.[32] Such longer
runs are also evident for Stephen's death resurfacing in 11:19 and
22:20, and for Paul's commission to preach to the gentiles informing
13:46, 22:1 and 28:28. It is notable that both these other repeated
'longer runs' are initiated by the activity of the heavenly Jesus; if the
Cornelius episode demonstrates such Christological activity, it will
fit with this wider narrative observation and contribute significantly
to our cumulative picture of an active Christology within Acts.
Although such interventions initially appear to be episodic, extension
by narrative retelling confirms them as pivotal for structuring narrative space within Acts. After all, Jesus himself enjoys the longest 'run'
of all within Acts (1:1; 28:31).

Introducing Cornelius-space (10:1–2)

Acts 10 introduces a new character, Cornelius. The narrator's opening
description of him begins to map his space.

First, Cornelius is in Caesarea. Caesarea has previously been
mentioned as a far horizon reached by the gospel (8:40); now it
becomes a narrative stage. The movement of 1:8, in the Lukan
economy of space, now reaches this predominantly gentile capital
of Judea,[33] and, in so doing, broadens the narrative's understanding
of Judea.[34]

Second, Cornelius is a centurion. While suggesting overtones of
Roman military oppression,[35] there is within Luke-Acts a 'narrative chain' of positive centurions (Luke 7:1–10; 23:47).[36] These
earlier centurions exemplify proper understanding of Jesus' space.
For the first, his desire that Jesus should not enter his house but
heal *in absentia* both highlighted the problematic nature of gentile
space and provoked Jesus' commendation, thereby anticipating the
absent but active Jesus of ascension geography. As such, Cornelius
as centurion suggests potentially insightful spatiality for auditors
of Acts.

---

[32] Rosenblatt 1990: 105.

[33] Hengel 1995: 53–63. Matson (1996: 107) risks overstatement when describing
Caesarea as 'a city loathed by the Jews and thus a conspicuous site for the start of
Christian missions'. He cites J. J. Scott 1991: 478, and quotes Kee 1990: 51 as supporting
this view, but the primary evidence corroborating it is relatively late.

[34] Cf. Béchard 1999: 688–9. Note, however, that certain contexts project Caesarea
as 'beyond' Judea (12:19).

[35] Matson 1996: 107 n. 90.   [36] Marguerat 2002: 52–3.

Third, Cornelius is 'devout' (εὐσεβής, Acts 10:2), praying continually to God. This piety is not abstract but, like Tabitha's, embodied: he gives 'alms generously to the people (τῷ λαῷ)'. If Cornelius is to be assessed by the Baptist's words to 'soldiers' in Luke 3:14,[37] then his initial spirituality is expansively repentant. Furthermore, Cornelius also 'feared God', together with his household.[38] Repeated mentions of this piety (10:2, 4, 22, 30) reinforce it within the narrative.

Fourth, despite the narrative employing maximal persuasive rhetoric to present Cornelius as positive within Jewish criteria, granting him a piety never ascribed to the Jewish leaders within Acts,[39] Cornelius is clearly a gentile. This disjuncture generates an unstable assessment of Cornelius and his space, presenting a kind of space not previously encountered within Acts. Rather than stressing the impressive reach of the gospel's grace at this stage in the narrative,[40] Cornelius-space in 10:1–8 disorientates auditors by unsettling conventional Jewish spatial categories. Within the narrative's expectations, this disorientation intimates that the only way that Cornelius-space can be understood is by applying ascension-geographical principles. As will be seen, heavenly intervention will initially heighten and then resolve these spatial tensions, thereby redrawing earthly spaces.

Thus, from the outset, Cornelius is a test case *par excellence* for ascension geography.[41] He exhibits contrary qualities of proximity and distance, not dissimilar to those seen in the Ethiopian (8:27–8). Importantly, however, Cornelius is grounded in a stationary place and is embedded within a household. His ambiguous spatiality therefore exerts a firstspace impact within the narrative world, something lacking in 8:26–39. Also, unlike the Ethiopian, Cornelius (presumably) could have been circumcised, had this been the route to resolving his spatial ambiguities. Auditors, however, have been primed by the preceding chapters to accept, even to expect, resolution to come from elsewhere, from another world order, from the realm of Christological heavenly thirdspace.[42]

---

[37] Spencer 1997: 109.
[38] Matson (1996: 86–134) explores this household dimension.
[39] Gowler 1991: 287.
[40] Cf. Barrett 1994: 493: 'The conversions of persons such as those described in 1 Cor. 6.19, 20 might have been more impressive.'
[41] Wilson (1973: 173) similarly claims Cornelius, albeit as exemplifying the gentile mission.
[42] Not that Cornelius is imagined as praying for such a resolution: rather, this is a reasonable expectation for auditors, given the preceding narrative.

Angelic vision and earthly response (10:3–8)

Therefore, unsurprisingly for auditors accumulating narrative space, an angelic vision begins to bring Cornelius within the nexus of ascension geography by both evoking and challenging limitations and potentialities within existing ascension geographies narrated earlier in Acts (e.g. 2:17, 39). Initially, Cornelius receiving the angel within his own domestic space ('coming in', εἰσελθόντα πρὸς αὐτόν, 10:3) heightens the earlier incongruities of Cornelius-space (10:1–2). The angel affirms Cornelius' existing spatiality, declaring that his prayers and alms 'have ascended (ἀνέβησαν) as a memorial before God' (10:4). The vision intimates, however, that Cornelius – at the divine behest – is about to be brought within *another* ascension network. He is to seek out 'Simon who is called Peter', a repeated designation throughout the incident (10:5, 18, 32; 11:13).

In the immediate cotext, this double-naming distinguishes the apostle from his Joppan host (cf. 10:6, 17, 32) but it continues beyond where the narrative requires such a distinction. As the only instance of Peter being called *Simon* in Acts,[43] this nomenclature recalls Peter's earlier relationship with the earthly Jesus in Luke's Gospel. It was Jesus who so changed Simon's name and gave him the spatial mandate threading through Luke 5:10; 6:14 and 22:31–2, a commission which here draws in Cornelius (10:42, 46–8). Within Acts, Peter has repeatedly been the main earthly producer and interpreter of ascension geography within different locales. For auditors, especially if familiar with Luke's Gospel, Cornelius is therefore told to summon not simply Peter, but also Peter's spatial connections with Jesus.

The angel's explicit departure (10:7; cf. 1:9–11; 10:16) leaves Cornelius with firstspace absence, but a thirdspace pregnant with potential consequence. Thirdspace sovereignty remains a heavenly prerogative, since Cornelius must now act on the precise (10:6!) directions of his now absent spatial instructor. The vision's purpose will become clearer, both to Cornelius and to auditors, as Acts 10 unfolds. Already, however, auditors anticipate and recognise that Cornelius needs Peter's interpretation, and Cornelius' prompt and obedient response (10:7–8) heightens expectation that he will appropriate the vision's spatiality in all three Sojan planes.

---

[43] *Pace* Rius-Camps and Read-Heimerdinger (2006: 247), who emphasise the allegorical qualities of *Peter*, although noting their later alternative reading regarding *Simon* (p. 297; cf. p. 254).

Peter's Christophany (10:9–16)

Claiming Peter's vision as a Christophany moves beyond explicit textual labelling, but sufficient narrative markers justify this designation.

First, and most emphatically, Peter receives his vision *from heaven*: 10:11 and 10:16 stress this provenance. Although these verses could simply indicate that the vision began and ended in the sky,[44] the voice (which Peter addresses as κύριε, 10:14) suggests a more theological reading of οὐρανός. Whereas the angel came *into* (εἰσελθόντα) Cornelius' space (10:3), the voice addresses Peter 'from heaven' (ἐκ τοῦ οὐρανοῦ, 11:9). Within Acts, both this phrase (2:2; cf. 2:33; 9:3; 22:6) and a heavenly voice are Christological markers, strongly suggesting that Peter is experiencing a Christophany.[45] Although not a vision of Christ *per se* (therefore preserving 1:11), the vision reveals *Jesus'* global influence (cf. 10:15).

Most commentators assume that Peter's vision comes from God, but 10:28 does not dictate this conclusion[46] and both the third-person reference to God in 10:15 and the sustained lack of any ascription to the voice (11:7, 9; cf. 11:16) indicate that Peter is better understood as addressing Jesus.[47] Why, then, is Jesus not mentioned explicitly, as he is in 7:55–6 and 9:3–16? Importantly, unlike Stephen, Saul or Ananias, *Simon* Peter has had – within Acts – an earthly discipleship encounter with Jesus. The narrative assumes this prior firstspace relationship and, indeed, preserves it by not mentioning Jesus by name lest the appearance of presence overwhelms the thirdspace balance engendered by 1:6–11.

Read thus, Peter's 'very strong negative reply', rather than causing logical inconsistency implied by Peter refusing God,[48] fits with Peter's previous personal experience of relating with Jesus.[49] This increases expectation that Jesus is, once more, about to correct Peter's understanding of space (cf. Luke 5:5–10; 22:33–4).

[44] So Haenchen 1971: 347, possibly because οὐρανός parallels γῆ in Acts 10:11. Elsewhere, however, Luke frequently uses γῆ as a counterpoint to heaven, e.g. 7:49.
[45] Rowe (2006: 238 n. 4) draws the same conclusion, based on Peter's Christological use of κύριος ('lord') in 10:36 and in Luke 5:8; 12:41 and 22:33.
[46] Within the narrative, Peter speaking of *God* in 10:28 can be understood best as appropriate terminology for communicating with someone characterised as a God-fearer (10:22), who is not yet acquainted with Jesus.
[47] Κύριε parallels *Simon* Peter's first address to Jesus in Luke's Gospel (5:8). Cf. Read-Heimerdinger 2002: 283–4. Rius-Camps and Read-Heimerdinger (2006: 253–5, 297, 299) judge that the voice is Jesus, but still refer to 'the divine command' (p. 254).
[48] Cf. Barrett (1994: 507–8), who pursues this assumption into its resultant difficulties.
[49] Spencer 1997: 110–11.

Such blurring of divine and Christological categories, titles and functions, as seen earlier in Acts, reflects the heavenly dynamic informing ascension geography. Perhaps unwittingly, Gaventa captures well this ambiguity: 'Peter then hears a voice instructing him to "Get up," as in the preceding story he instructed Aeneas and Tabitha to get up.'[50] Is 'he' Peter, or the heavenly voice (especially cf. Acts 9:34)? Such ambiguity, however, is not sustained; Gaventa continues to describe this as 'the divine command', without making any connection with her earlier advocacy of an active Christology blurring into theological categories.[51] Where other commentators lack even initial ambiguity, it is hard to judge whether 'divine' readings of the vision are cause or effect of a passive Christology in Acts. In contrast, however, recognising that across the Acts narrative the ascension blurs Christ's location with that of God preserves Christological heavenly thirdspace as both absent and active, as real-and-imaginary-and-more, able to shape earthly spaces into conformity with 1:6–11.

This Christological claim does not require Acts 10 to exhibit a 'double Christophany', as a slavish parallel to Acts 9, despite 10:9 firmly connecting Cornelius' vision with Peter's subsequent revelation. Although conforming to ascension geography, Cornelius' vision is not a Christophany; he still requires Peter's witness to Jesus (cf. 1:8). Furthermore – within the storyworld – given their profoundly different prior experience and discernment of heavenly beings, Cornelius' κύριε (10:4) is unlikely to be identical to Peter's κύριε (10:14). Although reflexively aiding each other's interpretation of space throughout Acts 10, they do not begin from equal positions.

Peter's vision concerns space and spatial relations. Its animal life is intended parabolically to map humanity.[52] A vision, almost by definition, communicates thirdspace, that is, a spatial vision beyond merely the material or the ideational,[53] or even the sum of their

---

[50] Gaventa 2003a: 166.

[51] Gaventa 2003a: 166 and, similarly, p. 141; cf. the more nuanced pp. 33–4. Furthermore, p. 166, despite 9:17, comments that 'both men [Peter, and Ananias in 9:10–16] assume they know more than God'.

[52] Thus οὐρανός, qualifying 'birds' in 10:12, refers simply to the sky ('air'), but the phrase could be an oblique reference to the gentile nations. Hurtado (1983: 80) reads the same phrase (albeit articular) as alluding to the gentile nations in the synoptic parable of the mustard seed (Luke 13:19 and par.; cf. Ezekiel 17:23; 31:6 and Daniel 4:12). Such an allusion in Acts 10:12 (and 11:6) fits with the vision's intended scope and consequences.

[53] Cf. the rigid logic pursued by Haenchen (1971: 348 n. 3) and Barrett (1994: 507–8).

parts. Indeed, both material and ideational space will be transformed by this visionary space as Acts 10 unfolds.[54]

Given that early Judaism assumed that contact with unclean persons caused defilement, 'it would be natural to assume the same with animals,'[55] and food restrictions would likewise limit social interaction with gentiles,[56] generating 'physical partition' lest there be 'defilement by association'.[57] The vision therefore challenges Peter's 'mental map', his secondspace assumptions, and how this interpretative grid informs his material (i.e. firstspace) relations. Despite the expansive potential of 1:8, Peter requires further clarification from above if he is to move beyond his frontier hostel in Joppa. Acts 10:15 provokes a different secondspace for viewing humanity: the connection with animals, the '*geography*' of unclean food',[58] is broken and rendered irrelevant.[59] 'You must not call profane' (Σὺ μὴ κοίνου) indicates that Peter should desist from 'what he is already doing'.[60] Instead, Christological cleansing is to govern Peter's understanding of people and places.[61] For the auditor, Peter the character is, of course, in a characteristic 'space-lag' somewhat behind the heavenly vision's spatiality; earlier latent spatial implications (e.g. 3:21–6; 4:24) are now expanding beyond Israel[62] to the wider world. Once again, heavenly intervention predicated upon the ascension (10:11; cf. 7:55–8:4; 9:3–20) expands mentality and practice, stimulating a distinctive Christofocal spatiality within Acts.[63]

Importantly, connecting the vision with Christological thirdspace casts Peter's resistance (10:14) as another – ironic – threefold denial of his Lord (10:16).[64] The Spirit's later command, 'Get up, go down and

---

[54] Such a spatial reading supplements and, to a degree, critiques as historicist the reading that Luke adopts 'a historian's approach, and thus the issue is one of hermeneutics and timing' (Witherington 1998: 354 n. 113).

[55] Witherington 1998: 350 n. 95; cf. House 1983: 150–1.   [56] J. J. Scott 1991: 480–1.

[57] House 1983: 150.   [58] To spatialise the title of Wenham 1981.

[59] Witherington 1998: 354 carefully traces these consequences regarding food fellowship.

[60] Bruce 1990: 256.

[61] This assumes, with Witherington 1998: 350, that 10:15 refers to Christ's death and its effects. Rius-Camps and Read-Heimerdinger (2006: 249) judge the hours in 10:3 and 10:9 to parallel deliberately the Lukan crucifixion account.

[62] House (1983: 152 n. 26) judges 'defilement by association' to be peculiar to Palestinian Judaism.

[63] Cf. Barrett 1994: 506, judging the open heaven as 'a standard feature of apocalyptic and other visions'.

[64] Witherington (1998: 350) makes this observation, but, since he does not consider Peter to be addressing Jesus, presumably he envisages Peter denying ('once again') some sort of ethos (i.e. a geography) instituted by Jesus. Noting Peter's bewilderment in 10:17, the 'illusion of transparency' concerning spatial ideas (Soja 1996: 63–4) which Witherington's reading presumes is unwarranted at this narrative juncture.

go' (ἀναστὰς κατάβηθι καὶ πορεύου, 10:20), given to a man of God in Joppa reluctant to align himself with a revealed spatial agenda, echoes Jonah 1:2 and 3:2 LXX (ἀνάστηθι καὶ πορεύθητι).[65] Peter is at a highly significant crossroads, and auditors do not know what will happen if Peter rejects the as yet unknown implication of the vision. Thus, setting increases tension at this relatively early stage of the narrative unit, reinforcing the vision's importance. Across Acts 10, however, Peter responds differently from Jonah, generating contrasts and similarities which communicate a spatial narrative.

Aftermath, and interlock of spaces (10:17–23a)

Peter's perplexity regarding the twice-repeated vision and dialogue highlights its probable importance and its confusing meaning.[66] Then ἰδού (NRSV 'suddenly') refocuses auditors' attention amid this narrative uncertainty.

Immediately 10:17b–19a interlocks Peter's uncertainty with those enquiring concerning his whereabouts. Heaven continues to direct earthly events so as to bring Peter and Cornelius together. The Spirit in 10:19b–20, as in 8:29, commands movement which specifically advances witness to Jesus in this immediate situation, articulating what 1:8 here requires of Peter. Rather than the Spirit explaining the vision immediately in 10:20, Peter the narrative character inhabits an uncertain space until 10:44. From 10:21 onwards, as Peter descends from his rooftop retreat, this space is progressively interlocked with that of Cornelius and becomes clearer as a result.

The initial progression occurs with an increasingly intimate first-space, beginning in 10:21–3. Further details regarding Cornelius in 10:22 advance this intimacy, expanding the narrator's earlier description of Cornelius' piety (10:2) and the angelic instruction he received (cf. 10:5–6). On both counts, the developing repetition illuminates the narrative's unfolding spatial implications.

First, Cornelius' envoys present Cornelius as 'well spoken of (μαρτυρούμενός) by the whole Jewish nation' (10:22), a secondspace warranty intended to appeal to Peter. Peter's contrasting 'witness' status in 10:39 will retrospectively indicate that their appeal is misplaced within the ideological perspective of Acts. Furthermore,

---

[65] Cf. Spencer 1997: 105, 112–13.
[66] Intensive (δια-) forms of various verbs and the particle ἄν highlight the uncertainty within 10:17. Regarding 'greatly puzzled' (διηπόρει), cf. 2:12; 5:24; Luke 9:7.

ascension geography has problematised previous appeals to the category 'Israel', requiring them to be reworked in view of the heavenly Christ and his earthly witnesses (1:6–11; 3:22–3). Thus, even while commending his piety, 10:22 provides an initial marker that Cornelius-space requires ascension realignment.

Cornelius' description as 'an upright and God-fearing man' (10:22) is perhaps also intended 'to encourage Peter's compliance by softening the impact of entering a Gentile's house'.[67] Despite considerable debate regarding the degree to which Jews and non-Jews would interact in the first century, and on what basis such interaction occurred,[68] clearly such relationships had problematic and ambiguous dimensions which would generate a more complex geography of interaction than can be reconstructed from extant historical records. These complexities cast Peter's interaction with Cornelius and his envoys – especially in the realm of hospitality – as freighted with theological-spatial significance.

Further detail in 10:22 regarding Cornelius' instruction 'by a holy angel' reveals that he expects 'to hear words (ῥήματα)' from Peter, a specificity absent in 10:5, and that Peter is to be summoned 'to (εἰς) his house'. Complying with this latter information will involve some sort of defilement for Peter.[69] Unsurprisingly, therefore, it dominates the narrative (cf. 10:25–7; 11:3, 12). It also establishes the transitional importance of Peter's extension of hospitality in 10:23a.[70]

The tanner's house

Some commentators judge that a tanner's house forms a dubious lodging for Peter in Joppa. Witherington, for example, suggests that 'there may ... be some intended irony here, since Peter had earlier protested his scrupulousness about food, all the while staying in the house of a man whose trade made him unclean!'[71] He adds: 'It is also possible to read this story as another example of Peter's well-known

---

[67] Matson 1996: 105–6.

[68] Cf., e.g., Conzelmann 1987: 82; Witherington 1998: 353 and Bockmuehl 1999: 164–5.

[69] Matson 1996: 105: 'Refusal to enter the house until invited to do so (vv. 17–18, 23a) highlights the problematic issue of space, this time from a gentile perspective.'

[70] Matson (1996: 106) risks thinning out the complexities of space prematurely when commenting that 'Peter's resistance to associating with Gentiles is now largely overcome'.

[71] Witherington 1998: 351.

tendency to vacillate about such matters (Galatians 2).'[72] Caution is necessary, however, before invoking a 'well-known tendency' to interpret a character's motivation within a particular narrative. Although later rabbinical texts would castigate such a choice of lodging, the narrative of Acts does not make such explicit judgements. Yet the venue is emphasised through redundant repetition (Acts 9:43; 10:6, 17, 32), which suggests some significance beyond local colour[73] or Lukan interest in the hosts of his principal characters (cf. 9:11; 21:6).[74]

Hypotheses concerning Joppa as the furthest boundary of Judea or as evoking Jonah have already been acknowledged; while suggestive, these theories are hard to tie down as explicitly resonant across Acts 10. Both hypotheses fit, however, within a spatial dynamic governed by an ascension matrix. Once confronted with the heavenly vision, Peter is caught on the horns of a 1:6/1:8 spatial dilemma which will be resolved only by continually unfolding heavenly thirdspace intervention. This intervention is only beginning with the dual vision and the Spirit's subsequent prompting of Peter.

In this complex and dynamic space, it is unreasonable to conclude that Peter's lodging with a tanner renders his resistance to the vision, especially his claim to be kosher in 10:14, as simply hypocritical. Such readings treat space as unproblematic and unreflexive, or assume that Peter has omniscient understanding of it. Instead of being considered simplistic, singular or positivistically 'flat',[75] space needs to be theorised as dynamic, even problematic, within lived experience. Spencer hints at such a reading, but without explicating it as spatial, proposing a reading which 'imagines more of a complex developmental *process* in Peter's socio-religious orientation, pushing certain radical boundaries here while toeing the party line there'.[76] Expressed in Sojan categories, Peter is struggling to live within ascension geography's thirdspace, that is,

---

[72] Witherington 1998: 351 n. 102; similarly p. 333.

[73] Spencer 1997: 103.   [74] Cf. Witherington 1998: 165–7.

[75] Barrett (1994: 487) suggests that 'Plümacher is probably right in thinking that residence with the tanner is after all not important. "Warum sollte Lk die Pointe der folgenden Vision des Petrus durch Vorwegnahme abschwächen?"' [Why should Luke soften the punchline of Peter's following vision through anticipation?] Such privileging of sequence unacceptably submerges the complexities of space. At the other extreme, Witherup (1993: 48) is too simplistic when suggesting that 'Peter's temporary residence provides a preview of the story about to unfold'. Tanner-space is not so transparent a servant of history, but neither is it oblique and inert in shaping the narrative.

[76] Spencer 1997: 113, emphasis original. His reading presupposes 'another interpretive approach [which] may prefer to appreciate and negotiate, rather than mitigate and obviate, apparent incongruities in the text'.

an-Other world, a meta-space of radical openness where everything can be found, where the possibilities for new discoveries and political strategies are endless, but where one must always be restlessly and self-critically moving on to new sites and insights, never confined by past journeys and accomplishments, always searching for differences, an Otherness, a strategic and heretical space 'beyond' what is presently known and taken for granted.[77]

Although more developmental than spatial, Spencer's enunciation does point towards these complexities of space: 'It may be illogical, to defend kosher laws on a tanner's roof, but realizing fallacy and hypocrisy is often a necessary step to transformation.'[78] There is also a resistant quality to unknown space, especially when existing space is encoded in regular, routinised practices. Again Spencer adumbrates this understanding but without elucidating its consequences for understanding space: 'Also major changes in worldview are as likely (if not more so) to come in fits and starts rather than once-for-all bolts of lightning.'[79]

Thus a thirdspatial perspective provides a more coherent examination of the tanner's house than previous atomistic attempts to probe individual details of the setting. For example, architectural inquiries intended to cast light on the size of the dwelling, or on the owner's consequent socio-economic status, stumble in the face of limited textual data and render only 'an incidental Firstspace tableau of geographical sites and situations'.[80] Jesus' ascension triggers a far more coherent reading of space, and one more comprehensive, reworking even a Joppan tanner's house.

Entering Cornelius-space (10:23b–27)

Peter then travels to Caesarea accompanied by 'believers [lit. brothers] from Joppa' (10:23). Although 11:12 clarifies that these (six) accomplices serve as witnesses, this does not establish the journey as 'an official action of the church'.[81] Rather, Peter's wisdom in taking these believers is precisely because this was *not* such an official action.[82]

---

[77] Soja 1996: 34.   [78] Spencer 1997: 113.   [79] Spencer 1997: 113.
[80] Soja 1996: 172. Cf., e.g., Barrett 1994: 510, interacting with Haenchen 1971: 348 n. 8, and Witherington 1998: 350–1 regarding 'gate' in 10:17.
[81] Conzelmann 1987: 82.   [82] Bruce 1990: 258: 'a wise precaution'.

That these brethren were Joppans further dilutes any Jerusalem-centred reading of Acts. At this crucial juncture in the narrative, Jerusalem sits in a tertiary relationship to the latest site of the Spirit's activity. This qualifies reading 11:18 as Jerusalem's affirmative sanction for a gentile mission. Instead, mission-space, being co-ordinated from heaven, stretches beyond and relativises Jerusalem's material and ideational spheres of influence.

The brethren do not demonstrate any foreknowledge, let alone sympathy,[83] with the journey's intention. Within the narrative, Peter offers them no explanation, and they re-enter the narrative only at 10:45, when it is they – not Peter – who are amazed at the Spirit's descent. Nevertheless, although appearing naïve regarding the direction of events, they help generate 'an occasion pregnant with social as well as personal significance, confirmed by multiple witnesses'.[84]

Peter's entry into Cornelius' house is narrated by a 'funnelling effect'[85] generated by successive spatial progressions. First Peter rises and goes away (10:23b), and then he enters Caesarea (10:24). Here the narrative focuses on Peter,[86] as Caesarea becomes a sustained setting for the first time in Acts (cf. 8:40; 9:30). Although the city is only the penumbra of Cornelius-space, arriving in 'Caesarea' denotes entry into a gentile spatial order.[87] Given that 10:24 'anticipates but does not fulfil' Peter's charge,[88] the result is heightened tension for auditors.

As one narrative space focuses down to one figure, another space broadens to the communal level; in his expectation, Cornelius has assembled around himself in his home those who constitute his first-space (10:24).[89] Cornelius-space is being defined by the narrator, prior to Peter's arrival, as more than an individual matter. This collective Cornelius-space will serve both as an audience for Peter

---

[83] *Contra* Bruce 1990: 258.   [84] Spencer 1997: 114.   [85] Matson 1996: 104.
[86] Against the NRSV's 'they entered' (εἰσῆλθον), 'he entered' (εἰσῆλεν) is to be preferred as the harder reading (Metzger 1994: 329).
[87] Kee 1990: 50–1, regarding the urban structure of Caesarea; cf. Hengel 1983: 112–15. Narratively, Eisen (2006: 183–4) positions Caesarea in geopolitical opposition to both Jerusalem and Joppa, such that Cornelius' house forms the focal point of the account.
[88] Matson 1996: 106.
[89] Commentators delimit this group in various ways. That some Jews might be among those invited (Fitzmyer 1998: 460) is possible (10:2, 22), but the narrative does not suggest it (cf. 10:28, 45; 11:3). Barrett's suggestion (1994: 513) that 'it is natural to suppose that … all were relatively "unobjectionable" Gentiles' also unnecessarily blunts the narrative's construction of space.

and as the foundation for a congregation.[90] Compared with the lone Ethiopian in Acts 8, Cornelius-space will generate *firstspace* gentile converts within Acts.

Cornelius' first action as Peter enters his space ('falling at his feet, [he] worshipped him', 10:25) is significant given its primacy effect as the narrative slows to maximise tension and significance, and following the previous descriptions of Cornelius from both the narrator (10:1–2) and characters (10:22). Peter's response (10:26) suggests that Cornelius misinterprets Peter's firstspace presence by equating it with the angelic thirdspace Cornelius encountered in his earlier vision.

This is, within the spatial ordering of Acts, a fundamental misunderstanding which must be corrected.[91] Gaventa underestimates the situation when commenting: 'Although this response is mistaken, and Peter moves quickly to correct it, it does not necessarily signal a profound misunderstanding on Cornelius' part (Stenschke 1999, 151–2).'[92] It is also insufficient to suggest that Cornelius 'shows his esteem for the heavenly authority attached to Peter's vision and mission',[93] still less that this action represents 'a normal Middle Eastern form of greeting for an important person',[94] or that 10:26 is 'Luke's way of illustrating his [Peter's] exemplary humility'.[95] Neither is the focus on Cornelius, as Spencer claims when identifying 'an elevation of Cornelius' socio-religious status' in 10:26, judged as paralleling Peter's speech-acts in 9:34, 40.[96] Spencer considers that Peter's reply expresses penitence concerning his previous 'reluctance to obey the heavenly vision', but this does not correlate with Peter's similar reaction in 3:12. Rather, in 10:26, as in 3:12 *and* 9:34, 40, Peter downplays *his* agency within heavenly thirdspace intervention. The focus falls instead on correct understanding of earthly categories – correct, that is, according to the heavenly vision, itself dependent

---

[90] Haenchen 1971: 350.

[91] Cf. 3:12; 12:21–3; 14:14–15; 16:30–2. Cf. also the humility espoused in Luke 9:46–8 and 22:24–7.

[92] Gaventa 2003a: 167. Gaventa also misrepresents Stenschke. Concerning 10:25, Stenschke (1999: 151–2) describes 'this failure [which] surfaced in the otherwise impeccable Cornelius' as a reaction within 'pagan categories' which is 'corrected forcefully' by Peter (10:26), a response which 'forbids overestimation of Cornelius' characterisation as δίκαιος'.

[93] Fitzmyer 1998: 461; similarly, Bruce 1990: 259.

[94] Witherington 1998: 352, who rejects this suggestion. Cf. Barrett 1994: 513, citing Liddell and Scott.

[95] Haenchen 1971: 350.   [96] Spencer 1997: 114.

upon the implications arising from the now heavenly Christ. Later invocations of οὐρανός in Acts (14:15; 17:24), although in very different circumstances, also correct confusions concerning human–divine relations. By these later places, Luke's interpretative structure has already been established, through a robust ascension geography.

On these grounds, Green's suggestion that Cornelius had no need of conversion to the God of Israel[97] requires qualification. Given the God of Israel's glorification of Jesus (3:13) and Jesus' consequent restructuring of earthly space (3:21–6), information which Cornelius lacks, a conversion of spatial categories is in view and this will have profound theological ramifications. Cornelius is, at this juncture, still outside of ascension geography. That Cornelius himself describes the 'angel of God' (10:3) as 'a man' in 10:30 provides some explanation for 10:25, and confirms that Cornelius requires clarification, even correction, regarding heavenly thirdspace. Acts 10:26 is Peter's first remedial step in this regard, asserting that he is no divine man (cf. Simon in 8:9, and Peter's consequent differentiation from him in 8:18–24). The auditor who recalls 3:12 might well be primed to expect further words from Peter here in Acts 10.

These immediate words are narrated but not told (10:27a). Instead, the narration slows further, foregrounding the spatial import of what is unfolding. First, the simple act of conversation is noteworthy (10:27a).[98] Next, Peter is *again* narrated as entering (εἰσῆλθεν, 10:27b; cf. 10:24, 25).[99] Finally, Peter discovers the nature of the firstspace he is entering: it is peopled with Cornelius' assembly. Within the narrative, Peter has not been forewarned of this eventuality, which moves the encounter from merely a private audience into a corporate dimension.[100]

Peter interprets Cornelius-space (10:28–9)

Peter's first action within Cornelius-space is, characteristically, to speak. Here, and until 11:17, Peter will be the interpreter of the heavenly ordering of earthly space. His first recorded words to Cornelius' gathering begin that function, based upon the spatial knowledge has thus far been revealed to him.

---

[97] Green 2002: 7.
[98] Heil (1999: 252) notes the frequent use of συν-related words in 10:23a–27.
[99] After 10:23a, this 'is the second effect of the vision that Luke carefully notes' (Fitzmyer 1998: 461).
[100] Matson 1996: 108–10.

Peter's earlier vision has provoked and legitimated his willing entry into Cornelius-space (10:29). Rather than exhibiting grudging 'minimalism',[101] Peter's words seek to understand a rapidly unfolding spatial vista. Within the diachronic confines of the narrative, Peter is dealing with a lack of knowledge as to why he has been summoned into this space. Only in the sense of reporting what is shared prior knowledge concerning such social interaction does Peter still declare what may be considered a Jewish spatiality in 10:28.[102] Prior to – as, indeed, during – his vision, Peter might well have reacted in such conventional spatial categories and responses, but, faced with Cornelius' assembly, Peter has translated his heavenly vision to the level of earthly ethics,[103] reading its earthly social significance by transposing it from animals to persons: just as food does not defile, neither does contact with non-Jews.

Acts 10:28b–29 therefore intimates the continuing spatial transformation in Peter's thinking, indicating his conformity to what the heavenly vision has revealed.[104] Peter has entered 'without objection' (10:29; cf. 10:20). Peter's dependence on the vision (especially 10:15) in these opening words suggests that, prior to it, for all the potentially expansive secondspace in his earlier proclamations (e.g. 2:39; 3:25–6), Peter himself had not grasped this import or its implications for gentiles. Rather than undermining these earlier intimations, this observation instead reaffirms the problematic nature of space and the need for a more developed heavenly thirdspace perspective. It is not that Peter is imperceptive or disingenuous;[105] rather, he is struggling to understand the theological complexities of the (embodied) space before him in the light of an ascension geography still being revealed to him. Simultaneously, the account is thematising an order of the world, with its stark contrasts, which is being violated and reworked in this incident. Rather than belittling Peter, the narrative presents him as coming to terms with the dynamic complexities of space, something which auditors will, in their turn, have to address in a variety of life situations.

---

[101] Cf. Gaventa 2003a: 168. Far less does 10:29 indicate that the apostles are generally stationary and Jerusalem-bound (cf. A. Clark 1998: 180).

[102] Cf. Fitzmyer 1998: 461: 'Peter still thinks like a Jew.' Peter's reference to 'God' (θεός) fits communication with a non-Jew (cf. Rius-Camps and Read-Heimerdinger 2006: 264).

[103] Marguerat 2002: 55.

[104] Κἀμοί 'probably has some adversative force – "but to me, God has shown …"' (Witherington 1998: 353); similarly, Barrett 1994: 515.

[105] As Spencer (1997: 115) suggests.

So far the vision has operated only to get Peter into Cornelius-space. At this juncture, Peter still does not know the nature of his summons.[106] There is more for him to understand about these new surroundings. Peter is willing to learn it from the person of Cornelius; 10:30–3 will provide Peter with still more understanding of the space he has entered.

Cornelius positions Peter-space (10:30–3)

Cornelius then recounts the vision already narrated in 10:3–6 (10:30–2). The variations anticipate the importance of Cornelius-space. First, Cornelius' description of 'dazzling clothes' is sufficiently close to 'white robes' of the messengers proclaiming Christological thirdspace in 1:10–11 to establish an inferential connection.[107] Further, specifying the location as 'in my house' and the messenger as being 'before me' (ἐνώπιόν μου, 10:30) both clarifies the location implicit in 10:3 and further justifies Peter's entry into Cornelius-space: some kind of heavenly agent has preceded Peter into this space with a word that dovetails with his own heavenly vision and subsequent word from the Spirit (10:32; cf. 10:18–20). Also, the messenger declared divine acceptance of Cornelius' piety (10:31; cf. 10:4), which connects Cornelius even more closely with the threefold declaration of 10:15. This is new and important information for Peter, as he seeks to understand this new space into which the Spirit has led him. Importantly, the content of Cornelius' prayers is not revealed: the focus is instead on their reception in the presence of God (ἐνώπιον τοῦ θεοῦ, 10:31).[108]

Not occurring in the LXX or the other Gospels, the phrase ἐνώπιον τοῦ θεοῦ is an echo chamber for the thirdspatial values and priorities of Luke-Acts. It echoes the heavenly realm of Gabriel (Luke 1:19), the

---

[106] Perhaps Peter has been summoned to perform a healing (Witherington 1998: 353); cf. 9:34; Luke 7:1–10.

[107] This conjecture is cautious, given the widespread expectation of angels being so attired (for which, see Bruce 1990: 259, 104; Witherington 1998: 353). Cf. Rius-Camps and Read-Heimerdinger (2006: 267), who claim – somewhat obliquely, via Luke 23:11 – that Cornelius saw Jesus.

[108] That Cornelius' alms have been '*remembered* before God' recalls the hope of Israel, expressed within Abrahamic covenantal horizons (Luke 1:54, 72), hopes which climax around Jesus (Luke 23:42; Acts 3:26). Peter's earlier proclamation in Acts 3:25 has previously positioned this covenant as being for Israel and 'all the families of the earth (γῆς)'. Cornelius' piety, now remembered before God, brings him – and his household – towards the orbit of what Peter has earlier proclaimed. Peter retrospectively clarifies this in 11:14.

sphere where even sparrows are remembered (Luke 12:6) but where deniers of Jesus will themselves be denied (Luke 12:9; cf. Acts 10:42) and where human exaltation will be revealed for what it truly is (Luke 16:15). It is the realm which determines what is right for the apostles to do (Acts 4:19). David found favour there (Acts 7:46), and 'in the presence (ἐνώπιον) of the angels of God' there is joy over one sinner who repents (Luke 15:10; cf. vv. 7 and 32). Now, most importantly for Acts 10, it is the realm where Cornelius' piety has found favour (10:31) and where – in a thirdspatial sense – Cornelius locates the assembly in his house (10:33).[109] In this latter reference, Cornelius primes Peter's understanding of Cornelius-space by interpreting the assembly as also ἐνώπιον τοῦ θεοῦ,[110] sparking Peter's unfolding address in 10:34–43. Although understated here (due to Cornelius' limited understanding at this stage in the encounter), this thirdspace is Christological as well as theological, given Christ's heavenly position (1:9–11; 7:55, 56).

The biggest cue for Peter's involvement in this place is the expansion from 10:22 found in Cornelius' request to hear 'all that the Lord has commanded you to say' (10:33). This not only establishes a rhetorically pregnant moment,[111] but also implies that Simon-Peter is going to speak what *Jesus* has commanded him to speak. Unwittingly, perhaps,[112] Cornelius invokes and anticipates the ascension geography that follows.

Peter positions Cornelius-space (10:34–5)

When Peter opens his mouth and speaks, his prophetic space-constituting speech-act declares that the geography of divine approval is now clarified to him as non-nationalistic. This realisation arises in part from his entry into this new (first)space, which has resulted in a

---

[109] Comparing ἐνώπιον τοῦ θεοῦ in 10:31 and 10:33, Hamm (2003: 222–3) comments: 'It is as if the preaching of the good news breaks down the division between the sacred and the profane.' Spatially, it also reconceptualises the earth–heaven distinction (cf., e.g., 10:44–8).

[110] The manuscript tradition marginalises the less religious D reading, 'before you' (Metzger 1994: 332).

[111] Soards 1994: 71.

[112] Fitzmyer (1998: 462) comments that 'Lord' 'may refer to the risen Christ, but on the lips of Cornelius who has not yet heard the Christian proclamation, it is probably better understood as referring to Yahweh'. While true of the character Cornelius, within the narrative 'Lord' has sufficient ambiguity, even reason, to refer to Jesus. Cf. 1:5, 8; 10:36, 42. D (etc.) have θεοῦ instead of κυρίου, the latter never being used by gentiles in D (Read-Heimerdinger 2002: 286–7).

'concretising'[113] of his heavenly vision within a new expanded conception of space. At root, his realisation – in this new space – is thirdspatial, driven from heaven. It breaks any synonymous immediacy of firstspace and secondspace lingering from 1:6–8: divine impartiality cannot be limited to Israel – indeed, to maintain such a spatiality would render God as one showing partiality – and the use of cultic terminology (δεκτός, 'acceptable') reflects the continuing relativising of spatial claims made by or for the Jerusalem Temple. This coheres in a possible criticism of the spatial limits inscribed in the Jewish theology of election, even if 10:34–5 'does not deny the unique status of the people of God in the Lukan narrative'.[114] Peter's spatial vision is of such a magnitude that, by implication, auditors might fairly adopt it for any other pragmatic boundaries placed on divine favour.

In short, Peter is unravelling the full implications of 1:6–11, of ascension geography. The process is still unfolding: thirdspatial heavenly intervention has yet to reach its climax in confirming these outworkings (10:44–6), but at this juncture 'God's decision is at least acknowledged'.[115]

Peter expounds ascension geography (10:36–43)

Peter then grounds God's decision within a Christological discourse. Although the varied syntactical and textual difficulties of 10:36–8 are well rehearsed within commentaries, the argument's 'general sense … is reasonably clear'.[116] For a spatial reading, the main observation is that the strong assertion concluding 10:36 (οὖτός ἐστιν πάντων κύριος), even if appearing grammatically parenthetical, is not parenthetical to Peter's argument.[117] Rather, it summarises 10:34–5: Jesus[118] is proclaimed 'Lord of all', understanding 'all' (πάντων) as indicating people, together with their constituent spatialities. Peter's assertion closely resembles the Septuagintal referent to God as 'Lord of all the earth', and in other ancient literature the phrase indicates divine or human ownership of property and/or political

---

[113] Marguerat 2002: 254: 'To travel, to speak at all, concretizes the revelation given to Peter' in 10:34.

[114] Pao 2000: 237.   [115] Gaventa 2003a: 170.

[116] Barrett 1994: 521; likewise, Witherington 1998: 356.

[117] Rowe 2005; 2006: 193–4 n. 114; cf. Barrett 1994: 522. Rowe (2006: 135–6 n. 36) asserts the cosmic dimensions of this lordship, not least given 10:38, seeing in 10:36 'the Christological counterpart' to Luke 10:21 and Acts 17:24.

[118] It is 'nigh impossible' for the antecedent of οὖτός to be 'the message' (Fitzmyer 1998: 464).

status.[119] In Acts 10, the setting sharpens the phrase's meaning, here uttered in the home of a Roman army officer.[120] Like the associated proclamation of 'peace' brought about 'by Jesus Christ',[121] Jesus' lordship – declared by Peter and underpinning the whole encounter – infuses all three Sojan dimensions, being presented as exercised over material space, ideational space and more. In its narrative cotext, within the last substantive speech in Acts by anyone present at the ascension,[122] this assertion forms a spatial claim which is proleptic for the ongoing narrative and for auditors, for places where Peter will be physically absent but where the apostolic witness will go forth towards the end of the earth.

A second universal Christological marker, Jesus as the God-appointed judge of the living and the dead (10:42), balances with the similar declaration in 10:36.[123] Yet between these markers, Jesus is pronounced within a distinctively Jewish context, his witnesses appointed to interpret his odyssey according to the prophets and divine vindication.[124] Nevertheless, these Jewish geographical markers have been realigned by the earlier exposition of ascension geography. 'Israel' (10:36) has been reworked by 1:6–11 (and 3:19–24, which also clarifies 'the prophets'), and 'Galilee' (10:37) recalls 1:11, 21–2. Peter's account therefore combines the specificity of Jesus' earthly (material) firstspace with an expanding and transformed secondspace conception of the world sealed by Jesus' ascension. Under Jesus' (heavenly) thirdspatial scope, the word to Israel in 10:36 becomes 'the word' also for the gentiles (10:44). Spencer claims that Peter's address here is typical of speeches in Acts, being 'thoroughly theocentric',[125] but it also exhibits a strong, albeit complementary, Christological focus, evident in the range of grammatical references to Jesus.[126] Peter's insight, its

---

[119]   Fitzmyer 1998: 463–4; Witherington 1998: 357.

[120]   Gaventa 2003a: 171. Perhaps the narrative characters would not have heard this implication, but its assertions would have been clearer for auditors (Rowe 2005: 292).

[121]   Fitzmyer (1998: 463) suggests that 'peace' alludes to Isaiah 52:7; cf. Nahum 1:15. Also, it would have potential political resonance for Roman ears (Gilbert 2003: 242).

[122]   Other than a terse sentence (12:17) and Peter's brief retrospective (15:7–11).

[123]   Tannehill 1990: 141.

[124]   Tannehill 1990: 142: 'Peter does not transform Jesus into a Gentile, living in a Gentile environment, in order to speak to Cornelius.' Cf. Trites 1977: 144–5.

[125]   Spencer 1997: 115.

[126]   Acts 10:36: name, and demonstrative pronoun; 10:38: name, accusative pronoun, relative pronoun, genitive (object) pronoun; 10:39: implied subject of verb, relative pronoun; 10:40: demonstrative pronoun, accusative pronoun; 10:41: dative (object) pronoun, accusative pronoun; 10:42: implied subject of verb, demonstrative pronoun, predicate participial phrase; 10:43: demonstrative pronoun (cf. Witherington 1998: 359), 'his name', object pronoun.

revelation for Cornelius, and its implications within the narrative are intensely Christological.

Given that this is Peter's last missionary address in Acts, it is fitting that a repetition of elements found in his earlier speeches provides a suitable summation of all that Peter has previously proclaimed and realigned. Indeed, the whole life-span of Jesus is summarised here, with its promised universal impact on people and places,[127] culminating in the witnesses sharing meals with the risen Jesus (10:41; cf. 1:4) and him commanding them 'to preach to the people' (10:42; cf. 1:8 and Luke 24:47–8!). Although Acts 10:42 expresses the scope of this proclamation within a more narrowly nationalistic reading of 1:8[128] 10:43 at least allows for a wider mental map ('everyone who believes in him'), one that will certainly arrive with the thirdspatial imposition of the Spirit which is about to interrupt Peter's address.

Thirdspatial intervention from heaven (10:44–6a)

While Peter is still speaking,[129] even this gentile location is overtaken by the Spirit. The close parallel between 10:44 and 10:33 indicates that it is Cornelius and his company who experience phenomena echoing the Day of Pentecost (10:45–6; cf. 11:15).[130] The Joppans accompanying Peter simply observe, 'astounded' (ἐξέστησαν) that the recipients of this thirdspatial intrusion are 'even (καὶ) gentiles'. This, the third incursion from heaven in Acts 10, unlike previously, does not turn back into heaven;[131] rather, the Spirit remains, decisively and thirdspatially influencing earthly orders of space on behalf of the absent Lord of all.

Acts has presented the heavenly Jesus as the one bestowing the Spirit (2:33), but commentators here in Acts 10 characteristically submerge this Christological aspect beneath divine sovereignty.[132] While God's role should not be ignored (11:17, 18; 15:8; also 2:17; cf. 2:33), the Christological import of 2:33 – and 11:16 – cannot be evacuated from

---

[127] Paul's final defence address, in Acts 26, especially v. 23, provides a parallel projection.

[128] Rius-Camps and Read-Heimerdinger 2006: 275–6.

[129] Note the present participle λαλοῦτος (Bruce 1990: 269).

[130] That 'just as we have' (10:47) and 'at the beginning' (11:15) refer to Pentecost is confirmed by 'gift' (δωρεά) in 10:45; 11:17. The only other occurrences of δωρεά also concern the Spirit's bestowal (2:38; 8:20).

[131] Eisen 2006:186, identifying a border-crossing into the human realm (*Reich*) and human space (*Raum*).

[132] E.g. Haenchen 1971: 359; Bruce 1990: 264; Barrett 1994: 529; Witherington 1998: 359; Marguerat 2002: 104 and Gaventa 2003a: 172.

analysis.[133] Earthly space ordered 'under heaven' in Acts cannot isolate either Christology or theology from the other in their connections with pneumatological activity. Conzelmann is helpfully nuanced at this juncture: 'Heaven itself points the way to the admission of the "Gentiles".'[134]

That this heavenly thirdspace reworks secondspace conceptions as well as firstspace relations is evident in the narrator characterising the astonished observers in relation to circumcision (10:45). By inference, their amazement arises because Cornelius and his house come under this heavenly blessing while remaining *un*circumcised (cf. 11:3). The spatiality drawn around circumcision can cut both ways in Acts. Although circumcision has previously been mentioned only at 7:8, and there positively in relation to the expansive Abrahamic secondspace vision (cf. 3:25–6), here this characterisation momentarily anticipates the shrunken understanding of divine space articulated in the criticism within 11:2–3. The absence of any recorded amazement at one of their own number being raised from the dead (9:38, 41) heightens the significance of the Joppans' astonished reaction in 10:45. Furthermore, this is the first time that the verb ἐξίστημι has been used of *believers* in Acts,[135] a measure of the import of this reordering of space.

Narrating the recipients as 'the gentiles' (10:45) confirms the importance of secondspace categories in this immediate interpretative response to the heavenly intervention within Cornelius' house. Such description completes the transposition from individual firstspace specificity ('Cornelius' in 'Caesarea', so important up to 10:33) back into the collectivity of Cornelius' household after 10:33 and here into the more abstracted realm of secondspace. By this change of spatial perspective, Acts 10 confirms a sea-change affecting the whole gentile world, not simply an isolated, localised or particularist event.[136]

Peter orders earthly space according to ascension geography (10:46b–48)

Whether addressing the household ('Be baptised') or the Joppans ('Baptise them'),[137] Peter's instruction in 10:48 reflects less his

---

[133] Marguerat (2002: 125) recognises two different Lukan 'discourses' concerning the Spirit as empowering *and* preceding believers, a double dynamic which applies to believer-spaces.

[134] Conzelmann 1987: 84.

[135] Cf. 2:7, 12; 8:9, 11, 13; 9:21. Its only other use is in 12:16.

[136] Cf. Haenchen 1971: 354.

[137] On the basis of analogy to 2:38 and 22:16, Bruce (1990: 265) considers the former to be more likely.

apostolic office in any abstract sense[138] and more his understanding of the unfolding situation. Peter continues to interpret the vibrant spatiality unfolding before his eyes and ears as he continues to speak. He is no 'prattling Peter' 'still partly out of step with God's agenda';[139] Peter knows what he is saying (cf. Luke 9:33–5), and declares what needs to be done in this dynamic space. He is flexible and discerning in his reading of it, answering (ἀπεκρίθη, Acts 10:46) the (vocal) situation unfolding before him.[140]

No-one should 'withhold' baptism from them (κωλῦσαι, 10:47, par. 11:17) precisely because of this heavenly thirdspatial intervention. If heaven has demonstrated a unity between Jew and gentile (10:44–5), implying that the recipients of its blessing have become part of the space proclaimed in 10:43, then this solidarity must be fully embodied on earth in the manner already outlined earlier in Acts, namely baptism and fellowship (10:47–8). 'Everything in the narrative conspires against maintaining the barrier between Jews and this Gentile.'[141] Furthermore, auditors, having already encountered the Ethiopian in Acts 8 through various confirmatory acts from heaven, are more informed than Peter the narrative character and are reassured that Peter's words at this critical juncture provide reliable interpretation.[142] Unlike 8:36, where the verb κωλύω was similarly used concerning baptism but on the lips of an outsider probing inwards towards a hoped-for expansive spatiality, here in 10:47 the question comes from the other side, expressed by an insider looking out onto an expansive spatiality unfolding before him. In both instances, categories of 'insider' and 'outsider' – and the spatiality they create and legitimate – are subverted by ascension geography's inclusive reach, which will

---

[138] Philip has already demonstrated that apostolic presence is not necessary for baptism.
[139] Spencer 1997: 116, likening Peter here with Luke 9:33–5. This comparison unnecessarily plays down the spatial developments and intimations informing this juncture in Acts 10. Furthermore, no such pejorative reading is made of Stephen, similarly 'interrupted' by heavenly thirdspace (7:55–6).
[140] The decision to baptise acts 'to ratify the divine decree', given the 'noisy divine approval' (Marguerat 2002: 104). Given 2:33, the decree and approval are Christological, as well as divine.
[141] Tannehill 1990: 133.
[142] If 10:45; 11:3 and 15:1, 5 suggest that some Jewish believers might have required further preparation for baptism, namely circumcision, then Haenchen (1971: 354) is right: 'The question is addressed to the six Jewish Christians, but at the same time to the reader … μήτι expects the answer "No!"'

echo throughout Acts, all the way to the cognate antonym ἀκωλύτως ('without hindrance', 28:31) which becomes the narrative's final word. More immediately, this inclusive subversion is demonstrated by the thirdspace connective from heaven – 'just as we have' in 10:47 – which is reprised in 11:15, 17 and 15:8, and inverted in 15:11. It is sealed through and in the 'name' of Jesus, 10:48 positioned by 10:43.[143] The entrance into believer-space is clarified as it is redrawn. Any sense of restraint based on circumcision (or any other restriction, beyond that established by ascension geography's new order of belief and repentance, as evidenced in 10:43 and 11:18) is to be resisted as unnecessarily restraining believer-space.[144] Nevertheless, material and relational difference is not obliterated. Nothing excludes circumcision, and 'just as we have' communicates simply that they have received the same Spirit, not that they have necessarily received it in the same way.

Given that Peter's vision ultimately addressed Jew–gentile separation, and that so much narrative time was dedicated to Peter's entry into Cornelius-space, Acts 10 fittingly concludes with him remaining in this new hybrid space. It is implicit that Peter accepted the household's hospitality offered 'for several days' (10:48b; Peter's companions disappear from the scene). The collective household remains in view, still functioning as τὰ ἔθνη, but now constituted within believer-space by thirdspace intervention (evident in the falling Spirit, the waters of baptism, and accepted hospitality). The narrative closure at 10:48 invites the auditor's imagination to inhabit those days spent at Cornelius' house, to create imaginatively the earthly ordering created by heavenly thirdspatial intervention.[145] If Luke has an interest in the hosts of his main characters,[146] then here is the narrative's most theologically significant host. If the influence of setting is taken seriously, then accepting hospitality from Cornelius' household not only indicates that Peter 'regards them as Christians in the full sense and as "clean"';[147] it also counters claims

---

[143]   The limited references to Jesus' 'name' beyond Acts 9 make this point especially noteworthy.

[144]   Jesus, in Luke's Gospel, anticipates such access, in embryo, in Luke 9:49–50 and 18:16.

[145]   Heil (1999: 256–7) positions Peter's actions as reflecting Jesus' instruction in Luke 9:4 and 10:7, and as informing a pattern for auditors involving table fellowship with the newly baptised to unite them into the broader believing community.

[146]   Bruce 1990: 237, 250.   [147]   Haenchen 1971: 354.

that the apostles remain Jerusalem-centred throughout Acts or, indeed, that the narrative itself is so centred. In terms of conventional Jewish mental maps, the space beneath Cornelius' roof *is* effectively the ends of the earth.

Postscript to a spatial reading of Acts 10

Acts 10 does not present some abstracted notion of secondspace unity detached from material encounters and embodied relationships. Rather, 'consistent with the entire narrative ... the inclusion of the Gentiles does not have to do only with a grudging admission to the circle of the baptized. Including Gentiles means receiving them, entering their homes, and accepting hospitality – even meals – in those homes.'[148] This is a rich spatiality, a lived experience with depth, being constructed within the narrative of Acts as the outworking of a foundational ascension geography. Heavenly thirdspace is being realised decisively on earth. Such reception and sharing are akin to the *koinonia* prominent earlier in Acts, and the focus upon *outsiders* marginalised by Jewish society mirrors similar Third-Gospel concern for marginalised *insiders*.[149] In short, the Lukan conception of gentile mission, at its outset, cannot be understood apart from such 'community-constituting practices' generating lived space, and affecting the spatiality of both Cornelius and Peter; there is no aspatial gentile mission in Acts, it *is* space.

Cornelius' household are the first *firstspace* gentile converts within the storyworld of Acts. Even if the Ethiopian was richly symbolic of the word's spread towards the end of the earth, it is noteworthy that Philip did not eat with him after his conversion (8:39). Furthermore, the Ethiopian generated nothing resembling the charge against Peter in 11:3, since he had no ongoing spatial impact which would unsettle Jerusalem believers. With Cornelius, however, 'Israel' itself (cf. 10:36) – defined by table fellowship as an expression of covenant – undergoes intimate redefinition by a succession of heavenly interventions provoking fellowship across previous divides according to the new spatial order established by the now heavenly Christ. The reflexive ordering of places anticipates, even demands, that there will be some sort of reaction among Jewish believers.

---

[148] Gaventa 2003a: 172; also 1986: 120.   [149] Tannehill 2005: 120.

4.   Peter-space and Cornelius-space, as perceived in Jerusalem (11:1–18)

Introduction

Acts 11:1–18 mediates the immediate consequences of the spatial transformation brought about in Acts 10, revisiting its momentous spatial restructuring from the perspective of a different place, that of Jerusalem believer-space. It demonstrates that different locales within ascension geography are usually interrelated and reflexively constructed (8:26–39, if anything, was the exception to this observation). Even Jerusalem is still being positioned properly within the unfolding ascension geography, indicating again that the conception of space projected in 1:8 depends upon, and demands, unified material and symbolic relations between places. Acts 11:1–18 demonstrates that this depends upon correct interpretation of the heavenly intervention establishing and upholding that spatial order. This discernment of space – within the narrative, let alone beyond the storyworld – is not resolved within believer-space until Acts 15 and, even then, its echoes extend into 21:20–6. Clearly, space is multiplex, and not something that is once-for-all understood and discerned. It is dynamic and reflexive, requiring believers to engage in continuing discernment of its mission of responding to spatialities and shaping their own according to ascension geography.

Accusation (11:1–3)

Acts 11 opens with word reaching back to Judea that 'the Gentiles had also accepted the word of God'. Narrated differently, the content of 11:1 could have formed a Lukan summary similar to 6:7 or 12:24, but instead it is oriented towards the reaction of Judean believers to spatial developments elsewhere.

Here, as elsewhere in Acts, 'the word of God' engenders a comprehensive spatiality, but secondspace conceptions are especially in view in 11:1, continuing the focus of 10:44–8a. First, 'the gentiles' (τὰ ἔθνη), as in 10:45, indicates that a class of people, not as particular individuals, are in view. Acts 11:1–18 focuses on what τὰ ἔθνη means, specifically within Jerusalem believer-space.[150] Second, 'Judea' (here

---

[150] That these matters arise within *Jerusalem* Judaism is not unsurprising (Bockmuehl 1999: 168).

including Jerusalem, 11:2) evokes 1:8 conceptual categories. Third, 11:1 parallels Jerusalem's relations with Samaria in 8:14, similarly addressing Jerusalem's reaction to ascension geography expanding into another 1:8 realm.

Perhaps ominously, 'nothing indicates this announcement was experienced as good news'.[151] Instead, when Peter returns to Jerusalem in 11:2, presumably after 'several days' (cf. 10:48),[152] a group 'criticised' him for his firstspace boldness. As will become apparent, a continuing word-play on this verb διακρίνω concerning gentile believer-space (cf. 10:20; 11:12; 15:9) bridges firstspace practices and secondspace prejudices as both aspects are ultimately overcome by heavenly thirdspace governing earthly praxis.

Most commentators judge these critics to be at least a sub-group within the Jerusalem believers who at this juncture articulate a conservatism concerning Torah observation centring on circumcision (cf. 15:1, 5).[153] They question the very spatial move – εἰσῆλθες – which Acts 10 stressed repeatedly (10:24, 25, 27), confirming that spatial order is integral to the narrative. Indeed, their whole charge exhibits a spatial logic: the entering precedes eating, and eating itself addresses a sensitive balance between 'profane' and 'fellowship' domestic space.[154] Thus the charges reassert Cornelius-space as alien space.[155] Even if by 11:18 the issue has become one of gentile admission into believer-space, these critics introduced it as a matter of believer-space (in the person of Peter) entering gentile-space.

Through hearing 'a subtle echo of Jesus' critics in 11:3',[156] auditors can also hear a subtle echo of Jesus' spatiality within Peter's new practices. Here rests another example of how, even under conditions

---

[151] Gaventa 2003a: 172.

[152] The longer D reading of 11:2 connects well with Jesus' prophecy in Luke 22:32 and other ministries to believers within Acts (Rius-Camps and Read-Heimerdinger 2006: 292–3). As such, it links Jesus' will with Peter's production of believer-space within Acts 10–11, but it is hard to see it as the preferred reading (Metzger 1994: 337–8).

[153] The Greek οἱ ἐκ περιτομῆς lacks the NRSV's insertion of 'believers', but its insertion makes cotextual sense. Bruce (1990: 267) suggests that the believers' public standing within Jerusalem might depend upon their strict adherence to the traditional Jewish lifestyle: 'It is probably no accident that, shortly after this, [in narrative terms] the elder Agrippa could count on public approval when he executed James the Zebedean and imprisoned Peter.'

[154] Matson 1996: 114–16. The charge that Peter ate *with* them (συνέφαλες) also reprises the συν-related words in 10:23–7, 41, 45 (Heil 1999: 258).

[155] The charges undermine Barrett's attempt (1994: 533) to lessen the magnitude of 10:48 by claiming that 'a Gentile in good standing with Jews, as Cornelius was, would not insult his guest with unclean food'.

[156] Tannehill 1990: 137; cf. Luke 5:30; 15:2; 19:7.

of firstspace absence, the narrative presents Jesus' will as continuing to shape earthly spatial relations. Perhaps auditors also recall a previous spatial charge laid in Jerusalem, albeit by false witnesses (6:13–14). Both 7:54 and 11:18 begin ἀκούοντες δὲ ταῦτα ('When they heard these things/this…'). Here, however, that parallel leads to comprehensive contrast; when it comes, the crowning resolution is a word from Jesus (11:17) rather than a Christophany, causing critics to glorify God (11:18), not murderously obliterate ascension-space.

Response (11:4–17)

Peter's response to this spatial accusation is to provide a 'step by step' explanation (καθεξῆς, 11:4). This explanation, laid out in 11:4–17, *constructs* space using narrative redundancy to develop a sustained and deepened sensitivity to the spatiality of events. Given the position of καθεξῆς ('orderly') in Luke 1:3, these spatial priorities in Acts 11 suggest that wider authorial intent includes a consciously produced narrative exposition of space, a *spatial* narrative.

To this end, Peter sustains and magnifies the heavenly emphasis identified in Acts 10. First, another οὐρανός *inclusio* positions Peter's vision (11:5, 10; cf. 10:11, 16). Second, according to 11:9, the voice which Peter heard came 'from (ἐκ) heaven'. This phrase is, elsewhere in Acts, consistently Christological (2:2; cf. 2:33; 9:3; 22:6). Third, Peter's retelling stresses details concerning the vision itself which reinforce its heavenly origins and intensify its thirdspace role. The unavoidable and carefully examined nature of the vision is emphasised ('it came close to me', 11:5; 'I looked at it closely', 11:6). Likewise, the breadth and uncleanness of the animal life in 11:6 includes 'beasts of prey', and Peter's rejection of the heavenly command carries amplified emphasis ('has ever entered my mouth', 11:8). Jerusalem is assured that nothing merely earthly could have persuaded Peter in his course of action. Fourth, Peter's potentially problematic location in a tanner's house is omitted. Without necessarily being suspicious,[157] this has the indirect effect of emphasising the heavenly aspect. Fifth, the synchronicity with the arriving envoys emphatically links the heavenly vision with what follows on earth (11:11; cf. 10:17). Further, as a passive with an unspecified subject, ἀπεσταλμένοι ('sent', 11:11) perhaps implies 'a collaborative sending by both divine … and human … agents'.[158]

---

[157] As Spencer (1997: 118) and Matson (1996: 119) intimate.
[158] Spencer 1997: 104.

On these grounds, Marguerat and Bourquin's otherwise excellent assertion of the dynamic and theologically significant role of setting in 10:1–11:18 is too earthbound when commenting that 'Acts 10–11 begins from two poles (Caesarea and Joppa) and ends up with one (Jerusalem)'.[159] Such a focus upon material firstspace should not detract from *heavenly* thirdspace as both catalyst and unifying locus in this section.

Peter's account addresses both the firstspace and the secondspace aspects of the controversy within 11:2–3. In 11:12 Peter accepts without apology the first(space) charge laid against him, using the same verb employed by his critics (11:3; cf. 11:8). Significantly, however, 'we entered' (εἰσήλθομεν, cf. the singular subjects in 10:24–7) positions Peter with his six companions within a shared action. More importantly, they had a thirdspace precedent for their firstspace innovation: according to 11:13, their unnamed host had already entertained an angel 'in his house', a sharp rejoinder to 11:3! As 11:13–15 recounts, he had summoned Simon-Peter to his household on the angel's instruction. Thus prevenient heavenly thirdspace is an additional strand to Witherington's identification of Peter as appealing to two different but important forms of proof – the testimony of witnesses in 11:12 and the evidence of confirmatory signs in 11:15.[160]

Peter also addresses his critics' secondspace concerns by maintaining their conceptual spatial categories. Cornelius remains unnamed, and no appeal is made to his piety; Peter's reply thereby establishes a broad principle concerning 'the gentiles', not particularist reasons for counting Cornelius as either an exception or an exemplar. Importantly, 11:14 introduces the verb σῴζω into the narrative for the first time since 4:12 with its mention of the household's hope of being 'saved'.[161] The global spatiality summed up before the Sanhedrin in 4:12 is now grounded within Cornelius-space. Such σῴζω-language – recounted in 11:14 as having been spoken by an angel – crowns the crescendo of increasing specificity regarding Peter's expected and eventual role within Cornelius-space played out across 10:5, 22 and 33.

---

[159] Marguerat and Bourquin 1999: 81. In contrast, Eisen (2006: 183–7) preserves the vertical and horizontal axes of the Cornelius incident, to the mutual illumination of each.

[160] Witherington 1998: 363.

[161] The following points stand, regardless of the intervening use of cognate nouns 'saviour' (5:31) and 'salvation' (7:25).

Tannehill suggests that 11:14 'may represent a gradual sharpening of Peter's perception of his own role in recent events ... Memory and recent events interact, producing new understanding.'[162] Importantly, this 'sharpening of perception' is spatial, involving deepening connections between different spaces reflecting Peter's unfolding grasp of ascension geography. With its roots in the (Jerusalem) Pentecost proclamation and its spatial outworkings (2:21, 40, 47), σῴζω-language further confirms a Christological impulse within the Cornelius incident. Peter's account in 11:15a reinforces the external sovereignty governing the Spirit's imposition, which repositions secondspace categories demarcating 'them' and 'us' (11:15b). There is no temporal privileging of those who received the Spirit 'at the beginning'; instead, the thirdspace imposition of ascension geography bridges both categories and any periodisation.

This connection is sealed by Peter's recollection and, importantly, his comprehension of 'the word (ῥήματος) of the Lord' (11:16). This agraphon is best ascribed to Jesus, finding its closest parallel in 1:5. Now Jesus' speech-act interprets and justifies both the heavenly imposition and the consequential restructuring of earthly space.[163] As an agraphon, especially at such a narrative crux, this contributes to reading 1:1 inceptively, and the emphasis on the one who spoke the word, who is now in heaven, reinforces a Christological reading of Peter's initial vision.[164]

Peter therefore emphatically denies his ability to 'hinder' (κωλῦσαι) God's prior, independent action (11:17).[165] Both 'outsider' and 'insider' have previously used κωλύω regarding access to baptismal water (8:36; 10:47); now the verb communicates the futility of keeping *God* within secondspace (conceptual) limits he has clearly

---

[162] Tannehill 1990: 144, 145.

[163] Cf. the agraphon of Jesus in 20:35 which crowns Paul's climactic description of Ephesian believer-space. Ascension geography remains inseparable from Jesus history: 'By withdrawing himself from our sight, Christ sends us back to the historical Jesus Christ as the *covenanted place* on earth and in time which God has appointed for meeting between man [*sic*] and himself' (Torrance 1976: 133).

[164] Cf. the interplay of the ministries of Jesus and the Spirit proposed by Bruce 1976–7, and, more recently, Larkin 2003. The Spirit maintains and enables the unity between ascension geography and Jesus history, mentioned above (cf. Torrance 1976: 130–5).

[165] Peter's appeal to ultimate origins ('God') need not deny the Christological mediation of the gift as expressed in 2:33. Rhetorically it sets up the first triadic occurrence of 'Lord Jesus Christ' within Acts in 11:17b (cf. 15:26 and 28:31), a triad predicated upon the climactic Pentecostal proclamation of Jesus' ascended status (2:36).

transcended. The use of 'gift' language parallels the defence of sovereign heavenly thirdspace made in 8:20 and, via 2:38, evokes Jesus' promise of the Spirit in 1:8.

Having discovered and enjoyed salvation geography within what he had previously perceived to be opposing space (*Gegensraum*), Peter's return to the place he left (*Ausgangsraum*) renders such borders permeable and continues the spatial transformation of that original ordering of place.[166] Peter's question therefore 'forces the issue',[167] crystallising his reply to both parts of the spatial charge laid against him in 11:3. It also provides an internal commentary upon, and climax to, Acts 8–11, wherein 'the opening of the heavenly world (cf. 7:56) overwhelms all earthly attempts to obstruct ... the progress of God's inclusive kingdom'.[168]

In the more immediate cotext, Marguerat identifies a 'narrative chain' of realisation through the Cornelius incident: 'The narrative chain leads us from ethics [10:28] to soteriology [15:9–10], by way of the image of God, of Christology and pneumatology, which all deepen meaning. This path is a veritable course in dogmatics.'[169] Read for its space, no one link in this chain can be isolated as *the* spatial component, or *the* geography. Rather, each part and the narrative whole are inherently spatial, together constituting what are essentially geographical 'dogmatics'. The hermeneutical key for the chain, 11:17, is Christological, in that 'the chain constructs a fundamental continuity of the Acts, not with Judaism, but with the action of God in Jesus Christ: the continuity with Jewish tradition passes through him'.[170] This Christological key is also clearly heavenly, and thirdspatial in its impact.

Acknowledgement (11:18)

The Jerusalem believers concur with Peter's spatial analysis. Those 'silenced' in 11:18 cannot continue to express an alternative exclusionary spatiality. Rather, simultaneously, they begin to glorify God for a divinely instituted and expansive spatiality which represents a mature outworking of the ascension geography paradigm outlined in

---

[166] Eisen 2006: 187.   [167] Gaventa 2003a: 173.
[168] Spencer 1997: 63, citing κωλύω, 'to prevent, hinder', in 8:36; [10:47] and 11:17. Come Acts 12, however, any incipient triumphalism within Spencer's reading will be qualified by continuing persecution.
[169] Marguerat 2002: 55.   [170] Marguerat 2002: 56.

1:6–11. Here in 11:18, 'there is room for neither Jewish nor apostolic opposition, only acquiescence and embrace'.[171]

This 'room' metaphor highlights a critical dimension to ascension geography, namely that its normative aspirations generate the judgement and rejection of alternative, incompatible spaces. In this regard, Peter's final rhetorical appeal (11:17) silences critics *within* Jerusalem's believer-space (11:18). Without presupposing a particular original situation for the narrative's composition, such silencing is also possible among auditors if they subscribe to the narrative's internal perspective whereby acknowledging a multiplicity of first-space forms and a secondspatial equality within believer-space does not preclude rejecting certain organisations of space as inappropriate 'under heaven'. Importantly, such experiential discernment of space is not always immediate or irreversible, as is registered here in 11:1–18 and, later, in Acts 15.[172]

Significantly, therefore, 11:18 provides only a provisional narrative resolution regarding ascension geography. On the one hand, previously antagonistic characters now declare the secondspace label 'the gentiles', which previously has been only narrated, not spoken (10:45; 11:1). Now it is internalised within Jerusalem believer-space, in accordance with the principles mapped out in 1:6–11. Their conclusion places no condition or limitation on the gentiles' conceptual inclusion and is geographically wider than 5:31 and theologically more expansive than 11:1. Given the Jerusalem setting, the lack of any mention of circumcision in 11:18 is telling. The shift in discourse within 11:1–18 from an issue internal to Judaism (control of spatial interaction with the uncircumcised) to a perspective that is distinctively 'Christian' (the manner by which gentiles may become believers, which will crystallise in this term in 11:26) highlights how different secondspace boundaries now govern their thinking.[173] Yet, on the other hand, the production of space within the narrative is not closed, nor is the conclusion unproblematic, not least because the narrative itself does not end here. Other resources and challenges for

---

[171] Rapske 1998: 241.

[172] Wilson (1983: 73) suggests that if 11:2 are the minority group of Jerusalem believers mentioned in 15:5, then 11:18 could be understood as a tactical silence on their part. Although not conclusive from the text, the dynamically produced complexities of space allow for such a reading. Concerning internal church tensions, see Rakotoharintsifa 1995; Penner 2004: 262–87.

[173] If 16:14–15, 40 forms a strong narrative parallel (as Eisen 2006: 185 suggests), then the taken-for-granted retelling of Paul's acceptance of hospitality from Lydia demonstrates the transformation of the spatial order within 10:1–11:18.

the production(s) of space, even by believers, remain in the later narrative.[174] Neither narrative nor spatiality stands still.

5.   Conclusion

Acts 11:18 functions as a terminus for the present close reading of Acts for its narrative spaces. Acts 9:32–11:18 has sustained and developed the absent-but-active Christology of Acts: Jesus still heals (9:34), and still acts thirdspatially in ordering earthly believer-space, even though his decisive return heralded in 1:11 has yet to be fulfilled.

This complex Cornelius narrative, wherein Luke skilfully manipulates space in all three Sojan dimensions, has demonstrated the value of using thirdspatial lenses to read Acts for its spaces. It has enabled an integrative, consistent and coherent understanding of the narrative's geography through spatiality's various manifestations across the geopolitical, topographical, architectural and cosmological spheres.

In terms of narrative insight, this lengthy episode has decisively clarified the ongoing implications of ascension geography, as outlined in 1:6–11. By 11:18, the believers' understanding of empirical and symbolic 'Israel' has been fundamentally redefined 'away from a strongly nomistic and nationalistic restoration'.[175] This restructuring has occurred at the ideational level, concerning the place of 'the gentiles', spurred by Peter's pioneering (firstspace) entry into Cornelius-space. This restructuring has been both provoked and interpreted by active heavenly intervention in a variety of guises, all of which have functioned thirdspatially. It has caused Peter to be a 'witness' (cf. 1:8), in his proclamation to the gentiles and also in what he saw (and interpreted) as the Spirit coming *to* the gentiles within Cornelius' house.

Peter also functioned as a witness to the Jerusalem believers in 11:1–18. The believers there eventually confirmed the Spirit's impulse to push the community (in spite of itself) beyond the firstspace bounds of Israel and beyond the secondspace limits of Torah as conventionally applied. Their acquiescence to this impulse, despite initial resistance, confirms the independence of the heavenly initiative but also

---

[174] R. P. Thompson (2006: 145–7) presents well this ongoing ambiguity inhabiting the apparent resolution found in 11:18.
[175] Turner 2000: 420. The same can, of course, be said regarding the Jerusalem mission in Acts 2–7: unavoidably it too redefines Jewish spaces.

embeds it within the community's reshaped secondspace and opened-up firstspace. If Acts 2–7 presented believer-space as a hybrid identity within Judaism, Acts 8:1–11:18 has also constructed its relationships *beyond* Judaism as hybrid in their orientation. The narrative is set for the description of the cosmopolitan Antioch church which will follow in 11:19–30. Now 'the end of the earth' seems conceptually possible, however distant in firstspace terms.

Therefore, at 11:18 the spatial ordering laid out in 1:6–11 appears complete, at least in embryo, from all three Sojan perspectives. The remaining narrative of Acts will not add anything substantially new to this embryonic vista, but instead – as the references to 'heaven' subside within the narrative – the rest of Acts will mature, defend and flesh out what Acts 1–11 has instilled 'under heaven'.

It is to an overall assessment of this spatial reading that the conclusion of this study will now attend.

8

CONCLUDING REFLECTIONS

1. Summary

This study has aimed to respatialise discourse concerning Acts and the ascension. This goal has been addressed in two parts: an overall review of the problem of narrative spatiality within Acts, focalised on Jesus' ascension, and an exegetical application of one geographical theory – that of thirdspace – to a reading of Acts 1:1–11:18.

The argument has been cumulative, with concluding summaries presenting findings of each chapter. Chapters 1 and 2 provided a general survey and evaluation of attempts to conceptualise the 'space' of the ascension (in both narrative and Christological terms) and the 'geography' of Acts. Various reductionistic readings of space in Acts scholarship were deduced, leading to the evaluation that insufficient attention had been paid to recent developments in geographical theory. It was suggested that Soja's concept of thirdspace would succeed in overcoming these reductions and would link three concerns whose interconnections have been neglected by Acts studies: Christ's ascension, narrative readings of Acts, and the production of space. Chapters 3–7 have applied Soja's theory to a reading of Acts 1:1–11:18.

Such a broad-ranging project extends beyond the present work, and justifies some wider reflection beyond its bounds. Finally, therefore, this chapter provides some retrospective and prospective reflections concerning the spatiality of Acts.

2. Retrospect

1. *Employing thirdspace as a reading method has illuminated a richer spatiality in Acts than that which has previously been identified.* The sustained exegesis in Part II has justified the application of this approach to Acts, and has confirmed that Acts can and should be

read for its internal narrative spatiality. Exegesis has corroborated the supposition from geographical theory that *any* narrative is inherently spatial. Soja's critique of historicism, and his desire to spatialise discourses, outlined in Part I, has found fruitful soil in the first half of Acts. A close reading of Acts has shown that the spatial dimension cannot and should not be downplayed in favour of time or marginalised in the interpretation of its theological message. This realisation is not surprising, given the wide interdisciplinary deployment of Soja's critique and vision.[1] Reading for space has not denied a temporal dimension within the Acts narrative. Instead, if, as has long been appreciated, Acts seeks to reconfigure time and history for its auditors, so too Acts impinges upon their construals of space and place. Space does not replace time but, rather, the believer-spaces in Acts examined here function to confirm the certainty of the earthly future promised in 1:11.

Reading for spatiality requires different conceptualisations, new vocabulary and redefined terms. As an evaluation of method, it has been apparent that, like Lefebvre and Harvey, Soja can be difficult to understand, sometimes conceptually obtuse. The persistent challenge has been to use Soja's analytical categories of firstspace, secondspace and thirdspace with maximal clarity and accuracy, so that they illuminate the spatiality of Acts rather than confuse it by introducing neologisms of questionable value. Soja's notion of thirdspace as 'simultaneously real and imagined and more',[2] although potentially mystic when declared in the abstract, has proved immensely useful for exploring the earthly influence of heaven within Acts in a deliberately non-reductive analytical framework which both contains and exceeds conventional ways of thinking about space. The exegesis in Part II has confirmed that *Thirdspace* presents a perspective rather than a taxonomy of space,[3] providing best traction within a broader definition of third spaces as 'produced by those processes that exceed the forms of knowledge that divide the world into binary oppositions'.[4] Part II has shown that it is neither necessary nor beneficial to parse out each of the three elements of Soja's trialectic at every narrative turn.

2. *Reading Acts through this particular spatial lens has broken new ground for understanding earthly space in relation to the post-ascension Christ in Acts.* The ascension account (1:6–11), read for its spaces,

---

[1] For instance, even accountancy has utilised Soja's framework: https://dspace.gla. ac.uk/bitstream/1905/144/1/99–4%5B1%5D.pdf (accessed July 2008).
[2] Soja 1996: 11.   [3] Soja 1999: 269–70.   [4] Rose 2000: 827.

provides an abiding spatiality across Acts 1–11 which can be termed an ascension geography. Christ's ascension is therefore not a discrete narrative feature concluded by 1:11 or only later alluded to in isolated verses such as 3:21. Instead, it exercises an unceasing influence over the whole narrative and its theology, an influence which previous scholarship has not pursued with sufficient rigour and consistency. As a result of the present reading, any reading for the spatiality of Acts cannot ignore the heavenly dimension of the narrative. Earthbound readings are no longer legitimate, given the rendering of space identified in this study.

References to οὐρανός ('heaven') are one conduit for this thirdspatial impulse within the narrative, the strategic importance of which has previously been downplayed, but ascension thirdspace cannot be reduced to a simple word study. The trailing off of οὐρανός references within Acts after 11:18 coincides with the climactic labelling of believers as 'Christians' in 11:26. This ascription reflects a distinctive community formation reflecting heavenly thirdspace, which combines Jew, gentile and 'more'. The 'and more' coheres within the label's acknowledgement of the Christ now in heaven who determines this hybrid identity within embodied earthly expressive organisations and emotional communities.[5] It crowns the preceding narrative even as it launches the ensuing narrative turn towards the Antioch-based missionaries and their ever-widening mission. Its recurrence in 26:28 bookends the intervening chapters and, like 26:19 and 26:23, reprises the wider narrative within the remit of heavenly thirdspace. Much more remains to be said concerning the spatiality of the rest of Acts, but the case has been made for setting 1:1–11:18 as foundational for establishing its roots within an ascension geography.

3. *Thirdspace has enabled new insight into the post-ascension Christ in Acts.* Moving beyond Chapter 1's identification of polarities of presence and absence, passivity and activity, a reading for thirdspace has revealed a narrative presentation of Jesus as absent-and-active-and-more. This Christological 'and more' resides in Jesus deconstructing such dualisms by continuing to order and challenge earthly spatialities within the narrative after his ascension. The heavenly Christ, hidden from sight and yet sovereign and transformative within earthly spaces, exemplifies and generates such non-reductive thirdspaces.

---

[5] Hetherington (1998: 83–100) maps such performative spaces; his formulations are suggestive for further reflections concerning the mimetic reconfigurations of ecclesial lived spaces within the auditors' worlds.

This impulse results in a functional blurring of the activities and titles associated with God and Jesus brought about by Jesus' ascension.[6] At certain junctures, this thirdspatial reading has highlighted a Christological dimension which commentators have frequently submerged within a broader theological interpretation (e.g. 7:55–6; 9:3–6, 10–16, 34); at other points the spatiality here identified suggests that other ambiguous texts should be understood Christologically (e.g. 1:24–5; 2:2, 5; 5:19–20; 10:10–16). The very ambiguity of these references, far from reducing the likelihood of a Christological referent, reflects Jesus' thirdspatial position and potentiality arising from his exaltation into heaven. While all such references need not be exclusively Christological, the interpretative onus rests upon those who would evacuate these terms of *any* Christological reference.

4. *This spatial dynamic installs the heavenly Jesus as an 'expanding symbol' with a 'fringe of unexhausted suggestions'[7] within Acts.* Jesus appoints Matthias, completes the twelve and positions the 120 (Chapter 3); he bestows the Spirit at Pentecost, triggering a spatial-theological judgement upon, and reconstituting of, 'Israel' (Chapter 4). Jesus directs Stephen-space, even to a martyr's death (Chapter 5), and then structures Philip-space in Samaria and beyond, and even arrests Saul's oppositional geography (Chapter 6), before reshaping the spatialities of Peter and the Jerusalem church towards Jew–gentile fellowship (Chapter 7). Jesus fulfils the functions associated with an expanding symbol and, analytically, this category for the ascended Jesus within Acts provides a better fit than Parsons's proposal of an 'empty center'.[8] Tannehill identifies Jesus' 'name' as an expanding symbol,[9] but the present study shows that this term better applies to Jesus himself and his wider post-ascension ordering of earthly space. Jesus' 'name' is just one function of this wider thirdspatial Christology within Acts.

5. *As such, believer-space within Acts engendered by the heavenly Christ is neither simply transparent nor oblique;[10] it is not immediately apparent at the outset of Acts.* Characters within the narrative, and auditors and readers following after them, need to work at discerning its contours and its openings. Because Christ's thirdspatial impulse

---

[6] Acts 3:21, for example, so often claimed as the linchpin for a passive absentee Christology, does not indicate Christological passivity within Acts any more than Acts commends divine passivity by virtue of *God* being in heaven.
[7] Brown 1950: 33–59 (43).   [8] Parsons 1987: 169. See Chapters 1 and 2 above.
[9] Tannehill 1984.
[10] Soja (1996: 62–6) describes these two illusions regarding space.

comes from an unseen heaven beyond human speculation, believers do not fully control or foresee the production of space within Acts. Indeed, the unseen but sovereign aspect of heaven is a key touchstone to establishing ascension geography as both material and ideational, *and more*. Ascension geography remains subject to surprising turns and prolepses, and its earthly decentring generates new alignments and elsewhere unseen possibilities. Recognising this supplements, and positions, any conventional geographical understanding of narrative diffusion across space (e.g. 1:8). Jesus' ascension calls both 'Israel' and 'the nations' into being in a new way.

6. *Theologically, however, believer-space in Acts does not remain as radically open as Soja would claim for his own method.*[11] From the narrator's point of view, at least, believer-spaces are constrained by their heavenly locus, and by the earthly teaching and ethic of 'this Jesus' mediated by his chosen Spirit-filled witnesses to other believers in new places, new believer-spaces. Acts also makes clear that the dynamics of space operating in a world not yet restored to the fullness foretold in 3:21 require believer-spaces to exercise a continuing self-critique of their own productions of space, but the narrative resolutely connects this critique with the earthly Jesus mediated through his witnesses. This divergence from Soja's agenda is a measure of the different presuppositional (theological) base underpinning Acts. This is not to claim that Acts presents a tight blueprint for believer-space; its believer-spaces are pluriform, evolving and non-exhaustive within the narrative.

7. *Apart from the possible exception of 8:39 (and, if so, 8:39* is *exceptional), salvation within Acts is found always within believer-space.* Such space is not an external support for the Christian life, such that discipleship can be abstracted from the collective concrete practices of believers; nor is believer-space a reservoir for grace, such that either grace or space enjoys a separate existence; rather, salvation within Acts can be said to *be* believer-space. Salvation and this production of space cohere inseparably within the narrative story-world and its projections for auditors, in an invitation to accept the authority of the story by entering into it and imaginatively inhabiting its claims within places and spaces beyond the narrative.

[11] Soja 1999: 269: 'There are no closures, no permanent structures of knowledge, no intrinsically privileged epistemologies. One must always be moving on, nomadically searching for new sources of practical knowledge, better approximations, carrying along only what was most useful from earlier voyages.' Such a vision must itself come under its own critique, but that lies beyond the scope of the present study.

3.   Prospect and openings

Famously, a 1562 second edition of the Geneva Bible rendered Matthew 5:9 as 'Blessed are the placemakers'. Beyond being a Matthean typo, such a maxim maps well the spatial ethos presented by Acts. The respatialised reading of Acts pursued here uncovers and provokes a mimetic reconfiguring of how places in the auditors' worlds are constructed and maintained. Skinner's conclusion that the text's understanding of custody spaces 'might also transfer to readers' perceptions of similar places of custody in the "real world"'[12] anticipates a wider narrative impulse influencing the formation of 'real-world' believer-spaces.

First, to reiterate, the insistently non-negotiable Christological and heavenly locus for thirdspace within Acts critiques all other thirdspace claims made over 'real-world' spaces. To resist, replace or domesticate the heavenly locus of the narrative's tenacious thirdspace is, in narrative terms, to be guilty of Simony, whether or not money has changed hands. Instead, the particularistic-but-absent Christofocal thirdspace commended within Acts translates into a resistance against alternative ownerships and allegiances and their rival spatial claims of both presence and absence. Yet resistance in the 'real world' cuts two ways: given the tardiness of the believers in Acts, even Peter, to grasp the implications of heavenly thirdspace within the narrative, especially as it orders the shape of the believing community, all 'real-world' embodiments claiming to reflect ascension geography must themselves retain a provisionality and remain subject to an ongoing revision, even a hermeneutic of suspicion. Earthly 'god tricks' (cf. Chapter 2) are not simply the concern of secular human geography; they are also a recognised, even expected, side-effect associated with believer-spaces seeking to (re)produce ascension geography. Auditors who are consciously engaging in such productions of space, duly sensitised, can mix humility with Christocentric hospitality in an ascension-driven ethic for life which appreciates the particularities of place within a pluriform expectation of what such lived places can look like.

Also, that the Acts narrative positions its auditors somewhere on an outward movement towards the end of the earth casts 'real-world' spatial relations as provisional and subject to dynamic change within this prior ordering of space. Those previously without a place find a

---

[12] Skinner 2003: 183.

secure home (cf. 8:26–40), whereas apparently solid ground melts away in an instant (cf. 9:3–6). As the one piece of teaching given to ordinary believers in Acts intimates, the co-ordinates of Acts project a nomadic quality to space, and a realisation that it will face opposition (14:22).

Consequently, any earthly locality's claims to a centring function, with its commensurate assertion of symbolic significance and territorial sovereignty, is rendered at best provisional by an ascension-geography critique. This humbling of earthly space does not seek to obliterate difference, since heavenly allegiance does not require earthly uniformity and indeed defies it as masking earthly thirdspace claims. Ascension geography instead maintains a vision for multiple and pluriform believer-spaces nevertheless unified by allegiance beyond themselves. There is a stubborn refusal to bring anyone back to Jerusalem under compulsion (cf. 9:2!), resulting in qualified freedom for firstspace diversity and creativity according to local conditions.

Taken together, these pointers suggest horizons for ways to 'see' believer-space commensurate with the Acts narrative. Such a vision, a perennial desire for geographers and artists alike, lies at the heart of the geographical imagination.[13] Without Acts, Jerusalem, Judea and Samaria would be far less visible, vision towards the end of the earth much impoverished. Because of Acts, Jesus' ascension casts all places as non-neutral, either conforming to, or resisting, his ordering of spaces as presented in its twenty-eight chapters and overflowing into 'real' worlds. All earthly places, with their associated spatialities ever generating a thousand new and sinuous places, remain – for believers – subject to the continuous Christofocal assessment and critique of Acts. By inference, also, according to Acts, the scholarly discipline of geography cannot isolate itself from a theological critique. In these ways, the dynamic spatiality witnessed in Acts generates life-sized horizons for its auditors.

First, on a scholarly level, the spatiality of the whole of Acts deserves more thorough narrative-critical examination, and requires parallel analyses employing other spatialised interpretative lenses. The few excursions made here into Greco-Roman parallels and social-scientific approaches suggest that these interpretative lenses also have an important part to play in discerning the spatiality of Acts. While the present study commends thirdspace as a useful

[13] At the time of writing, D. Cosgrove 2008 is a recent exemplar of this broader geographical project.

hermeneutical lens for conducting spatialised exegesis, it does not control or exhaust the spatiality of the text. Spatiality (as Soja acknowledges) is not the monopoly domain of any one method or perspective.

Second, regarding ecclesial praxis, the focus of both thirdspatial theory and the spatiality here uncovered in Acts, a focus on 'lived space', should provoke, position and encourage self-conscious reflection upon contemporary believer-spaces. Such nascent reflection is evident both in the so-called 'Emerging Churches'[14] and within more mainstream ecclesial life.[15]

Third, more expansively, a spatialised reading of Acts widens the aperture of the word for the auditors' broader worlds. The narrative's relentless optimism that the unconstrained word will reach all spaces (albeit seasoned with the realism of 14:22) seeks to overflow into auditors' understanding of every place. Such refusal to constrict the word not only allows for public theology, it expects it. Gender, ethnicity, race and other status constructs are discounted as barriers against Jesus' expansive reach, but the constructions of such concepts themselves come under transformation by heavenly thirdspace.

Mixing insight with overstatement, John Berger declared: 'Prophecy now involves a geographical rather than historical projection; it is space not time that hides consequences from us.'[16] Without creating a dichotomy between space and time, Berger's instinct is apposite for exploring the myriad pluriform spatial implications arising from Acts. To highlight just one, the Acts narrative, *as* narrative, offers important resources for a distinctively Christian post-9/11 (and, in the UK, post-7/7) approach to territoriality and place. In January 2008, for example, the British media reported and raised fears that multicultural policies were generating 'no-go' areas for Christians within some British towns and cities.[17] While such matters are complex and defy simplistic analyses, a narrative-theological reading of the spatiality within Acts feeds into

---

[14] For instance, Sweet, McLaren, and Haselmayer (2003: 286–7) sketch the trialectics of 'thirding'. The adoption of such approaches requires logical, scriptural and historical nuance, which will necessitate sustained readings of scripture. Cf. Carson 2005: 125–56.

[15] E.g. Dawson (2004: 185–210), who grounds the ascension's impact on the earthly church in practical and provocative ways but, as Chapter 1 noted, does not connect the ascension with Acts as a narrative whole.

[16] Berger 1969: 46.

[17] An article by Michael Nazir-Ali, the Bishop of Rochester, in the *Sunday Telegraph* on 6 January 2008, initiated the debate. For it, and subsequent statements issued by the Bishop, see www.rochester.anglican.org/bishop_michael_addressarticles. htm (accessed July 2008).

debates surrounding the limits of multiculturalism (and the visionary possibilities of omniculturalism[18]). The narrative spaces of Acts guard against the evacuation and separation from certain locations which have fed into the development of such fears, and offer resources for a non-triumphalistic coexistence and transformative re-engagement with the otherness and diversity which such places require.

In sum, the spatial riches of Acts will be further illuminated by a broad coalition of approaches positioning one another's findings. As Chapter 2 highlighted, there is a growing trend to read biblical texts (and not exclusively narratives) for their spaces. The contribution of this study is therefore located within a wider paradigm shift which is still under way. In these senses, the task of reading for space within Acts is only just begun.

Such a conclusion fits with Soja's final words in *Thirdspace*: 'Only one ending is possible: **TO BE CONTINUED** ...'[19] Here Soja deliberately reflects his roots, the final chapter of Lefebvre's *The Production of Space* being entitled 'Openings and Conclusions'.[20] At the close, Lefebvre envisions 'the creation (or production) of a planet-wide space as the social foundation of a transformed everyday life open to myriad possibilities – such is the dawn now beginning to break on the far horizon'.[21] Describing it as 'the same dawn as glimpsed by the great utopians',[22] both Soja and Lefebvre occupy similar space to Luke.

The final word, however, concerns Luke. This study has advanced understanding of the ascension in Acts, its place within the narrative, and the role of geography in exegeting it. It has shown that Jesus' ascension in Acts not only happens within the narrative, it also structures it. The ascension's impact extends far beyond 'obvious' (but isolated) proof-texts such as 3:21, and that narrative consideration actually redefines previously passive 'absentee' interpretations of such texts. The thesis has been demonstrated that Jesus' ascension (understood as 1:6–11) orders space across Luke's narrative; if such an analytical separation can be made, this is both a theological insight and a geographical observation. This means that the 'geography' of Acts cannot be reduced to the earthbound, or to 'obvious' (but again, isolated) verses such as 1:8. Instead, the geography of Acts must be

---

[18] I explore a Trinitarian omnicultural model in a different context in Sleeman 1996: 187–8, 207–13.
[19] Soja 1996: 320, bold capitalisation and ellipsis original.
[20] Lefebvre 1991: 401–23.   [21] Lefebvre 1991: 422.   [22] Lefebvre 1991: 422.

viewed in the thirdspatial light of the heavenly Christ. Likewise, within Acts, Jesus' continuing activity cannot be reduced simply to the Spirit and/or the church as his replacement. Luke's Christology and, with it, his geography, are more complex than such binary explanations.

While Luke does not write within explicit thirdspatial categories, it is the closing contention of this study that such an analytic framework appropriately expounds the spatiality of Acts. Geography and theology have been shown to be integrally entwined within Acts such that the spatial can no longer be ignored in reading Acts as a narrative. A widened discourse is required. If Luke can be called 'the first historian' of the church, he also lays claim to be the first Christian geographer.

BIBLIOGRAPHY

Aay, H., and S. Griffioen (1998), *Geography and Worldview: A Christian Renaissance*. Lanham, MD: University Press of America.

Alexander, Loveday C. A. (1993), *The Preface to Luke's Gospel: Literary Convention and Social Context in Luke 1:4 and Acts 1:1*. Cambridge: Cambridge University Press.

—— (1995a), '"In Journeyings Often": Voyaging in the Acts of the Apostles', in *Luke's Literary Achievement: Collected Essays*, ed. C. M. Tuckett, pp. 17–49. Sheffield: Sheffield Academic Press.

—— (1995b), 'Narrative Maps: Reflections on the Toponymy of Acts', in *The Bible in Human Society: Essays in Honour of John Rogerson*, ed. M. Daniel, R. Carroll, David J. A. Clines and Philip R. Davies, pp. 17–57. Sheffield: Sheffield Academic Press.

—— (2003), 'Mapping Early Christianity: Acts and the Shape of Early Church History'. *Interpretation* 57(2), pp. 163–73.

—— (2005), *Acts in its Ancient Literary Context: A Classicist Looks at the Acts of the Apostles*. London: T. & T. Clark International.

Alexander, Philip S. (1982), 'Notes on the *Imago Mundi* in the Book of Jubilees'. *Journal of Jewish Studies* 33, pp. 197–213.

—— (1990), 'Review of Alain Desremaux and Francis Schmidt, *Moïse Géographe: Recherches sur les Représentations Juives et Chrétiennes de L'espace*'. *Journal of Jewish Studies* 41(1), pp. 120–2.

—— (1992), 'Geography and the Bible (Early Jewish)', in *The Anchor Bible Dictionary*, vol. II, ed. David Noel Freedman, pp. 977–88. New York: Doubleday.

—— (1997), 'Jerusalem as the Omphalos of the World: On the History of a Geographical Concept'. *Judaism* 46, pp. 147–58.

Allen, John (2003), *Lost Geographies of Power*. Oxford: Blackwell.

Allen, O. Wesley Jr (1995), *The Death of Herod: The Narrative and Theological Function of Retribution in Luke-Acts*. Atlanta, GA: Scholars Press.

Anderson, Benedict (1983), *Imagined Communities: Reflections on the Origin and Spread of Nationalism*. London: Verso.

Anderson, Janice Capel (1994), 'Reading Tabitha: A Feminist Reception History', in *The New Literary Criticism and the New Testament*, ed. Elizabeth Struthers Malbon and Edgar V. McKnight, pp. 108–44. Sheffield: Sheffield Academic Press.

Anderson, Kevin L. (2006), *'But God Raised Him from the Dead': The Theology of Jesus' Resurrection in Luke-Acts*. Milton Keynes: Paternoster.

Anonymous (1987), 'History', in *The Eerdmans Bible Dictionary*, ed. Allen C. Myers, p. 490. Grand Rapids: Eerdmans.

Arnold, Bill T. (1996), 'Luke's Characterizing Use of the Old Testament in the Book of Acts', in *History, Literature and Society in the Book of Acts*, ed. Ben Witherington III, pp. 300–23. Cambridge: Cambridge University Press.

Baker, Christopher Richard (2007), *The Hybrid Church in the City: Third Space Thinking*. Aldershot: Ashgate.

Bal, Mieke (1995), *Narratology: Introduction to the Theory of Narrative*. Trans. Christine van Boheemen. Toronto: University of Toronto Press.

Balch, David L. (2003), 'The Cultural Origin of "Receiving All Nations" in Luke-Acts: Alexander the Great or Roman Social Policy?', in *Early Christianity and Classical Culture: Comparative Studies in Honor of Abraham J. Malherbe*, ed. John T. Fitzgerald, Thomas H. Olbricht and L. Michael White, pp. 483–500. Atlanta, GA: Society of Biblical Literature.

Baly, Denis (1957), *The Geography of the Bible: A Study in Historical Geography*. London: Lutterworth Press.

(1987), *Basic Biblical Geography*. Philadelphia: Fortress Press.

Bar-Efrat, Shimon (1989), *Narrative Art in the Bible*. Sheffield: Almond Press.

Barnes, Trevor (2000a), 'Quantitative Revolution', in Johnston, Gregory, Pratt and Watts, eds., *Dictionary of Human Geography*, pp. 664–7.

(2000b), 'Situated Knowledge', in Johnston, Gregory, Pratt and Watts, eds., *Dictionary of Human Geography*, pp. 742–3.

Barrett, C. K. (1979), 'Light on the Holy Spirit from Simon Magus (Acts 8, 4-25)', in *Les Actes des Apôtres: Traditions, Redaction, Théologie*, ed. J. Kremer, pp. 281–95. Leuven: Leuven University Press.

(1988), 'The Gentile Mission as an Eschatological Phenomenon', in *Eschatology and the New Testament: Essays in Honour of George Raymond Beasley-Murray*, ed. W. Hulitt Gloer, pp. 65–75. Peabody, MA: Hendrickson.

(1991), 'Attitudes to the Temple in the Acts of the Apostles', in *Templum Amicitiae: Essays on the Second Temple Presented to Ernst Bammel*, ed. William Horbury, pp. 345–67. Sheffield: Sheffield Academic Press.

(1994), *A Critical and Exegetical Commentary on the Acts of the Apostles*, vol. I: *Preliminary Introduction and Commentary on Acts I–XIV*. Edinburgh: T. & T. Clark.

Barton, Stephen C. (1995), 'Historical Criticism and Social-Scientific Perspectives in New Testament Study', in *Hearing the New Testament: Strategies for Interpretation*, ed. Joel B. Green, pp. 61–89. Grand Rapids: Eerdmans; Carlisle: Paternoster Press.

Bauckham, Richard (1995), 'James and the Jerusalem Church', in *The Book of Acts in its First Century Setting,* vol. IV: *Palestinian Setting*, ed. Richard Bauckham, pp. 415–80. Grand Rapids: Eerdmans; Carlisle: Paternoster Press.

(1996), 'James and the Gentiles (Acts 15:13–21)', in *History, Literature and Society in the Book of Acts*, ed. Ben Witherington III, pp. 154–84. Cambridge: Cambridge University Press.

(1998), *The Gospels for All Christians: Rethinking Gospel Audiences*. Edinburgh: T. & T. Clark.

(2000), 'What if Paul had Travelled East rather than West?', in *Virtual History and the Bible*, ed. J. Cheryl Exum, pp. 171–84. Leiden: Brill.

(2001), 'The Restoration of Israel in Luke-Acts', in *Restoration: Old Testament, Jewish and Christian Perspectives*, ed. James M. Scott, pp. 435–87. Leiden: Brill.

(2003), *Bible and Mission: Christian Witness in a Postmodern World*. Carlisle: Paternoster Press.

Beale, Gregory K. (2004), *The Temple and the Church's Mission: A Biblical Theology of the Dwelling Place of God*. Downers Grove, IL: InterVarsity Press.

Béchard, Dean Philip (1999), 'The Theological Significance of Judaea in Luke-Acts', in *The Unity of Luke-Acts*, ed. Joseph Verheyden, pp. 675–91. Leuven: Leuven University Press.

Bekker-Nielsen, T. (1988), 'Terra Incognita: The Subjective Geography of the Roman Empire', in *Studies in Ancient History and Numismatics Presented to Rudi Thomsen*, ed. Askel Damsgaard-Madsen *et al.*, pp. 148–61. Århus: Århus University Press.

Berger, John (1969), *The Moment of Cubism and Other Essays*. London: Weidenfeld & Nicholson.

Berquist, Jon L. (2002), 'Critical Spatiality and the Construction of the Ancient World', in Gunn and McNutt, eds., *'Imagining' Biblical Worlds*, pp. 14–29.

Berquist, Jon L., and Claudia V. Camp, eds. (2007), *Constructions of Space*, vol. I: *Theory, Geography, and Narrative*. New York and London: T. & T. Clark.

Beutler, Johannes (1981), 'Μάρτυς, -υρος, ὁ', in *Exegetical Dictionary of the New Testament*, vol. II, ed. Horst Balz and Gerhard Schneider, pp. 393–5. Grand Rapids: Eerdmans.

Billinge, Mark, Derek Gregory, and Ron Martin (1984), *Recollections of a Revolution: Geography as Spatial Science*. London: Macmillan.

Blue, Brad (1998), 'The Influence of Jewish Worship on Luke's Presentation of the Early Church', in Marshall and Peterson, eds., *Witness to the Gospel*, pp. 473–97.

Bobrinsky, B. (1963), 'Worship and the Ascension of Christ'. *Studia Liturgica* 2, pp. 108–23.

Bock, Darrell (1998), 'Scripture and the Realisation of God's Promises', in Marshall and Peterson, eds., *Witness to the Gospel*, pp. 41–62.

Bockmuehl, Marcus (1999), 'Antioch and James the Just', in *James the Just and Christian Origins*, ed. Bruce Chilton and Craig A. Evans, pp. 155–98. Leiden: Brill.

Bolt, Peter (1998), 'Mission and Witness', in Marshall and Peterson, eds., *Witness to the Gospel*, pp. 191–214.

Borgen, Peder (1997), *Philo of Alexandria: An Exegete for His Time*. Leiden: Brill.

Brawley, Robert L. (1987), *Luke-Acts and The Jews: Conflict, Apology, and Conciliation*. Atlanta, GA: Scholars Press.

(1990), *Centering on God: Method and Message in Luke-Acts*. Louisville, KY: Westminster/John Knox Press.

(1999), 'Abrahamic Covenant Traditions and the Characterization of God in Luke-Acts', in *The Unity of Luke-Acts*, ed. Joseph Verheyden, pp. 109–32. Leuven: University Press.

Brown, Edward Killoran (1950), *Rhythm in the Novel*. Toronto: University of Toronto Press.

Brown, Malcolm, and Shirley Seaton (1994), *Christmas Truce: The Western Front, December 1914*. Basingstoke: Papermac.

Bruce, F. F. (1976–7), 'Christ and the Spirit in Paul'. *Bulletin of the John Rylands (University) Library* 59, pp. 259–85.

—— (1987), 'Stephen's Apologia', in *Scripture: Meaning and Method: Essays Presented to Anthony Tyrrell Hanson for his Seventieth Birthday*, ed. Barry P. Thompson, pp. 37–50. Hull: Hull University Press.

—— (1989), 'Philip and the Ethiopian'. *Journal of Semitic Studies* 34(2), pp. 377–86.

—— (1990), *The Acts of the Apostles: The Greek Text with Introduction and Commentary*, 3rd edn. Grand Rapids: Eerdmans; Leicester: Apollos.

Brueggemann, Walter (1997), *Theology of the Old Testament: Testimony, Dispute, Advocacy*. Minneapolis: Fortress Press.

Buckwalter, H. Douglas (1996), *The Character and Purpose of Luke's Christology*. Cambridge: Cambridge University Press.

Burgess, Andrew (2004), *The Ascension in Karl Barth*. Aldershot: Ashgate.

Burridge, Richard (2004), *What Are the Gospels? A Comparison with Graeco-Roman Biography*. Grand Rapids: Eerdmans.

Calvin, John (1965), *Calvin's New Testament Commentaries: Acts 1–13*. Trans. John W. Fraser and W. J. G. McDonald. Grand Rapids: Eerdmans; Carlisle: Paternoster Press.

Camp, Claudia V. (2002), 'Storied Space, or, Ben Sira "Tells" a Temple', in Gunn and McNutt, eds., *'Imagining' Biblical Worlds*, pp. 64–80.

Carroll, J. T. (1988), *Response to the End of History: Eschatology and Situation in Luke-Acts*. Atlanta, GA: Scholars Press.

Carson, Donald A. (2005), *Becoming Conversant with the Emerging Church: Understanding a Movement and its Implications*. Grand Rapids: Zondervan.

Chance, J. Bradley (1988), *Jerusalem, the Temple, and the New Age in Luke-Acts*. Macon, GA: Mercer University Press.

Chibici-Reveanu, Nicole (2007), 'Ein Himmlischer Stehplatz: Die Haltung Jesus in der Stephanusvision (Apg. 7.55–56) und Ihre Bedeutung'. *New Testament Studies* 53(4), pp. 459–88.

Clark, Andrew (1998), 'The Role of the Apostles', in Marshall and Peterson, eds., *Witness to the Gospel*, pp. 169–90.

Clark, Martin (1991), 'Developments in Human Geography: Niches for a Christian Contribution'. *Area* 23, pp. 339–44.

Clark, Martin, and Matthew T. Sleeman (1991), 'Writing the Earth, Righting the Earth: Committed Presuppositions and the Geographical Imagination', in *New Words, New Worlds: Reconceptualising Social and Cultural Geography*, ed. Chris Philo, pp. 49–60. Lampeter: Social and Cultural Geography Study Group.

Clarke, Katherine (1999), *Between Geography and History: Hellenistic Constructions of the Roman World*. Oxford: Clarendon Press.

Coggins, R. J. (1982), 'The Samaritans and Acts'. *New Testament Studies* 28, pp. 423–34.

Cole, Tim (2003), *Holocaust City: The Making of a Jewish Ghetto*. New York and London: Routledge.

Conzelmann, Hans (1960), *The Theology of St Luke*. London: Faber.
(1987), *The Acts of the Apostles*. Philadelphia: Fortress Press.
Cosgrove, Charles H. (1984), 'The Divine ΔEI in Luke-Acts: Investigations into the Lukan Understanding of God's Providence'. *Novum Testamentum* 26(2), pp. 168–90.
Cosgrove, Denis (2000), 'Sense of Place', in Johnston, Gregory, Pratt and Watts, eds., *Dictionary of Human Geography*, pp. 731–4.
(2008), *Geography and Vision: Seeing, Imagining and Representing the World*. London: I. B. Tauris.
Crang, Mike (1998), *Cultural Geography*. London: Routledge.
Crang, Phil (2000), 'Cultural Turn', in Johnston, Gregory, Pratt and Watts, eds., *Dictionary of Human Geography*, pp. 141–3.
Cresswell, Tim (1996), *In Place / Out of Place: Geography, Ideology and Transgression*. Minneapolis: University of Minnesota Press.
(2004), *Place: A Short Introduction*. Oxford: Blackwell.
Croatto, J. Severino (2005), 'Jesus, Prophet Like Elijah, and Prophet-Teacher Like Moses in Luke-Acts'. *Journal of Biblical Literature* 124 (3), pp. 451–65.
Curtis, A. H. W. (1990), 'Theological Geography', in *A Dictionary of Biblical Interpretation*, ed. R. J. Coggins and J. L. Houlden, pp. 687–9. London: SCM Press.
Dahl, Nils A. (1966), 'The Story of Abraham in Luke-Acts', in *Studies in Luke-Acts: Essays Presented in Honor of Paul Schubert, Buckingham Professor of New Testament Criticism and Interpretation at Yale University*, ed. Leander E. Keck and J. Louis Martyn, pp. 139–58. London: SPCK.
Darby, H. C. (1962), 'The Problem of Geographical Description'. *Transactions of the Institute of British Geographers* 30, pp. 1–14.
Darr, John A. (1992), *On Character Building: The Reader and the Rhetoric of Characterization in Luke-Acts*. Louisville, KY: Westminster/John Knox Press.
(1998), *Herod The Fox: Audience Criticism and Lukan Characterization*. Sheffield: Sheffield Academic Press.
(1998), 'Irenic or Ironic? Another Look at Gamaliel before the Sanhedrin', in *Literary Studies in Luke-Acts: Essays in Honor of Joseph B. Tyson*, ed. Richard P. Thompson and Thomas E. Phillips, pp. 121–39. Macon, GA: Mercer University Press.
Davies, D. J. (1995), 'Rebounding Vitality: Resurrection and Spirit in Luke-Acts', in *The Bible in Human Society: Essays in Honour of John Rogerson*, ed. M. Daniel, R. Carroll, David J. A. Clines and Philip R. Davies, pp. 205–24. Sheffield: Sheffield Academic Press.
Davies, J. G. (1958), *He Ascended into Heaven. A Study in the History of Doctrine*. London: Lutterworth.
(1969), 'Ascension of Christ', in *A Dictionary of Christian Theology*, ed. Alan Richardson, pp. 15–16. London: SCM Press.
Davies, Philip R. (2002), 'Space and Sects in the Qumran Scrolls', in Gunn and McNutt, eds., *'Imagining' Biblical Worlds*, pp. 81–98.
Davies, W. D. (1974), *The Gospel and the Land: Early Christianity and Jewish Territorial Doctrine*. Berkeley, CA: University of California Press.

Dawson, Gerrit Scott (2004), *Jesus Ascended: The Meaning of Christ's Continuing Incarnation*. London: T. & T. Clark International.

Dean-Otting, Mary (1984), *Heavenly Journeys: A Study of the Motif in Hellenistic Jewish Literature*. Frankfurt: Verlag Peter Lang.

Dear, Michael J. (1994), 'Postmodern Human Geography: A Preliminary Assessment'. *Eerkunde* 48(1), pp. 2–13.

Denova, Rebecca I. (1997), *The Things Accomplished among Us: Prophetic Tradition in the Structural Pattern of Luke-Acts*. Sheffield: Sheffield Academic Press.

Derrett, J. Duncan M. (1982), 'Simon Magus (Acts 8, 9–24)'. *Zeitschrift für die neutestamentliche Wissenschaft und die Kunde der älteren Kirche* 73, pp. 52–68.

deSilva, D. A. (1997), 'Heaven, New Heavens', in *Dictionary of the Later New Testament and its Developments*, ed. Ralph P. Martin and Peter H. Davids, pp. 439–43. Downers Grove, IL: InterVarsity Press.

Doble, Peter (2000), 'Something Greater than Solomon: An Approach to Stephen's Speech', in *The Old Testament in the New Testament: Essays in Honour of J. L. North*, ed. Steve Moyise. Sheffield: Sheffield Academic Press.

Downing, F. Gerald (1990), 'Historical-Critical Method', in *A Dictionary of Biblical Interpretation*, ed. R. J. Coggins and J. L. Houlden, pp. 284–5. London: SCM Press.

Drinkard, Joel F., Jr (1992), 'Direction and Orientation', in *The Anchor Bible Dictionary*, vol. II, ed. David Noel Freedman, p. 204. New York: Doubleday.

Driver, Felix (1991), 'Morality, Politics, Geography?: Brave New Worlds', in *New Words, New Worlds: Reconceptualising Social and Cultural Geography*, ed. Chris Philo, pp. 61–4. Lampeter: Social and Cultural Geography Study Group.

— (1992), 'Geography's Empire: Histories of Geographical Knowledge'. *Environment and Planning 'D': Society and Space* 10, pp. 23–40.

Duncan, James, and Derek Gregory (1999), 'Introduction', in *Writes of Passage: Reading Travel Writing*, ed. James Duncan and Derek Gregory, pp. 1–13. London and New York: Routledge.

Dunn, James D. G. (1996), *The Acts of the Apostles*. Peterborough: Epworth Press.

Edelman, Lee (1994), *Homographesis: Essays in Gay Literary and Cultural Theory*. New York: Routledge.

Eisen, Ute E. (2006), *Die Poetik der Apostelgeschichte: Eine Narratologische Studie*. Göttingen: Vandenhoeck & Ruprecht.

Elbert, Paul (2004), 'An Observation on Luke's Composition and Narrative Style of Questions'. *Catholic Biblical Quarterly* 66(1), pp. 98–109.

Elden, Stuart (1997), 'What about Huddersfield?', *Radical Philosophy* 84, pp. 47–8.

— (2001), 'Politics, Philosophy, Geography: Henri Lefebvre in Recent Anglo-American Scholarship'. *Antipode* 33(5), pp. 809–25.

Ellis, Earle E. (1991), '"The End of the Earth" (Acts 1:8)'. *Bulletin for Bible Research* 1, pp. 123–31.

Esler, Philip F. (1987), *Community and Gospel in Luke-Acts: The Social and Political Motivations of Lucan Theology*. Cambridge: Cambridge University Press.

Estrada, Nelson P. (2004), *From Followers to Leaders: The Apostles in the Ritual of Status Transformation in Acts 1–2*. Sheffield: Sheffield Academic Press.

Evans, Craig A. (1993a), '"He Set His Face": On the Meaning of Luke 9:51', in *Luke and Scripture: The Function of Sacred Tradition in Luke-Acts*, ed. Craig A. Evans and James A. Sanders, pp. 93–105. Minneapolis: Fortress Press.

(1993b), 'The Function of the Elijah/Elisha Narratives in Luke's Ethic of Election', in *Luke and Scripture: The Function of Sacred Tradition in Luke-Acts*, ed. Craig A. Evans and James A. Sanders, pp. 70–83. Minneapolis: Fortress Press.

(1993c), 'The Twelve Thrones of Israel: Scripture and Politics in Luke 22:24–30', in *Luke and Scripture: The Function of Sacred Tradition in Luke-Acts*, ed. Craig A. Evans and James A. Sanders, pp. 154–70. Minneapolis: Fortress Press.

(1997), 'Aspects of Exile and Restoration in the Proclamation of Jesus and the Gospels', in *Exile: Old Testament, Jewish, and Christian Conceptions*, ed. James M. Scott, pp. 299–328. Leiden: Brill.

Evans, Craig A., and Stanley E. Porter, eds. (2000), *Dictionary of New Testament Background: A Compendium of Contemporary Biblical Scholarship*. Downers Grove, IL: InterVarsity Press.

Farrow, Douglas (1999), *Ascension and Ecclesia: On the Significance of the Doctrine of the Ascension for Ecclesiology and Christian Cosmology*. Edinburgh: T. & T. Clark.

(2005), 'Andrew Burgess, *The Ascension in Karl Barth*'. *International Journal of Systematic Theology* 7(2), pp. 205–8.

Fay, Ron C. (2006), 'The Narrative Function of the Temple in Luke-Acts'. *Trinity Journal* n.s. 27(2), pp. 255–70.

Felder, Cain Hope (1995), 'Racial Motifs in the Biblical Narratives', in *Voices from the Margin: Interpreting the Bible in the Third World*, ed. R. S. Sugirtharajah, pp. 172–88. Maryknoll, NY: Orbis Books; London: SPCK.

Finger, Reta Halteman (2007), *Of Widows and Meals: Communal Meals in the Book of Acts*. Grand Rapids: Eerdmans.

Fitzmyer, Joseph A. (1998), *The Acts of the Apostles: A New Translation and Commentary*. New York: Doubleday.

Flanagan, James W. (1999), 'Ancient Perceptions of Space / Perceptions of Ancient Space'. *Semeia* 87, pp. 15–43.

(2000), 'Space', in *Handbook of Postmodern Biblical Interpretation*, ed. A. K. M. Adam, pp. 239–44. St Louis: Chalice.

(2001), 'Mapping the Biblical World: Perceptions of Space in Ancient Southwestern Asia', in *Humanities Group Working Papers*, ed. Jacqueline Murray, pp. 1–18. Windsor, Ont.: University of Windsor.

Fletcher-Louis, Crispin H. T. (1997), *Luke-Acts: Angels, Christology and Soteriology*. Tübingen: Mohr Siebeck.

Foucault, Michel (1980a), 'Questions on Geography', in *Power/Knowledge: Selected Interviews and Other Writings 1972–1977*, ed. Colin Gordon, pp. 63–77. New York: Pantheon Books.

(1980b), 'The Eye of Power', in *Power/Knowledge: Selected Interviews and Other Writings 1972–1977*, ed. Colin Gordon, pp. 146–65. New York: Pantheon Books.

Franklin, Eric (1975), *Christ the Lord: A Study in the Purpose and Theology of Luke-Acts*. London: SPCK.

Fuller, G. C. (1994), 'The Life of Jesus, after the Ascension (Luke 24:50–53; Acts 1:9–11)'. *Westminster Journal of Theology* 56, pp. 391–8.

Gage, Warren Austin, and John Randolph Beck (1994), 'The Gospel, Zion's Barren Woman and the Ethiopian Eunuch'. *Crux* 30(2), pp. 35–43.

Gallagher, Robert L. (2004), 'From "Doingness" to "Beingness": A Missiological Interpretation (Acts 4:23–31)', in *Mission in Acts: Ancient Narratives in Contemporary Context*, ed. Paul Hertig and Robert L. Gallagher, pp. 45–58. Maryknoll, NY: Orbis Books.

Garrett, Susan R. (1989), *The Demise of the Devil: Magic and the Demonic in Luke's Writing*. Minneapolis: Fortress Press.

Gaventa, Beverly Roberts (1986), *From Darkness to Light: Aspects of Conversion in the New Testament*. Philadelphia: Fortress Press.

(1988), 'Towards a Theology of Acts: Reading and Rereading'. *Interpretation* 42, pp. 146–57.

(2003a), *Abingdon New Testament Commentaries: The Acts of the Apostles*. Nashville: Abingdon Press.

(2003b), 'The Presence of the Absent Lord: The Characterization of Jesus in the Acts of the Apostles'. Unpublished paper presented at the November 2003 Annual Meeting of the Society of Biblical Literature.

(2004), 'Theology and Ecclesiology in the Miletus Speech: Reflections on Content and Context'. *New Testament Studies* 50, pp. 36–52.

Gehring, Roger W. (2004), *House Church and Mission: The Importance of Household Structures in Early Christianity*. Peabody, MA: Hendrickson.

Giddens, Anthony (1984), *The Constitution of Society: Outline of the Theory of Structuration*. Cambridge: Polity Press.

Giessler-Wirsig, Eva (2001), 'History, Auxiliary Sciences to', in *The Encyclopedia of Christianity*, vol. II, ed. Erwin Fahlbusch, Jan Milic Lochan, John Mbiti, Jaroslav Pelikan and Lukas Vischer, pp. 559–62. Trans. Geoffrey W. Bromiley. Grand Rapids: Eerdmans; Leiden: Brill.

Gilbert, Gary (2002), 'From Eschatology to Imperialism: Mapping the Territory of Acts 2', in *The Gospels According to Michael Goulder: A North American Response*, ed. Christopher A. Rollston, pp. 84–110. Harrisburg, PA: Trinity Press International.

(2003), 'Roman Propaganda and Christian Identity in the Worldview of Luke-Acts', in *Contextualising Acts: Lukan Narrative and Greco-Roman Discourse*, ed. Todd Penner and Caroline vander Stichele, pp. 233–56. Atlanta, GA: Society of Biblical Literature.

Giles, Kevin N. (1985), 'Luke's Use of the Term *Ekklesia* with Special Reference to Acts 20:28 and 9:31'. *New Testament Studies* 31, pp. 135–42.

(1992), 'Ascension', in *Dictionary of Jesus and the Gospels*, ed. Joel B. Green, Scot McKnight and I. Howard Marshall, pp. 46–50. Downers Grove, IL: InterVarsity Press.

(1995), *What on Earth is the Church? A Biblical and Theological Inquiry*. London: SPCK.

Goulder, Michael D. (2002), 'Appendix: Michael Goulder Responds', in *The Gospels According to Michael Goulder: A North American Response*, ed. Christopher A. Rollston, pp. 137–52. Harrisburg, PA: Trinity Press International.

Gowler, David B. (1991), *Host, Guest, Enemy and Friend: Portraits of the Pharisees in Luke and Acts*. New York: Peter Lang.

Grant, Robert M. (1992), 'Early Christian Geography'. *Vigiliae Christianae* 46, pp. 105–11.

Green, Joel B. (1991), 'The Death of Jesus and the Rending of the Temple Veil (Luke 23:44–49): A Window into Luke's Understanding of Jesus and the Temple', in *The Society of Biblical Literature 1991 Seminar Papers*, ed. Eugene H. Lovering Jr, pp. 543–57. Atlanta, GA: Scholars Press.

(1994), 'The Demise of the Temple as "Cultural Center" in Luke-Acts: An Exploration of the Rending of the Temple Veil (Luke 23:44–49)'. *Revue Biblique* 101(4), pp. 495–515.

(1997a), 'Acts of the Apostles', in *Dictionary of the Later New Testament and its Developments*, ed. Ralph P. Martin and Peter H. Davids, pp. 7–24. Downers Grove, IL: InterVarsity Press.

(1997b), *The Gospel of Luke*. Grand Rapids: Eerdmans.

(2002), 'Doing Repentance: The Formation of Disciples in the Acts of the Apostles'. *Ex Auditu* 18, pp. 1–23.

Gregory, Derek (1994), *Geographical Imaginations*. Oxford: Blackwell.

(2000a), 'Imaginative Geographies', in Johnston, Gregory, Pratt and Watts, *Dictionary of Human Geography*, pp. 372–3.

(2000b), 'Structuration Theory', in Johnston, Gregory, Pratt and Watts, eds., *Dictionary of Human Geography*, pp. 798–801.

Gunn, David M., and Paula M. McNutt, eds. (2002), *'Imagining' Biblical Worlds: Studies in Spatial, Social and Historical Constructs in Honor of James W. Flanagan*. London: Sheffield Academic Press.

Haar, Stephen (2003), *Simon Magus: The First Gnostic?* Berlin and New York: Walter de Gruyter.

Habel, Norman C. (1995), *The Land is Mine: Six Biblical Land Ideologies*. Minneapolis: Fortress Press.

Haenchen, Ernst (1971), *The Acts of the Apostles: A Commentary*. Oxford: Blackwell.

Hamm, Dennis (1986), 'Acts 3.1–10: The Healing of the Temple Beggar as Lucan Theology'. *Biblica* 67, pp. 304–19.

(2003), 'The Tamid Service in Luke-Acts: The Cultic Background Behind Luke's Theology of Worship (Luke 1:5–25; 18:9–14; 24:59–53; Acts 3:1; 10:3, 30)'. *Catholic Biblical Quarterly* 65, pp. 215–31.

Haraway, Donna J. (1991), *Simians, Cyborgs, and Women: The Reinvention of Nature*. London: Free Association Books.

Harley, J. B. (1989), 'Deconstructing the Map'. *Cartographica* 26(2), pp. 1–20.

Harvey, David (1969), *Explanation in Geography*. London: Edward Arnold.
   (1973), *Social Justice and the City*. London: Edward Arnold.
   (1990), *The Condition of Postmodernity: An Enquiry into the Origins of Cultural Change*. Oxford: Basil Blackwell.
   (1996), *Justice, Nature and the Geography of Difference*. Oxford: Blackwell.
Hastings, Adrian (2000), 'History', in Hastings, Mason and Pyper, eds., *The Oxford Companion to Christian Thought*, pp. 299–302.
Hastings, Adrian, Alistair Mason, and Hugh Pyper, eds. (2000), *The Oxford Companion to Christian Thought*. Oxford: Oxford University Press.
Hays, Daniel J. (2003), *From Every People and Nation: A Biblical Theology of Race*. Leicester: Apollos.
Hedrick, C. W. (1981), 'Paul's Conversion/Call: A Comparative Analysis of the Three Reports in Acts'. *Journal of Biblical Literature* 100(3), pp. 415–32.
Heil, John Paul (1999), *The Meal Scenes in Luke Acts: An Audience-Oriented Approach*. Atlanta: Society of Biblical Literature.
Hengel, Martin (1979), *Acts and the History of Earliest Christianity*. Trans. John Bowden. London: SCM.
   (1983), *Between Jesus and Paul: Studies in the Earliest History of Christianity*. Trans. John Bowden. London: SCM Press.
   (1995), 'The Geography of Palestine in Acts', in *The Book of Acts in its First Century Setting*, vol. IV: *Palestinian Setting*, ed. Richard Bauckham, pp. 27–78. Grand Rapids: Eerdmans; Carlisle: Paternoster Press.
Henkel, Reinhard (2001), 'Geography of Religion', in *The Encyclopedia of Christianity*, vol. II, ed. Erwin Fahlbusch, Jan Milic Lochan, John Mbiti, Jaroslav Pelikan and Lukas Vischer, pp. 385–6. Trans. Geoffrey W. Bromiley. Grand Rapids: Eerdmans; Leiden: Brill.
Hennesey, James (1987), 'History', in *The New Dictionary of Theology*, ed. Joseph A. Komonchak, Mary Collins and Dermot A. Lane, pp. 469–72. Dublin: Gill & Macmillan.
Hetherington, Kevin (1998), *Expressions of Identity: Space, Performance, Politics*. London: Sage.
Hiebert, David (2000), 'Ethnicity', in Johnston, Gregory, Pratt and Watts, *Dictionary of Human Geography*, pp. 235–8.
Horton, Fred L., Jr, and Jeffrey A. Blakely (2000), '"Behold, Water!" Tell El-Hesi and the Baptism of the Ethiopian Eunuch (Acts 8:26–40)'. *Revue Biblique* 107(1), pp. 56–71.
Houlden, J. L. (1991), 'Beyond Belief: Preaching the Ascension (II)'. *Theology* 94, pp. 173–80.
House, Colin (1983), 'Defilement by Association: Some Insights from the Usage of ΚΟΙΝΟΣ / ΚΟΙΝΟΩ in Acts 10 and 11'. *Andrews University Seminary Studies* 21(2), pp. 143–53.
Hurtado, Larry W. (1983), *Mark*. Peabody, MA: Hendrickson.
Inge, John (2003), *A Christian Theology of Place*. Aldershot: Ashgate.
Jacob, Christian (1999), 'Mapping in the Mind: The Earth from Ancient Alexandria', in *Mappings*, ed. Denis E. Cosgrove, pp. 24–49. London: Reaktion.
Jedin, Hubert, Kenneth Scott Latourette, and Jochen Martin (1970), *Atlas zur Kirchengeschichte: Die Christlichen Kirchen in Geschichte und Gegenwart*. Freiburg: Herder.

Jeremias, Joachim (1969), *Jerusalem in the Time of Jesus*. London: SCM Press.

Jervell, Jacob (1972), *Luke and the People of God: A New Look at Luke-Acts*. Minneapolis: Augsburg.

— (1998), *Die Apostelgeschichte*. Göttingen: Vandenhoeck & Ruprecht.

Johnson, Andy (2004), 'Resurrection, Ascension and the Developing Portrait of the God of Israel in Acts'. *Scottish Journal of Theology* 57(2), pp. 146–62.

Johnson, Luke Timothy (1977), *The Literary Function of Possessions in Luke-Acts*. Missoula, MT: Scholars Press.

— (1992), *The Acts of the Apostles*. Collegeville, MN: Liturgical Press.

Johnston, Ron J., Derek Gregory, Geraldine Pratt, and Michael Watts, eds. (2000), *The Dictionary of Human Geography*, 4th edn. Oxford: Blackwell.

Kee, Howard Clark (1989), *Knowing The Truth: A Sociological Approach to New Testament Interpretation*. Minneapolis: Fortress Press.

— (1990), *Good News to the Ends of the Earth: The Theology of Acts*. London: SCM Press; Philadelphia: Trinity Press International.

Kent, John (1983), 'History', in *A New Dictionary of Christian Theology*, ed. Alan Richardson and John Bowden, pp. 258–61. London: SCM Press.

Kilgallen, John J. (2004), 'The Speech of Stephen, Acts 7:2–53'. *Expository Times* 115(9), pp. 293–7.

King, Martin Luther, Jr (1999), '"There Comes a Time When People Get Tired" (Montgomery, Alabama, 5 December 1955)', in *The Penguin Book of Twentieth-Century Speeches*, ed. Brian MacArthur, pp. 265–7. London: Penguin.

Kitchen, J. Howard (1955), *Holy Fields: An Introduction to the Historical Geography of the Holy Land*. London: Paternoster Press.

Kodell, J. (1974), '"The Word of God Grew": The Ecclesial Tendency of Logos in Acts 6:7; 12:24; 19:20'. *Biblica* 55, pp. 505–19.

Köstenberger, Andreas J., and Peter T. O'Brien (2001), *Salvation to the Ends of the Earth: A Biblical Theology of Mission*. Downers Grove, IL: InterVarsity Press.

Kreiswirth, Martin (1984), 'Centers, Openings, and Endings: Some Faulknerian Constants'. *American Literature* 56, pp. 38–50.

Lake, Kirsopp, and Henry Joel Cadbury (1933), *The Beginnings of Christianity*, Part I, *The Acts of the Apostles*, vol. IV: *English Translation and Commentary*. London: Macmillan.

Lake, Robert W. (1999), 'Postmodern Urbanism?' *Urban Geography* 20(5), pp. 393–5.

Lane, William L. (1974), *The Gospel of Mark*. Grand Rapids: Eerdmans.

Larkin, William J., Jr (1997), 'Ascension', in *Dictionary of the Later New Testament and its Developments*, ed. Ralph P. Martin and Peter H. Davids. Downers Grove, IL: InterVarsity Press.

— (2003), 'The Spirit and Jesus "on Mission" in the Postresurrection and Postascension Stages of Salvation History: The Impact of the Pneumatology of Acts on Its Christology', in *New Testament Greek and Exegesis: Essays in Honor of Gerald F. Hawthorne*, ed. Amy M. Donaldson and Timothy B. Sailors, pp. 121–39. Grand Rapids and Cambridge: Eerdmans.

Larsson, Edvin (1993), 'Temple-Criticism and the Jewish Heritage: Some Reflections on Acts 6–7'. *New Testament Studies* 39, pp. 379–95.

Latham, H. (1926), *The Risen Master: A Sequel to Pastor Pastorum.* Cambridge: Deighton Bell.

Laytham, D. Brent (2002), 'Response to Green'. *Ex Auditu* 18, pp. 24–8.

Lefebvre, Henri (1991), *The Production of Space.* Trans. Donald Nicholson-Smith. Oxford: Blackwell.

Ley, David (1974), 'The City and Good and Evil: Reflections on Christian and Marxist Interpretations'. *Antipode* 6(1), pp. 66–73.

Ley, David, and Martyn S. Samuels, eds. (1978), *Humanistic Geography: Prospects and Problems.* London: Croom Helm.

Lieu, Judith M. (2004), *Christian Identity in the Jewish and Graeco-Roman World.* Oxford: Oxford University Press.

Lincoln, Andrew T. (1981), *Paradise Now and Not Yet: Studies in the Role of the Heavenly Dimension in Paul's Thought with Special Reference to His Eschatology.* Cambridge: Cambridge University Press.

Livingstone, David N. (1992), *The Geographical Tradition: Episodes in the History of a Contested Enterprise.* Oxford: Blackwell.

—— (1998), 'Geography and the Natural Theology Imperative', in Aay and Griffioen, eds., *Geography and Worldview*, pp. 1–17.

Lohfink, Gerhard (1971), *Die Himmelfahrt Jesu: Untersuchungen zu den Himmelfahrts- und Erhöhungstexten bei Lukas.* Munich: Kösel-Verlag.

—— (1975), *Die Sammlung Israels: Eine Untersuchung zur lukanischen Ekklesiologie.* Munich: Kösel-Verlag.

—— (1976), *The Conversion of St Paul: Narrative and History in Acts.* Trans. Bruce J. Malina. Chicago: Franciscan Herald.

—— (1999), *Does God Need the Church? Toward a Theology of the People of God.* Trans. Linda M. Maloney. Collegeville, MN: Liturgical Press.

Long, Burke O. (2002), 'Embodied Typology: Modeling the Mosaic Tabernacle', in Gunn and McNutt, eds., *'Imagining' Biblical Worlds,* pp. 117–38.

Longenecker, Bruce W. (2004), 'Lukan Aversion to Humps and Hollows: The Case of Acts 11.27–12.25'. *New Testament Studies* 50, pp. 185–204.

Lundgren, Sten (1971), 'Ananias and the Calling of Paul in Acts'. *Studia Theologia* 25, pp. 117–22.

McIver, Robert K. (1999), 'Review of A. W. Zwiep, *The Ascension of the Messiah in Lukan Christology'. Review of Biblical Literature* 1, pp. 297–8.

McKelvey, R. J. (1969), *The New Temple: The Church in the New Testament.* Oxford: Oxford University Press.

McKnight, Scot (2001), 'Jesus and the Twelve'. *Bulletin of Biblical Research* 11(2), pp. 203–31.

MacLean, A. J. (1915), 'Ascension', in *Dictionary of the Apostolic Church*, ed. James Hastings, pp. 95–9. Edinburgh: T. & T. Clark.

MacRae, George (1973), '"Whom Heaven Must Receive until the Time": Reflections on the Christology of Acts'. *Interpretation* 27, pp. 151–65.

Maddox, Robert (1982), *The Purpose of Luke-Acts.* Göttingen: Vandenhoeck & Ruprecht; Edinburgh: T. & T. Clark.

Maile, John F. (1986), 'The Ascension in Luke-Acts'. *Tyndale Bulletin* 37, pp. 29–59.

Malbon, Elizabeth Struthers (1992), 'Narrative Criticism: How Does the Story Mean?' in *Mark and Method: New Approaches in Biblical Studies*, ed. Janice Capel Anderson and Stephen D. Moore, pp. 23–49. Minneapolis: Fortress Press.

Malina, Bruce J., and Jerome H. Neyrey (1991), 'Conflict in Luke-Acts: Labelling and Deviance Theory', in *The Social World of Luke-Acts: Models for Interpretation*, ed. Jerome H. Neyrey, pp. 97–122. Peabody, MA: Hendrickson.

Marguerat, Daniel (2002), *The First Christian Historian: Writing the 'Acts of the Apostles'*. Trans. Ken McKinney, Gregory J. Laughery and Richard Bauckham. Cambridge: Cambridge University Press.

(2003), 'Magic and Miracle in the Acts of the Apostles', in *Magic in the Biblical World: From the Rod of Aaron to the Ring of Solomon*, ed. Todd Klutz, pp. 100–24. London: T. & T. Clark International.

Marguerat, Daniel, and Yvan Bourquin (1999), *How to Read Bible Stories: An Introduction to Narrative Criticism*. Trans. John Bowden. London: SCM Press.

Marshall, I. Howard (1980), *The Acts of the Apostles*. Leicester: Inter-Varsity Press; Grand Rapids: Eerdmans.

(1999), '"Israel" and the Story of Salvation: One Theme in Two Parts', in *Jesus and the Heritage of Israel: Luke's Narrative Claim on Israel's Legacy*, ed. David P. Moessner, pp. 340–57. Harrisburg, PA: Trinity Press International.

(2007), 'Acts', in *Commentary on the New Testament Use of the Old Testament*, ed. G. K. Beale and D. A. Carson, pp. 513–606. Grand Rapids: Baker.

Marshall, I. Howard, and David Peterson, eds. (1998), *Witness to the Gospel: The Theology of Acts*. Grand Rapids and Cambridge: Eerdmans.

Martin, Clarice J. (1995), 'The Acts of the Apostles', in *Searching the Scriptures*, vol. II: *A Feminist Commentary*, ed. Elizabeth Schüssler Fiorenza, pp. 763–799. London: SCM Press.

Martín-Asensio, Gustavo (1999), 'Participant Reference and Foregrounded Syntax in the Stephen Episode', in *Discourse Analysis and the New Testament: Approaches and Results*, ed. Stanley E. Porter and Jeffrey T. Reed, pp. 235–57. Sheffield: Sheffield Academic Press.

Massey, Doreen (1984), 'Introduction: Geography Matters', in *Geography Matters! A Reader*, ed. Doreen Massey and John Allen, pp. 1–11. Cambridge: Cambridge University Press, in association with the Open University.

Matson, David Lertis (1996), *Household Conversion Narratives in Acts: Pattern and Interpretation*. Sheffield: Sheffield Academic Press.

Matthews, Victor H. (2003), 'Physical Space, Imagined Space, and "Lived Space" in Ancient Israel'. *Biblical Theology Bulletin* 33(1), pp. 12–20.

Mayer, Edgar (1996), *Die Reiseerzählung des Lukas (Lk 9,51–19,10): Entscheidung in der Wüste*. Frankfurt and Bern: Peter Lang.

Meeks, Wayne A. (1983), *The First Urban Christians: The Social World of the Apostle Paul*. New Haven, CT, and London: Yale University Press.

Meer, F. van der, and Christine Mohrmann (1958), *Atlas of the Early Christian World*. Trans. Mary F. Hedlund and H. H. Rowley. London and Edinburgh: Nelson.

Meier, John P. (2001), 'Jesus, the Twelve and the Restoration of Israel', in *Restoration: Old Testament, Jewish and Christian Perspectives*, ed. James M. Scott, pp. 365–404. Leiden: Brill.

Menoud, Philippe H. (1962), '"Pendant quarante jours" (Actes I 3)', in *Neotestamentica et Patristica: Eine Freundesgabe, Herrn Professor Dr Oscar Cullmann zu seinem 60. Geburtstag überreicht*, ed. Oscar Cullmann, pp. 148–56. Leiden: Brill.

(1978a), 'During Forty Days (Acts 1:3)', in Menoud, *Jesus Christ and the Faith: A Collection of Studies*, pp. 167–79. Trans. Eunice M. Paul. Pittsburgh, PA: Pickwick Press.

(1978b), 'The Acts of the Apostles and the Eucharist', in Menoud, *Jesus Christ and the Faith: A Collection of Studies*, pp. 84–106. Trans. Eunice M. Paul. Pittsburgh, PA: Pickwick Press.

Metzger, Bruce M. (1969), 'The Meaning of Christ's Ascension', in *Search the Scriptures: New Testament Studies in Honor of Raymond T. Stamm*, ed. J. M. Myers, O. Reimherr and H. N. Bream, pp. 118–28. Leiden: Brill.

(1994), *A Textual Commentary on the Greek New Testament*. Stuttgart: German Bible Society.

Mittmann, Siegfried, and Götz Schmitt, eds. (2001), *Tübinger Bibelatlas*. Stuttgart: Deutsche Bibelgesellschaft.

Moessner, David P. (1989), *Lord of The Banquet: The Literary and Theological Significance of the Lukan Travel Narrative*. Minneapolis: Fortress Press.

Monmonier, Mark (2000), 'Cartography', in Johnston, Gregory, Pratt and Watts, *Dictionary of Human Geography*, pp. 61–4.

Morgan, Robert (1990), 'Historicism', in *A Dictionary of Biblical Interpretation*, ed. R. J. Coggins and J. L. Houlden, pp. 290–1. London: SCM Press.

Moule, C. F. D. (1957), 'Expository Problems: The Ascension – Acts 1:9'. *Expository Times* 68, pp. 205–9.

(1966), 'The Christology of Acts', in *Studies in Luke-Acts: Essays Presented in Honor of Paul Schubert, Buckingham Professor of New Testament Criticism and Interpretation at Yale University*, ed. Leander E. Keck and J. Louis Martyn, pp. 159–85. London: SPCK.

(1977), *The Origin of Christology*. Cambridge: Cambridge University Press.

Moxnes, Halvor (2000), 'Placing Jesus of Nazareth: Toward a Theory of Place in the Study of the Historical Jesus', in *Text and Artifact in the Religions of Mediterranean Antiquity: Essays in Honour of Peter Richardson*, ed. Stephen G. Wilson and Michel Desjardins, pp. 158–75. Waterloo, Ont.: Wilfrid Laurier University Press.

(2001a), 'Kingdom Takes Place: Transformation of Place and Power in the Kingdom of God in the Gospel of Luke', in *Social Scientific Models for Interpreting the Bible: Essays by the Context Group in Honour of Bruce J. Malina*, ed. John J. Pilch, pp. 176–209. Leiden: Brill.

(2001b), 'The Construction of Galilee as a Place for the Historical Jesus – Part 1'. *Biblical Theology Bulletin* 31(1), pp. 26–37.

(2001c), 'The Construction of Galilee as a Place for the Historical Jesus – Part 2'. *Biblical Theology Bulletin* 31(2), pp. 64–77.

Nave, Guy D., Jr (2002), *The Role and Function of Repentance in Luke-Acts*. Atlanta, GA: Society of Biblical Literature.

Neirynck, Frans (1999), 'Luke 4:16–30 and the Unity of Luke-Acts', in *The Unity of Luke-Acts*, ed. Joseph Verheyden, pp. 357–95. Leuven: Leuven University Press.

Neudorfer, Heinz-Werner (1998), 'The Speech of Stephen', in Marshall and Peterson, eds., *Witness to the Gospel*, pp. 275–94.

Nicolet, Claude (1991), *Space, Geography, and Politics in the Early Roman Empire*. Trans. Hélène Leclerc. Ann Arbor, MI: University of Michigan Press.

Niehr, Herbert (1999), 'Host of Heaven', in *Dictionary of Deities and Demons in the Bible*, 2nd edn., ed. Karel van der Toorn, Bob Becking and Pieter W. van der Horst, pp. 428–30. Leiden: Brill.

Nolland, John (1998), 'Salvation-History and Eschatology', in Marshall and Peterson, eds., *Witness to the Gospel*, pp. 63–81.

O'Day, G. R. (1992), 'Acts', in *The Women's Bible Commentary*, ed. C. A. Newsom and S. H. Ringe, pp. 305–12. Louisville: Westminster/ John Knox Press; London: SPCK.

O'Donovan, Oliver (1989), 'The Loss of a Sense of Place'. *Irish Theological Quarterly* 55(1), pp. 39–58.

(1996), *The Desire of the Nations: Rediscovering the Roots of Political Theology*. Cambridge: Cambridge University Press.

Olliver, Alice (1989), 'Christian Geographers' Fellowship Conference Report'. *Area* 23, pp. 101–10.

O'Reilly, Leo (1987), *Word and Sign in the Acts of the Apostles: A Study in Lucan Theology*. Rome: Editrice Pontificia Università Gregoriana.

O'Toole, Robert F. (1979), 'Luke's Understanding of Jesus' Resurrection-Ascension-Exaltation'. *Biblical Theology Bulletin* 9, pp. 106–14.

(1981), 'Activity of the Risen Jesus in Luke-Acts'. *Biblica* 62, pp. 471–98.

Panier, Louis (1991), 'Portes ouvertes à la Foi. La mission dans les Actes des Apôtres'. *Lumière et vie* 205, pp. 103–21.

Pao, David W. (2000), *Acts and the Isaianic New Exodus*. Tübingen: Mohr (Siebeck).

Park, Chris (1994), *Sacred Worlds: An Introduction to Geography and Religion*. London: Routledge.

Parsons, Mikeal C. (1987), *The Departure of Jesus in Luke-Acts: The Ascension Narratives in Context*. Sheffield: JSOT Press.

(1988), 'The Text of Acts 1.2 Reconsidered'. *Catholic Biblical Quarterly* 50, pp. 58–71.

(1990), 'Christian Origins and Narrative Openings: The Sense of a Beginning in Acts 1–5'. *Review and Expositor* 87, pp. 403–22.

(1998), 'The Place of Jerusalem on the Lukan Landscape: An Exercise in Symbolic Cartography', in *Literary Studies in Luke-Acts: Essays in Honor of Joseph B. Tyson*, ed. Richard P. Thompson and Thomas E. Phillips, pp. 155–71. Macon, GA: Mercer University Press.

(2006), *Body and Character in Luke and Acts: The Subversion of Physiognomy in Early Christianity*. Grand Rapids: Baker Academic.

Penner, Todd (2004), *In Praise of Christian Origins: Stephen and the Hellenists in Lukan Apologetic Historiography*. New York and London: T. & T. Clark International.

Petersen, Norman R. (1978), *Literary Criticism for New Testament Critics*. Philadelphia: Fortress Press.

Peterson, David (1998a), 'The "Locus" of the Church: Heaven or Earth?' *Churchman* 112(3), pp. 199–213.

(1998b), 'The Worship of the New Community', in Marshall and Peterson, eds., *Witness to the Gospel*, pp. 373–95.

(1998c), 'Luke's Theological Enterprise: Integration and Intent', in Marshall and Peterson, eds., *Witness to the Gospel*, pp. 521–44.

(2004), 'Atonement Theology in Luke-Acts: Reflections on its Background', in *The New Testament in its First Century Setting: Essays on Context and Background in Honor of B.W. Winter on his 65th Birthday*, ed. P.J. Williams, Andrew D. Clarke, Peter M. Head and David Instone-Brewer, pp. 56–71. Grand Rapids: Eerdmans.

Phillips, Thomas E. (2003), 'Creation, Sin and Its Curse, and the People of God: An Intertextual Reading of Genesis 1–12 and Acts 1–7'. *Horizons in Biblical Theology* 25(2), pp. 146–60.

(2006), 'The Genre of Acts: Moving Towards a Consensus?' *Currents in Biblical Research* 4(3), pp. 365–96.

Plymale, Steven F. (1991), *The Prayer Texts of Luke-Acts*. New York: Peter Lang.

Porter, R.J. (1988), 'What Did Philip Say to the Eunuch?' *Expository Times* 100, pp. 54–5.

Porter, Stanley E. (2007), 'Magic in the Book of Acts', in *A Kind of Magic: Understanding Magic in the New Testament and its Religious Environment*, ed. Michael Labahn and Bert Jan Lietaert Peerbolte, pp. 107–21. London: T. & T. Clark.

Powell, Mark Allan (1990), *What is Narrative Criticism? A New Approach to the Bible*. London: SPCK.

Pratt, Geraldine (1999), 'Geographies of Identity and Difference', in *Human Geography Today*, ed. Doreen Massey, John Allen and Philip Sarre, pp. 151–67. Oxford: Polity Press.

Pred, Allan (1990), *Making Histories and Constructing Human Geographies: The Local Transformation of Practice, Power Relations, and Consciousness*. Boulder, CO: Westview Press.

Rakotoharintsifa, A. (1995), 'Luke and the Internal Divisions in the Early Church', in *Luke's Literary Achievement: Collected Essays*, ed. C.M. Tuckett, pp. 165–77. Sheffield: Sheffield Academic Press.

Raphael, C. Nicholas (1992), 'Geography and the Bible (Palestine)', in *The Anchor Bible Dictionary*, vol. II, ed. David Noel Freedman, pp. 964–77. New York: Doubleday.

Rapske, Brian (1998), 'Opposition to the Plan of God and Persecution', in Marshall and Peterson, eds., *Witness to the Gospel*, pp. 235–56.

Rapuano, Yedudah (1990), 'Did Philip Baptize the Eunuch at Ein Yael?' *Biblical Archaeology Review* 16(6), pp. 44–9.

Ravens, David (1995), *Luke and the Restoration of Israel*. Sheffield: Sheffield Academic Press.

Read-Heimerdinger, Jenny (2002), *The Bezan Text of Acts: A Contribution of Discourse Analysis to Textual Criticism*. Sheffield: Sheffield Academic Press.

Reimer, Ivoni Richter (1995), *Women in the Acts of the Apostles: A Feminist Liberation Perspective*. Trans. Linda M. Maloney. Minneapolis: Fortress Press.

Reinhartz, Adele (2000), 'Better Homes and Gardens: Women and Domestic Space in the Books of Judith and Susanna', in *Text and Artifact in the Religions of Mediterranean Antiquity: Essays in Honor of Peter Richardson*, ed. Stephen G. Wilson and Michel Desjardins, pp. 325–39. Waterloo, Ont.: Wilfrid Laurier University Press.

Resseguie, James L. (2004), *Spiritual Landscape: Images of the Spiritual Life in the Gospel of Luke*. Peabody, MA: Hendrickson.

   (2005), *Narrative Criticism of the New Testament: An Introduction*. Grand Rapids: Baker Academic.

Rhoads, David (1982), 'Narrative Criticism and the Gospel of Mark'. *Journal of the American Academy of Religion* 50(3), pp. 411–34.

Richard, Earl (1978), *Acts 6:1–8:4: The Author's Method of Composition*. Missoula, MT: Society of Biblical Literature.

   (1979), 'The Polemical Character of the Joseph Episode in Acts 7'. *Journal of Biblical Literature* 98, pp. 255–67.

   (1982), 'The Creative Use of Amos by the Author of Acts'. *Novum Testamentum* 24, pp. 37–53.

Rius-Camps, Josep, and Jenny Read-Heimerdinger (2004), *The Message of Acts in Codex Bezae: A Comparison with the Alexandrian Tradition*, vol. I: *Acts 1.1–5.42: Jerusalem*. London: T. & T. Clark International.

   (2006), *The Message of Acts in Codex Bezae: A Comparison with the Alexandrian Tradition*, vol. II: *Acts 6.1–12.25: From Judaea and Samaria to the Church in Antioch*. London: T. & T. Clark International.

Robbins, Vernon K. (1991), 'Luke-Acts: A Mixed Population Seeks a Home in the Roman Empire', in *Images of Empire*, ed. Loveday C. A. Alexander, pp. 202–21. Sheffield: JSOT Press.

Römer, T., and J. D. Macchi (1995), 'Luke, Disciple of the Deuteronomistic School', in *Luke's Literary Achievement: Collected Essays*, ed. C. M. Tuckett, pp. 178–87. Sheffield: Sheffield Academic Press.

Romm, James S. (1992), *The Edges of the Earth in Ancient Thought: Geography, Exploration, and Fiction*. Princeton: Princeton University Press.

Rose, Gillian (1993), *Feminism and Geography: The Limits of Geographical Knowledge*. Cambridge: Polity Press.

   (2000), 'Third Space', in Johnston, Gregory, Pratt and Watts, eds., *Dictionary of Human Geography*, p. 827.

Rosenblatt, Marie Eloise (1990), 'Recurring Narration as a Lukan Literary Convention in Acts: Paul's Jerusalem Speech in Acts 22:1–22', in *New Views on Luke and Acts*, ed. Earl Richard, pp. 94–105. Collegeville: Liturgical Press.

Rosner, Brian (1998), 'The Progress of the Word', in Marshall and Peterson, eds., *Witness to the Gospel*, pp. 215–33.

Rowe, C. Kavin (2005), 'Luke-Acts and the Imperial Cult: A Way through the Conundrum?' *Journal for the Study of the New Testament* 27(3), pp. 279–300.

(2006), *Early Narrative Christology: The Lord in the Gospel of Luke*. Berlin and New York: Walter de Gruyter.

(2007), 'Acts 2.36 and the Continuity of Lukan Christology'. *New Testament Studies* 53(1), pp. 37–56.

Sack, Robert David (1986), *Human Territoriality: Its Theory and History*. Cambridge: Cambridge University Press.

(1997), *Homo Geographicus: A Framework for Action, Awareness, and Moral Concern*. Baltimore: Johns Hopkins University Press.

Salmon, Marilyn (1988), 'Insider or Outsider? Luke's Relationship with Judaism', in *Luke-Acts and the Jewish People: Eight Critical Perspectives*, ed. J. B. Tyson, pp. 76–82. Minneapolis: Augsburg.

Sayer, Andrew (1991), 'Behind the Locality Debate: Deconstructing Geography's Dualisms'. *Environment and Planning 'A'* 23, pp. 283–308.

Schille, G. (1966), 'Die Himmelfahrt'. *Zeitschrift für die neutestamentliche Wissenschaft und die Kunde der älteren Kirche* 57, pp. 183–99.

Schnabel, Eckhard J. (2004a), *Early Christian Mission*, vol. I: *Jesus and the Twelve*. Downers Grove, IL: InterVarsity Press.

(2004b), *Early Christian Mission*, vol. II: *Paul and the Early Church*. Downers Grove, IL: InterVarsity Press.

Schneider, G. (1980–2), *Die Apostelgeschichte*. Freiburg, Basle and Vienna: Herder.

Scott, J. Julius, Jr (1978), 'Stephen's Defense and the World Mission of the People of God'. *Journal of the Evangelical Theological Society* 21(2), pp. 131–41.

(1991), 'The Cornelius Incident in Light of its Jewish Setting'. *Journal of the Evangelical Theological Society* 34(4), pp. 475–84.

Scott, James M. (1994), 'Luke's Geographical Horizon', in *The Book of Acts in its First Century Setting*, vol. II: *Graeco-Roman Setting*, ed. David W. J. Gill and Conrad Gempf, pp. 483–544. Grand Rapids: Eerdmans; Carlisle: Paternoster Press.

(1995), *Paul and the Nations: The Old Testament Background of Paul's Mission to the Nations with Special Reference to the Destination of Galatians*. Tübingen: Mohr (Siebeck).

(1997), 'Geographical Aspects of Noachic Materials in the Scrolls at Qumran', in *The Scrolls and the Scriptures: Qumran Fifty Years After*, ed. Stanley E. Porter and Craig A. Evans, pp. 368–81. Sheffield: Sheffield Academic Press.

(2000), 'Geographical Perspectives in Late Antiquity', in Evans and Porter, eds., *Dictionary of New Testament Background*, pp. 411–14.

(2002), *Geography in Early Judaism and Christianity*. Cambridge: Cambridge University Press.

Seccombe, David (1981), 'Luke and Isaiah'. *New Testament Studies* 27, pp. 252–59.

(1998), 'The New People of God', in Marshall and Peterson, eds., *Witness to the Gospel*, pp. 349–72.

Selman, M. R. (1969), 'The Intention of the Ascension Narratives in Luke 24:50–53 and Acts 1:1–12'. Master of Arts dissertation, University of Bristol.

Sennett, Richard (1994), *Flesh and Stone: The Body and the City in Western Civilisation*. London: Faber & Faber.

Shahar, Yuval (2004), *Josephus Geographicus: The Classical Context of Geography in Josephus*. Tübingen: Mohr (Siebeck).

Shaw, Bernard (1988), *Androcles and the Lion: An Old Fable Renovated*. London: Penguin.

Shiell, William David (2004), *Reading Acts: The Lector and the Early Christian Audience*. Leiden: Brill.

Shurmer-Smith, Pamela, and Kevin Hannam (1994), *Worlds of Desire, Realms of Power: A Cultural Geography*. London: Edward Arnold.

Skinner, Matthew L. (2003), *Locating Paul: Places of Custody as Narrative Settings in Acts 21–28*. Atlanta, GA: Society of Biblical Literature.

Sleeman, Matthew (1996), 'The Geography of Citizenship Strategies in a Rural South Australian Aboriginal Community, 1940–1993'. PhD dissertation, University of Cambridge.

(2006), '"Under Heaven": The Narrative-Geographical Implications of the Ascended Christ for the Believers (and Their Mission) within Acts 1:1–11:18'. PhD dissertation, University of London.

(2007), 'Mark, the Temple and Space: A Geographer's Response'. *Biblical Interpretation* 15, pp. 338–49.

Smith, Abraham (1995), 'A Second Step in African Biblical Interpretation: A Generic Reading Analysis of Acts 8:26–40', in *Reading from this Place*, vol. I: *Social Location and Biblical Interpretation in the United States*, ed. Fernando F. Segovia and Mary Ann Tolbert, pp. 213–28. Minneapolis: Fortress Press.

Smith, David M. (1984), 'Recollections of a Random Variable', in Billinge, Gregory and Martin, eds., *Recollections of a Revolution*, pp. 117–33.

Smith, Graham (2000), 'Geopolitik', in Johnston, Gregory, Pratt and Watts, *Dictionary of Human Geography*, p. 311.

Smith, Susan J. (1994), 'Soundscape'. *Area* 26(3), pp. 232–40.

(1999), 'The Cultural Politics of Difference', in *Human Geography Today*, ed. Doreen Massey, John Allen and Philip Sarre, pp. 129–50. Oxford: Polity Press.

Soards, Marion L. (1994), *The Speeches in Acts: Their Content, Context, and Concerns*. Louisville, KY: Westminster/John Knox Press.

Soja, Edward W. (1989), *Postmodern Geographies: The Reassertion of Space in Critical Social Theory*. London: Verso.

(1996), *Thirdspace: Journeys to Los Angeles and Other Real-and-Imagined Places*. Oxford: Basil Blackwell.

(1999), 'Thirdspace: Expanding the Scope of the Geographical Imagination', in *Human Geography Today*, ed. Doreen Massey, John Allen and Philip Sarre, pp. 260–77. Oxford: Polity Press.

Spencer, F. Scott (1992a), 'The Ethiopian Eunuch and His Bible: A Social-Science Analysis'. *Biblical Theology Bulletin* 22, pp. 155–65.

(1992b), *The Portrait of Philip in Acts: A Study of Roles and Relations*. Sheffield: Sheffield Academic Press.

(1997), *Acts*. Sheffield: Sheffield Academic Press.

Squires, John T. (1993), *The Plan of God in Luke-Acts*. Cambridge: Cambridge University Press.

(1998), 'The Plan of God', in Marshall and Peterson, eds., *Witness to the Gospel*, pp. 19–37.

Stanton, Graham N. (1990), 'Historical Jesus', in *A Dictionary of Biblical Interpretation*, ed. R. J. Coggins and J. L. Houlden, pp. 285–90. London: SCM Press.

Stenschke, Christoph W. (1998), 'The Need for Salvation', in Marshall and Peterson, eds., *Witness to the Gospel*, pp. 125–44.

(1999), *Luke's Portrait of Gentiles Prior to Their Coming to Faith*. Tübingen: Mohr (Siebeck).

Sterling, Gregory E. (1999), '"Opening the Scriptures": The Legitimation of the Jewish Diaspora and the Early Christian Mission', in *Jesus and the Heritage of Israel: Luke's Narrative Claim on Israel's Legacy*, ed. David P. Moessner, pp. 199–217. Harrisburg, PA: Trinity Press International.

Strauss, Mark L. (1995), *The Davidic Messiah in Luke-Acts: The Promise and its Fulfilment in Lukan Christology*. Sheffield: Sheffield Academic Press.

Sweeney, J. P. (2002), 'Stephen's Speech (Acts 7:2–53): Is it as "Anti-Temple" as is Frequently Alleged?' *Trinity Journal* 23(2), pp. 185–210.

Sweet, Leonard, Brian D. McLaren, and Jerry Haselmayer (2003), *A is for Abductive: The Language of the Emerging Church*. Grand Rapids: Zondervan.

Swete, H. B. (1910), *The Ascended Christ: A Study in the Earliest Christian Teaching*. London: Macmillan.

Sylva, Dennis D. (1987), 'The Meaning and Function of Acts 7:46–50'. *Journal of Biblical Literature* 106(2), pp. 261–75.

Talbert, Charles H. (1974), *Literary Patterns, Theological Themes, and the Genre of Luke-Acts*. Missoula, MT: Society of Biblical Literature and Scholars Press.

Tannehill, Robert C. (1984), 'The Composition of Acts 3–5: Narrative Development and Echo Effect', in *The Society of Biblical Literature 1984 Seminar Papers*, ed. Kent Harold Richards, pp. 217–40. Chico, CA: Scholars Press.

(1986), *The Narrative Unity of Luke-Acts: A Literary Interpretation*, vol. I: *The Gospel According to Luke*. Philadelphia: Fortress Press.

(1990), *The Narrative Unity of Luke-Acts: A Literary Interpretation*, vol. II: *The Acts of the Apostles*. Philadelphia: Fortress Press.

(2005), 'Do the Ethics of Acts Include the Ethical Teaching of Luke?', in *Acts and Ethics*, ed. Thomas E. Phillips, pp. 109–22. Sheffield: Sheffield Phoenix Press.

Theissen, Gerd (1978), *Sociology of Early Palestinian Christianity*. Trans. John Bowden. Philadelphia: Fortress Press.

Thompson, K. C. (1964), *Received up into Glory. A Study of Ascension*. London: Faith Press.

Thompson, Michael B. (1998), 'The Holy Internet: Communication between Churches in the First Christian Generation', in *The Gospels for All Christians: Rethinking Gospel Audiences*, ed. Richard Bauckham, pp. 49–70. Edinburgh: T. & T. Clark.

Thompson, Richard P. (2006), *Keeping the Church in its Place: The Church as Narrative Character in Acts*. New York and London: T. & T. Clark.

Thomson, J. Oliver (1948), *History of Ancient Geography*. Cambridge: Cambridge University Press.

Tiede, David L. (1981), 'Acts 1:6–8 and the Theo-Political Claims of Christian Witness'. *Word and World* 1(1), pp. 41–51.

(1986), 'The Exaltation of Jesus and the Restoration of Israel in Acts I'. *Harvard Theological Review* 79, pp. 278–86.

Torrance, Thomas F. (1976), *Space, Time and Resurrection*. Edinburgh: Handsel Press.

Townsend, John T. (1998), 'Acts 9:1–29 and Early Church Tradition', in *Literary Studies in Luke-Acts: Essays in Honor of Joseph B. Tyson*, ed. Richard P. Thompson and Thomas E. Phillips, pp. 87–98. Macon, GA: Mercer University Press.

Trites, Allison A. (1977), *The New Testament Concept of Witness*. Cambridge: Cambridge University Press.

(1978), 'The Prayer Motif in Luke-Acts', in *Perspectives on Luke-Acts*, ed. Charles H. Talbert, pp. 168–86. Edinburgh: T. & T. Clark.

Troeltsch, Ernst (1913), 'Historiography', in *Encyclopaedia of Religion and Ethics*, vol. VI, ed. James Hastings, pp. 716–23. Edinburgh: T. & T. Clark.

Tuckett, C. (2001), *Christology and the New Testament: Jesus and His Earliest Followers*. Edinburgh: Edinburgh University Press.

Turner, Max (1998), 'The "Spirit of Prophecy" as the Power of Israel's Restoration and Witness', in Marshall and Peterson, eds., *Witness to the Gospel*, pp. 327–48.

(2000), *Power from on High: The Spirit in Israel's Restoration and Witness in Luke-Acts*. Sheffield: Sheffield Academic Press.

Tyson, J. B. (1988), 'The Problem of Jewish Rejection in Acts', in *Luke-Acts and the Jewish People: Eight Critical Perspectives*, ed. J. B. Tyson, pp. 124–37. Minneapolis: Augsburg.

Valentine, Gill (1999), 'Imagined Geographies: Geographical Knowledges of Self and Other in Everyday Life', in *Human Geography Today*, ed. Doreen Massey, John Allen and Philip Sarre, pp. 47–61. Oxford: Polity Press.

van der Horst, Peter W. (1985), 'Hellenistic Parallels to the Acts of the Apostles (2.1-47)'. *Journal for the Study of the New Testament* 25, pp. 49–60.

van Stempvoort, P. A. (1958/9), 'The Interpretation of the Ascension in Luke and Acts'. *New Testament Studies* 5, pp. 30–42.

Vanderkam, James C. (1994), 'Putting Them in Their Place: Geography as an Evaluative Tool', in *Pursuing the Text: Studies in Honour of Ben Zion Wacholder on the Occasion of His Seventieth Birthday*, ed. John C. Reeves and John Kampen, pp. 46–69. Sheffield: Sheffield Academic Press.

Volf, Miroslav (1998), *After Our Likeness: The Church as the Image of the Trinity*. Grand Rapids: Eerdmans.

Walker, Peter W. L. (1990), *Holy City, Holy Places? Christian Attitudes to Jerusalem and the Holy Land in the Fourth Century*. Oxford: Clarendon Press.

Wall, Robert W. (1998), 'Israel and the Gentile Mission in Acts and Paul: A Canonical Approach', in Marshall and Peterson, eds., *Witness to the Gospel*, pp. 437–57.

Wallace, Richard, and Wynne Williams (1998), *The Three Worlds of Paul of Tarsus*. London: Routledge.

Walton, Steve (1999), 'Where Does the Beginning of Acts End?' in *The Unity of Luke-Acts*, ed. Joseph Verheyden, pp. 447–67. Leuven: Leuven University Press.

(2004a) Ὁμοθυμαδόν in Acts: Co-Location, Common Action or "Of One Heart and Mind"?' in *The New Testament in its First Century Setting: Essays on Context and Background in Honor of B. W. Winter on His 65th Birthday*, ed. P. J. Williams, Andrew D. Clarke, Peter M. Head and David Instone-Brewer, pp. 89–105. Grand Rapids: Eerdmans.

(2004b), 'A Tale of Two Perspectives? The Place of the Temple in Acts', in *Heaven on Earth: The Temple in Biblical Theology*, ed. T. Desmond Alexander and Simon Gathercole, pp. 135–49. Carlisle: Paternoster Press.

Wasserberg, Günter (1998), *Aus Israels mitte – Heil für die Welt: eine narrative-exegetische Studie zur Theologie des Lukas*. Berlin: de Gruyter.

Weatherly, Jon A. (1994), *Jewish Responsibility for the Death of Jesus in Luke-Acts*. Sheffield: Sheffield Academic Press.

Weaver, John B. (2004), *Plots of Epiphany: Prison-Escape in the Acts of the Apostles*. Berlin: de Gruyter.

Wenham, Gordon J. (1981), 'The Theology of Unclean Food'. *Evangelical Quarterly* 53, pp. 6–15.

Werlen, Benno (1993), *Society, Action and Space: An Alternative Human Geography*. Trans. Gayna Walls. London and New York: Routledge.

Whitelam, Keith W. (2007), 'Lines of Power: Mapping Ancient Israel', in *To Break Every Yoke: Essays in Honor of Marvin L. Chaney*, ed. Robert Coote and Norman K. Gottwald, pp. 40–79. Sheffield: Sheffield Phoenix Press.

Wilken, Robert L. (1992), *The Land Called Holy: Palestine in Christian History and Thought*. New Haven, CT: Yale University Press.

Williams, Rowan (1983), 'Ascension of Christ', in *A New Dictionary of Christian Theology*, ed. Alan Richardson and John Bowden, pp. 44–5. London: SCM Press.

Wilson, Stephen G. (1973), *The Gentiles and the Gentile Mission in Luke-Acts*. Cambridge: Cambridge University Press.

(1983), *Luke and the Law*. Cambridge: Cambridge University Press.

Witherington III, Ben (1998), *The Acts of the Apostles: A Socio-Rhetorical Commentary*. Grand Rapids: Eerdmans; Carlisle: Paternoster Press.

Witherup, Ronald D. (1992), 'Functional Redundancy in the Acts of the Apostles: A Case Study'. *Journal for the Study of the New Testament* 48, pp. 67–86.

(1993), 'Cornelius Over and Over and Over Again: "Functional Redundancy" in the Acts of the Apostles'. *Journal for the Study of the New Testament* 49, pp. 45–66.

Woodward, David (2000), 'Cartography, History of', in Johnston, Gregory, Pratt and Watts, eds., *Dictionary of Human Geography*, pp. 64–8.

Wright, John Kirtland (1925), *The Geographical Lore at the Time of the Crusades*. New York: American Geographical Society.

Wright, N. T. (2003), *The Resurrection of the Son of God*. London: SPCK.

Yamasaki, Gary (2007), *Watching a Biblical Narrative: Point of View in Biblical Exegesis*. London: T. & T. Clark.

Ziesler, J. A. (1979), 'The Name of Jesus in the Acts of the Apostles'. *Journal for the Study of the New Testament* 4, pp. 28–41.

Zwiep, Arie W. (1996), 'The Text of the Ascension Narratives (Luke 24.50–3; Acts 1.1–2, 9–11)'. *New Testament Studies* 42, pp. 219–44.

(1997), *The Ascension of the Messiah in Lukan Christology*. Leiden: Brill.

(2004), *Judas and the Choice of Matthias: A Study of Context and Concern of Acts 1:15–26*. Tübingen: Mohr (Siebeck).

INDEX OF BIBLE REFERENCES

21:27, 31 *97–8*
21:28 *142*
21:30 *98*
21:38 *82, 98, 155*
22:1 *223*
22:1–22 *222–3*
22:3 *98, 130, 214*
22:6 *60, 226, 248*
22:8 *100*
22:14 *128*
22:16 *100, 242*
22:17–18 *16*
22:17–21 *154, 170, 200*
22:19 *206*
22:20 *223*
22:21 *103, 214*
22:22 *98*
23:6 *208*
23:8 *112*
23:11 *17, 200, 206, 211*
24–8 *34*
24:5 *100*
24:11 *189*
24:15 *208*
24:23 *195*
26:6–7 *208*
26:9 *100*
26:13 *60*
26:16–17 *211*
26:19 *257*
26:20 *206*
26:23 *206, 208, 241, 257*
26:24 *141*
26:26 *113, 120*
26:28 *141, 257*
27:12 *118*

27:43 *195*
28:14–15 *72*
28:15 *208*
28:17 *34*
28:20 *208*
28:23 *194*
28:24 *210, 212*
28:26–7 *167*
28:27 *156*
28:28 *223*
28:31 *66, 223, 244, 250*

Romans
  8:17 *201*

1 Corinthians
  15:8 *16*

Galatians
  1:21 *214*

Ephesians
  2:13, 17 *103*

Philippians
  3:10 *201*

Colossians
  3:1 *20*

1 Thessalonians
  1:10 *16*

Revelation
  3:4 *85*
  11:13 *85*

GENERAL INDEX

Principal references are indicated by bold type.